Advancing Equity and Inclusion in Early Childhood Education

Amber Friesen
San Francisco State University, USA

Maryssa K. Mitsch
San Francisco State University, USA

Karina Du
San Francisco State University, USA & University of California, Berkeley, USA

A volume in the Advances in
Early Childhood and K–12
Education (AECKE) Book Series

Published in the United States of America by
    IGI Global
    Information Science Reference (an imprint of IGI Global)
    701 E. Chocolate Avenue
    Hershey PA, USA 17033
    Tel: 717-533-8845
    Fax: 717-533-8661
    E-mail: cust@igi-global.com
    Web site: http://www.igi-global.com

Library of Congress Cataloging-in-Publication Data

Names: Friesen, Amber, editor. | Mitsch, Maryssa Kucskar, 1987- editor. |
  Du, Karina, 1991- editor.
Title: Advancing equity and inclusion in early childhood education / Edited
  by Amber Friesen, Maryssa Mitsch, Karina Du.
Description: Hershey, PA : Information Science Reference, [2024] | Includes
  bibliographical references and index. | Summary: "This edited book can
  provide a means to consider the ways in which early childhood education
  can advance equitable access and inclusion for all young children and
  their families, and to highlight ways in which this is being confronted
  within teacher preparation programs, teacher development, policy, and
  research"-- Provided by publisher.
Identifiers: LCCN 2024010150 (print) | LCCN 2024010151 (ebook) | ISBN
  9798369309247 (hardcover) | ISBN 9798369344590 (paperback) | ISBN
  9798369309254 (ebook)
Subjects: LCSH: Early childhood education. | Educational equalization. |
  Inclusive education.
Classification: LCC LB1139.23 .A33 2024 (print) | LCC LB1139.23 (ebook) |
  DDC 372.21--dc23/eng/20240308
LC record available at https://lccn.loc.gov/2024010150
LC ebook record available at https://lccn.loc.gov/2024010151

British Cataloguing in Publication Data
A Cataloguing in Publication record for this book is available from the British Library.

All work contributed to this book is new, previously-unpublished material.
The views expressed in this book are those of the authors, but not necessarily of the publisher.

For electronic access to this publication, please contact: eresources@igi-global.com.

Advances in Early Childhood and K-12 Education (AECKE) Book Series

Jared Keengwe
University of North Dakota, USA

ISSN:2329-5929
EISSN:2329-5937

MISSION

Early childhood and K-12 education is always evolving as new methods and tools are developed through which to shape the minds of today's youth. Globally, educational approaches vary allowing for new discussions on the best methods to not only educate, but also measure and analyze the learning process as well as an individual's intellectual development. New research in these fields is necessary to improve the current state of education and ensure that future generations are presented with quality learning opportunities.

The **Advances in Early Childhood and K-12 Education (AECKE)** series aims to present the latest research on trends, pedagogies, tools, and methodologies regarding all facets of early childhood and K-12 education.

Coverage

- Diverse Learners
- Early Childhood Education
- Learning Outcomes
- Literacy Development
- Performance Assessment
- Special Education
- STEM Education
- Urban K-12 Education

IGI Global is currently accepting manuscripts for publication within this series. To submit a proposal for a volume in this series, please contact our Acquisition Editors at Acquisitions@igi-global.com or visit: http://www.igi-global.com/publish/.

Titles in this Series

For a list of additional titles in this series, please visit:
http://www.igi-global.com/book-series/

Parental Influence on Educational Success and Wellbeing
Ana Maria Gamez (California Baptist University, USA)
Information Science Reference • copyright 2024 • 472pp • H/C (ISBN: 9798369314517)
• US $245.00 (our price)

Cultivating Literate Citizenry Through Interdisciplinary Instruction
Chyllis E. Scott (University of Nevada, Las Vegas, USA) Diane M. Miller (University of
Houston-Downtown, USA) and Matthew Albert (University of Nevada, Las Vegas, USA)
Information Science Reference • copyright 2024 • 318pp • H/C (ISBN: 9798369308431)
• US $235.00 (our price)

Using STEM-Focused Teacher Preparation Programs to Reimagine Elementary Education
Emily Cayton (Campbell University, USA) Miriam Sanders (Texas A&M University, USA)
and John A. Williams (Texas A&M University, USA)
Information Science Reference • copyright 2024 • 362pp • H/C (ISBN: 9781668459393)
• US $215.00 (our price)

Modern Early Childhood Teacher Education Theories and Practice
Mihaela Badea (Petroleum-Gas University of Ploiesti, Romania) and Mihaela Suditu
(Petroleum-Gas University of Ploiesti, Romania)
Information Science Reference • copyright 2024 • 331pp • H/C (ISBN: 9798369309568)
• US $230.00 (our price)

Emergent Practices of Learning Analytics in K-12 Classrooms
Nurdan Kavaklı Ulutaş (Izmir Demokrasi University, Turkey) and Devrim Höl (Pamukkale
University, Turkey)
Information Science Reference • copyright 2024 • 268pp • H/C (ISBN: 9798369300664)
• US $235.00 (our price)

701 East Chocolate Avenue, Hershey, PA 17033, USA
Tel: 717-533-8845 x100 • Fax: 717-533-8661
E-Mail: cust@igi-global.com • www.igi-global.com

Table of Contents

Detailed Table of Contents

Chapter 1

Patricia K. Hampshire, Mississippi State University, USA
Juli L. Pool, Boise State University, USA
Deb R. Carter, Boise State University, USA
Sylvia Horning, Boise State University, USA
Shamaria Mosley, Mississippi State University, USA

The goal of this book chapter is to further push the boundaries of how we define inclusive early learning environments. In a field challenged by an ongoing lack of resources, teacher shortages, and issues surrounding the importance of early education, the authors of this chapter want to provide ideas that promote hope. In environments where emerging curriculum is used, the focus is on the process of learning and the understanding that each child has unique strengths. Given its focus on the strengths and interests of each individual child, this approach offers opportunities to create inclusive learning environments for all children, including those with exceptional learning needs. The use of emergent curriculum in early childhood environments promotes the use of access, participation, and supports that are needed for children with exceptionalities to be successful in an inclusive classroom. The authors utilize a case study to illustrate how emergent learning environments can be designed to include all learners exploring and learning through play.

Chapter 2

Melissa C. Walter, Northern Illinois University, USA
Ruby Batz, University of Nevada, Reno, USA
Melissa M. Burnham, University of Nevada, Reno, USA
Lisa B. Fiore, Lesley University, USA

This chapter chronicles the transformative journey of a group of early childhood education (ECE) teacher educators as they critically examined the construction of early childhood teacher preparation courses. Rooted in critical pedagogy, their process demanded deep self-reflection and an acknowledgement of the oppressive systems within the field. Initially pursuing a linear checklist approach to cultivating inclusive practices, the team's extensive discussions and readings revealed the limitations of this method. Instead, they embraced a non-linear, formative spiral model, reflecting ongoing learning and reflection over time. Divided into four elements–identity and self-reflection, course syllabi, course design, and course content–-their approach aims to inspire faculty to confront biases, elevate marginalized voices, and reshape the ECE landscape. The authors invite readers into this ongoing journey, emphasizing the need for continuous introspection and collective effort to foster equity and inclusion in ECE.

Chapter 3

Monica R. Brown, University of Nevada, Las Vegas, USA
Monique Matute-Chavarria, New Mexico State University, USA
Pricella Morris, University of Nevada, Las Vegas, USA

Early childhood (EC) education is integral to the overall well-being of all young children. However, many children (e.g., Black and those with disabilities) experience an ECE system that is not equitable. In this chapter, presented are 1) the inherent flaws in ECE policies, 2) program inequities, 3) the potential benefits of equitable ECE policies and programs for Black children, and 4) recommendations for ECE stakeholders (i.e., educators, Black families, and policymakers) for addressing inequitable ECE as they contemplate a reconceptualization of ECE policies and educational programs for young Black children with and without disabilities.

Chapter 4

*Karina Du, San Francisco State University, USA & University of
California, Berkeley, USA*

Family partnerships are critical to supporting the learning and development of young children, including those with disabilities. However, systemic inequities create barriers for families to meaningfully engage in the special education process, especially for those from nondominant backgrounds. The family systems theory (FST) is a framework used to understand the dynamic nature of a family system by understanding an individual with a disability as interrelated to the rest of the family unit. The author offers a reconceptualization of the framework by embedding intersectionality within family inputs to honor families' multiple, overlapping identities. Funds of knowledge, culturally responsive teaching and reflective practice are offered as tools to strengthen understanding and responsiveness to children and families with intersectional identities.

Chapter 5

*John Kim, San Francisco State University, USA & University of
California, Berkeley, USA*

This chapter addresses an equity-centered approach to family-professional partnerships on augmentative and alternative communication (AAC) service delivery for young children with complex communication needs (CCN). Despite the recognition of family-centered practices as best practices, families often voice their frustrations when attempting to implement AAC in their homes, especially for families with culturally and linguistically diverse backgrounds. The aims of this chapter are (a) to discuss the current state of the field in family-centered AAC practices; (b) to describe family perspectives of AAC implementation in the home; and (c) to describe how "participatory help-giving AAC practices" can bridge the equity gap in AAC service delivery. Moreover, this chapter aims to discuss the foundational principle of participatory help-giving AAC practices as a form of equity between practitioners and families across the assessment, recommendation, and intervention phases in clinical practice.

This chapter explores the experiences and integration of approaches and selfcare techniques of teachers in their TK–12 credential programs and human service workers in providing trauma-informed care or teaching. Focus groups and interviews were used to collect the data from human service providers and TK–12 teachers currently enrolled in credential programs or working in care systems in California. Content analysis of the rich data elevated the voices of these teachers and service providers and the massive gaps in skill development, preparedness, and care to provide heart work and trauma informed care in their classrooms, care systems and communities. The results suggested that the abusive and toxic relationship of working in the education or care systems is a foundational element that impacts and harms both teachers, providers and their students or clients—which stifles the access and effectiveness of trauma informed practices. These stories of adults doing heart work in care systems shows equitable, inclusive care for the adults is where to start.

Chapter 8

Maria del Rosario Zavala, San Francisco State University, USA
Jennifer Ward, Kennesaw State University, USA
Courtney Koestler, Ohio University, USA
Tonya Bartell, Michigan State University, USA

Early childhood mathematics instruction is child-centered and play-based, supporting children to learn foundational mathematical concepts like counting, quantity, and pattern through hands-on experiences. Recent work in ethnic studies and social justice shows that young children are keenly aware of their own identities, empathic, and ready to take action in the world in age-appropriate ways. How might this research inform our understanding of mathematics instruction in early childhood inclusion spaces? Mathematics for social justice is a way to support identity development and mathematics learning, while challenging the medical models of mathematics that dominate special education discourses. In this chapter, the authors introduce principles for social justice mathematics for early childhood. They build on Learning for Justice's social justice standards and illustrate them through a classroom vignette. They conclude with advice to educators about engaging with social justice mathematics through attention to context, content, and the "who, when, and how" of social justice mathematics lessons.

Chapter 9

Jacqueline Anton, San Francisco State University, USA & University of California, Berkeley, USA

Sara Ucar, San Francisco State University, USA & University of California, Berkeley, USA

Mayumi Hagiwara, San Francisco State University, USA

Early intervention and early childhood special education are shifting to more inclusive and equity-empowered systems. High-quality inclusion challenges dominant norms around dis-ability and ableism to honor the strengths, preferences, and support needs of young children and their families. Equity-empowered systems promote high expectations and facilitate culturally responsive family-centered education aligned with anti-bias and anti-racist education frameworks. Research shows that promoting self-determination for children with dis-abilities can increase access to inclusive settings and enhance anti-bias and anti-racism by elevating individual and communal voices. This chapter proposes promoting self-determination as an emancipatory practice in early childhood and links high-quality inclusion with opportunities to engage in self-determined action. Further, the chapter proposes the promotion of self-determination as a culturally responsive practice aligned with anti-bias and anti-racism frameworks. Recommendations for practice and implications for future research are also discussed.

Angi Stone-MacDonald, California State University, San Bernardino,
USA
Serra Acar, University of Massachusetts, Boston, USA
Eunsuk Kim, University of Massachusetts, Boston, USA

This chapter examines how preservice early intervention (EI) practitioners become empowered as reflective practitioners through their internship, coursework, and their real-world experiences in an urban early childhood inclusive education program where over 70% of the students are from minoritized and underrepresented groups. The authors draw on two studies about students using professional, practical, and personal experiences to make their decisions in their EI and early childhood settings and use feedback and reflective practice. They examine how the reflective practice and feedback support non-traditional students who are entering EI after other educational work. One study focuses more on their development of their reflective practice and the other study focuses more on the important role of field experiences in preparing high-quality early childhood practitioners who are ready to work with the diversity found amongst children and families in an urban area.

Chapter 11

Kofi LeNiles, Towson University, USA
Katherine Orlando, Towson University, USA

This chapter offers dynamic pedagogies, reflective activities, and strategies for early childhood educators who want to deepen their cultural competence. By being culturally aware and competent, early childhood educators can better serve the needs of their young learners (birth up to age 8) and help them reach their full potential. To truly revolutionize teaching and learning in early childhood settings, it is crucial for educators to engage in intentional, continuous, and inquiry-based professional development and learning. This chapter shares both theoretical concepts and practical activities to empower early childhood educators to enhance their professionalism beyond traditional professional development and learning activities.

346

Preface

Welcome to *Advancing Equity and Inclusion in Early Childhood Education.* As editors, we are thrilled to present this collaborative effort aimed at addressing persistent and systemic societal inequities that affect access and inclusion in early learning environments.

In recent years, there has been growing recognition of the profound impact high-quality early childhood education can have on a child's education, health, and family outcomes. However, despite this awareness, disparities persist, disproportionately affecting children and families from traditionally marginalized groups.

At this critical juncture, our field has the opportunity to make significant strides toward equity and inclusion. With a focus on universal access to early childhood learning environments, both locally and nationally, we have the chance to reshape the landscape of early childhood education.

This edited volume explores various facets of professional preparation, development, research, and policy, all through the lens of equity and inclusion. Our goal is to provide a comprehensive resource for individuals supporting young children from diverse backgrounds and abilities, as well as their families.

We are committed to amplifying a range of voices in this endeavor. By including chapters from practicing educators, family members, and experts with diverse perspectives, we aim to foster meaningful dialogue and action.

Our target audience encompasses professionals and students across disciplines who work with young children and families. Whether you are involved in teacher preparation programs, policy development, or research and evaluation, we believe this book will offer valuable insights and guidance.

We envision this book being used in a variety of contexts, from informing educational programs to guiding policy decisions and professional development initiatives. Our hope is that it will inspire continued innovation and collaboration in the pursuit of equity and inclusion for all young children.

Thank you for joining us on this journey. Together, we can create a more equitable and inclusive future for early childhood education.

ORGANIZATION OF THE BOOK

Chapter 1: "Promoting Inclusion in Emergent Early Childhood Learning Environments" ventures into redefining inclusive early learning environments within a field often constrained by resource scarcity and teacher shortages. By emphasizing emergent curriculum, which prioritizes each child's unique strengths and interests, the chapter advocates for inclusive learning environments for all children, including those with exceptional learning needs. Through a case study, the authors illustrate how emergent learning environments foster inclusivity by accommodating diverse learners, promoting access, participation, and support needed for success.

Chapter 2: "Confronting Bias in Early Childhood Teacher Preparation: A Journey of Reflection and Transformation" narrates the profound evolution of Early Childhood Education (ECE) teacher educators as they scrutinize the structures of early childhood teacher preparation courses. This journey, rooted in critical pedagogy, entails introspection and recognition of oppressive systems within the field. Initially, the educators pursued a linear approach to inclusive practices but found its limitations through extensive discussions and readings. They embraced a non-linear, formative spiral model, divided into four elements: Identity and Self-Reflection, Course Syllabi, Course Design, and Course Content. The chapter aims to inspire faculty to confront biases, amplify marginalized voices, and reshape the ECE landscape through ongoing introspection and collective efforts.

Chapter 3: "Identifying Policy Flaws: Addressing Educational Inequities in Early Childhood Education for Young Black Children" delves into the systemic inequities present in early childhood education (ECE) policies and programs, particularly concerning Black children and those with disabilities. The chapter outlines inherent flaws in ECE policies, program inequities, potential benefits of equitable policies and programs for Black children, and recommendations for stakeholders to address these inequities. By reconceptualizing ECE policies and programs, the chapter advocates for a more equitable and inclusive educational landscape for young Black children.

Chapter 4: "An Intersectional Approach to Forming Meaningful Family Partnerships" scrutinizes systemic barriers that hinder meaningful family engagement in special education processes, particularly for families from nondominant backgrounds. The chapter proposes a reconceptualization of the Family Systems Theory (FST) by integrating intersectionality within family inputs, honoring families' multiple identities. It suggests utilizing funds of knowledge, culturally responsive teaching, and reflective practice to strengthen understanding and responsiveness to families with intersectional identities, thereby fostering meaningful family partnerships.

Chapter 5: "Participatory Help-Giving AAC Practices: Bridging the Equity Gap in Family Centered AAC Services in Early Intervention" advocates for equity-centered family-professional partnerships in augmentative and alternative communication

(AAC) service delivery for young children with complex communication needs (CCN). The chapter discusses current challenges in AAC implementation at home, especially for culturally and linguistically diverse families, and proposes "participatory help-giving AAC practices" as a means to bridge the equity gap. It emphasizes equitable collaboration between practitioners and families throughout the assessment, recommendation, and intervention phases to enhance AAC service delivery.

Chapter 6: "Teachers are Allowed to Be Human Starting with Trauma-Informed Care of Educators who Care for Youth" investigates the integration of trauma-informed care approaches and self-care techniques for teachers and human service workers in educational and care systems. Through focus groups and interviews, the chapter highlights gaps in skill development and preparedness among educators and service providers, influenced by abusive and toxic work environments. It underscores the importance of equitable, inclusive care for adults as a foundational step towards effective trauma-informed practices in educational and care systems.

Chapter 7: "Preparing a New Generation of Practitioners: An Equity- and Inclusion-Focused ECSE and SW Personnel Preparation Program" outlines Project ARISE, a preservice personnel preparation program aimed at training Early Childhood Special Educators and Social Workers to serve young children with disabilities, particularly those with early childhood mental health needs, in inclusive learning environments. The chapter discusses the rationale, roadmap, reflections, and lessons learned from Project ARISE, offering insights for developing similar programs to address shortages of high-quality ECSE and SW personnel reflective of diverse communities.

Chapter 8: "Mathematics for Social Justice: Building on Students' Agency, Empathy, and Mathematics Ingenuity" introduces social justice mathematics principles for early childhood education, challenging traditional approaches dominated by medical models. The chapter advocates for child-centered, play-based mathematics instruction that supports identity development and challenges dominant norms. Drawing on Learning for Justice's Social Justice Standards, it provides a classroom vignette and guidance for educators on engaging with social justice mathematics to promote agency, empathy, and mathematical ingenuity in young learners.

Chapter 9: "Promoting Self-Determination as an Emancipatory Practice in Early Childhood Inclusion" explores the shift towards inclusive and equity-empowered early childhood education systems, emphasizing the promotion of self-determination as an emancipatory practice. The chapter discusses how promoting self-determination for children with disabilities aligns with anti-bias and anti-racism frameworks, enhancing access to inclusive settings and amplifying individual and communal voices. Recommendations for practice and future research are provided to support high-quality inclusion aligned with culturally responsive practices.

Chapter 10: "Becoming Reflective Early Intervention Practitioners in an Urban Area" examines the development of reflective practitioners among preservice early intervention (EI) practitioners in urban early childhood inclusive education programs. Drawing on studies about reflective practice and field experiences, the chapter highlights the role of reflective practice and feedback in supporting non-traditional students entering EI. It emphasizes the importance of field experiences in preparing high-quality early childhood practitioners ready to work with diverse children and families in urban settings.

Chapter 11: "They Who Learn Teach: Self-Directed Activities for Early-Childhood Educators to Deepen Their Cultural Competence" offers pedagogies and activities to enhance cultural competence among early childhood educators. By engaging in intentional, continuous, and inquiry-based professional development, educators can better serve the needs of young learners and promote their full potential. The chapter provides theoretical concepts and practical activities to empower educators in deepening their cultural competence beyond traditional professional development activities.

IN CONCLUSION

In conclusion, this edited reference book offers a comprehensive exploration of critical issues and innovative practices in early childhood education and intervention. Through the diverse perspectives of our esteemed contributors, we have delved into topics ranging from confronting bias in teacher preparation to promoting self-determination in early childhood inclusion. Each chapter provides valuable insights, research findings, and practical strategies that contribute to the ongoing dialogue surrounding equity, inclusion, and social justice in early childhood education.

As editors, we are immensely grateful to the authors for their dedication, expertise, and passion in addressing these vital issues. Their contributions have enriched this book and advanced our collective understanding of how to create more equitable and inclusive early childhood environments. We also extend our gratitude to the reviewers who provided invaluable feedback and guidance throughout the publication process.

It is our sincere hope that this book serves as a valuable resource for educators, researchers, policymakers, and practitioners committed to promoting equity and inclusion in early childhood settings. By engaging with the ideas presented in these chapters, we can work together to build a more just and inclusive future for all young children and their families.

We invite readers to join us in continuing these important conversations, exploring new avenues of research and practice, and striving towards a more equitable and inclusive early childhood landscape.

Thank you for your interest in this book, and may it inspire meaningful change in the field of early childhood education.

Amber Friesen
San Francisco State University, USA

Maryssa K. Mitsch
San Francisco State University, USA

Karina Du
San Francisco State University, USA & University of California, Berkeley, USA

Chapter 1
Promoting Inclusion in Emergent Early Childhood Learning Environments

Patricia K. Hampshire
Mississippi State University, USA

Juli L. Pool
Boise State University, USA

Deb R. Carter
https://orcid.org/0000-0001-6211-6584
Boise State University, USA

Sylvia Horning
Boise State University, USA

Shamaria Mosley
Mississippi State University, USA

ABSTRACT

The goal of this book chapter is to further push the boundaries of how we define inclusive early learning environments. In a field challenged by an ongoing lack of resources, teacher shortages, and issues surrounding the importance of early education, the authors of this chapter want to provide ideas that promote hope. In environments where emerging curriculum is used, the focus is on the process of learning and the understanding that each child has unique strengths. Given its focus on the strengths and interests of each individual child, this approach offers opportunities to create inclusive learning environments for all children, including those with exceptional

DOI: 10.4018/979-8-3693-0924-7.ch001

learning needs. The use of emergent curriculum in early childhood environments promotes the use of access, participation, and supports that are needed for children with exceptionalities to be successful in an inclusive classroom. The authors utilize a case study to illustrate how emergent learning environments can be designed to include all learners exploring and learning through play.

INTRODUCTION

The inclusion of young children with diverse abilities continues to be one of the most pressing challenges in education today (Odom et al., 2011; Sullivan-Sego et al., 2016). Programming must not only be developmentally appropriate, but it should also include opportunities for nurturing relationships with typical peers. Additionally, the National Association for the Education of Young Children (NAEYC; 2020) states that "developmentally appropriate practices must include learning experiences that are meaningful, accessible, and responsive to children both individually and collectively" (pg. 5). For early childhood educators who lack focused preparation in working with individuals with diverse needs, the challenge becomes one of resources and training. For families of young children with diverse learning needs, options for childcare and early education become limited. Further, early care options where educators are versed in inclusive methods remain rare, and in some areas, non-existent.

INCLUSION AND TEACHER TRAINING

Inclusion is defined as the "values, policies, and practices" that allow young children with disabilities to be "full members of families, communities, and society" (DEC/NAEYC, 2009, p. 2). Inclusive education emphasizes the idea that all children should be "welcomed as valued and contributing members" of the school (TASH, 2021). The benefits of inclusion for all children is well documented in the literature, including access to peer models for working on social emotional learning (SEL) goals, emergence in language-rich environments, opportunities to work on self-help skills, and access to challenging curricula (Parlakian, 2021). For typically developing peers, benefits include an appreciation for difference and diversity, exposure to differentiated approaches to learning content, and participating and contributing to a more diverse world (Lawrence et al., 2016). To this end, the benefits of inclusive learning environments are positive for both children and adults as society continues to push the boundaries of social justice for all marginalized populations.

Inclusive education is a necessary component when fostering equity and diversity for all students. Gutierrez (2009) shares that the definition of equity includes a "classroom environment that invites participation" (p. 5). In the field of early childhood education (ECE), there is a significant shortage of professionals who are trained in supporting children with mild to moderate disabilities (Kwon et al., 2017). With a lack of trained professionals, young exceptional learners often have restrictions on achievement in the classroom. According to the Department of Education and Human Services (2015), "early childhood providers and teachers may lack knowledge and competencies in child development, early childhood pedagogy, and individualizing instruction" (p. 2). This affects all children and presents a barrier to high-quality inclusive early learning. Recognizing this shortage is pivotal to ensuring that all young learners receive the education they need to be successful in inclusive environments.

It is important to remember that children with exceptionalities require additional support to be successful in inclusive classrooms. Aspects of equity related to achievement, including active engagement, confidence, and success (Gutierrez, 2009) must also be considered as we determine which supports are needed and in what format. Many ECE teachers, however, do not have the training and knowledge necessary to address the unique needs of children with disabilities in their program (Kwon et al., 2017; Mitchell & Hedge, 2007). This is often the result of requirements for ECE teacher preparation that do not include learners who need more focused support. The result is a lack of knowledge and experience in inclusive education, which directly impacts teachers' beliefs regarding their own capabilities and strategies for integrating exceptional young learners into the classroom (Dignath et al., 2022). The need for comprehensive teacher preparation on inclusion is essential to improving practices in early childhood programs and creating a more supportive environment for all children. Reexamining the way we prepare and support ECE professionals to include practices that promote inclusive pedagogy is one positive step in addressing these pressing needs.

Reimagining the Inclusive Early Learning Space

The goal of inclusion in early childhood is to create integrated learning environments for children with exceptionalities alongside their typically developing peers. One such setting that appears to be a natural fit for inclusion are classrooms based in emergent philosophies. Emergent curriculum is a philosophy of teaching and planning in early childhood curriculum that is based on children's interests and wonders. Inspired by Loris Malaguzzi, the founder of Reggio Emilia schools in Italy, this philosophy is a blend of theory and practice that challenges educators to see children as competent and capable learners in the context of group work (Fraser

& Gestwicki, 2002). Emerging learning environments align with inclusion as they are naturally individualized. Emergent curriculum is rooted in careful planning by teachers following the close observation of individual children. The goal of the emergent curriculum is to respond to every child's interests through open-ended and self-directed engagement (Jones, 2012). In environments where emergent curriculum is used, the focus is on the process of learning and the understanding that each child has unique strengths. Given its focus on the strengths and interests of each individual child (Jones, 2012), this approach offers opportunities to create inclusive learning environments for all children, including those with exceptional learning needs. The use of emergent curriculum in early childhood environments promotes access, participation, and supports that are needed for children with exceptionalities to be successful in an inclusive classroom. Maintaining high-quality inclusive classrooms requires educators to create supports across all areas of development so children can genuinely participate and achieve their individual goals.

Emergent curriculum is not accidental, as it emerges from intentional observation and documentation of children by teachers and is an extension of children's inquiry. Central to this approach is a strong image of the child who is seen as capable, curious, intelligent, and bringing their own prior knowledge. When the voice of the child is present in the classroom, we acknowledge the dimension of power (Tang, et. al., 2017) as we strive towards a more equitable approach to education. Through teachers' close observations, they notice not only what children are doing, but how they are playing and what they are saying. This practice enables teachers to develop responsive observation-based curriculum (Stacey, 2018). An important aspect of emergent curriculum is building and sustaining meaningful relationships and the importance of social learning. This is supported through key relationships where children, teachers, parents, and administrators engage and interact with one another and the environment.

The Three Teachers

Relationships are at the very heart of the curriculum and are reflected in an environment that encircles the child with three "teachers," (Biermeier, 2015). The three teachers are meaningful and intentional interactions and relationships based on partnerships with parents, teachers, and the environment itself. Parents are the child's first teacher(s) and advocates for their learning. As active participants in their child's learning, parents also need to have a sense of belonging within the environment. Effective inclusion requires the active, authentic, and meaningful participation and partnership between families and teachers. Families provide insight and expertise on their child that is vital for an inclusive program to provide support and plan for meaningful activities and opportunities for children. Educators learn from this expertise and extend their strength-based view of the child to the family. This mutual sharing and learning from each other about the child helps build a respectful collaboration and partnership.

The role of the teacher in emergent curriculum programs is that of a guide that learns alongside children, instead of as an instructor that provides children with information (Carter & Curtis, 2017). As a guide, the teacher (1) observes, interacts with, and listens to the children to learn more about their wonders and interests, (2) plans curriculum and prepares the environment that facilitates the children's deep exploration, (3) documents the children's words, actions, interests, experiences, and activities, and (4) interprets what is happening with the children and to make predictions and projections about how to go forward with the curriculum (Edwards, 2012; Stacey, 2018). In this role, educators provide opportunities to extend a child's learning based on individual and group interests. They also work together with families, colleagues, and children to create a mutual community of learners to build and maintain social relationships (Fraser & Gestwicki, 2002). As a result, relationships serve as the foundation for creating environments that are flexible and are designed to reflect children's individual interests and strengths.

When the environment is viewed as the third teacher, it reflects on the image of the child as rich, strong, and powerful and allows the child to be actively engaged in learning (Fraser & Gestwicki, 2002). The use of open-ended materials that are readily available in the environment shows the value and importance of creativity and the belief that children can lead their learning.

Emergent learning environments provide opportunities for all children to build knowledge around individual interests and prior experiences. By building on children's interests and ideas, the emergent curriculum respects the voice of children while meeting standards across learning domains, as well as multiple modalities for learning (Stacey, 2018). Through play-based learning, children have opportunities to establish relationships with peers and teachers through collaborative learning and meaningful and engaging play. Working together in groups and building connections with peers provides children with opportunities to navigate and develop meaningful social relationships. The environment as the third teacher provides space for children to work with peers as they develop their inquiry and ideas together in large or small groups as well as areas that support independent play. Educators make learning visible to children, families, and the community by creating meaningful documentation that shows the learning journey. Reviewing documentation with children provides opportunities for them to reflect on their work or the work of others and expand on their learning (Fraser & Gestwicki, 2002). By creating rich environments, play-based learning is promoted, and educators can support children's developmental needs by following and building on the inquiries and wonders of the children.

The Value of Play-Based Learning in Emergent Curriculum

As a central component of emergent learning models, play is integral to the cognitive, physical, social and emotional well-being of children (Ginsburg, 2007) and contributes to the development of social skills through purposeful verbal inter-action, cooperation, and collaboration (Smilansky & Shefatya, 1990). Play-based learning is an essential component in emergent learning spaces where children are encouraged to explore and engage in their environment independently. Most young children spend their day engaging in a world of play as they learn about themselves and explore their environments. Play is often defined as a self-initiated activity that is intrinsically motivating and satisfying (Hansen et al., 1999) and characterized as: (1) controlled by the players; (2) concerned with process rather than product; (3) nonliteral; (4) free of externally imposed rules; and (5) incorporating active engage-ment on the part of the players (Passmore & Hughes, 2020). For each young child, their experiences with play vary. In some cases, individuals with exceptionalities may struggle to express their feelings or pick up on the social cues of others. While others may have restricted or unusual interests and experience limiting reciprocity in relationships (Trawick-Smith, 2014). Children with exceptional learning needs may not use play in ways that are most beneficial to them (Lantz, n.d.). Oftentimes, these children are observed playing alone in repetitive, stereotyped manners. Given the value of play in early childhood pedagogy and theory, it is imperative that all young children have access to learning through play-based support.

As a vehicle for learning, play provides a platform that is both engaging and motivating for young children who are seeking to understand the world around them. Research suggests a connection between play-based learning and gains in young children's self-regulation skills (Pyle & DeLuca, 2017), social competence (Chau et al., 2022), language and communication (Ercis, Ahmet, & Levent, 2021), vocabulary acquisition (Van Oers & Duijkers, 2013), mathematical understanding and spatial relationships (Levine et al., 2012), and emergent literacy skills (Nicolopoulou et al., 2015). When considering the overall benefits of play, children with exceptionali-ties would benefit from environments that not only have a strong focus on play but supports in place to further individual student growth in this area. Given that many young children with exceptionalities show marked delays in the social domain (e.g., delayed toy play skills, struggles related to peer engagement), practitioners must rely on current and ongoing research in the space of play interventions to identify strategies that may be effectively embedded in their classroom.

INCLUSIVE EMERGENT PLAY-BASED LEARNING IN ACTION

When reimagining any learning environment, models and examples can be helpful in supporting practitioners to apply content in meaningful ways. In this section of the chapter, one such model will be described to illustrate how emergent learning environments can incorporate all learners while taking a strengths-based approach to intervention for students with exceptional needs. Mrs. Jewel's preschool learning environment will be described and used as an example for how these ideas could look in practice. In addition, one of Mrs. Jewel's students will be described to demonstrate specific inclusive practices in this setting.

Mrs. Jewel is an early childhood educator who works in a local early learning center and currently leads a classroom for young children 2-3 years of age. Her classroom is designed to incorporate emergent curriculum and a play-based philosophy. Through close observation and interaction with the children Mrs. Jewel creates and builds the curriculum based on the children's wonders and inquiries. This includes the use of open-ended materials and loose parts (i.e., materials with varied properties that can be moved and manipulated in many ways such as blocks, digging and dumping tools, rocks, buttons, sand, leaves…) to create an environment that will encourage growth and a love of learning. By providing materials that are inspired by the children, Mrs. Jewel creates spaces that are tailored to meet the needs of each individual child. This classroom is highly dedicated to each child's unique needs and supporting them through a strength-based approach.

Mrs. Jewel designed the classroom environment to invite the children to explore a variety of natural and open-ended materials available. For example, she may arrange on a table a few clear tubs of flowers, petals, rocks, twigs, and shells to see how children explore nature. She then sits at the table alongside the children and asks guiding questions and listens to the children's wonderings. She documents how the children interact with the materials, what questions they are asking, how they are working together, etc. The free-flowing environment invites both children and adults to investigate. Open spaces provide opportunities for building large structures while smaller, cozy spaces invite children to curl up with pillows or their favorite stuffies. Natural light is abundant in the classroom, and Mrs. Jewel makes use of the light to reduce the use of fluorescent lights. She has also draped tulle from the ceiling, which has been lined with twinkle lights to create a calming atmosphere that adds just enough light. Muted and soft colors have been selected for the classroom to reduce visual noise within the environment. Mrs. Jewel provides opportunities for children to choose how and if their work is displayed in the classroom, as well as where they would like it to be displayed.

In this classroom, all furniture is sized based on the age of the children and encourages student independence and the ability to choose their own materials. To support the interests and abilities of all children, multiple spaces were created, including a small world table, sensory table, art area, block play, home area, and quiet spaces. Children have access to a variety of natural and authentic materials in each space and the freedom to use the materials in any area of the classroom to support their continued exploration.

In Mrs. Jewel's classroom, there are children representing a variety of cultures, races, ethnicities, socioeconomic status, and ability levels. Mrs. Jewel has several children in the classroom with exceptional learning needs. One three-year-old student, Sebastian, was recently diagnosed with Autism Spectrum Disorder (ASD). Sebastian has one older and one younger sibling who also live in his home. Sebastian attends an all-day emergent early learning program that is supportive of creating inclusive environments for all children. Sebastian began receiving services for early intervention (i.e., IDEA Part C services) when he was 18 months old for speech and language. He is now participating in Speech therapy and Occupational therapy in his classroom at the early learning center.

Sebastian's unique learning needs inspired Mrs. Jewel to intentionally think about whether her classroom was truly inclusive of all learners. Mrs. Jewel had never worked with a child with ASD, so she reached out to both the child's family and her colleagues to ensure she was incorporating supports that would engage Sebastian. Mrs. Jewel also spent a lot of time observing Sebastian in the learning environment to determine his strengths and areas of need.

The Power of Observation and Documentation

One of our best tools as early educators is observation. Through observation, we gain insight into a child's interests, dislikes, fears, motivators, and learning patterns. An observation that includes all the developmental domains helps to provide a comprehensive understanding of how a child learns best and in what context. Given the role that play has in early learning, observations focused in this area are essential. By identifying the types of play materials, the child prefers, the teacher gains insight that can be used to help motivate an isolated child. During initial observations, early educators should note the types of play materials a child is typically drawn to. For example, do they tend to play with toys that light up or have lots of pieces? Are there play items the child avoids or appears agitated by? Does the child run away or cover their ears when a toy is making a loud noise? When working to expand play-based skills, it is important to work with toys the child already has some experience with, as this sets the stage for increasing the skill set and building on success.

Central to these observations is gathering information about how the child engages with not only the environment and play materials, but adults and peers as well (Gargiulo & Kilgo, 2011). Given that play provides an opportunity for improving social competence, understanding how the child relates to those in their environment is essential. For example, is there a teacher that the child appears to be most comfortable with? When playing with toys, does the child tolerate interruptions easily from a specific peer or adult? Does the child initiate play with any specific peers or avoid someone in particular? Documenting this additional "data" can help inform plans for engagement and where to start when working on more collaborative forms of play.

Children's development extends across a vast variety of developmental domains including social/emotional, communication, and cognitive skills (Moore, 2017). Play has a pivotal role in nurturing these developmental domains. Collaborative play teaches children social norms and empathy. Research suggests that the advancement of brain development (cognitive function and self-regulatory skills) hinges significantly on play quality (Hakkarainen & Bredikyte, 2010). The framework of play promotes the development of problem-solving, coping, and understanding the perspective of their peers (Ali et al., 2018). Through play, children develop language skills that enable them to express their thoughts and ideas. Concurrently, the cognitive domain is stimulated, as play helps cultivate imaginative scenarios as well as creativity (Sansanwal, 2014). Physical development is refined through active play as children engage in gross and fine motor skills (Ali et al., 2018). Running, climbing, and manipulating objects enhance a child's physicality (Ali et al., 2018). In summary, play promotes cognitive exercises that stimulate growth across a child's developmental domains (Tomporowski et al., 2015).

When learning how developmental domains and play relate, it is pivotal that observers know what play-related skills look like. Carefully observing, analyzing, and documenting these play-related skills across developmental domains, practitioners, educators, and parents can cultivate interventions to enhance the play experiences for children. One way to document what we learn during these observations is through Learning Stories. Learning Stories are a narrative tool used to record a child's life in the classroom and school community based on the teacher's observations (NAEYC, 2022). This tool provides observers with a lens to analyze and document the development of these skills within the realm of play while also ensuring that the home culture of the child is valued. Learning Stories have several key components including photos or videos based on the observation, an analysis of the observation, a plan for extending learning, the family's perspective on their child's learning, and links to evaluation tools. By utilizing tools that promote family voice we also further promote equity through the lens of identity (Tang, et al, 2017). When conducting observations, early childhood educators should take note (i.e., through written or voice recorded formats) of the following areas:

Sharing and Collaborative Play: The ability to share and collaborate signifies a child's social development (Jung & Sainato, 2013). Collaborative play enhances sharing and communication with peers. An observer may note if a child shares blocks or a puzzle with a peer.

Independent Toy Play Skills: Selecting and personalizing toys demonstrates a child's autonomy (Paterson & Arco, 2007). For example, a child independently choosing blocks to complete a structure that he or she is building showcases independence.

Social Bids to Peers: Engaging in social interaction through verbal cues is pivotal for play (Dueñas et al., 2021). Another key aspect is the child initiating communication with their peers. This may look like a child inviting a peer to join them in completing a puzzle.

Preference for Specific Toys: Knowing a child's preference for toys enhances play engagement. This may look like a child gravitating towards the art center instead of the dramatic play center. This may indicate the child has a particular interest in sensory-based activities (Conine & Vollmer, 2019).

Avoidance of Specific Toys: When observing play it is important to recognize toys or spaces that cause discomfort. Loud noise or flashing lights may not be conducive to the play environment (Shillingsburg et al., 2014).

Perseveration with Specific Toys: While observing it is important to notice repetitive engagement with a specific toy. For example, building and unbuilding blocks demonstrate a perseverative play pattern (Raulston & Machalicek, 2018).

In essence, play operates as a multifaceted tool that fosters the integration of physical, social, and emotional development. Play also contributes to the enrichment of communication and cognitive development of children. Play is integral to the growth of children across diverse developmental domains. By carefully observing and analyzing these play-related skills across developmental domains, practitioners, educators, and parents can cultivate play experiences and interventions, when appropriate, to enhance the play experiences for children.

In her classroom, Mrs. Jewel intentionally observes and provides respectful attention to her student's' words, actions, and creations. She believes it is important to focus on the process of learning, not teaching. She inquires, explores, and researches alongside children and provides opportunities for children to discover the answers to their questions.

When Sebastian first joined the classroom, Mrs. Jewel spent a lot of time observing his play skills and preferences in the environment. During these observations, she learned many important things that helped her to tailor the environment to meet his individual needs. For example, throughout the day, Sebastian does not actively engage in the environment or with his peers. In the classroom, he frequently paces the threshold between the carpet and tile for 3-5 minutes while flapping his hands. During open play time in the classroom, Sebastian can be found lining up crayons, emptying and refilling baskets with loose parts, or stacking translucent blocks on the light table. Sebastian prefers to engage in these activities by himself and struggles to share highly preferred materials.

Based on these observations, Mrs. Jewel spends some time thinking about how she might prepare the physical environment to better meet the needs of students like Sebastian. Her goal is to build on his strengths while helping to provide opportunities for growth and independence.

PREPARING PHYSICAL ENVIRONMENTS TO SUPPORT INCLUSION

Like Sebastian, some students need more support in the physical environment to ensure they are successful in inclusive spaces. Physical modifications include changes to the environment, including adaptations to lighting, selection and arrangement of materials and furniture, selection of seating options, and intentional use of visual supports and environmental cues (Rausch et al., 2021; Sandall et al., 2019). The intentional selection of materials that align with children's interests, that promote peer interaction, and that support access can promote children's motivation and enhance learning and achievement. This aligns with Developmentally Appropriate Practice recommendations (NAEYC, 2020) to provide "a rich variety of materials, challenges, and ideas that are worthy of children's attention" (p. 22), to select materials that are "based on careful observation of children's play choices" (p. 21), and to intentionally rotate and revisit materials periodically to "provide children with opportunities to reflect and re-engage with the learning experiences" (p. 22).

In planning to support Sebastian's engagement in the classroom, Mrs. Jewel paid special attention to his high preference materials and created a basket of preferred items. For Sebastian, this included materials that allowed him to engage in repetitive and calming movements and activities such as crayons, markers, magnet tiles, clothes pins, and modeling clay. This basket of materials was available to Sebastian throughout the day and was utilized specifically during challenging activities, as well as to begin planned play interventions.

The use of visual supports, such as visual schedules, visual scripts, or picture cues can promote children's independence and task engagement, encourage social interaction, and promote new skills such as play skills (Gauvreau & Schwartz, 2013).

Educators teaching in play-based environments should remember that traditional methods that are language-based have been found to be less effective for many students with exceptionalities who often have difficulty understanding abstract concepts and words with dual meanings (Mesibov et al., 2004). Taking advantage of some students' preference for visual stimuli, teachers structuring materials for learners through this modality is an increasingly common practice (Mesibov & Shea, 2010; National Research Council, 2001). Using visually structured activities provides students with cues to assist them in responding efficiently. In effective visually structured activities, the materials are organized and presented in a planned, sequential, and logical way.

Mrs. Jewel utilized visual supports as well as temporal modifications, adjusting the timing and order of routines and activities, to support Sebastian's independence and engagement in the classroom. Recognizing that transitions were difficult for Sebastian, Mrs. Jewel began by carefully reviewing the daily schedule to identify ways to reduce the number of transitions that Sebastian engaged in each day. She scheduled Sebastian's diaper changes right before snack and mealtimes so that diaper changes became part of existing transitions rather than additional transitions he had to experience throughout the day.

While Mrs. Jewel used a visual schedule with her entire class, she individualized the schedule for Sebastian by using real objects. In particular, the schedule used real three-dimensional objects that cued Sebastian to transition to a specific activity. For example, a diaper was used to prompt him to go to the bathroom. Mrs. Jewel also broke down Sebastian's day into manageable chunks by including only three activities at a time and then taking them away as they were completed. Additionally, Mrs. Jewel integrated preference and sensory breaks into Sebastian's individual object schedule. She included preferred play materials, embedding three intentional play opportunities into Sebastian's morning routine. She also built intentional sensory breaks into the schedule, ensuring Sebastian's access to regulating activities such as hugs and squeezes from his teacher, or brief time to rock or jump on the trampoline. Sensory breaks, integrated throughout the schedule, provided interspersed breaks to enhance learning, reduce distress, and promote self-regulation.

By establishing environmental supports in the classroom, Mrs. Jewel began seeing more engagement with materials and a general sense of calm in how Sebastian transitioned throughout his day. One area that also started to change was Sebastian's tolerance for peers in his personal play space as he appeared more comfortable with children playing in closer proximity. However, Sebastian still struggled with sharing highly preferred items, resulting in grabbing toys from peers or simply leaving the play environment and self-stimulating. Mrs. Jewel decided that she needed to look more closely at the social environment in her classroom to support Sebastian in establishing relationships with both adults and peers.

PREPARING SOCIAL ENVIRONMENTS
TO SUPPORT INCLUSION

The social environment refers to the way that a classroom learning environment influences and supports interactions that occur throughout the day among children, educators, and family members. A prepared and well-designed social environment helps foster positive peer to peer relationships, as well as positive interactions between adults and children. Research has shown the careful and intentional planning, designing, and facilitating of child social interactions is foundational to maximizing active engagement, collaborative participation, and creating an environment that promotes relationship building and fosters healthy social interactions (Orr, 2009; Reska et al., 2012). Effective interactions are one of the most crucial ingredients for both social and whole child development. The next section will discuss how educators, peers, and family members can support the social environment.

Educators

Educators must be flexible and able to adapt and modify the environment and their instructional approach for children who need more support to have effective and successful interactions (Barton et al., 2015). Social modifications include using "social scripts to support communication and problem solving, use of 'buddy' systems, and reinforcement of specific social skills that encourage a sense of belonging and meaningful friendships" (Rausch et al., 2021, p. 17). The use of modifications to the social environment, explicit teaching and modeling of social skills, scaffolding, and embedded opportunities to practice with peers ensure a continuum of supports are provided (Barton et al., 2015).

Social Scripts

Scripted stories, also referred to as social scripts, personal stories, or personal narratives, are tools that can be used for teaching social skills to children. The goals of a scripted story are to: (1) describe a confusing or difficult social situation for the child, (2) help the child understand a social routine, (3) increase understanding of specific situations, (4) provide suggestions for appropriate behaviors, and (5) support the child in understanding the thoughts, feelings, and behavior of others ("Tip sheets - inclusive child care", 2020). In other words, social scripts promote true social understanding.

Currently, Sebastian's family has been experiencing some life transitions that affect consistency across social environments. Anticipating an upcoming move the family was making, Mrs. Jewel worked with Sebastian's family to develop a social story to emotionally prepare him for this change. Mrs. Jewel asked the family to take pictures of the new house they were moving to and also send pictures of their current living space. She then developed a social story that incorporated pictures of these spaces and Sebastian and his family to show them in the new environment. Pictures also included key comfort items like Sebastian's stuffed crocodile to give him an "anchor" item to connect with. Mrs. Jewel asked Sebastian's family to read this social story daily in the weeks leading up to the move. She also read the story at school a few days prior to the move to ensure he was processing the new information across environments.

Explicit Teaching and Modeling

Emergent learning environments offer a variety of open-ended materials and activities, child choice (in how and what they want to discover and learn), and activities that require collaborative social skills. Inevitably, there are children in the inclusive emergent learning environment whose needs are not met and need more direct support in the form of explicit teaching and modeling. Intentional and strategic modeling and scaffolding support children's success with interactions and collaborations.

Teach Friendship and Play Skills. Educators need to be intentional about teaching friendship skills and concepts of friendships (e.g., reciprocity, how to manage interactions). Children with (and without) disabilities may need to be taught and supported in how to ask a friend to play and how to share materials. Educators might need to offer instruction on how to connect with peers, as well as give the time and support within play activities to create these important relationships.

In Mrs. Jewel's classroom, she emphasizes the importance of community and treating all of your friends with kindness. During morning group meetings, Mrs. Jewel will pick a topic or specific skill to focus on with the students. Recently, she chose to teach a lesson on sharing. She read a book to the students about the importance of sharing and then engaged in some role play based on scenarios they might encounter. In the role play, she emphasized behaviors she wanted to see and also those that were problematic in forming relationships with peers. Throughout the week, Mrs. Jewel then looked for opportunities to reinforce students when she saw sharing behaviors. When students engaged in the opposite behavior, Mrs. Jewel provided feedback to students and modeled a more appropriate way of engaging with peers. Mrs. Jewel also recognized that not all her students would get the information they needed in this format and in some cases, additional foundational skills would need to be taught first.

Some children, like Sebastian, may need more foundational social skills such as allowing other children to play in his space or use his preferred materials. Entering into the play of young children can be tricky. For children with exceptionalities who engage in stereotypic and repetitive play, allowing peers or adults into their play may be especially challenging. Once teachers have spent time observing young children in play settings to identify motivators and preferred items, finding ways to "teach" within those play scenarios is essential.

Least-to-Most Prompting (LtM) Least-to-Most (LtM), or the system of least prompts (SLP), refers to a prompting hierarchy in which the lowest levels of prompting are provided until targeted behaviors are achieved (Barton et al., 2019). For example, the teacher may first wait to see if the child can perform the behavior independently, based only on the natural cue in the environment, before offering a gesture or indirect verbal prompt, only moving to more intrusive prompts such as modeling or physical assistance, if the child needs this additional level of support to respond correctly. LtM prompting is particularly effective for play interventions, as it is easily faded and does not interrupt the flow of play while allowing for independence on behalf of the child (Barton, 2015). Davis-Temple, Jung, and Sainato (2014) used an LtM prompting hierarchy to promote on-task and independent behavior of young children learning to play a board game; the study concluded that prompt fading is an effective measure for teaching play skills. Research in this area also emphasizes the importance of having specific play targets to increase play diversity in young children with autism (Barton et al., 2019).

Pivotal Response Training (PRT) When an educator observes a young child engaging in repetitive play in isolation in the classroom, they may begin by inserting themselves into the scenario by playing alongside the child using similar or shared materials. If the child shows some interest, the teacher may model an action with a toy similar to see if the child is paying attention or to begin prompting imitation or even engagement. If the child is not attending to the teacher or appears uninterested, the teacher may go a step further into their play using strategies found in Pivotal Response Training (Koegel et al., 1987). In this case, the teacher may block a child's access to an item needed while engaging in a repetitive or restricted activity, holding access contingent on a targeted action (e.g., imitating a play action) or verbalization. In either of these scenarios, the teacher's engagement in the play space is short to begin with and would increase over time as the child becomes more tolerant and open to bids for interaction.

Given Sebastian's preference to play alone with highly preferred items in repetitive ways (e.g., dumping and filling baskets), Mrs. Jewel decided that she needed to begin intervening to promote more social engagement in the classroom. Since Sebastian did not have "typical" toy play skills that would invite a peer to play with him, Mrs. Jewel decided that she would start with teaching him some basic play sequences through imitation. Using a PRT model, Mrs. Jewel would wait until Sebastian was engaged in repetitive play in isolation and then quietly enter into his play. First, she played alongside him with the same materials modeling different actions looking for him to mimic actions. When she realized this was not happening and she needed to be more direct, she began modeling and then prompting him to do the same (increasing prompts from least to most). At first, she needed to provide some additional partial physical prompting or a gesture. Over time, once Sebastian anticipated the expectations of these interactions, he needed less support and mimicked the different actions and at times built on them. Utilizing a Least-to-Most approach Mrs. Jewel supported Sebastian until he demonstrated a readiness for prompt fading.

Teach Children How to Recognize Emotions Emotions impact attention, memory, and learning; the ability to build relationships; and physical and mental health (Tominey et al., 2017). Developing emotional intelligence enables children to recognize, name, and manage their emotions effectively. Children with these skills are better able to pay attention, are more engaged, have more positive relationships, are more empathic, and are also better able to regulate their behaviors (Eggum et al., 2011; Raver et al., 2007; Rivers et al., 2012; Tominey et al., 2017).

Children who are unable to understand, label, and/or identify their own feelings have a hard time accurately identifying how others are feeling as well. Tominey at al. (2017) describe five skills that can be taught and modeled to promote emotional intelligence: (1) recognizing emotions in oneself and others; (2) understanding the causes and consequences of emotions; (3) labeling emotions accurately; (4) expressing emotions in ways that are appropriate for the time, place, and culture; and (5) regulating emotions. Instructional strategies such as singing songs (e.g., "If You're Happy and You Know It"); using puppets/toys to act out and talk through emotions; and playing games to teach and practice how to take turns, win and lose, share, and negotiate can be used to support children in learning about emotions.

Mrs. Jewel recognized the need for embedding social emotional) teaching opportunities throughout her students' day. Managing "big feelings" in the classroom was an ongoing need for her students, especially those who did not have siblings at home with whom to practice some of these skills. Mrs. Jewel utilized morning meetings to introduce new topics and explore areas related to social and emotional self-regulation. She intentionally set up activities like games that required turn taking to give students the opportunity to practice new skills and put names to emotions that were challenging for them. Mrs. Jewel sent home ideas for working on these skills at home in her weekly newsletter in an attempt to create consistency across activities, environments, and caregivers.

Embedded Opportunities to Interact

An instructional method that educators (and parents) can use to meet children's needs is embedded learning opportunities. Embedded learning opportunities (ELOs) align with research supported practices (DEC, 2014; NAEYC, 2020) and occur in three parts: antecedent, target behavior, and consequence (Coogle et al., 2021). In the first part, an adult provides a prompt or other cue (antecedent) to elicit a targeted behavior or skill in a child. Second, the child either initiates the target behavior spontaneously or with support from the adult (i.e., prompted and/or modeled by the adult). The ELO concludes with the delivery of a motivating consequence (i.e., desired activity, material, and/or action). ELOs allow educators to provide multiple intentional opportunities for children to practice targeted skills with support across activities, routines, and environments (DEC, 2014; Johnson et al., 2015). Systematically embedding planned social interactions throughout the day provides increased opportunities for learning positive social behaviors.

Prior to beginning instruction on social behaviors or embedding planned interactions, educators need to attend to particular components of the classroom (Joseph & Strain, 2010). First, an inclusive classroom where children with exceptionalities are meaningfully included in natural proportions is an important component (Causton & Tracy-Bronson, 2015). Second, the pre-selection and presence of cooperative-use toys and materials will increase the opportunities for social interaction. Cooperative-use toys and materials are those that encourage two or more children playing together. Third, educators should look at classroom routines and determine where they can embed social interaction instruction and practice opportunities throughout the day. **Figure 1** provides an example of how social interactions can be embedded into classroom routines. Lastly, and arguably the most important, educators need to create a social environment with a sense of belonging and a climate of friendship.

During open play time, Mrs. Jewel sets up highly preferred materials at the table for Sebastian to engage with. Sitting near him, she observes him engaging with the materials, adding items (e.g., rolling pin) slowly to extend his play. Once he was comfortable, she invited one of his trusted peers to join. Very quickly it became apparent that Sebastian was agitated, and he began taking items from his friend and vocally stimming. Thinking on her feet, Mrs. Jewel grabbed two trays, putting the same items on each one in front of the two children. Sensing the clear boundary of what was his, Sebastian calmed down and began engaging again with the modeling clay.

Peers

Implementing a "buddy system," or peer intervention, is another modification that can be made to the social environment (Prendeville et al., 2006; Rausch et al., 2017). Engaging with peers can be challenging for children with ASD and other disabilities. Children may lack the skills needed to effectively interact with peers. In these cases, educators identify a peer or "buddy" to work alongside the child needing support. The selected peer should be socially competent and able to maintain positive social interactions and contact (Prendeville et al., 2006). The peer provides a model for communication and interaction patterns, as well as support in play skills by assisting with organizing play, offering suggestions, and exchanging ideas about what they are doing (Prendeville et al., 2006; Rausch et al., 2017). Suggestions for embedding the "buddy system" are included in Figure 1.

Families

Consistency is important for all children, but for children with exceptionalities, consistency is essential. For children to thrive, they need to know what is expected in the classroom, in the home, and in the community. If expectations change everywhere they go, they may become confused, which can lead to maladaptive behaviors such as challenging behavior and improper social skills (Rausch et al., 2017). Educators and families can work together to create consistency across the various social environments.

Routines and Expectations

Consistent and predictable routines help prepare children for each part of the day, know what to expect, aid in transitions, and maximize autonomy. When children are part of familiar activities and routines, they develop relationships with the people they interact with and gain a sense of belonging and self-confidence. "Environments that are engaging, predictable, and characterized by ongoing positive adult-child interactions are necessary for promoting children's social and emotional development and preventing challenging behavior" (Hemmeter et al., 2006, p. 592). Children are more likely to engage in prosocial behavior when they know what to do, when to do it, how to do it, and what is expected.

Communicating with families about classroom routines and expectations can open an important dialogue about developmentally appropriate behavior expectations for young children and effective ways to encourage young children to follow the routines and expectations. This dialogue allows opportunities to discuss similarities and differences between the home and school environment, which allows everyone to work together to be as consistent as possible and to help children navigate the expectations across environments.

Mrs. Jewel also partnered with Sebastian's family to support consistency in routines across school and home environments. One example of this is Sebastian's healthy sleep routine. Mrs. Jewel talked with the family about their sleep routines at home, including learning about what was working for them and what was challenging for them. She shared the same about his sleeping routines at school. Together, they developed a consistent and effective sleep routine that could be used consistently across environments. At home and at school, they read a book to support relaxation, played white noise from a free downloadable app, added black-out curtains, and used a sensory compression bed sheet. At school, this all occurred directly after snack. At home, the family included a bath before Sebastian's story. The consistency across home and school supported Sebastian and his family in creating a successful sleep routine.

Teachers can create a positive social environment by interacting with children in ways that make them feel valued, seen, and heard. By carefully observing children in their play and intentionally planning for instruction and embedding opportunities for meaningful social interactions, teachers can maximize active engagement and collaborative participation for all children. In addition, when teachers work with families to establish supports across environments (e.g., home, school), we create more consistency and less confusion. In this same sense, by sharing the responsibility for planning and implementation, we empower families as agents of change and partners in the education of their child. A prepared social environment promotes relationship building and fosters healthy social interactions for all children.

CONCLUSION

Mrs. Jewel's journey of reflection focused on creating a more inclusive learning environment has helped her to also grow as a teacher. After 20 years in the field of ECE, she is constantly reminded of the importance of creating and maintaining intentional and supportive partnerships with all members of the community (e.g., children, families, educators). Parents are encouraged to participate in classroom activities and events are scheduled as a way to invite families into the environment to engage with their children. The early learning center Mrs. Jewel works in has begun work on creating more classrooms that meet the needs of more diverse learners. Her center director has asked Mrs. Jewel to partner with her colleagues as they begin their own personal reflection and find new ways to support inclusion center wide.

REFERENCES

Ali, E., Constantino, K. M., Hussain, A., & Akhtar, Z. (2018). The effects of play-based learning on early childhood education and development. *Journal of Evolution of Medical and Dental Sciences*, 7(43), 6808–6811. 10.14260/jemds/2018/1044

Barton, E., Pribble, L., & Joseph, J. (2015). Evidenced-based practices for successful inclusion. In Barton, E., & Smith, B. (Eds.), *The preschool inclusion toolbox: How to build and lead a high-quality program* (pp. 113–132). Brookes.

Barton, E. E., Gossett, S., Waters, M. C., Murray, R., & Francis, R. (2019). Increasing play complexity in a young child with autism. *Focus on Autism and Other Developmental Disabilities*, 34(2), 81–90. 10.1177/1088357618800493

Biermeier, M. A. (2015). Inspired by Reggio Emilia: Emergent curriculum in relationship-driven learning environments. *Young Children*, 70(5), 72–79.

Carter, M., & Curtis, D. (2017). *Learning together with young children: A curriculum framework for reflective teachers*. Redleaf Press.

Causton, J., & Tracy-Bronson, C. P. (2015). *The educator's handbook to inclusive school practices*. Brookes.

Chau, L., Yuen, M., Chan, P., Liu, S., Chan, K., Lee, D., & Hsieh, W. Y. (2022). Play-based parent training programme supporting Hong Kong kindergarten children in social competence development. *British Journal of Guidance & Counselling*, 50(3), 386–399. 10.1080/03069885.2022.2030464

Conine, D. E., & Vollmer, T. R. (2019). Relative preferences for edible and leisure stimuli in children with autism. *Journal of Applied Behavior Analysis*, 52(2), 557–573. 10.1002/jaba.52530468244

Coogle, C. G., Lakey, E. R., Ottley, J. R., Brown, J. A., & Romano, M. K. (2021). Embedded learning opportunities for children with and without disabilities. *Young Children*, 76(4), 8–15.

Davis-Temple, J., Jung, S., & Sainato, D. M. (2014). Teaching young children with special needs and their peers to play board games: Effects of a least to most prompting procedure to increase independent performance. *Behavior Analysis in Practice*, 7(1), 21–30. 10.1007/s40617-014-0001-827019792

Dignath, C., Rimm-Kaufman, S., van Ewijk, R., & Kunter, M. (2022). Teachers' Beliefs About Inclusive Education and Insights on What Contributes to Those Beliefs: A Meta-analytical Study. *Educational Psychology Review*, 34(4), 2609–2660. 10.1007/s10648-022-09695-0

Dueñas, A. D., D'Agostino, S. R., & Plavnick, J. B. (2021). Teaching Young Children to Make Bids to Play to Peers With Autism Spectrum Disorder. *Focus on Autism and Other Developmental Disabilities*, 36(4), 201–212. 10.1177/10883576211023326

Edwards, C. (2011). The Hundred Languages of Children: *The Reggio Emilia Experience in Transformation*. ProQuest Ebook Central, https://ebookcentral.proquest.com/lib/cudenver/detail.action?docID=820317

Eggum, N. D., Eisenberg, N., Kao, K., Spinrad, T. L., Bolnick, R., Hofer, C., Kupfer, A. S., & Fabricius, W. V. (2011). Emotion understanding, theory of mind, and prosocial orientation: Relations over time in early childhood. *The Journal of Positive Psychology*, 6(1), 4–16. 10.1080/17439760.2010.53677622518196

Ercis, S., Sirinkan, A., & Önal, L. (2021). Investigation of the Effect of Inclusive Play and Special Movement Education to Social Communication in Disadvantaged and Peer Children in Preschool (Erzurum Sample). *Journal of Educational Issues*, 7(3), 1–9. 10.5296/jei.v7i3.19155

Fraser, S., & Gestwicki, C. (2002). *Authentic Childhood: Exploring Reggio Emilia in the Classroom*. Delmar/Thomson Learning.

Gargiulo, R. M., & Kilgo, J. L. (2011). *An introduction to young children with special needs*. Birth Through Age Eight.

Gauvreau, A. N., & Schwartz, I. S. (2013). Using visual supports to promote appropriate behavior in young children with Autism and related disorders. *Young Exceptional Children Monograph Series*, 15, 29–44.

Ginsburg, K. R. (2007). The importance of play in promoting healthy child development and maintaining strong parent-child bonds. *Pediatrics*, 119(1), 182–191. 10.1542/peds.2006-269717200287

Gutierrez, R. (2009). Framing equity: Helping students "play the game" and "change the game". *Teaching for Excellence and Equity in Mathematics*, 1(1), 5–7.

Hakkarainen, P., & Bredikyte, M. (2010). Strong foundation through play-based learning. *Psychological Science and Education*, 3, 58–64.

Hemmeter, M. L., Ostrosky, M., & Fox, L. (2006). Social and emotional foundations for early learning: A conceptual model for intervention. *School Psychology Review*, 35(4), 583–601. 10.1080/02796015.2006.12087963

Johnson, J., Rahn, N., & Bricker, D. (2015). *An activity-based approach to early intervention* (4th ed.). Brookes.

Jones, E. (2012). The emergence of emergent curriculum. *Young Children*, 67(2), 66–73.

Joseph, G., & Strain, P. (2010). *Module 2 handout 2.3: Social emotional teaching strategies - You've got to have friends*. The Center on the Social and Emotional Foundations for Early Learning. http://csefel.vanderbilt.edu/modules/module2/handout3.pdf

Jung, S., & Sainato, D. M. (2013). Teaching play skills to young children with autism. *Journal of Intellectual & Developmental Disability*, 38(1), 74–90. 10.310 9/13668250.2012.73222023157647

Koegel, R. L., O'dell, M. C., & Koegel, L. K. (1987). A natural language teaching paradigm for nonverbal autistic children. *Journal of Autism and Developmental Disorders*, 17(2), 187–200. 10.1007/BF014950553610995

Kwon, K. A., Hong, S. Y., & Jeon, H. J. (2017). Classroom readiness for successful inclusion: Teacher factors and preschool children's experience with and attitudes toward peers with disabilities. *Journal of Research in Childhood Education*, 31(3), 360–378. 10.1080/02568543.2017.1309480

Lantz, J. (n.d.). *Play time: An examination of play intervention strategies in children with Autism Spectrum Disorders*. IIDC. https://www.iidc.indiana.edu/pages/Play -Time-An-Examination-Of-Play-Intervention-Strategies-for-Children-with-Autism -Spectrum-Disorders>

Lawrence, D., Smith, S., & Banerjee, R. (2016). Preschool inclusion: Key findings from research and implications for policy. *Child Care and Early Education Research Connections*, 1-15.

Levine, S. C., Gibson, D. J., & Berkowitz, T. (2019). Mathematical development in the early home environment. In *Cognitive foundations for improving mathematical learning* (pp. 107–142). Academic Press. 10.1016/B978-0-12-815952-1.00005-0

Mesibov, G. B., Shea, V., & Schopler, E. (2004). *The TEACCH approach to autism spectrum disorders*. Springer. 10.1007/978-0-306-48647-0

Mitchell, C. L., & Hedge, V. A. (2007). Beliefs and practices of in-service preschool teachers in inclusive settings: Implications for personnel preparation. *Journal of Early Childhood Teacher Education*, 28(4), 353–366. 10.1080/10901020701686617

Moore, R. C. (2017). *Childhood's domain: Play and place in child development* (Vol. 6). Routledge. 10.4324/9781315121895

NAEYC. (2020). *Developmentally Appropriate Practice: A position statement of the National Association for the Education of Young Children*. NAEYC. https://www.naeyc.org/resources/position-statements/dap/contents

NAEYC. (2021). *Learning Stories: Observation, Reflection, and Narrative in Early Childhood Education. Association for the Education of Young Children*. NAEYC. https://www.naeyc.org/resources/pubs/yc/summer2021/learning-stories

National Research Council. (2001). *Educating children with autism*. Committee on Educational Interventions for Children with Autism. Division of Behavioral and Social Sciences and Education. Washington, DC: National Academy Press.

Nicolopoulou, A., Cortina, K. S., Ilgaz, H., Cates, C. B., & de Sá, A. B. (2015). Using a narrative-and play-based activity to promote low-income preschoolers' oral language, emergent literacy, and social competence. *Early Childhood Research Quarterly*, 31, 147–162. 10.1016/j.ecresq.2015.01.00625866441

Odom, S., Buysse, V., & Soukakou, E. (2011). Inclusion for young children with disabilities: A quarter century of research perspectives. *Journal of Early Intervention*, 33(4), 344–356. 10.1177/1053815111430094

Orr, R., Williams, M. R., & Pennington, K. (2009). Institutional efforts to support faculty in online teaching. *Innovative Higher Education*, 34(4), 257–268. 10.1007/s10755-009-9111-6

Parlakian, R. (2021). Promoting inclusion in infant toddler settings. *Young Children*, 90–94.

Passmore, A. H., & Tejero Hughes, M. (2022). Using eCoaching to Support Mothers' Pretend Play Interactions at Home. *Early Childhood Education Journal*. 10.1007/s10643-022-01420-436439906

Paterson, C. R., & Arco, L. (2007). Using video modeling for generalizing toy play in children with autism. *Behavior Modification*, 31(5), 660–681. 10.1177/014544550730165117699123

Prendeville, J., Prelock, P., & Unwin, G. (2006). Peer play interventions to support the social competence of children with autism spectrum disorders. *Seminars in Speech and Language*, 27(1), 32–46. 10.1055/s-2006-93243716440243

Pyle, A., & DeLuca, C. (2017). Assessment in play-based kindergarten classrooms: An empirical study of teacher perspectives and practices. *The Journal of Educational Research*, 110(5), 457–466. 10.1080/00220671.2015.1118005

Raulston, T. J., & Machalicek, W. (2018). Early intervention for repetitive behavior in autism spectrum disorder: A conceptual model. *Journal of Developmental and Physical Disabilities*, 30(1), 89–109. 10.1007/s10882-017-9566-9

Rausch, A., Joseph, J., Strain, P. S., & Steed, E. A. (2021). Fostering engagement within inclusive settings. *Young Children*, 76(4), 16–21.

Raver, C. C., Garner, P. W., & Smith-Donald, R. (2007). The roles of emotion regulation and emotion knowledge for children's academic readiness: Are the links causal?

Reska, S. S., Odom, S. L., & Hume, K. A. (2012). Ecological features of preschools and the social engagement of children with autism. *Journal of Early Intervention*, 34(1), 40–56. 10.1177/1053815112452596

Rivers, S. E., Brackett, M. A., Reyes, M. R., Mayer, J. D., Caruso, D. R., & Salovey, P. (2012). Measuring emotional intelligence in early adolescence with the MSCEIT-YV: Psychometric properties and relationship with academic performance and psychosocial functioning. *Journal of Psychoeducational Assessment*, 30(4), 344–366. 10.1177/0734282912449443

Sandall, S. R., Schwartz, I. S., Joseph, G. E., & Gauvreau, A. N. (2019). *Building blocks for teaching preschoolers with special needs* (3rd ed.). Brookes.

Sansanwal, S. (2014). Pretend play enhances creativity and imagination. *Journal of Arts and Humanities*, 3(1), 70–83.

Shillingsburg, M. A., Bowen, C. N., & Shapiro, S. K. (2014). Increasing social approach and decreasing social avoidance in children with autism spectrum disorder during discrete trial training. *Research in Autism Spectrum Disorders*, 8(11), 1443–1453. 10.1016/j.rasd.2014.07.013

Smilansky, S., & Shefatya, L. (1990). *Facilitating play: a medium for promoting cognitive, socio-emotional, and academic development in young children*. Psychological & Educational Publications.

Stacey, S. (2018). *Emergent curriculum in early childhood settings: From theory to practice* (2nd ed.). Redleaf Press.

Tang, G., Savic, M., El Turkey, H., Karakok, G., Cilli-Turner, E., & Plaxco, D. (2017). Inquiry as an access point to equity in the classroom. In *Proceedings of the 20th Annual Conference on Research on Undergraduate Mathematics Education* (pp. 1098-1106). IEEE.

TASH. (2021). *TASH position statement with policy recommendations on inclusive education.* TASH. https://tash.org/tash-position-statement-with-policy-recommendations-on-inclusive-education/

Tip sheets - inclusive child care. (2020). Center for Inclusive Child Care. https://www.inclusivechildcare.org/sites/default/files/courses/swf/Social%20Scripts.pdf

Tominey, S. L., O'Bryon, E. C., Rivers, S. E., & Shapses, S. (2017). Teaching emotional intelligence in early childhood. *Young Children*, 72(1), 6–12.

Tomporowski, P. D., McCullick, B., Pendleton, D. M., & Pesce, C. (2015). Exercise and children's cognition: The role of exercise characteristics and a place for metacognition. *Journal of Sport and Health Science*, 4(1), 47–55. 10.1016/j.jshs.2014.09.003

Trawick-Smith, J. (2014). *The physical play and motor development of young children: A review of literature and implications for practice.* Center for Early Childhood Education, Eastern Connecticut State University.

Van Oers, B., & Duijkers, D. (2013). Teaching in a play-based curriculum: Theory, practice and evidence of developmental education for young children. *Journal of Curriculum Studies*, 45(4), 511–534. 10.1080/00220272.2011.637182

Chapter 2
Confronting Bias in Early Childhood Teacher Preparation:
A Journey of Reflection and Transformation

Melissa C. Walter
Northern Illinois University, USA

Ruby Batz
University of Nevada, Reno, USA

Melissa M. Burnham
https://orcid.org/0000-0002-2570-0092
University of Nevada, Reno, USA

Lisa B. Fiore
https://orcid.org/0000-0002-9692-3613
Lesley University, USA

ABSTRACT

This chapter chronicles the transformative journey of a group of early childhood education (ECE) teacher educators as they critically examined the construction of early childhood teacher preparation courses. Rooted in critical pedagogy, their process demanded deep self-reflection and an acknowledgement of the oppressive systems within the field. Initially pursuing a linear checklist approach to cultivating inclusive practices, the team's extensive discussions and readings revealed the limitations of this method. Instead, they embraced a non-linear, formative spiral model,

DOI: 10.4018/979-8-3693-0924-7.ch002

reflecting ongoing learning and reflection over time. Divided into four elements– identity and self-reflection, course syllabi, course design, and course content--their approach aims to inspire faculty to confront biases, elevate marginalized voices, and reshape the ECE landscape. The authors invite readers into this ongoing journey, emphasizing the need for continuous introspection and collective effort to foster equity and inclusion in ECE.

INTRODUCTION

The historical roots of the early childhood education (ECE) field are deeply entrenched in privileged Eurocentric viewpoints, which have profoundly shaped its practices, epistemologies, and assumptions regarding young children and families. This Eurocentric framework has traditionally centered on an idealized image of the White, middle-class, monolingual, neurotypical, and cisgender child, while simultaneously focusing on the adults who perpetuate this narrow perspective (Perez & Saavedra, 2017). This paradigm has fostered a system that not only marginalizes, but also actively neglects the diverse experiences of historically marginalized children and families, perpetuating cycles of inequality and exclusion (e.g., Escayg, 2019; Souto-Manning & Rabadi-Raol, 2018; Perez & Saavedra, 2017). This narrow lens not only shapes pedagogical approaches and curriculum content, but it also permeates throughout teacher preparation programs, professional development initiatives, and educational policies.

The Eurocentric framework of ECE tends to prioritize individualistic and developmentalist perspectives, focusing on child outcomes and readiness for academic success, often at the expense of holistic and culturally responsive practices. The predominant focus on individual socio-biological mechanisms has overshadowed an essential exploration of existing and historical systems of inequity. This omission has allowed racism, ableism, and other systems of domination to persist as either invisible or irrelevant forces within the field (Souto-Manning & Rabadi-Raol, 2018; Perez & Saavedra, 2017). This approach perpetuates systemic inequities by neglecting to address broader social, economic, and political factors that influence children's educational experiences. While critical ECE scholars have persistently challenged the alliances and complicities inherent in the foundational concepts and methodologies within the ECE field (e.g., Bloch, 1992; Ferri & Bacon, 2011; Cannella & Viruru, 2004; Kessler & Swadener, 1992), issues of racism and bias remain deeply ingrained within ECE training, demanding rigorous critical examination. (e.g., Escayg, 2019; NAEYC, 2019).

There has been a growing recognition recently of the need to collectively problematize and interrogate issues of racism, ableism, and other forms of systemic domination within ECE. Initiative such as the Division for Early Childhood (DEC) Racial Equity Point of View (2023) and the National Association for the Education of Young Children's (NAEYC) Position Statement on Advancing Equity in Early Childhood Education (2019) represent important steps towards acknowledging and confronting systemic injustices within the field. However, translating these declarations into meaningful action requires a concerted effort to dismantle entrenched biases. This oversight has hindered the ability of pre-service and in-service ECE educators to fully grapple with the complexities of their role in fostering an inclusive and equitable learning environment.

To effect real change within the ECE system, it is imperative to recognize that equitable practices cannot exist without directly addressing the injustices experienced by historically marginalized children (Souto-Manning & Rabadi-Raol, 2018). Faculty members in ECE programs share a public responsibility to prepare competent educators equipped to address chronic social issues. As pre-service teachers construct and reconstruct their understanding of themselves and the world, faculty teaching in early childhood teacher education programs must proactively confront the full spectrum of historical and contextual challenges present in ECE. This necessitates not only acknowledging and dismantling racist and biased perspectives embedded in hegemonic dominant ECE practices, theories, and methodologies, but also fostering a curriculum and learning environment that actively champions equity, inclusion, and social justice. By doing so, ECE can evolve into a more equitable and culturally responsive field, better positioned to meet the needs of all children and families.

This chapter articulates the process undertaken by a group of ECE teacher educators as they critically examined the construction of early childhood teacher preparation course syllabi, content, and pedagogy. The impetus for this process was driven by the realization that ECE courses often perpetuate privileged identities, perspectives, and practices within the field of ECE. Our work resonates with the principles of critical pedagogy's culture circles (Souto-Manning, 2010), as spaces to seize and explore relevant issues demanding deep self-reflection, humility, and an acknowledgment of the oppressive systems entrenched within our field, the research base, and the academy.

Initially, our aim was to engage in a time-bound process with a tangible product upon completion: a checklist that could serve as a practical resource for faculty striving to cultivate more inclusive practices in their ECE programs. However, after several months of intensive reading and profound, reflective discussions, we came to recognize the limitations of a linear checklist. Instead, a non-linear, formative spiral emerged as the model best representing our emerging, continuous thought process. It is important to note that while we are sharing our process and model as they exist in a specific moment in time, these continue to be evolving and are therefore not "finished." Our model encapsulates a dynamic process in which scholars engage in *ongoing learning and reflection over time* to shape their perspectives, identities, and practices. Our model encompasses four core elements:

1. **Identity and Self-Reflection**: This central point involves self-situation and scrutinizing one's positionality and social location. We engage in critical introspection regarding how our social location influences our pedagogy.

2. **Course Syllabi**: Here, we delve into a critical analysis of power dynamics in our course syllabi, considering who and what is centered and why and identifying opportunities for democratic processes and empowerment. We consider aspects of a syllabus (e.g., structure, tone, policies) that can contribute to dynamics that maintain oppressive, biased systems and how we can ensure opportunities for dialogue and democracy.

3. **Course Design**: This element focuses on *how* the course is taught, centering the intentionality of each faculty member in designing a course that seeks to interrupt inequality and injustice for their students. We concentrate on creating equitable learning spaces for our students, considering hidden curriculum, the knowledge and skills that matter for student success but aren't explicitly taught, and power dynamics that are inherently embedded in higher education (Calarco, 2020).

4. **Course Content**: This aspect focuses on what is taught, emphasizing the elevation and centralization of epistemologies, methodologies, critical scholarship, and voices not commonly centered in course materials. We ask ourselves who and what is (un)valued, (in)visible, and (un)heard in our courses.

In this chapter, we invite readers into our journey, sharing ongoing efforts to confront bias and break down barriers in our ECE courses, our scholarship, and our lives. Throughout this narrative, we emphasize the importance of continuous learning and personal growth. To support readers in exploring the concepts discussed, we offer resources such as the glossary and recommended reading list. These resources provide additional insights and information for readers at various levels of familiarity with the subject matter. While we aim to meet readers where they are in their understanding, we recognize this chapter represents just the beginning of a reflective journey. It is essential to acknowledge that we cannot provide everything needed in this discussion. Our intention is to initiate a reflective journey that encourages ongoing learning and engagement with these critical topics.

We begin by describing ourselves and sharing the social location and positions from which we have engaged in this work. Next, we describe the dynamics of our collegial atmosphere – one that fosters vulnerability, self-disclosure, and growth through professional development and resource sharing – as integral to guiding our thinking, teaching, and learning. We articulate how the initial virtual meetings were motivated by a short-term plan to interrogate the construction of our course syllabi and to "decolonize" our teaching. As we began our research, creating a growing list of items to consider and participating in professional development webinars in the areas of decolonization and antiracist teaching, we experienced two pivotal conceptual breakthroughs:

1. **Shifting from decolonization to decentering.** Although initially tasked with "decolonizing the syllabus," our collective reflection, discussion, and extensive reading led us to a profound realization. We recognized that our mission extended beyond decolonization (Tuck & Yang, 2012). Instead, our aim was to decenter Eurocentric epistemologies and methodologies that have long dominated our courses and the field of ECE.

2. **Moving beyond the checklist**. We recognized that this transformative work surpasses the confines of a simple checklist. A checklist implies a finite list of tasks that can be checked off, implicitly perpetuating some of the historical and attitudinal issues we had been discussing (e.g., Eurocentrism, capitalism, selfishness). Our journey demanded a more nuanced and holistic approach.

Through these revelations, we forged a path that transcended traditional boundaries, embracing a holistic perspective that mirrors the complexity of our endeavor. Ultimately, we created a dynamic tool--the non-linear formative spiral—an embodiment of our collective work. We enthusiastically present this model with readers, offering a detailed description of each component followed by brief, illustrative vignettes that provide insight into how we have personally implemented the model in our teaching and scholarship. Importantly, we firmly believe our work is far from concluded or ever will be. As we continue to co-create new insights through our teaching and reflection, we invite readers to join us in this transformative process. Our intention is to extend the reach and stimulate critical reflection within the field of ECE. It is vital to recognize that the voices and perspectives in our courses exert a profound influence on students as they shape and cultivate their professional identities.

We conclude the chapter by detailing our experiences navigating this transformative process and highlighting significant signposts we've encountered along the journey. Our approach involves deep self-reflection, humility, and a recognition that we are engaged in this work while navigating multiple systems of oppression as we work and live. Collectively, the authors of this chapter embody diverse perspectives and identities that contribute to the social locations that influence this dialogue. We aim to reflect on the personal experiences of engaging in this work, acknowledging the unique perspectives each faculty member in the group offers. For the White faculty, this entails an exploration of our positions and the privileges we hold as faculty members, shedding light on the complexities of our involvement. We also highlight the perspectives of BIPOC scholars that have significantly influenced the direction of our collective work, underlining the critical role of resource sharing and diverse viewpoints in shaping our trajectory.

This work can begin and evolve in our courses, but it must be accompanied by the pursuit of justice, equity, belonging, and inclusion in our personal lives, our field of expertise, and our institutions. We wholeheartedly invite readers to join in the roles of educators, activists, and advocates, united in our shared mission for transformation. We are grounded in the hope that our role as early childhood teacher educators is a vital force—focused on making early childhood education better for all children and families, moving ever closer to an equitable and just society.

The Journey of Reflection and Transformation

An Ordinary Group of ECE Teacher Educators

In the process of sharing our transformative journey, it is vital to recognize the diverse perspectives and social locations of the authors deeply engaged in this work. Acknowledging our backgrounds enriches the context of our collaborative efforts:

- First Author: I am an assistant professor of Human Development and Family Sciences with a background in ECE. I identify as a White, Christian, cis-gender, heterosexual woman, who is a wife and mother, not living with a disability. My research focuses on nurturing high-quality interactions between caregivers and young children, spanning various caregiver settings and workforce development.

- Second Author: I am an assistant professor of special education and a former preschool and early intervention teacher. I am an immigrant to the U.S. racialized as a Latina, non-disabled, bilingual cisgender woman of color. My doctoral education was grounded in positivist understandings of child development disability, but I was fortunate enough to learn critical theories about child development and learning. I consider myself a critical early childhood special educator.

- Third Author: I am a Professor, department chair, and lifelong academic, trained in the field of human development, family science, and ECE. I am a 51-year-old, English-speaking, white, cis-gender woman, married to a woman, spiritual, but not religious, raised Christian (Catholic), born in America of western European, colonial ancestors, who is not living with a disability. I am grateful to live and work on the unceded, traditional homelands of the Numu, Wašiw, Newe, and Nuwu peoples.

- Fourth Author: I am Professor and Chair of Education with a background in developmental and educational psychology. I identify as a White, Jewish, cis-gender, heterosexual woman, and I am also a mother and a wife. My research interests typically center child and family trauma and resilience, most recently exploring oppressive systems and structures related to poverty, homelessness, and gender-based violence locally and globally.

Despite diversity in our social identities, academic backgrounds, and research interests, we share a common ground as ECE teacher educators. In hindsight, there is irony evident in a group of like-minded ECE faculty members choosing to participate in a larger group of like-minded professionals to explore and improve teaching in higher education. The "like goes with like" principle has positive and negative associations with representativeness and bias (Gilovich & Savitsky, 2012), and yet in the spring of 2020 a group of five[1] ECE professors teaching at four different institutions volunteered to constitute a committee focused on "revolutionizing syllabi" used in teacher preparation programs. The impetus to do so was strong – the murder of George Floyd and subsequent riots and protests, witnessed by far more observers than active participants amid the early stage of a global pandemic. This collective moment stirred a surge of motivation among many individuals, compelling them to actively seek out ways to initiate and inspire change. Such action felt good. Such action felt positive. Such action felt necessary to support a nation's democratic foundation – however wobbly – in hopes that it would survive.

The consortium we engaged with naturally facilitated our committee's efforts by offering a structured monthly timeline and built-in accountability, ensuring our progress could be shared transparently with the larger group. The Collaborative for Understanding the Pedagogy of Infant/Toddler Development (CUPID), welcomed our efforts, aligning with the consortium's stated goal of improving "practice in the field of infant/toddler care and education by improving our own teaching" (https://cupidconsortium.org/).

Initial Goals and Evolution Over Time: Conceptual Shift from Decolonizing to Decentering

Our committee aimed to examine syllabi from our own courses, analyzing assignments, materials, and language for subsequent translation into a checklist that fellow CUPID members could use as they examined and considered changing their syllabi. Our committee met and discussed our ideas, and yet we felt less tethered than floating for many of the first meetings. On the surface, the professors that met differed in our specific ranks, roles, ages, and geographic locations, but it was the perspective of one member, the second author, who joined the work shortly after we began meeting that dramatically impacted what we were doing and why we were doing the work. Her scholarship is deeply rooted in pedagogy aimed at centering critical theories and non-dominant communities in research and practice. Rather than attempting to spread benevolence through revised course syllabi and related content and assignments, this member encouraged us to begin interrogating our work and reckoning with the systems of oppression that had maintained power dynamics that were reflected in coursework that perpetuated these very systems.

A simple, yet profound example of examining systemic oppression involves the concept of poverty – a term used frequently in courses that prepare aspiring early childhood practitioners for work with children and families. Rather than perpetuating the acknowledgement of "poor" as an adjective (sometimes made more clinical/less uncomfortable through the synonym "low income") or fact of life that "just is" for many people around the world, we can engage students in a deeper examination of poverty through the lens of lived experiences. This shift in perspective can transform students' understanding and create opportunities for dialogue on related topics such as trauma, immigration, and resilience. It also encourages critical reflection on policy and legislative decision-making practices, redirecting the focus from the individual to the systemic factors that impact children and families. In *I, Rigoberta Menchu* (Burgos-Debray, 2009), Rigoberta describes life on a *finca*:

We slept in the same clothes we worked in. That's why society rejects us…They say we

Indians are dirty, but it's our circumstances which force us to be like that…if we have time, we go to the river every week, every Sunday, and wash our clothes. These clothes have to last us all week because we haven't any other time for washing and we haven't any soap either. That's how it is. We sleep in our clothes, we get up the next day, we tidy ourselves up a bit and off to work, just like that. (p. 55)

A greater awareness of perspectives and differences has helped us in our professional practices and personal relationships with each other, as described throughout this chapter.

During the initial months of our conversations and relationship-building, we committed to learning together and reflecting together, and intentionally acknowledging the lenses, or theory, through which we were perceiving information. We met up monthly to read, discuss, learn from, and challenge each other to learn from critical ECE-related educators across disciplines. We participated in professional development webinars together, which made our physical distance from each other irrelevant, thanks to technology that brought us into the same virtual space. We reflected upon content and shared readings and conference sessions with each other, causing us to actively consider the "why?" and "so what?" underlying our professional practices and the impact that our decisions would have on our students' development and, by extension, that of the children and families with whom they would work.

One of the pivotal moments in our work was recognizing that it was less accurate to frame our efforts as "decolonizing," (Tuck and Yang, 2012) and more accurate to broaden the scope of the work by centering perspectives typically kept in the margins or ignored entirely (Perez & Saavedra, 2017). We recommitted to these efforts each and every time we met, and our energy reserves renewed even though the work was often difficult and resulted in disequilibrium that would eventually lessen as we gained more confidence in our abilities and trust in each other as collaborators and friends.

Beyond the Checklist: Embracing a Holistic Approach

Influenced by our collective, mutually reciprocal learning meeting to meeting, we made the decision to dispense with the checklist as our primary goal. We grew to recognize that a checklist implied that one would be "finished" with their own personal and professional efforts to center and elevate non-dominant communities and perspectives once they had finished checking a finite number of boxes on a static document. We also agreed with the argument made by authors Tuck and Yang (2012) that the term "decolonization" is not the same as activities that are launched in an attempt to make change, even if intended to improve society, higher education, and human experiences.

We chose instead to focus on identifying an image or concept that represented the life-long, often bumpy process of learning, un-learning, and re-learning that we came to appreciate as educators committed to civic engagement for ourselves and the students with whom we teach and learn. It was difficult to articulate what we were looking for and what qualities we were seeking aside from a non-linear, start-to-finish representation. It was after we participated in a webinar together and were processing the content together that we landed on the visual model that most effectively embraced our learning journey and our relative entry points into the collaborative learning experience. We recognized that our search for a model paralleled aspects of what we teach students about universal design and multiple entry points into curriculum, and we finally felt comfortable with a visual model that best represented our continuous learning.

Development of the Non-Linear Formative Spiral Model

The non-linear spiral model that we all agreed fit our learning experience and incorporated our future learning efforts is different from the notion of "spiral curriculum," in which concepts or topics are taught and then revisited at a specific later time to intentionally build upon previous learning. That type of spiral is often depicted as a cyclone or conical swirl, with a distinct top and bottom. Our preferred spiral is similar to that of a nautilus seashell cut in half, or a spiral cloud or galaxy formation (see Figure 1). The most important feature of the spiral is represented in the different points along the fluid, constantly evolving line that moves and refreshes as it continues to develop. We wanted the image to reflect the inclusive learning experience that we had been encountering, and the underlying premise to note is that people may enter the learning (spiral) from whichever entry point they choose or fall into as a starting point. The very process of exploring the different points along the spiral incorporates the influence of previous learning and experiences, all of which revolve around self-reflection and situating. It is through the exploration and reflection that occurs during the learning journey that transformation is possible.

Figure 1. Non-linear formative spiral model

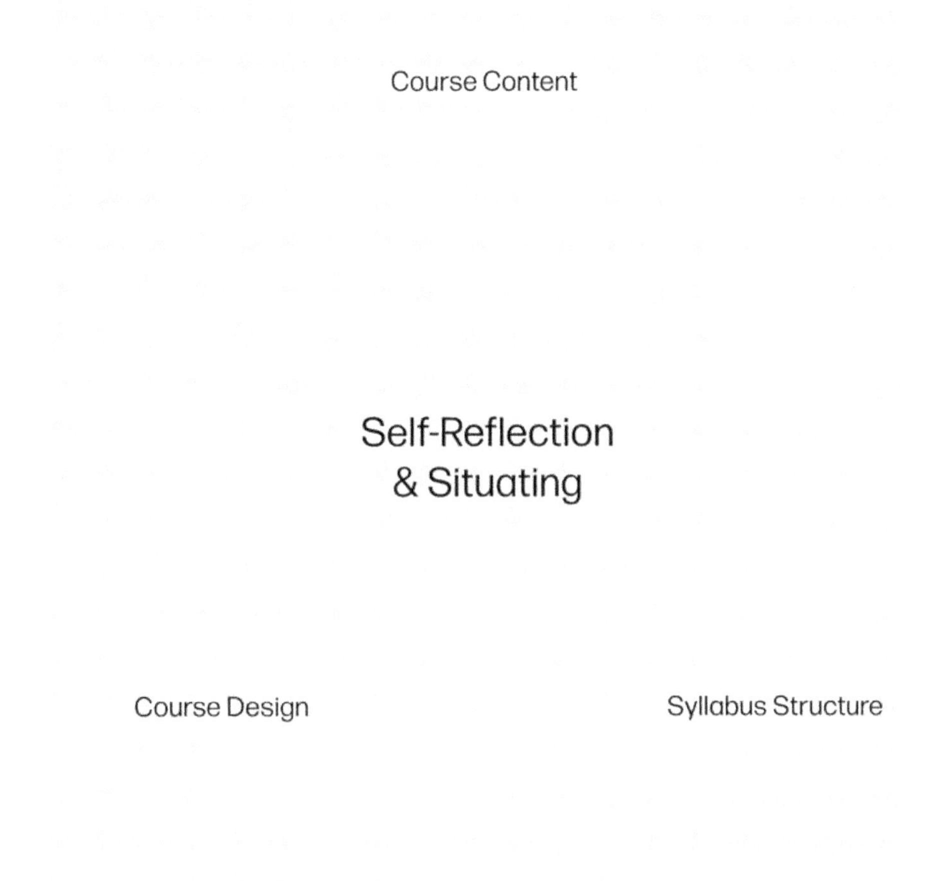

Course Content

Self-Reflection & Situating

Course Design   Syllabus Structure

Note. This figure illustrates the non-linear spiral that best represents our ongoing transformative journey. This approach allows various entry points for transforming our courses. Whether we focus on reshaping syllabus structure (e.g., policies and language), addressing power dynamics in course design, or elevating marginalized voices in course content, each path leads back to the central element of self-reflection and situating oneself. This pivotal self-work has a ripple effect, reverberating across our professional and personal lives, influencing our course development and broader aspects of our lives. [Credit and special thanks to the third author's nephew, Willie Shaw, for his transformation of our Prezi model into this graphic.]

Elements of the Transformative Process

Identity and Self-Reflection

The non-linear spiral model that emerged has several possible entry points, with identity and self-reflection at the center–a grounding point to which we return again and again. Regardless of where we begin, critical self-examination and reflection ground us and inform our growing understanding, humility, and competence. The identity and self-reflection process begins with the naming of our own social identities and personal history that informs our perspective on the world and our work. Naming and reflecting on our social identities can be facilitated by the use of tools such as the Social Identity Wheel, developed by the Arizona State University Intergroup Relations Center and adapted by multiple universities (e.g., Center for Service-Learning and Civic Engagement, n.d.). The wheel prompts us to list our visible and invisible identities such as gender, socioeconomic status, ability, first language, sexual orientation, age, and national origin. After listing these, reflection prompts encourage us to consider the identities we think about most often and least often, and which have the strongest impact on how we view ourselves. This exercise inevitably uncovers privileges we have been afforded based on the social identities that we hold.

Knowledge of our social identities is necessary, but not sufficient, in the identity and self-reflection process. In a manner similar to that articulated by Reyes et al. (2021), our collaborative process includes negotiation of humility and epistemic findings, as well as examination of how our "interests and commitments enhance or jeopardize this work" (p. 131). Naming our identities and reflecting on each is just a first step. The harder work comes with a critical examination of the histories of these identities, both in our personal journeys and in the larger historical context. For example, how has this identity contributed to the oppression of others? How has this identity been oppressed historically? How have I, as a person holding this identity, contributed to the oppression of others, wittingly or unwittingly?

It is also critical to reflect on our social location and consider how our social location might affect our views of students and pedagogical choices. Social location is shaped by our diverse identities and defines our standing in the world, dictating access to power or lack thereof. It is an intersectional framework encompassing identities and associated privilege or marginalization, which ultimately shapes our social experiences. Social location deeply influences how others perceive and treat us, our interactions, teaching approaches, and research methodologies. Therefore, it is essential that we continuously reflect on our social positioning and how it impacts our teaching. For example, one author reflected that many aspects of her social identity are privileged, which can prevent her from recognizing barriers her students with marginalized identities often experience. As we continue the journey, we come back to the identity and self-reflection process in an iterative fashion. Learning that occurs as part of the process will point to key reflection points that raise awareness and deepen understanding of both ourselves and the experiences of others with different identities.

Identity and Self-Reflection in Practice: Second Author's Reflection. Understanding one's social location is crucial in navigating systems and recognizing disparities in power and privilege. Throughout our semester, I guide my students in exploring their social locations through an intersectional lens, illuminating how these factors shape their interactions in diverse contexts. For example, as an instructor, I acknowledge the power dynamics inherent in our classroom from the outset. In our class, I am the person with more power, given the inherent design of a college course. Therefore, establishing a space that actively uncovers the hidden curriculum fosters equitable learning opportunities (Calarco, 2020). For instance, soliciting anonymous mid-semester feedback empowers students to voice concerns without fear of reprisal, fostering a sense of mutual respect and responsibility in our learning community.

It is important to understand our social locations when we work with others so students can critically engage with prevailing ideologies, such as the pervasive deficit-based portrayal of children and families living in poverty, which often perpetuates deficit-based narratives about them. Through self-reflection, students examine their own social locations and power dynamics in relation to these dominant discourses. What is their relationship with "poverty"? What are the ideas they grew up hearing from society about "poverty"? Were such depictions dignifying and respectful? What counternarratives can we find about such deficit-based portrayals of families and children living in poverty? This introspection enables them to discern between deficit-based and asset-based perspectives, empowering them to engage constructively with readings and real-world contexts involving children and families living in poverty.

Influential dominant and essentialist narratives about the "culture of poverty," which pathologize the language and culture of children and their families living in poverty, have been heavily criticized and contested (e.g., Dudley-Marling & Lucas, 2009; Gorski, 2012). However, such essentialist narratives still remain widely used. Therefore, students need the opportunity to understand that poverty is a multidimensional factor that significantly influences health and educational outcomes, in which racism alongside other systems of domination contribute to and perpetuate economic and financial inequality (Gorski, 2012). Overall, by foregrounding the intersection of social location and power dynamics through critical self-reflection, students develop a nuanced understanding of societal structures and their roles within them, fostering a more inclusive and empathetic approach to their professional practice.

Course Syllabi Analysis: Examining Power Dynamics and Hidden Curriculum

Our original goal was to create a checklist to interrogate the syllabi in our courses with a critical lens. As we deepened our understanding of the workings of power and privilege in the field, in university systems, and broader society, this goal shifted. Nonetheless, an analysis of the syllabus is one important component of the process as it reflects inherent power dynamics and hidden curriculum. The hidden curriculum, conceptualized by Phillip Jackson in 1968, refers to the unspoken competencies and skills implicitly expected of students from preschool to graduate school, significantly influencing their educational experiences and outcomes. This covert curriculum shapes children's social perceptions and norms from an early age, perpetuating educational inequalities across socio-economic backgrounds. For instance, middle-class families equip their children with assertive help-seeking strategies that yield academic advantages, while historically marginalized students face stereotype threats and feelings of imposter syndrome in higher education settings. Recognizing the nuances of the hidden curriculum empowers students to navigate systemic inequities, fostering critical awareness and self-advocacy skills (Calarco, 2020). Furthermore, it places a profound responsibility on educational institutions and teacher educators to cultivate inclusive, equitable learning environments. Addressing the hidden curriculum is paramount for fostering justice and enabling all students to thrive academically and personally.

Here, we are examining the "attitude" of the syllabus. What does the syllabus say about how we approach this course, view university students, and our commitment to continuous confrontation of bias and continuous learning? Who is centered? Who is provided with an invisible advantage or disadvantage? It is well documented that middle-class students, from preschool to graduate school (Calarco, 2018; Carlarco, 2020; Stockstill, 2023), learn to challenge rules and request assistance, accommodations, and attention in excess of what is fair or required—opportunities not known by every student. Therefore, unpacking the explicit and implicit rules embedded in the syllabus is necessary to provide all students with equitable learning opportunities. The following list specifies considerations for inclusion when interrogating and revising a syllabus. Many of these ideas derive from the work of the Faculty Center for Ignatian Pedagogy at Loyola University (2024) on "Decolonizing your Syllabus," and The Social Justice Syllabus Design Tool (Taylor et al., 2019). As previously mentioned, the initial goal of our faculty group was to develop a checklist to revise our syllabi; however, upon deep reflection, we realized that a checklist implies the ability to indicate something is complete. Instead, our intention in providing the following list of considerations is to offer readers reflective questions to initiate an introspective journey into their teaching policies and practices, fostering ongoing growth and development.

Does the syllabus:

- include a policy for ongoing student feedback? How will students receive feedback, and how often?
- include a policy for student agreement regarding the contents of the syllabus. Are the contents mutually agreeable? Do changes need to be made?
- include a policy for students' voice/voting on how to complete key components of the course (i.e., final paper vs. exam)? If there is space for student voice in determining key components of the course, include it.
- include a policy for student voting on classroom guidelines/agreements? In a discussion-based course, this is particularly important. Having student agreements that students help to develop on how people are expected to contribute is important in developing a sense of shared community. For example, how will we work together to prevent a student from dominating contributions to class discussions?
- provide clarity about what information needs to be known outside of prerequisites for successful course completion? Include ways to access this information if oppression may have prevented students from previously acquiring this information. This prompts us to consider the "hidden curriculum" that can prevent full access to the course by all individuals.
- give multiple, flexible methods and times for students to contact you? Develop a policy for communication outside of class time, since limited in-person office hours restrict accessibility. If a student emails you, when can they expect a response? If a student works full-time, can they contact you after hours?
- offer opportunities for retaking/resubmitting missed or late work that are available from the beginning to all students? A firm policy of "no late or make-up work" may limit course accessibility for students who experience a life event during the semester.
- offer opportunities to catch up if students fall behind due to technological barriers or other personal deterrents? Such opportunities should be available to all students, not only those trained to request such help.
- present course modules in a learning management system that are accessible, clear, inclusive, welcoming, and supportive for all learners to follow for either asynchronous or synchronous courses?
- include language about your responsibility to alert students early in the semester if course requirements are not met?
- include a reflection of how university statement (s) related to equity, inclusion, justice, and anti-racism come to life in class?

- include a reflection of how land acknowledgments require an ongoing effort to be in good standing with the people and the histories of those whose lands are occupied?

The syllabus provides the opportunity for instructors to set the stage for learning, to acknowledge our commitment to anti-racist pedagogies, and to give students a voice in co-constructing the learning journey we are undertaking together. Gannon (2016) notes that a syllabus is a "document that talks about possibilities rather than prohibitions. It allows students to see why they get to take our course, not why they have to" (par. 16). A syllabus that centers inclusion, belonging, and our commitment to acknowledging and disrupting the status quo is the goal, but it is essential to recognize that the syllabus is just a document filled with empty signifiers that mean nothing if the statements are not actively reckoned with during the implementation of the course.

Course Syllabus Analysis in Practice: First Author's Reflection. As I prepare for a new semester, I begin by revisiting my previous syllabus and reflecting on the questions raised in this section of the chapter. I ask myself how things went the last time I taught the course and how they could be improved this semester. While acknowledging the biases in student evaluations of teaching (Heffernan, 2021), especially for women and faculty of color, I find value in reviewing their feedback to gain insight into their perspectives and experiences with the course.

More significantly, I actively seek to incorporate student voice and choice into the upcoming semester's syllabus, recognizing the underlying power dynamics inherent in traditional educational structures. One method I employ is creating and distributing an "interactive syllabus" (McHendry, G., n.d.) about a week before the semester commences. Using my university's online survey management system, I develop the interactive syllabus, which presents content followed by related questions prompting students to share insights about themselves, their learning objectives, concerns, and aspirations. This interactive approach serves multiple purposes: it allows me to familiarize myself with students before the course begins, giving them a voice in shaping their learning experience, and it highlights the hidden curriculum embedded within course design. By actively listening to and incorporating student feedback, I am to disrupt traditional power dynamics and empower students to play a collaborative role in shaping the course and syllabus.

On the first day of class, we review the revised syllabus and engage in open discussion about its policies, providing further opportunities for student input and addressing aspects of the hidden curriculum. This discussion helps expose and challenge underlying power dynamics and expectations that may be implicit in the course structure. Importantly, the first day is not the only occasion for students to voice their desires and needs. Throughout the semester, I check in with students to ensure ongoing dialogue and to continue to address power dynamics and hidden curriculum elements that may arise. Previously, I administered an anonymous mid-term plus/delta survey to gather feedback on course progress and solicit suggestions for improvement. However, recognizing that waiting until mid-semester might delay addressing certain concerns, I now collect anonymous feedback when we are 25% into the course. This approach allows students to adapt to the course structure while providing sufficient time for me to implement their suggestions and make necessary adjustments, thereby further challenging traditional power dynamics and enriching the learning experience.

Course Design: Embracing Multiple Pedagogical Approaches

In designing and implementing a course, instructors must utilize multiple pedagogical approaches rather than defaulting to just one instructor-preferred style. Our course design tells the story of our commitment to change and our commitment to the learning of all students, not just those who comply with the colonial conceptualization of a "good student.". This requires that we use a variety of means to present material and encourage student learning of key outcomes. Although the concept of students having different "learning styles" has long been debunked (e.g., Newton, 2015), the science of learning does support the importance of presenting course material in multiple ways to facilitate deep learning. For example, mixing a traditional lecture with video clips, regular breaks, short discussions, and meaningful references to current events is more effective and inclusive than a teaching style of a simple lecture with call-and-response prompts. Effective university instruction embraces multiple pedagogical strategies. Instruction that centers on belonging, inclusion, and anti-racist practice mandates it. Here are some considerations as we critically examine our course design:

- What epistemologies and world views inform your teaching? What epistemologies and world views are silenced?
- What is your pedagogical approach and theoretical stance... How might these approaches and theories perpetuate harm to the marginalized and minoritized?
- Does your course design suggest a "banking" model of education (Freire, [1970] 2000), one where student learning extends only to receiving, filing, or storing the "deposits" of the teacher(s), or are the instructor and students in a mutual learning community?
- Are you fostering dialogue-based learning that favors aggressive debate/hostile discussion?
- Is it possible to use open-access resources or a no-cost text?

- Have you designed group discussion agreements that hold space for the marginalized and minoritized?
- What does your course do to recenter and open the learning experience to all students?

When considering our pedagogical approaches, we aspire to a fully inclusive model of education that celebrates differences in how students approach learning, honors their backgrounds and personal histories, and includes them as an active part of the learning process.

Course Design in Practice: Fourth Author's Reflection. Over time, I've adopted new practices under the broader approach to teaching and learning in the classes that I teach. It's my intention to model – and articulate my pedagogical choices with the teacher candidates in the classes – ways of teaching that, in turn, impact our individual and group learning. The primary emphasis for me at this time is related to equity and accessibility. I want to ensure that all students can access course materials with little to no financial stress, and that content is accessible with the aid of captions and/or audio supports to the greatest extent possible. Some concrete examples include a decision to reduce or eliminate the material costs that students incur by taking a required course. I now select eBooks available through our university library instead of requiring one or more textbooks. I upload links to journal articles or PDFs (adhering to copyright standards), videos (e.g., YouTube, podcasts, webinar recordings), and primary sources through libraries and foundations whose collections include images and audio recordings of people sharing their own stories, rather than authors/researchers sharing others' stories or interpreting them through their own filters and related (though perhaps implicit or unintentional) biases. I also include a "keyword" or "featured vocabulary" guide for students so they can familiarize themselves with academic/specific terms that they may be unfamiliar with, need a reminder about, or wish to explore further as their own curiosity prompts them.

Another example is incorporating collaborative assignments and peer feedback into required course experiences. Collaborative assignments, while sometimes challenging for students due to difficulty scheduling outside work sessions or navigating personality differences, provide students with practice working as part of a team, listening and/or speaking respectfully, and learning from others' lived experiences. Instead of assigning groups or having students choose groups, I use a random assignment tool (brown paper bag with items in it that students hand-pick to be sorted into thematic groups), which eliminates the power dynamic of the professor making the decision and social pressures to be included in any particular group. During the first week of class, the students and I co-construct a feedback protocol to be utilized and shared with groups. The feedback sheet features categories such as, "I really liked…," "You could increase accessibility by…," and "Room to grow…," and I gather all feedback sheets after group presentations and compile groups' feedback from (anonymous) classmates into one comprehensive document for each group. I also include a synthesis that incorporates my own guidance and suggestions.

I hope that the greatest impact resulting from these simple design elements is that students recognize – in the moment or in the future – that knowledge is shared, something to be questioned and revisited and valued, and should be accessible to everyone. As students recognize the power of their own thinking and gain comfort sharing their ideas, their motivation grows to contribute to the teaching and learning contexts in which they participate. This includes a focus on course content and decisions about what is being taught – explicitly or implicitly – in classrooms and school communities.

Course Content: Elevating Marginalized Voices

Another component of the process that became abundantly clear as we began excavating the levels of change needed for transformation is the course content itself. By course content, we mean elements such as whose ideas are being taught, which theories guide the work, what researchers and methods are the focus, and a consideration of which perspectives on ECE are being centered and which have been excluded. Examining the answers to these questions is a humbling process. Many of us come from higher education programs that may not have taught us about "non-mainstream" theoretical orientations and research by marginalized and minoritized scholars. The "canon" of developmental and early childhood education literature and theory is largely limited to Western, Educated, Industrialized, Rich, and Democratic (WEIRD; Henrich et al., 2010) researchers and theorists who typically studied WEIRD infants and young children from a positivist paradigm. To elevate the voices of scholars and Indigenous knowledge that have been excluded requires our learning. This process requires us first to know what we don't know and then to seek out the knowledge we're lacking.

Elevating the marginalized voice requires us to become seekers, to look beyond the "top ten" lists and reading lists from our own educational experiences. It requires us to dive deeply into the formal, academic literature and relevant knowledge outside of the academic literature. It may require reading the dissertations of emerging scholars and reading poetry and elder accounts of knowledge passed down in cultures with a storytelling rather than written tradition of transferring knowledge. Naturally, this journey is not a process that can be completed a week prior to the beginning of the semester or term. It is a lifelong process of seeking and engaging with knowledge in ways that feel uncomfortable and are different from the traditional (White, Euro-centric) ways of preparing a reading list. It may mean turning away from a textbook that centers WEIRD scholarship and theory or, at the very least, adding additional readings to provide a full account of the topic. It may mean demanding that publishers provide textbooks that are designed with previously minoritized scholarship and theory at the core. It may require attending mainstream professional and academic conferences (such as the Society for Research on Child Development or NAEYC) and conferences that center work that questions mainstream assumptions (such as Reconceptualizing Early Childhood Education). At the very least, this aspect of the work requires us to expand our knowledge and to seek out silenced voices. Land and Frankowski (2022), in their discussion of citational practices, note that:

> *Citational practices turn toward pedagogies when we take questions of circulation, erasure and refusal as ethical and political responses to pedagogy's push for ongoingness through emphasizing the ethic of want (Land et al., 2020): we want to keep asking who and what we give air to; we want to keep noticing and presencing against macro and minute erasures; we want to constantly ask how we need to stop citing, who we need to enter into citational relation with, and how to cite well—with care, accountability and reciprocity in contemporary times. (p. 455, emphasis in original)*

Land and Frankowski (2022) challenge us as professional educators to question the centering of voices that have always been centered and to think beyond what we have traditionally taught, considering postdevelopmental perspectives and different epistemologies and ontologies. Here are some considerations as we critically examine our course content:

- Who and what is (un)valued, (in)visible, and (un)heard in the learning materials?
- Do the learning materials have real application to those who experience marginalization today?
- Do the learning materials include BIPOC cultures and represent BIPOC scholars and perspectives with dignity?
- Do the learning materials expose students to the lived experiences of BIPOC communities, beyond academic articles and texts?
- Do you acknowledge and communicate to students the limitations of the literature and influences of racism and oppression in the field?
- Do you intentionally and critically review learning materials to examine messages that reinforce anti-Black racism and oppression?

Course Content in Practice: Third Author's Reflection. I am currently revising an introductory ECE textbook. Previous editions of this textbook have centered the dominant narratives of the field…stories of quality, child development milestones, and White, European theorists among them. As a result of reflecting on course content, I have dug into a new (to me) world of literature to center and uplift. I am introducing readers to the dominant narratives and adding counterpoints and different perspectives. So, for example, I discuss Piaget and Vygotsky in the theory chapter with slight edits to reduce their presence, and I have added postfoundational and critical theories and an introduction to paradigm. It is not just a matter of replacing what exists; it is explaining that what exists is just one way of knowing using one particular paradigm. My intention is to introduce students to other ways of knowing and other paradigms rather than simply centering positivism and empirical science as the gold standard (only) method of understanding the world. The same chapter contains a brief history of the field. Rather than regurgitating the same key points, I intentionally centered the important contributions of silenced and forgotten women of color who were doing the work at the same time as the White women who have been centered at the forefront of the field in the early 1900s. I added a critical examination of Head Start and its origins in a deficit orientation, and a critical discussion of the early research used to justify the importance of ECE. So, I discuss the dominant narrative and also intentionally counter it to foster critical thinking. It is a much less decisive introductory textbook as a result. Instead of declaring things as truth, I am introducing nuance and criticality.

Now that we have described the components of the model that emerged from our ongoing collaborations and some reflective examples of what each component looks like in practice, we will turn toward key reflections on the processes and commitments to ourselves and each other. These commitments led to personal and professional transformations and deepening understandings.

Navigating the Transformative Process

Collegial Atmosphere and Professional Development

Expanding knowledge is a natural outcome of expanding relationships with others, and it is because of this phenomenon that our work together has flourished over time. What began as a task – born out of a desire to contribute to a national (and global) effort to reduce racism and increase equity and accountability – quickly became a rewarding, supportive endeavor. Each participant in our learning group understood the general culture of higher education because of our similar professional backgrounds and practices, and yet our experiences within our respective institutions varied due to our roles and our institutional community cultures and geographic regions.

While we had no formal protocol to guide our virtual meetings, we fell into a pattern of checking in with each other at the beginning of each meeting, and it was these check-ins that provided opportunities to connect as human beings: as voters concerned about the political climate and how decisions would impact current and future education for all citizens; as women with loved ones, including children of various ages; as professionals navigating tenure, union, and governance processes. With shared knowledge of, passion for, and investment in early childhood education, we reaffirmed our appreciation for critical thinking that parallels hooks's (2010) description of young children as "relentless interrogators" whose energy is fueled by curiosity and discovery. As our interconnectedness deepened, we committed to engaging in shared external professional development opportunities facilitated by professional organizations (e.g., Reconceptualizing Early Childhood Education, Society for Research in Child Development, SAGE). It was after one webinar, specifically, that we noted a breakthrough with regard to our respective understanding about our process and goals (see Brown, et al., 2021).

Conceptual Breakthroughs and Revelations

The most striking breakthrough that shifted the scope of our work was linked to a realization about our own roles in the oppressive systems that we were attempting to highlight and interrupt in our courses (design and content). One group member noted in a Zoom meeting chat: "...we have been perpetuating the oppression by disseminating the same narrative we learned" (M. Burnham, personal communication, November 10, 2022). As teacher educators, we had successfully progressed through the linear and hierarchical education system as students to attain "required" degrees and "necessary" experiences that gained us entry into the higher education system as professors. Our collaborative work provided us with a new perspective, and we were surprised at how the awareness of our positions and roles in sustaining the power dynamics in higher education felt quite shocking and uncomfortable. Being shocked and uncomfortable is a function of privilege and a part of the process (Oluo, 2018).

Along with this revelation came the recognition that each of us was at a different point or level of awareness and the reckoning that we were experiencing as being complicit in maintaining oppression and inequity. Our discomfort included acknowledgment of privilege and positionality, and while we had all worked hard to obtain our professional roles, we became increasingly adept at articulating the entry points and journeys that we had, which varied from those others had, based on our respective personal and social identities, as well as socioeconomic realities. None of us had ever taken a graduate class that examined systems of oppression and links to systems and citizens, and we grew to appreciate the gap – intentional or ignorant – that exists in most teacher education programs, specifically, and higher education programs, more broadly. We realized that until more students are exposed to coursework and fieldwork that challenges the beliefs and values that are taught in the dominant cultural narrative in the United States, then they would also be complicit in perpetuating inequitable and oppressive systems by virtue of following the rules, playbook, or whatever systemic guide is provided to them along their academic journeys. We renewed our commitment, again and again, to do what we could in our respective roles and workplaces so that we could interrupt and interrogate the systems of oppression with a long-term goal of elevating children and families respectfully and accurately from a strengths-based perspective.

How We Built a Sense of Community and Actualized Commitment

Our commitment to this transformative work was not confined to individual efforts, but thrived on collective growth, and our journey toward confronting biases and reshaping our teaching methodologies was intricately tied to fostering a robust sense of community within our group. Two of us began this work as full professors, and two are still in the pre-tenure process. The positions and privileges afforded to full professors in the academy are well known and provided us with the ability to devote time to this work, which had no known conclusion point or product. This is a privilege not afforded to the untenured, so the full professors among us tried to create space and boundaries, allowing for all to contribute in a way that worked for each and guarded the time of those who needed it most.

Through regular (monthly) virtual meetings and open discussions, we cultivated an atmosphere where we felt safe expressing vulnerabilities and uncertainties with one another. This sense of safety was essential in fostering genuine commitment and accountability among group members. We recognized that accountability necessitates a supportive network where vulnerability and growth through professional development are encouraged. Professional development initiatives and resource-sharing acted as catalysts for our work, facilitating continuous learning and reflection. We soon recognized that our collective learning extended beyond formal settings, encompassing informal exchanges and reflections that challenged and enriched our understanding in both our personal and professional lives.

Challenges and Successes in Embracing Multiple Perspectives and Remaining Open to Criticism

Navigating the complexities of embracing multiple perspectives while remaining open to criticism presented both challenges and successes. Initially tasked with "decolonizing the syllabus," our progression toward "decentering" Eurocentric perspectives marked a significant conceptual breakthrough. It wasn't merely a change in terminology, but a paradigm shift, highlighting the need to move beyond rectifying colonial legacies and actively centering marginalized perspectives. This shift was a key success that brought into focus the "interdependent nature of theory and practice [as] the vital link between critical thinking and practical wisdom" (Kantawala, 2022, p. 4) and defined the trajectory of our work.

Creating a culture that welcomed critique and vulnerability was instrumental in our transformative process. Encouraging open dialogue and constructive feedback fostered an environment where diverse perspectives were valued and respected. Remaining open to criticism and diverse viewpoints posed challenges, as it often led to discomfort and dissonance. We frequently reminded one another of the importance of "sitting with" those feelings of discomfort and acknowledging them. Acknowledging and embracing this discomfort as an integral part of growth allowed us to navigate challenging conversations with openness, within the context of the emotionally safe and vulnerable learning community we had built. It was through these moments of discomfort that we confronted our biases, expanded our perspectives, and embraced a more inclusive approach to education. Recognizing vulnerability as a strength rather than a weakness was crucial in our journey. It allowed us to acknowledge gaps in our understanding, fostering humility and openness that propelled us towards continuous learning and improvement and a steadfast commitment to inclusive practices.

Central Role of Self-Reflection and Situating

Situating oneself and engaging in self-reflection form the bedrock of this transformative work. It is the central component of the spiral model, and, in parallel process, was imperative to our work as a collaborative team. The process of critically examining one's positionality and social location allows for a deeper understanding of the lenses through which we perceive the world. This introspection is not merely a self-assessment that can be completed; it is a journey into recognizing how our identities, experiences, and cultural contexts shape our perspectives. By acknowledging the profound impact of these factors, we gain insights into our roles within larger systems of oppression. Self-reflection becomes a compass guiding us through this transformative journey. It prompts us to examine our biases, privileges, and contributions to systemic inequalities. Understanding our own cultural contexts and biases enables us to actively challenge them (Reyes, et al., 2021). This process is iterative, requiring continual reevaluation and growth. Situating oneself and engaging in self-reflection, therefore, are not just starting points; they are on-going practices crucial to confronting biases, fostering inclusivity, and reshaping educational landscapes.

Accountability in Teaching, Research, and Practice

In our pursuit of accountability, we consistently prioritized the elevation and centralization of marginalized voices in teaching, research, and practice. Our commitment extended beyond a mere acknowledgement of diverse perspectives; it was woven into considerations of our pedagogy and methodologies. Recognizing the profound impact our courses have on students' professional identities, we acknowledge the responsibility to challenge biases and create inclusive spaces. This awareness drove our commitment to continual improvement and active engagement with critical perspectives, using the non-linear spiral model to guide this work. Accountability in our work is not a one-time commitment, but an ongoing, iterative process. It involves regularly revisiting and reassessing our approaches, acknowledging our positions within systems of oppression, and actively addressing these power dynamics in our educational practices.

One of the simplest practices that helped us resolve our evolving understanding of our work and positions within the many systems in which we live and teach (e.g., education, government) was to ask ourselves "what lenses are we looking through?" when we were examining or discussing a situation or topic. When we paused to acknowledge factors that could be influencing our perceptions, the very act of noticing was helpful in interrupting the ordinary practices to which we had become accustomed. For example, were we able to note our biases when conducting observations of teacher candidates or home visits with families? Did we recognize the frameworks that exist that position some people and/or communities as problematic (a.k.a., "damaged"), or did we only perceive deficits based on our assumptions? Because we had established trust in each other and our shared process, we felt more comfortable with our commitment to an evolving, longer journey together, and we knew that we would provide each other with critical responses to our interpretations in the spirit of growing in our work. This, in turn, would positively impact the work we do with teacher candidates and others in the education, human services, and related classes that we teach in our institutions of higher education.

Signposts Along the Journey

The transformative journey toward inclusivity and equity isn't linear and it is never complete; rather, it is marked by key signposts. These signposts, representing pivotal moments and realizations, guide us through the complexity of this work. They illuminate critical reflections and actions that propel us forward.

- **Moments of conceptual shifts**: Instances where the group collectively experienced paradigm shifts, like transitioning from "decolonization" to "decentering." The very idea of "decolonization" as a goal illustrates the infancy of our starting point and the hubris of a largely white group of scholars, thinking that decolonization was not only possible but the correct goal. Gently, the second author fostered a deepening of understanding and a conceptual shift to our true goal of decentering the white perspective. And then we realized the enormity of the task, because once you see it, it can't be unseen.

- **Epiphanies in learning**: Realizations that challenged conventional wisdom or deeply entrenched biases, leading to expanded perspectives and deeper understanding. One epiphany occurred during a meeting when we zoomed out from the minute details toward a broader perspective. One faculty member reflected that she will never forget the moment when, upon zooming out, we started generating a list of oppressive systems in which we, and our work, were embedded. The list included higher education itself and its furtive, oppressive stance toward non-white students and scholars, how funding agencies and publishers largely define the work that gets done and disseminated, and the research methods and statistics that literally center the mean. This epiphany led to a dawning realization that the work must begin with us, but it cannot end with us. A critical mass of emerging and existing scholars is necessary to create a tipping point that will lead to true transformation. We stand on the shoulders of academics who have been dispatching a call to action for several decades, and we aim to join them in elevating this call.

- **Community reflections**: Moments of vulnerability and open dialogue within the group, fostering trust and openness. One vivid example of this occurred when one member expressed discomfort after a presentation due to a conflict between their social beliefs and those of the presenter. This member was vulnerable in disclosing her discomfort, stemming from personal convictions and her own social location. As a group, we navigated this situation by encouraging a reflective mindset, valuing diverse viewpoints without compromising our own beliefs or casting judgment. These moments of open reflection and exchange allowed us to cultivate a space of trust and understanding within our community. Another moment of vulnerability came with the discussion of one member's public comment given at a local school board meeting that was overrun with groups present to demand that the district eliminate its diversity, equity, and inclusion initiatives…knowing it was the right thing to do, and being both terrified and terrorized in doing so (with audience members writing down her name on an enemy list and threatening to contact her chair/dean). Allyship involves joining alongside those who have been fighting for justice long before our awakening. It means brave action and standing aside to make way for marginalized voices.

CONCLUSION

The quest for justice is an ongoing lifetime process. It requires a commitment to justice through both our professional and personal lives. Transformative practices are not immediate, not spontaneous. Enacting justice in institutions of higher education and preparing ECE professionals requires radically changing the systems, structures, policies, norms, discourses, and beliefs to reimagine a different world. They require continuous inquiry, flexibility, interdependency, and commitment to equity to prevent the invisible reproduction of socially unjust systems (Souto-Manning, 2010).

Our transformative journey towards confronting biases in early childhood teacher preparation has been marked by profound shifts, collaborative learning, and continuous reevaluation. Beginning with the intention to scrutinize course syllabi, our focus expanded beyond hubristic and misnamed "decolonization" efforts. The journey was characterized by pivotal moments of conceptual shifts–from a narrow focus on rectifying settler colonial legacies to a holistic approach centered on elevating marginalized perspectives. Throughout this journey, our group experienced epiphanies that reshaped our understanding of biases and systemic inequities. Moments of discomfort and vulnerability became gateways to growth, fostering a culture where diverse perspectives were embraced and critiques were welcomed. Central to our progress were moments of community reflection, where open dialogue and shared insights propelled our collective learning. Trust, vulnerability, and a commitment to ongoing growth were integral to our approach.

It is again crucial to acknowledge that our journey toward equity and inclusivity is not confined to a linear trajectory. The transformative process does not have a fixed endpoint; it is a continual, non-linear progression. We've come to embrace the idea that growth is iterative, involving continual reentry into reflection spaces and reassessment of practices. This ongoing work involves revisiting and revising our approaches, continually interrogating biases, and actively addressing power dynamics within early childhood education. The non-linear nature of this journey liberates us from the constraints of predetermined outcomes, allowing for perpetual learning and evolution.

Invitation to Readers to Join the Mission for Transformation

As ECE teacher educators, our role extends beyond imparting knowledge; it is about shaping the ethos of ECE. We recognize the profound impact our courses have in shaping future educators, and by extension, the lives of children and families they will serve. Our responsibility lies in fostering inclusive spaces that challenge biases, elevate marginalized voices, and cultivate critical thinking. This process also includes confronting the inequitable ways that "identity still influences the distribution of outcomes in society" (Steele, 2010, p. 4). We aim to model inclusivity in our courses, equipping future educators with the tools to navigate complex social landscapes and disrupt systemic inequalities within educational settings. Through our continuous commitment to transformative practices, we aspire to redefine the role of educators in promoting equity, justice, and inclusivity within the field of ECE.

The work described in this chapter is part of a collaborative, ongoing effort to examine current and historical interconnected systems of inequity that maintain oppressive systems that impact children and families in the United States – in ECE settings as well as institutions of higher education and the broader society. Our writing is also an invitation for action and reflection to interrogate and interrupt these systems. We believe that the process and questions within these pages will help transform awareness into advocacy strengthened by understanding about how biases and narrow perspectives affect humanity.

We invite you to consider ways that you would consider sharing and applying ideas – including pitfalls and humbling moments that result from reckoning with historical privilege and oppression – in your own community. How might you explore and create new opportunities for pre- and in-service practitioners to interpret and critique the contents of this chapter? We invite you to contribute to a greater awareness of individual and collective experiences – an awareness that celebrates inherent strengths in a diverse citizenry, and centers children and families as cornerstones of our global community.

REFERENCES

Bloch, M. (1992). Critical perspectives on the historical relationship between child development and early childhood education research. In Kessler, S., & Swadener, E. B. (Eds.), *Reconceptualizing the early childhood curriculum: Beginning the dialogue* (pp. 3–20). Teachers College Press.

Brown, M. A., Jirard, S. A., Beemyn, G., & Ansara, G. (2021). *How to decolonize and decisnormatize curricula* [Webinar]. Sage. https://www.socialsciencespace.com/2021/04/watch-the-webinar-decolonizing-and-decisnormatizing-curricula/

Burgos-Debray, E. (2009). *I, Rigoberta Menchú: An Indian woman in Guatemala* (Wright, A., Trans.). Verso.

Calarco, J. M. (2018). *Negotiating opportunities: How the middle class secures advantages in school*. Oxford University Press.

Calarco, J. M. (2020). *A field guide to grad school: Uncovering the hidden curriculum*. Princeton University Press.

Cannella, G. S. (1997). *Deconstructing early childhood education: Social justice and revolution*. Peter Lang.

Cannella, G. S., & Viruru, R. (2004). *Childhood and postcolonization: Power, education, and contemporary practice* (1st ed.). Routledge., 10.4324/9780203463536

Center for Service-Learning and Civic Engagement. (n.d.). *Social identity wheel*. MSU. https://communityengagedlearning.msu.edu/upload/toolkits/Social-Identity-Wheel.pdf

Dudley-Marling, C., & Lucas, K. (2009). Pathologizing the language and culture of poor children. *Language Arts*, 86(5), 362–370.

Escayg, K. A. (2019). "Who's got the power?": A critical examination of the anti-bias curriculum. *International Journal of Child Care and Education Policy*, 13(1), 1–18.

Faculty Center for Ignatian Pedagogy. (2024). *Decolonizing your syllabus*. LUC. https://www.luc.edu/fcip/anti-racistpedagogy/anti-racistpedagogyresources/decolonizingyoursyllabus/#:~:text=Overall%2C%20it%20means%20shifting%20your,of%20Color%20(BIPOC)%20people%20are

Ferri, B. A., & Bacon, J. (2011). Beyond inclusion: Disability studies in early childhood teacher education. *Promoting Social Justice for Young Children*, 137-146.

Freire, P. (2000). *Pedagogy of the oppressed* (30th anniversary edition). [Original work published in English 1970]. *Continuum*.

Gannon, K. (2016, October 28). What goes into a syllabus. *The Chronicle of Higher Education*, 63(9), A40.

Gilovich, T., & Savitsky, K. (2012). Like goes with like: The role of representativeness in erroneous and pseudo-scientific beliefs. In Gilovich, T., Griffin, D., & Kahneman, D. (Eds.), *Heuristics and biases: The psychology of intuitive judgment* (pp. 617–624)., 10.1017/CBO9780511808098.036

Gorski, P. C. (2012). Teaching against essentialism and the "culture of poverty". In *Cultivating social justice teachers* (pp. 84–107). Routledge.

Heffernan, T. (2021). Sexism, racism, prejudice, and bias: A literature review and synthesis of research surrounding student evaluations of courses and teaching. *Assessment & Evaluation in Higher Education*, 47(1), 144–154.

Henrich, J., Heine, S. J., & Norenzayan, A. (2010). Most people are not WEIRD. *Nature*, 466, 29. 10.1038/466029a20595995

hooks, b. (2010). *Teaching critical thinking: Practical wisdom*. Routledge.

Kantawala, A. (2022). Action and reflection as "living theory and practice" (hooks, 2013). *Art Education*, 75(2), 4–7.

Kessler, S. A., & Swadener, B. B. (1992). *Reconceptualizing the early childhood curriculum: Beginning the dialog*. Teachers College Press.

Land, N., & Frankowski, A. (2022). (Un)finding childhoods in citational practices with postdevelopmental pedagogies. *Contemporary Issues in Early Childhood*, 23(4), 452–466. 10.1177/14639491221106500

Land, N., Vintimilla, C. D., & Pacini-Ketchabaw, V. (2020). Propositions toward educating pedagogists: Decentering the child. *Contemporary Issues in Early Childhood*, 23(2), 109–121.

McHendry, G. (n.d.). Interactive syllabus. *Interactive Syllabus*. https://www.interactivesyllabus.com/

NAEYC. (2019). *Position Statement on Advancing Equity in Early Childhood Education*. National Association for the Education of Young Children. https://www.naeyc.org/sites/default/files/globally-shared/downloads/PDFs/resources/position-statements/advancingequitypositionstatement.pdf

Newton, P. M. (2015). The learning styles myth is thriving in higher education. *Frontiers in Psychology*, 6, 1908. 10.3389/fpsyg.2015.0190826696947

Oluo, I. (2018). *So you want to talk about race*. Seal.

Pérez, M. S., & Saavedra, C. (2017). A call for onto-epistemological diversity in early childhood education and care: Centering global South conceptualizations of childhood/s. *Review of Research in Education*, *41*, 1–29. https://doi./10.3102/0091732X16688621org

Reyes, C.C., Haines, S.J., & Clark/Keefe, K. (2021). *Humanizing methodologies in educational research: Centering non-dominant communities.* Teachers College Press.

Souto-Manning, M. (2010). *Freire, teaching, and learning: Culture circles across contexts* (Vol. 350). Peter Lang.

Souto-Manning, M., & Rabadi-Raol, A. (2018). (Re)centering quality in early childhood education: Toward intersectional justice for minoritized children. *Review of Research in Education*, *42*(1), 203–225. 10.3102/0091732X187595

Steele, C. M. (2010). *Whistling Vivaldi: How stereotypes affect us and what we can do*. W.W. Norton & Company.

Stockstill, C. (2023). *False starts: The segregated lives of preschoolers*. NYU Press.

Taylor, S. D., Veri, M. J., Eliason, M., Hermoso, J. C. R., Bolter, N. D., & Van Olphen, J. E. V. (2019). The social justice syllabus design tool: A first step in doing social justice pedagogy. *Journal Committed to Social Change on Race and Ethnicity*, *5*(2), 133–166.

Tuck, E., & Yang, K. W. (2012). Decolonization is not a metaphor. *Decolonization*, *1*(1), 1–40.

ADDITIONAL READINGS

Adair, J. K., & Colegrove, K. S. S. (2021). *Segregation by experience: Agency, racism, and learning in the early grades*. University of Chicago Press.

Allen, R. L. (2005). Reassessing the internal (neo) colonialism theory. *The Black Scholar*, *35*(1), 2–11.

Blanchard, S. B., Newton, J. R., Didericksen, K. W., Daniels, M., & Glosson, K. (2021). Confronting racism and bias within early intervention: The responsibility of systems and individuals to influence change and advance equity. *Topics in Early Childhood Special Education*, *41*(1). 10.1177/0271121421992470

Brady, J. (2022). Exploring the role of Black feminist thought in pre-service early childhood teacher education: On the possibilities of embedded transformative change. *Contemporary Issues in Early Childhood*, *23*(4), 392–407.

Garba, T., & Sorentino, S. (2020). Slavery is a metaphor: A critical commentary on Eve Tuck and K. Wayne Yang's "Decolonization is not a metaphor.". *Antipode*, 52(3), 764–782.

Pérez, M. S., Saavedra, C. M., & Habashi, J. (2017). Rethinking global north onto-epistemologies in childhood studies [Special issue]. *Global Studies of Childhood*, 7(2).

Sykes, M., & Ostendorf, K. (Eds.). (2022). *Child care justice: Transforming the system of care for young children*. Teachers College Press.

Wilkerson, I. (2020). *Caste: The origins of our discontents*. Penguin Random House.

KEY TERMS AND DEFINITIONS

Anti-Racist Pedagogy: An educational practice that actively confronts and dismantles systemic racism within learning environments through inclusive teaching methods, curriculum, and policies.

BIPOC: An acronym for Black, Indigenous, and People of Color used to recognize and center the experiences and identities of individuals who belong to racial and ethnic groups that have been historically marginalized.

Colonization: The imposition of European American knowledge, beliefs, power structures and policies, rooted in imperialism, white supremacy, and exploitation, and often directed at Indigenous communities.

Critical Pedagogy: An educational philosophy and approach based on scholar and activist Paulo Freire's work that aims to empower learners by encouraging them to think critically about societal issues, fostering a deeper understanding of power structures, inequities, and injustices, and inspiring action for social change.

Decentering: Intentionally shifting away from dominant, often Eurocentric, perspectives to give equitable recognition and value to marginalized or non-dominant perspectives, cultures, and epistemologies.

Epistemology: The study of knowledge, including how knowledge is created, acquired, and validated within learning environments.

Hidden Curriculum: Implicit, embedded features of "doing school" that reflect culturally dominant norms for ways of being in relationship to learning; the unofficial rules, structures, and routines that go unnamed and privilege culturally dominant groups.

Positionality: An individual's social, cultural, and personal contexts that shape their viewpoints and understanding of the world.

Situating: Positioning oneself within broader social, cultural, and historical contexts to understand how personal experiences and identities influence perspectives and actions.

Social Identity: An individual's self-perception and affiliations with specific social groups (e.g., race, ethnicity, gender, religion, sexual orientation), shaping their interactions and perceptions within society.

Social Location: An individual's position within social structures, determined by various factors such as gender, race, socioeconomic status, and other social identities, influencing access to resources, power, and opportunities within society.

WEIRD: An acronym for Western, Educated, Industrialized, Rich, and Democratic used in social science to describe a population that is often overrepresented in studies, leading to potential biases in findings due to lack of diversity in samples.

ENDNOTES

[1]   Our group initially included five members; one member participated in the initial convenings, but life events led to discontinuation. We acknowledge and honor her contributions and participation in our learning process.

Chapter 3
Identifying Policy Flaws:
Addressing Educational Inequities in Early Childhood Education for Young Black Children

Monica R. Brown
https://orcid.org/0000-0002-8011-7772
University of Nevada, Las Vegas, USA

Monique Matute-Chavarria
http://orcid.org/0000-0002-9086-3429
New Mexico State University, USA

Pricella Morris
http://orcid.org/0009-0001-7309-7566
University of Nevada, Las Vegas, USA

ABSTRACT

Early childhood (EC) education is integral to the overall well-being of all young children. However, many children (e.g., Black and those with disabilities) experience an ECE system that is not equitable. In this chapter, presented are 1) the inherent flaws in ECE policies, 2) program inequities, 3) the potential benefits of equitable ECE policies and programs for Black children, and 4) recommendations for ECE stakeholders (i.e., educators, Black families, and policymakers) for addressing inequitable ECE as they contemplate a reconceptualization of ECE policies and educational programs for young Black children with and without disabilities.

DOI: 10.4018/979-8-3693-0924-7.ch003

INTRODUCTION

Access to and participation in early childhood education (ECE) programs are foundational to children's later success (McCoy et al., 2017). Children who do not have access to EC programs find adjusting to the school environment at grade level challenging (Ansari, 2018). Additionally, children entering kindergarten and first grade may struggle academically due to delayed social adjustment to their school environment (Elliott et al., 2015). EC programs also prepare children emotionally and are vital to attaining academic success. According to Wu et al. (2020), emotional intelligence reduces tendencies for disruptive behavior, negative attitudes, and abuse. Being equipped emotionally sets the pace for creating and sustaining positive relationships and making intelligent choices (Wu et al., 2020).

Early childhood education (ECE) is all-encompassing; it equips students with sound cognitive, emotional, and social skills essential in the next stage of learning and beyond (Iruka & Morgan, 2014). Therefore, it is equally important that *all* young children, regardless of race, gender, ability status, and/or economic status, have equitable EC experiences. Unfortunately, this has not been true for *all* children. If the pandemic revealed anything, it was that not all young children experience ECE programs in the same ways. For example, although young Black children access and participate in ECE programs in similar numbers to other groups (NCES, 2022), the ways they experience the programs are not the same, and their access to does not always meet their needs (Ferette, 2021). These are flaws in the Individuals With Disabilities Education Act (IDEA) and the system.

The ECE system and policies have been inequitable, unjust, and flawed for some (i.e., Black children with and without dis/abilities) young children for some time (Bassok & Galdo, 2016). The National Academies of Sciences, Engineering, and Medicine (NASEM, 2022) identified challenges in the ECE sector, such as "pre-existing structural flaws, and inequalities such as lack of high-quality care among low-income, rural populations, and communities of color" (NASEM, 2022, p. 2), to name a few. This is not a fact that was unknown to educators and policymakers. For example, young Black children have consistently had less affordable childcare, less access to childcare subsidies, and access to fewer childcare programs in their communities (Sethi et al., 2020). Likewise, young Black children continue to experience barriers in accessing ECE settings because of disparate treatment (e.g., higher suspension and expulsion rates; Sethi et al., 2020). Furthermore, the removal from ECE placements due to suspension and expulsion denies them those enriching ECE experiences.

Because we purport to care about the current and future well-being of all young children, especially those with disabilities, and place high importance on EC education, it is imperative that we reimagine ECE policies and practice so that *all* young children benefit (i.e., quality access and participation) and not just a few. Therefore, in this chapter we will discuss 1) the inherent flaws in ECE policies [i.e., IDEA], 2) program inequities, 3) the potential benefits of equitable ECE policies and programs for Black children, and 4) recommendations for ECE stakeholders (i.e., educators, Black families, and policymakers) for addressing inequitable ECE as they contemplate a reconceptualization of ECE policies and educational programs for young Black children with and without disabilities.

ECE INEQUITIES AND YOUNG BLACK CHILDREN

If acted on now, early childhood education can have a significant impact on the life and achievement (i.e., physical, cognitive, communication, social, emotional, and adaptive development; Barnard-Brak et al., 2021; Evans et al., 2016) of young children (i.e., ages 3-5) and their future, particularly Black children (McCoy et al., 2017) with and without disabilities. For example, research has indicated that Black children are more likely to access low-quality early childhood programs (Barnett et al., 2013) that can impact their academic outcomes (Iruka & Morgan, 2014). Conversely, access to high-quality ECE and early childhood special education (ECSE) can boost cognitive and social skills and help mitigate disparities in early learning experiences for young Black children (Fischberg, 2017). Likewise, Wright and Ford (2016) reported that ECE assists Black children in gaining access to learning. Ansari et al. (2019), reported that ECE enabled children to be academically sound. They reported that children (i.e., ages 3-5) who engaged in ECE exhibited superior achievement in academic subjects (e.g., math, literacy, and language skills) at grade level compared to their peers who did not participate in ECE. The benefits of ECE programs for all children are not in dispute. Additionally, it can benefit young Black children in their trajectory in school. Unfortunately, despite all that is known regarding the benefits of ECE for young Black children, disparities are still present.

Young Black Children

Over the years, researchers have established the importance of providing an enriched early childhood experience for young Black children (Barnett et al., 2013). In 2019, Black children accounted for 63.9% of the 3-5-year-old enrollment in ECE programs (NCES, 2022). Prior to the pandemic, they were participating in early childhood education (ECE) at rates like their Asian and bi/multi-racial peers. However, for young Black children ages 3 -5, the pandemic resulted in an overall decline in ECE participation. Although many wanted to blame the pandemic closures for young Black children's decline in ECE participation, prior to 2020 many preschools in Black communities were under-resourced, and the teachers were often not qualified (Cascio, 2021). The pandemic just exacerbated the existing inequities (Friedman-Krauss & Barnett, 2020), potentially creating a wider gap (e.g., rates of suspensions and expulsions; Iruka et al., 2022) between young Black children and some of their peers.

Young Black Children With Disabilities

Ford (2020) noted that Black children experienced two pandemics simultaneously during the pandemic, one racial and the other Covid-19. If this is true, then Black children with disabilities experienced three pandemics simultaneously (i.e., race, Covid-19, and disability). They were already labeled as vulnerable children because of their race and disability. The pandemic further highlighted the inequities they were already experiencing in the larger education system, the early childhood system, and the special education system under The Individuals with Disabilities Education Act (IDEA, 2004). Because the data does not report the impact of race plus disability with respect to 3-5-year-olds, it is difficult to determine the exact experiences of this specific demographic (i.e., 3-5-year-old Black children with disabilities). However, one might assume that young Black children with disabilities experienced the inequities experienced by children with disabilities, as well as those experienced by Black children.

IDEA, YOUNG BLACK CHILDREN, AND THE IMPLICIT PROMISES

For almost five decades, lawmakers and educators have confirmed the importance of early childhood education (ECE) for *all* children, particularly those who possess multiple vulnerabilities (e.g., racially/ethnically diverse, disability, low SES; Schochet et al., 2020). They agree that ECE is so important to the overall well-being (i.e., academic, social, emotional, behavioral; Gillispie, 2021) of children that lawmakers have been intentional about making ECE services available to *all* children, including those with disabilities. In theory, The IDEA (2004) promised *all* communities a fair chance at ECE for their children. However, IDEA has fallen short for many children with disabilities, specifically Black children. The well-intentioned laws and policies of ECE (and ECSE) for young Black children with and without disabilities have not lived up to the implicit promises (e.g., equity, inclusion, access, proportional treatment) made to all children, including those with disabilities.

The Promises

IDEA (2004) mandates that students with disabilities, ages 3 - 21 years old, receive a free and appropriate public education (FAPE). Part B of the IDEA was passed in 1986, approximately 11 years after the original enactment of the law. One goal of Part B is to support early childhood (i.e., ages 3-5) education special education (ECSE) programs and related services for *all* children with disabilities and to assist states with the operation of ECSE services for young children and their families. Despite the implicit promises and protections mandated in IDEA, the carve-out provisions of Part B (i.e., 3-5-year-olds), and its documented benefits, *all* children with disabilities have not had positive experiences. IDEA has not protected young children with disabilities, Black children, or Black children with disabilities from disparate treatment (e.g., disproportionality in exclusion and over-identification and placement) in ECE programs. In fact, IDEA may be viewed by some as an *anti*-Black law.

IDEA AS AN *ANTI*-BLACK LAW

Dumas and ross (2016) defined *anti*blackness as a type of oppression that degrades the cultural wealth of Black individuals through policies and practices. IDEA perpetuates *anti*blackness by not substantively addressing the inequitable ECE experiences of young Black children. For example, many young Black children are often placed in more restrictive environments and experience exclusionary practices (Meek et al., 2020). This exclusionary practice limits young Black children's access to and participation in quality ECE programs (Meek et al., 2020).

Additionally, young Black children are expelled and suspended at disproportionate rates, even those with disabilities (Meek et al., 2021). Additionally, they are not afforded the free appropriate public education (FAPE) granted by IDEA. This could be detrimental for those young Black children in need of ECE services. Although the ruling of Brown vs. Board of Education was established almost 70 years ago, making school segregation illegal, IDEA has become a form of de facto segregation for young Black children. When the young Black child is labeled, removed to a special education placement, and suspended and expelled disproportionately; they are segregated from the rest of the school population as well as a certain type of instruction. If these *anti*black policies and practices are allowed to continue, young Black children will continue to suffer.

Broken Law: Black Children's Experiences

Since the reauthorization of IDEA in 2004, young Black children between the ages of 3-5 years old have been *over*represented (i.e., labeled and placed) in specific special education categories (e.g., developmental delay; Wright & Counsell, 2018). Grindal et al. (2019) reported that *over*representation might be attributed to racial bias, as Black children are inappropriately referred based on their perceived challenging behaviors or lower academic skills. These perceptions often lead to practices that impede Black children's rights within the law. It has been decades since the authorization of the law, yet its promises have not manifested for Black children. The truth is that young Black children are not experiencing ECE in the same ways as other young children with disabilities. In the next sections, we discuss the ways young Black children experience ECE under IDEA. See Figure 1 for a representation of the brokenness of ECE under IDEA for young Black children.

Figure 1. ECE experiences of young black children under IDEA

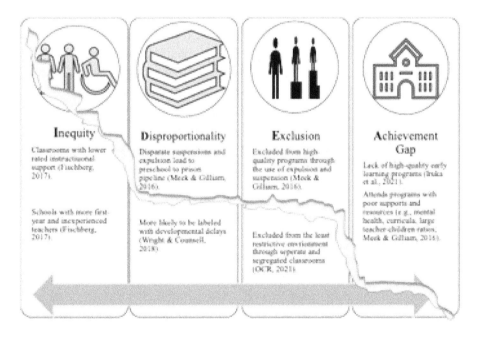

Inequity

Inequity refers to something that is unfair or unjust. ECE programs are inequitable for young Black children. For example, Fischberg (2017) reported that Black children from low-income homes were more likely to experience a) ECE classrooms with lower ratings of instructional support, b) schools with more first-year and inexperienced teachers, and c) higher teacher turnover. These things contribute to young Black children being behind in their academic and social-emotional skills when they enter kindergarten (Fischberg, 2017).

Disproportionality

An example of disproportionality experienced by young Black children is regarding suspensions and expulsions. According to the Office for Civil Rights (OCR, 2021b), 1.5 million preschoolers were enrolled during the 2017-2018 school year. Nearly 23% of them were served under IDEA. OCR (2021b) reported that 2,822 were suspended, and another 306 were expelled during that school year. They identified disparities in expulsion rates for children with disabilities, but Black preschoolers were disproportionately suspended and expelled during that school year. Black preschoolers comprised just over 18% of enrollment but accounted for 38.2% of the expulsions (OCR, 2021b). Disproportionate suspensions for Black preschoolers were more alarming. During the same school year, their suspensions were 2.5 times their total preschool population (43.3% and 18.2%, respectively; OCR, 2021b). Of the 2,822 preschoolers suspended, Black preschoolers accounted for 1,221 of them. Due to disproportionate suspensions, there were an additional 600 instances where Black preschoolers lost access to ECE.

There is no data that looks at the intersection of race and disability (i.e., Black 3-5-year-olds with a disability) at this age, but both are vulnerable populations. ECE programs were designed for all children, especially the most vulnerable. According to the Equal Justice Society (EJS, 2021), when preschoolers lose access due to suspensions and expulsions,

a) their future academic foundation is weak, b) their long-term, overall health is impacted, and c) they miss out on a critical time when they should be developing life-long socio-emotional behaviors and academic attitudes. These punitive and exclusionary practices deny young Black children the opportunity of receiving appropriate education and access to high-quality ECE programs. This may lead young Black children into the preschool-to-prison pipeline (Neitzel, 2018).

Exclusion

Merriam-Webster (n.d.). defines exclusion as shutting or keeping someone out of something or someplace. Young Black children experience one form of exclusion/ separation in terms of the settings where they receive ECE services. This exclusion or separation may not be intentional, but it is real. In most instances, Black children are placed in separate classes at higher rates compared to their White peers (NCLD, 2020). For example, OCR (2021a) reported that 24% of young children received services in separate classes (i.e., placements where children with disabilities receive services in restricted environments that do not include their typical peers; NCLD, 2020). When young Black children are excluded/separated from certain EC settings, it places them at a disadvantage for potential lifelong negative effects (i.e., high school dropout, poor academic outcomes, incarceration; Meek & Gilliam, 2016).

Achievement Gap

According to Kalil (2015), disparities in educational achievement are established early in a child's life. Once these gaps are established, the potential for a child's upward mobility decrease significantly. Therefore, it is imperative that all children have access to high-quality ECE programs, as it sets a foundation in the early years of learning (Dobbins et al., 2016). According to Fischberg (2017), access to higher-quality ECE programs can boost young Black children's cognitive and social skills, as well as mitigate disparities in early learning experiences.

However, Black children often do not have access to high-quality ECE programs (Fischberg, 2017). Instead, many Black children experience preschool/ECE through daycare or in-home programs (Kenly & Klein, 2020). When Black children attend lower-quality programs, their readiness for kindergarten (Kenly & Klein, 2020) is impacted.

It should also be noted that high-quality ECE as defined by policy or organizations (e.g., National Association for the Education of Young Children [NAEYC, 2019]), may not be consistent with what Black families consider high quality. It would be prudent to gain an understanding of what their conceptions are regarding high quality programs so that ECE can be reconceptualized to meet the needs of the Black child and their family. Until the current conceptualization and implementation of ECE under IDEA are addressed, young Black children with and without disabilities will not benefit like some other children. Instead, they will continue to experience a system that denies them an opportunity to thrive.

ADDRESSING THE FLAWS CRITICALLY

Using Black Critical Theory (BlackCrit; Dumas & Ross, 2016) and Disability Critical Race Theory (DisCrit; Annamma et al., 2016), IDEA has been reconceptualized for a more equitable positioning for young Black children. BlackCrit clarifies and acknowledges the disregard and marginalization (Dumas & ross, 2016) young Black children experience in ECE spaces. Specifically, the framing of *anti*blackness within BlackCrit and DisCrit sheds light on the inequities and harmful policies that IDEA has on young Black children.

In addition, Annamma et al. (2016) DisCrit acknowledges the physical and mental impact of being labeled due to race and ability. For example, young Black children with disabilities are multiply marginalized due to race and dis/ability. The impact of these marginalized experiences can often alienate children from the educational system, which can have a detrimental impact on their future successes. Furthermore, this conceptual framework uses tenet 5 (i.e., consider legal and historical aspects of dis/ability and race; Conner et al., 2015) to examine and challenge how IDEA is currently implemented and its impact on young Black children with disabilities.

Policy Reconceptualization

Since the inception of IDEA 50 years ago, educators and policymakers have grappled with the inequities in the ways the law is implemented. For young Black children, IDEA represents inequity, disproportionality, exclusion, as well as achievement and other (e.g., discipline, opportunity, value, etc.) gaps. In the following sections, we reconceptualize IDEA(A) to be inclusivity, diversity, equity, and accessibility, so that young Black children with and without disabilities and their families get to experience ECE in the same ways as other young children and their families. Finally, action. We know what needs to be done. Now is the time to act. Figure 2 represents actions EC educators can take to ensure equity for young Black children. In the following sections, we discuss a new IDEA(A).

Figure 2. IDEA reconceptualized: Actions for equitable ECE for young Black children

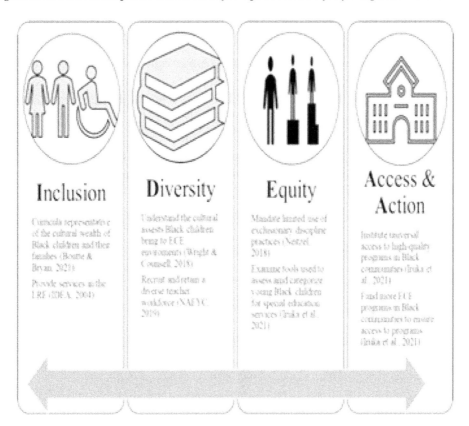

Inclusivity

For IDEA to really be inclusive, ECE programs need to mandate curricula that are representative of Black children with and without disabilities to create a sense of belonging. Additionally, as young Black children continue to diversify ECE programs, it is vital that they have access to the LRE (i.e., fewer Black children in segregated classrooms) to be truly inclusive. Moreover, more practices should be implemented that represent their diverse culture.

Diversity

To address the cultural aspects of ECE, educators need to a) analyze ECE practices and policies that are implicitly and explicitly *anti*black, b) intentionally focus on equity and justice in ECE spaces, and c) implement materials and curricula of Black culture. For example, the policies and practices should directly work to dismantle racism, *anti*blackness, and inequities young Black children and their families experience. Educators must work to understand the cultural assets (e.g., creative imagination, risk-taking, and thinking outside the box; Wright & Counsell, 2018) that Black children bring to schools (Wright & Counsell, 2018). Therefore, to truly exemplify a diverse environment, it is vital that educators understand these cultural assets and be responsive to Black students.

Equity

For IDEA (2004) to be truly equitable, ECE programs must ensure that *all* young Black children and their families have equitable opportunities. Therefore, programs need to examine how young Black children are assessed for special education services (Iruka et al., 2021). Programs also need to examine how they categorize young Black children with disabilities (Iruka et al., 2021). Furthermore, states must provide better funding to lower-resourced programs (Iruka et al., 2021) to provide young Black children with high-quality early learning experiences.

Accessibility and (Action)

For ECE under IDEA (2004) to be truly accessible, young Black children should be able to access and participate in high-quality programs. States must provide universal access to high-quality preschool programming in Black communities (Iruka et al., 2021). Additionally, the profession must work to diversify its educators (Paschall et al., 2020). Currently, just 9% of EC educators are Black (Zippia: The Career Expert, 2022). Finally, it is imperative that salaries are evened out and increased across the states (i.e., the average salary is $31,000; Zippia: The Career Expert, 2022) so that potential educators view it as a viable option for a career. This will allow the profession to potentially recruit and retain Black EC educators, as it is important for young Black children to see them in these spaces.

Once young Black children can access these spaces, EC educators must ensure that their policies and practices reflect high-quality early education (Iruka et al., 2021) for young Black children and their families. One way would be for educators to reflect on their implicit biases and seek trainings that prepare them to respond positively to the cultural behaviors (e.g., expressive body language, expressive individualism; Durden & Curenton, 2017; Wright & Counsell, 2018) that young Black children bring into the EC classroom. Finally, Durden and Curenton (2017) indicated that for young Black children to have quality learning experiences, teaching practices must be culturally appropriate. Thus, educators must examine the curricula, assessment tools, and practices that perpetuate *anti*blackness. We offer additional recommendations for EC educators and policymakers in the following sections.

RECOMMENDATIONS FOR ECE STAKEHOLDERS

Early education stakeholders (i.e., educators, families, policymakers) have been aware of these inequities for many years. Unfortunately, though, they have been unsuccessful in alleviating the differences experienced by vulnerable children (i.e., Black, and those with disabilities) when they engage with the ECE system. It is past the time that ECE stakeholders reflect on the inequities and disadvantages that young Black children have experienced for several decades. To mitigate some of the challenges experienced by young Black children, policymakers need to rethink local, state, and federal policies that are currently impacting young Black children in ECE programs. This is their opportunity to reimagine IDEA and how it continues to impact young Black children with disabilities in disparate ways. This reimagining could ensure that the inequity issues in Part B with respect to ECE programs are addressed.

This is a critical time for ECE and the educators charged with providing equitable educational spaces for young Black children with and without disabilities. Educators must create inclusive environments that mitigate some of the disparities young Black children often face in ECE spaces. Now is the time for educators to examine their pedagogies to determine how they may impact young Black children's outcomes. Table 1 provides additional recommendations for those interested in the EC experiences of Black preschool children. The recommendations are not exhaustive. They only provide a starting point for EC educators, Black families, and policymakers.

Table 1. Recommendations for ECE stakeholders

Stakeholders	Recommendations
Early Childhood Educators	• Develop cultural competence and sociopolitical consciousness around Black culture (Ladson-Billings, 2021). • Implement culturally relevant practices that reflect Black culture (Ladson-Billings, 2021). • Utilize Black culture as a central component when developing curricula (Boutte & Bryan, 2021). • Evaluate the perceptions and biases brought to EC spaces and consider how they impact the ways educators interact with young Black children. • Take this opportunity to reset and reimagine (Ladson-Billings, 2021) EC pedagogies and curriculum. • Utilize a strengths-based approach in EC spaces (Wright & Counsel, 2018). • Behave as if Black families know Black children best.
Black Families	• Advocate for resources for their child(ren) (e.g., technology equipment, internet resources, community resources). • Insist on two-way communication from early childhood educators. • Utilize parental safeguards to advocate for equitable EC experiences. • Hold educators accountable for implementing policies and laws. • Utilize social networks (i.e., community, faith-based organizations, recreation centers, support groups) to support advocacy efforts. • Collaborate with other Black families to create a coalition to ensure all Black children receive an equitable education.
Policymakers	• Revisit current laws and policies to address inequities, flaws, and injustices present in them. • Create actionable steps to equitable early learning and quality programs for young Black children. • Provide adequate funding to support high-quality EC programs for vulnerable communities (i.e., low-income, rural, disability, minoritized; Meek et al., 2020). • Reauthorize IDEA to reflect the need of the growing diverse population and address the disparities experienced by children and their families from minoritized backgrounds. • Prioritizing access to high-quality EC education for young Black children (Meek et al., 2020). • Provide policy briefs that are jargon-free and accessible for Black families.

CONCLUSION

ECE education is important to the overall well-being of all children (Gillispie, 2021). However, not all children get to experience ECE programs to the same degree as other children. It is true that young Black children participate in ECE programs at rates like most other young children (i.e., White and Latinx children). It is also true that the ECE programs accessible to young Black children and their families does not meet their needs (Ferrette, 2021). That is, there are not enough high-quality programs, as determined by Black families, available for the number of young Black children who need them.

IDEA made promises to *all* children regarding ECE. Now is the time to re-imagine an ECE system that provides equitable experiences for young Black children. Most importantly, now is the time for action. Laws and policy statements are wonderful, but without action, they are just words on a piece of paper.

REFERENCES

Ansari, A. (2018). The persistence of preschool effects from early childhood through adolescence. *Journal of Educational Psychology*, 110(7), 952–973. 10.1037/edu000025530906008

Ansari, A., Pianta, R. C., Whittaker, J. V., Vitiello, V. E., & Ruzek, E. A. (2019). Starting early: The benefits of attending early childhood education programs at age 3. *American Educational Research Journal*, 56(4), 1495–1523. 10.3102/0002831218817737

Barnard-Brac, L., Morales-Alerman, M. M., Toment, K., & McWilliam, R. A. (2021). Rural and racial/ethnic differences in children receiving early intervention services. *Family & Community Health*, 44(1), 52–58. 10.1097/FCH.0000000000000028533214410

Barnett, S., Carolan, M., & Johns, D. (2013). *Equity and Excellence: African-American Children's Access to Quality Preschool*. Center on Enhancing Early Learning Outcomes. http://ceelo.org/wp-content/uploads/2013/11/CEELO-NIEERequity Excellence-2013.pdf

Bassok, D., & Galdo, E. (2016). Inequality in preschool quality? Community-level disparities in access to high-quality learning environments. *Early Education and Development*, 27(1), 128–144. 10.1080/10409289.2015.1057463

Boutte, G., & Bryan, N. (2021). When will Black children be well? Interrupting anti-black violence in early childhood classrooms and schools. *Contemporary Issues in Early Childhood*, 22(3), 232–243. 10.1177/1463949119890598

Cascio, E. U. (2021). *Covid-19, early care and education, and child development.* Dartmouth College and National Bureau of Economic Development. https://www.nber.org/sites/default/files/2021-10/cascio_seanWP_oct2021_revised.pdf

Dobbins, D., McCready, M., Rackas, L., & Child Care Aware of America. (2016). *Unequal access: Barriers to early childhood education for boys of color [Issue Brief].* Robert Wood Johnson Foundation. https://www.childcareaware.org/wp-content/uploads/2016/10/UnequalAccess_BoysOfColor.pdf

Durden, T. R., & Curenton, S. M. (2017). Pathways to excellence – what we know works for nurturing Black children's success. In Iruka, I. U., Cureton, S. M., & Durden, T. R. (Eds.), *African American Children in Early Childhood Education: Making the case for policy investments in families, schools, and communities* (Vol. 5, pp. 35–55). Emerald Group Publishing. 10.1108/S2051-231720170000005003

Elliott, S. N., Frey, J. R., & Davies, M. (2015). Systems for assessing and improving students' social skills to achieve academic competence. In Durlak, J. A., Domitrovich, C. E., Weissberg, R. P., & Gullotta, T. P. (Eds.), *Handbook of social and emotional learning: Research and practice* (pp. 301–319). The Guilford Press.

Evans, D. L., Feit, M. D., & Trent, T. (2016). African American parents and attitudes about child disability and early intervention services. *Journal of Social Service Research*, 42(1), 96–112. 10.1080/01488376.2015.1081118

Ferrette, T. (2021). *Roots of discipline-induced trauma for Black children in early childhood settings*. The Center for Law and Social Policy. https://www.clasp.org/publications/fact-sheet/roots-discipline-induced-trauma-black-children-early-childhood-settings/

Fischberg, J. (2017). *The crisis in Black education: Early disparities*. Rubicon Programs. https://rubiconprograms.org/news/blog/the-crisis-in-black-education-early-disparities

Ford, D. Y. (2020, September 14). *Miseducating Black students as a form of educational malpractice and professional betrayal.* https://www.diverseeducation.com/demographics/african-american/article/15107747/miseducating-black-students-as-a-form-of-educational-malpractice-and-professional-betrayal

Friedman-Krauss. A., & Barnett, S. (2020). Access to high-quality early education and racial equity. Rutgers Graduate School of Education. *National Institute for Early Education Research,* 1-3. https://nieer.org/wp-content/uploads/2021/02/Special-Report-Access-to-High-Quality-Early-Education-and-Racial-Equity.pdf

Gillispie, C. (2021). *Our youngest learners: Increasing equity in early intervention*. The Education Trust. https://edtrust.org/wp-content/uploads/2014/09/Increasing-Equity-in-Early-Intervention-May-2021.pdf

Grindal, T., Schifter, L. A., Schwartz, G., & Hehir, T. (2019). Racial differences in special education identification and placement: Evidence across three states. *Harvard Educational Review*, 89(4), 525–553. 10.17763/1943-5045-89.4.525

Individuals with Disabilities Education Act, 20 U.S.C. § 1400 (2004).

Iruka, I. U., Gardner-Neblett, N., Telfer, N. A., Ibekwe-Okafor, N., Curenton, S. M., Sims, J., Sansbury, A. B., & Neblett, E. W. (2022). Effects of racism on child development: Advancing antiracist developmental science. *Annual Review of Developmental Psychology*, 4(1), 109–132. 10.1146/annurev-devpsych-121020-031339

Iruka, I. U., James, C., Reaves, C., & Forte, A. (2021). *Black child national agenda: America must deliver on its promise.* Equity Research Action Coalition, Frank Porter Graham Child Development Institute, The University of North Carolina at Chapel Hill. https://equity-coalition.fpg.unc.edu/resource/black-child-national -agenda-america-must-deliver-on-its-promise/

Iruka, I. U., & Morgan, J. (2014). Patterns of quality experienced by African American children in early education programs: Predictors and links to children's preschool and kindergarten academic outcomes. *The Journal of Negro Education*, 83(3), 235–255. 10.7709/jnegroeducation.83.3.0235

Kalil, A. (2015). Inequality begins at home: The role of parenting in the diverging destinies of rich and poor children. In Amato, P., Booth, A., McHale, S., & Van Hook, J. (Eds.), *Diverging destinies: Families in an era of increasing inequality* (pp. 63–82). Springer. 10.1007/978-3-319-08308-7_5

Kenly, A., & Klein, A. (2020). Early childhood experiences of black children in a diverse midwestern suburb. *Journal of African American Studies*, 24(1), 129–148. 10.1007/s12111-020-09461-y

Ladson-Billings, G. (2021). I'm here for the hard re-set: Post pandemic pedagogy to preserve our culture. *Equity & Excellence in Education*, 54(1), 68–78. 10.1080/10665684.2020.1863883

McCoy, D. C., Yoshikawa, H., Ziol-Guest, K. M., Duncan, G. J., Schindler, H. S., Magnuson, K., Yang, R., Koepp, A., & Shonkoff, J. P. (2017). Impacts of early childhood education on medium-and long-term educational outcomes. *Educational Researcher*, 46(8), 474–487. 10.3102/0013189X1773773930147124

Meek, S., Iruka, I. U., Allen, R., Yazzie, D., Fernandez, V., Catherine, E., McIntosh, K., Gordon, L., Gilliam, W., Hemmeter, M. L., Blevins, D., & Powell, T. (2020). Fourteen priorities to dismantle systemic racism in early care and education. The Children's Equity Project. https://fpg.unc.edu/sites/fpg.unc.edu/files/resource-files/ 14-priorities-equity-121420.pdf

Meek, S., Iruka, I. U., Catherine, E., Yazzie, D., Gilliam, W., McIntosh, K., Fernandez, V., Blevins, D., Jimenez Castellanos, O., & Garcia, G. (2021). Advancing equity in early care and education systems with the american rescue plan act. The Children's Equity Project. https://childandfamilysuccess.asu.edu/cep/initiatives/ advancing-equity-through-american-rescue-plan-

Meek, S. E., & Gilliam, W. S. (2016). *Expulsion and suspension in early education as matters of social justice and health equity.* (Discussion Paper). Washington, DC. National Academy of Medicine. 10.31478/201610e

Merriam-Webster. (n.d.). Inclusion. In *Merriam-Webster.com com dictionary*. Merriam-Webster. https://www.merriam-webster.com/dictionary/inclusion

National Academies of Sciences, Engineering, and Medicine. (2022). *Addressing the Impact of COVID-19 on the Early Care and Education Sector*. Washington, DC: The National Academies Press. https://doi.org/10.17226/26463

National Association for the Education of Young Children. (2019). *Early learning program accreditation standards and assessment items*. NAEYC. https://www.naeyc.org/sites/default/files/globally-shared/downloads/PDFs/accreditation/early-learning/standards_assessment_2019.pdf

Neitzel, J. (2018). Research to practice: Understanding the role of implicit bias in early childhood disciplinary practices. *Journal of Early Childhood Teacher Education*, 39(3), 232–242. 10.1080/10901027.2018.1463322

Paschall, K., Madill, R., & Halle, T. (2020). *Demographic characteristics of the early care and education workforce: Comparisons with child and community characteristics*. OPRE Report #2020-108. Washington, DC: Office of Planning, Research, and Evaluation, Administration for Children and Families., U.S. Department of Health and Human Services.

Schochet, O. N., Johnson, A. D., & Phillips, D. A. (2020). The effects of early care and education settings on the kindergarten outcomes of doubly vulnerable children. *Exceptional Children*, 87(1), 27–53. 10.1177/0014402920926461

Sethi, S., Johnson-Staub, C., & Robbins, K. G. (2020). *An anti-racist approach to supporting child care through COVID-19 and beyond*. The Center for Law and Social Policy (CLASP). https://www.clasp.org/publications/report/brief/anti-racist-approach-supporting-child-care-through-covid-19-and-beyond/

Wright, B., & Counsell, S. (2018). *The brilliance of Black boys: Cultivating school success in the early grades*. Teachers College Press.

Wright, B. L., & Ford, D. Y. (2016). "This little light of mine": Creating early childhood education classroom experiences for African American boys prek-3. *Journal of African American Males in Education*, 7(1), 5–19.

Wu, M. Y. H., Alexander, M. A., Frydenberg, E., & Deans, J. (2020). Early childhood social-emotional learning based on the Cope-Resilience program: Impact of teacher experience. *Issues in Educational Research*, 30(2), 782–807.

Zippia: The Career Expert. (2022). *Early childhood teacher demographics and statistics in the US*. Zippia. https://www.zippia.com/early-childhood-teacher-jobs/demographics/

Chapter 4
An Intersectional Approach to Forming Meaningful Family Partnerships

Karina Du

San Francisco State University, USA & University of California, Berkeley, USA

ABSTRACT

Family partnerships are critical to supporting the learning and development of young children, including those with disabilities. However, systemic inequities create barriers for families to meaningfully engage in the special education process, especially for those from nondominant backgrounds. The family systems theory (FST) is a framework used to understand the dynamic nature of a family system by understanding an individual with a disability as interrelated to the rest of the family unit. The author offers a reconceptualization of the framework by embedding intersectionality within family inputs to honor families' multiple, overlapping identities. Funds of knowledge, culturally responsive teaching and reflective practice are offered as tools to strengthen understanding and responsiveness to children and families with intersectional identities.

INTRODUCTION

All practitioners of the early childhood ecosystem are responsible for advancing equitable practices to support the learning and development of all young children (National Association for the Education of Young Children [NAEYC], 2019). These practices honor children's identities, elevate the diverse communities they belong

DOI: 10.4018/979-8-3693-0924-7.ch004

to, and dismantle structural inequities that create barriers for children and families. This includes establishing reciprocal family partnerships, where family strengths, identities, and knowledge can be elevated to ensure children, including those with disabilities, and their families have what they need to thrive. When family-centered practices are established, families can engage in active decision-making, share their priorities and goals, and advocate for their child's learning and development (Division for Early Childhood [DEC], 2014).

Family partnerships also support the inclusion of young children with disabilities and their families. According to the Division of Early Childhood and the National Association for the Education of Young Children's (2009) joint position statement on early childhood inclusion, early education professionals must support children within the context of their families and communities. They define early childhood inclusion as embodying

the values, policies, and practices that support the right of every infant and young child and his or her family, regardless of ability, to participate in a broad range of activities and contexts as full members of families, communities, and society. (p. 2)

For programs to be inclusive, services and support acknowledge and respond to the needs of children, in relation to the family and communities in which children belong.

Systemic inequities create barriers for meaningful family partnerships. Child development frameworks often center White, middle class, suburban, nondisabled, English-speaking, and nuclear family structures, failing to acknowledge the complex identities young children and their families may experience (Derman-Sparks et al., 2020). Families from historically marginalized communities, including those who are of color (Kayser et al., 2021; Yull et al., 2014), multilingual (Kayser et al., 2021; Ortega, 2014), refugees (Haines et al., 2015), and/or disabled (Gerzel-Short et al., 2019; Kalyanpur & Harry, 2012), may experience additional barriers when collaborating with teachers. In addition, families who hold multiple marginalized identities may experience additional barriers due to the intersections of those identities (Crenshaw, 1989). Early educators must actively engage in family-centered practices that respond to the individualized context of each family unit, while acknowledging the complexities when their identities overlap.

The Family Systems Theory (FST) is a framework for understanding the interactive and dynamic nature of a family system (Turnbull et. al 1984, 2015). Family members are seen as interrelated and interdependent, adapting and responding to changes within the family unit and external environment. Although the existing framework acknowledges the dynamic nature of the family system when supporting a child with a disability, it does not explicitly address the additional layers of complexities when families hold multiple and marginalized identities or when those identities overlap.

In this chapter, the author introduces the topic of intersectionality, focusing on the role of race and disability in special education. Next, the author reviews challenges to family partnerships, focusing on how special education systems distort family identity and experiences. Then, the author introduces and reconceptualize the FST by applying an intersectional lens within family inputs as a way to understand how holding multiple minoritized identities can compound, influencing the family unit, and subsequently processes, outputs, and changes. Utilizing families' funds of knowledge, the author discusses how the framework can be utilized to elevate the assets each family brings through their intersectional experiences. Lastly, implications for research and practice are offered, focusing on the role of reflective practice, culturally responsive teaching. By understanding a family's intersectional experiences, practitioners can strengthen family engagement practices to better support families of color who have children with disabilities. The following questions guide the chapter: How can the FST be reconceptualized to elevate the lived experiences of families and children with intersectional identities? What strategies can help deepen engagement between families and schooling for those with multiple and marginalized identities?

INTERSECTIONALITY

Language holds great weight in education and various terms can hold different connotations (Nieto & Bode, 2018). Additionally, language is nuanced and consistently changes over time in response to social, economic, and political events (2018). The language the author uses around race and disability is guided by how people themselves choose to identify and attempt to utilize the most accurate terms. The author does not mean to suggest that these are the most "politically correct" terms nor does she mean to impose usage of certain identity markers over others. The author also recognizes individuals may choose to identify in other ways. The terms are based on her own identities as a nondisabled, woman of color, current research trends, and conversations with members across various communities. The author explicitly names her own positionality and subjectivity in recognition that they influence the lens in which she approaches her inquiry process (Peshkin, 1988) and attempt to manage her bias (Maxwell, 2013).

The author refers to race as a socially constructed concept utilized to categorize people based on *perceived* biological differences, and is reflective of history, politics, and shared social traditions that systemically advantage some and disadvantage others (Annamma et el al., 2013; Coates et al., 2022; Zack, 2023). Similarly, disability is also an evolving and socially constructed concept (World Health Organization, 2011). For example, the term "special needs" was once commonly used in referring to individuals with disability (Ladau, 2021). However, disability advocates have argued against this term as euphemistic, and now reclaim the term "disability" and their identity. The author utilizes the United Nations' (2006) human rights model of disability that defines persons with disabilities as "those who have long-term physical, mental, intellectual or sensory impairments which in interaction with various barriers may hinder their full and effective participation in society on an equal basis with others" (p. 12). This definition acknowledges the physical and mental impairment or conditions that may influence one's access and participation, when experienced with societal barriers that can cause or exacerbate restrictions (World Health Organization, 2011). The human rights model of disability corresponds with inclusive equality as it recognizes that disability is a social construct and offers legal and political protection of human rights (Degener & de Castro, 2022). Establishing a shared definition of race and disability allows to examine how these entities can be mutually reinforcing as minoritized identities.

Within early education, families are multidimensional and individuals often identify with multiple social and cultural groups, such as race, class, gender, and disability (NAEYC, 2019). According to Crenshaw (1989), intersectionality recognizes that social identity groups may overlap, leading to additional oppression due to the interdependent nature of those identities. Crenshaw introduced the concept of intersectionality when referring to the double discrimination that Black women experience due to racism and sexism by examining feminist theory and antiracist politics across legal cases. Because only single identities, specifically race or gender, were analyzed in these cases, courts found that discrimination had not been committed, as the single-axis framework did not allow individuals to account for the combined effects of race and gender. The framework only focused on the experiences of the most privileged members of each minority group, further marginalizing those who are multiply-burdened. Utilized across a wide variety of disciplines, the field of intersectional studies has emerged consisting of intersectional engagement around application, theory, praxis, and a fusing of the three (Cho et al., 2013). When working with families who hold multiple social identities, acknowledging their intersections can help better understand how these identities can further shape their interactions, experiences, and adaptations to change.

Within special education, racism and ableism intersect and create notions of normalcy that ultimately guide how children are expected to behave, learn, and interact (Annamma et al., 2013; Brown et al., 2010). Disability is often rooted in deficit perspectives, as it situates the individual as in need of a cure or intervention, reinforcing notions of normalcy (Kalyanpur, 1999). The disabled individual is seen as the cause for exclusion, rather than the structures and systems that oppress and marginalize. Additionally, child development frameworks often normalize White and Eurocentric norms, othering and creating deficit-based perspectives for children of color (Beneke & Cheatham, 2020). For example, Bronfenbrenner's (1986) ecological systems theory is prominent in the field of early education. The theory provides a systems model for understanding individual development by examining the various layers of influences stemming from the microsystem, which includes immediate relationships such as family and school, to the macro- and chronosystems that acknowledge overall culture and environmental events that occur throughout their lifetime. Critics such as Vélez-Agosto et al. (2017) argued that the model fails to acknowledge how culture permeates all levels of the system, including most immediate relationships and interactions. They argued that culture becomes a part of everyday activities, actions, and routine, and these are largely influenced by shared identities such as race, language, and immigration status. Though these frameworks can provide one lens to understand learning and development, when normalized in the field, they may impede to acknowledge other ways of seeing and knowing about how children grow and develop, especially when there are deviations from dominant culture. The intersections between race and disability reinforce and maintain dominant culture within early education systems.

Disparities in access to special education services are also represented across disability and race. Asian, Latinx, and Black children are less likely to receive early intervention and early childhood special education services than White children with similar disabilities (Dawn et al., 2017; Friedman-Krauss & Barnett, 2023). Additionally, Black and Latinx children are also less likely to receive services in inclusive environments (Friedman-Krauss & Barnett, 2023; Grindal et al., 2018), despite legislation that emphasizes the importance of educating students in the least restrictive environment possible (Individuals with Disabilities Education Act [IDEA], 2004). The intersections between disability and race raise issues of inequity and systems that further maintain and perpetuate harmful practices impacting families from nondominant communities.

Early educators are responsible for engaging in more equitable practices to ensure all young children can thrive. As such, teachers can actively interrogate and process through their own implicit biases, influencing how they connect with children and families and respond to the identities and experiences they bring into early learning settings. Implicit biases are involuntary and unconscious beliefs that guide individuals' perceptions and attitudes towards others (Iruka et al., 2020). Without spaces for critical self-reflection, biases can perpetuate negative stereotypes. In this regard, Gilliam et al. (2016) found that White teachers were more likely to track Black boys, expect challenging behaviors, and hold them to lower expectations than White children. This study is in alignment with statistics that Black children are 3.4 times more likely to experience suspension than White children (U.S. Department of Education, Office of Special Education and Rehabilitative Services, Office of Special Education Programs, 2021) and are also more likely to qualify for services under the emotional disturbance category than any other racial groups (Lambert et al., 2021; U.S. Department of Education, Office of Special Education and Rehabilitative Services, Office of Special Education Programs, 2021). The role of implicit bias can have detrimental effects on children's learning if explicit efforts are not made to interrogate them.

FAMILY PERSPECTIVES ON NAVIGATING SPECIAL EDUCATION

Parent participation is a critical component of the IDEA (2004), which mandates free appropriate public education to eligible children with disabilities. However, White middle-class norms influence the policies and practices around special education, leading to deficit-views for racially minoritized children and families (Kalyanpur & Harry, 2012; Trainor, 2010). Under IDEA, parents are guaranteed the right to engage in decision-making rights in the special education process by accessing educational records, discussing placement decisions, codeveloping the education program, and engaging in legal processes around compliance (Banks et al., 2023). However, families may not have the social and cultural capital, privileged by hegemonic systems, that are needed to participate as IDEA and schools suggest (Cioè-Peña, 2020). Differences in expectations around family roles and participation in school, different values in learning goals, and language accessibility can lead to deficit-based assumptions around family engagement, especially families from nondominant cultures.

Families of color who have children with disabilities report language and communication barriers, cultural variances on views of family involvement, and mismatched expectations for children's learning and development as continued challenges to family partnerships (Burke & Goldman, 2018; Cavendish & Connor, 2018; Chu S., 2014). These biases and assumptions influence how families are expected to participate and engage in home-school partnerships, including the navigation of special education processes.

In a small study of Chinese-American parents of children with disabilities and their teachers, Chu S. (2014) found challenges to teacher-family interactions, including unstated assumptions around communication and general communication and language barriers. The largest disconnect was mismatched expectations around children's needs and instruction. One parent reported feeling they needed to be "obedient" and "deferent" (Chu S., 2014, p. 243) to the American education system. She spoke of learning about the laws, her rights, and how to advocate as she went:

There are a lot of people who have doctoral degrees in Angel ISD, they must know something around there. So, they know somebody breaks the law. The school is worried that I (Wangli) may go to sue them [principal and teachers]. (Chu S., 2014, p. 241)

Chu S. (2014) found that, in addition to establishing clearer communication expectations and needs, cultural sensitivity was also needed to account for the sociocultural influences of young children's home lives (Vygotsky, 1978).

The navigation of accessing services through formalized meetings, including the Individualized Education Program (IEP), also challenges meaningful family partnership. Buren et al. (2018) conducted a metasynthesis of 18 qualitative research studies on home-school partnerships focusing on families across racial and linguistic backgrounds. Families reported cultural differences across communication and advocacy, alienation due to missing information, lack of translation services, confusion about their rights as parents, disrespect from school personnel, and general lack of support. Families also reported consistent exclusion from the decision-making process within IEP meetings. This is especially alarming as parents have the right to participate in the identification (i.e., eligibility), assessment or educational placement of their child and other matters relating to your child's free appropriate public education (IDEA, 2004). For families holding nondominant identities, this is also an issue of equity pertaining to parental rights around their children's schooling.

Families also actively engage to make sense of the bureaucracy and navigation of the special education system. Cavendish and Connor (2018) conducted a mixed-methods study on Black and Latino families, students, and teachers on children's IEP transitions. They found a significant gap between policy and implementation for parent and student involvement in the IEP process. Compliance with the law was seen as a central focus of IEP meetings. One mother shared that, "maybe because of my limitations in terms of language, sometimes they do not take me into account" (Cavendish & Connor, 2018, p. 38). Though asked to attend meetings, parents did not feel included in the cocreation of the IEP, often resuming the "passive role" (Cavendish & Connor, 2018, p. 39) and simultaneously reporting challenges with language and how emotionally draining it was that meetings always focus on children's deficits.

In their study of Chinese, Vietnamese, and Haitian immigrant parents, Rossetti et al. (2020) found similar barriers regarding the need for language accommodations for IEPs, along with the needs for accountability and outreach to strengthen relationships with families. One family discussed not having an interpreter, and another reported the constant fight with school:

> *It seems as if parents are always butting heads and going to war with the school, when the appropriate and the right thing to do is simply provide that service, because, if appropriate services are provided at an appropriate time, students are able to thrive. (p. 248)*

Participants also reported wanting to learn more about becoming advocates in how to navigate the special education system, despite feelings of unresponsiveness from schools. The authors suggested the need to value different cultural norms and increase collaboration to strengthen family engagement.

THE FAMILY SYSTEMS THEORY

The FST is an approach to understanding the family as an interrelated system, each with its own characteristics and complexities (Turnbull et al., 1984, 2015). The family unit is meant to be understood as one dynamic system, both impacting and being impacted by its environment. Additionally, the system is not meant to be reality, but a way of knowing about the family and understanding family experience as a unit. Although the framework was originally developed for practitioners to better understand family experiences when the family has a child with a disability, it can be applied to all families as a way to understand how families function in relation to individual members (Dunst, 2017). It can also provide the context in developing more family-centered practices.

The FST is composed of four interrelated components: Inputs, processes, outputs, and changes (Turnbull et al., 1984, 2015). Inputs refer to the characteristics of the family, including those that affect the family unit as a whole as well as individual members, including disability, health status, race, gender, and socioeconomic and cultural background. Family inputs contextualize the various events and experiences that may shape families, such as their interactions. The process refers to the nature of relationships held across members, such as marital, sibling or extended family members. These interactions fluctuate by the degree of cohesiveness and adaptability of families. They also influence the outputs or activities in which they engage together. Outputs, or functions, fulfill the individual and collective needs of the family and can reflect the resources, concerns, and priorities of the family, such as finances, education, health, socialization, and family identity. Lastly, changes within the life cycle refers to developmental events or transitions that occur to families over time. These changes can be developmental in nature, such as learning about a child's disability, or include transitions such as moving from an Individualized Family Service Plan to an IEP. Changes in the family life cycle can affect the characteristics of families and their daily functioning. Within the FST, each part of the system is interrelated and transitions within one component can alter the others, impacting the family unit as a whole.

Currently, the family systems perspective is often used in early intervention and special education as a tool to help prepare teachers in understanding the experiences of families who have children with disabilities (Dunst, 2017; McBride & Brotherson, 1997). Additionally, existing models of family partnerships often fail to address the intersectional identities and experiences of families of marginalized backgrounds (Baquedano-Lopez et al., 2013). Centering disability intersectionality within inputs of the FST allows to construct a deeper understanding of each family unit and how they experience intersecting systems of privilege and oppression. This will also allow to better strengthen the understanding of family dynamics to connect with families more authentically. The following questions guide the chapter: How can the FST be reconceptualized to elevate the lived experiences of families and children with intersectional identities? What strategies can help deepen engagement between families and schooling for those with multiple, marginalized identities?

RECONCEPTUALIZING FAMILY SYSTEMS THEORY WITH AN EMPHASIS ON INTERSECTIONALITY

The FST can be utilized as a tool to understand the dynamics and complexities of a family system, when supporting a family who has a child with a disability (Turnbull et al., 1984, 2015). The author argues that the FST can be reconceptualized by explicitly acknowledging intersecting identities within family inputs. Characteristics of the family may include group size, composition, socioeconomic status, geography, race, and cultural backgrounds, and individual characteristics may include values, health status, and disability (Turnbull et al., 2015). Addressing intersectionality within family and individual characteristics allows to begin understanding how these multidimensional identities can influence the other components of the FST, including family interactions, functions, and transitions in the life cycle, as they all overlap.

In an example of a child with a disability, it may be improbable to get a full depiction or context of how they are positioned or understood within their family unit if only characteristics as singular identities are considered. However, identifying multiple characteristics across the individual and family and learning how these structures, identity groups, and belief systems intersect can facilitate a more holistic understanding of inputs and ultimately the child and family. This knowledge can lead to family interactions as researchers learn more about which relationships are important, the various roles individuals hold, and how relationships generally function.

Each family may negotiate different relationships based on their own culture or identities, equating to a variety of family structures (Fujiura, 2014). Addressing intersections within family inputs can also strengthen ways researchers understand family processes by expanding the subsystem of relationships important to families. This may include intergenerational relationships such as grandparents, cluster households or extensions of families beyond the nuclear household (Rios-Aguilar & Kiyama, 2012) and nonfamily households (Altman & Blackwell, 2014). Nontraditional members may be strong avenues of support that families identify as critical to their functioning.

Family processes can influence and are also influenced by outputs and how families engage in activities or access resources to meet their family needs. Various sources of identities, such as race, language or socioeconomic background, compounded with disability can influence what services or support families may need or access. Using an intersectional lens, these spaces of connection may stem from informal support such as community-based organizations like churches (Cook & Williams, 2015). Cook and Williams (2015) identified that fictive kinship can serve as a protective factor for Black women. These networks are often found in the church and faith, providing emotional, spiritual, and intellectual spaces for women of color to explore their possibilities. An intersectional lens shows activities and functions in which families engage, demonstrating their advocacy, coping, and navigation of special education systems.

Lastly, family life cycle or transitions can shift characteristics across inputs and outputs. As disability and identities are fluid, families may experience changes in their inputs that may affect the overall family system. For example, as Rios and Tu (2023) pointed out, transitions such as an IEP meeting where progress, goals, and services for children are discussed can become sources of stress for families. In their study of Asian families with children with intellectual and developmental disabilities, the authors found that families reported stress before, during, and after the IEP meeting due to preparation, anxiousness from being outnumbered or having their suggestions embraced, and uncertainty of outcomes of the meeting. They suggested schools provide resources to support families throughout the IEP process, such as information or consultation meetings around special education processes, collaborating with community partners, and providing training to staff in working with families with various identities. These outputs can be tools to provide more family-centered support for families navigating the special education process.

Beneke et al. (2021) conducted focus groups centering the experiences of 33 "Mothers of Color," who had young children with disabilities, on the intersections of ableism and racism. The author followed Beneke et al.'s lead by capitalizing "Mothers of Color" as they refer to a specific group of self-identified mothers who engaged as participants. In the study, the authors sought to understand how participants made meaning of competence in schooling and conceptualized justice in early childhood. They found that participants believed early education upholds whiteness and narrow beliefs of ability, reinforcing deficit beliefs that their children of color are less human, and worthy of exclusion and punishment. One participant shared:

We are in a society that seems to have a formula for developing the ideal child. Like, if you do this and this right, then your child will achieve this and have this opportunity and it just does not work that way. Yeah, I think he is shown a lot of growth, but it is all come at a price for him emotionally. I want him to be considered as a whole person; really hard, because they want to focus on the deficit and what he cannot do. (p. 334)

This mother sought for her child to be seen and appreciated for who he is, not who he can be. In response to institutionalized practices, mothers advocated for authentic respect and care for their children, rejected exclusionary systems, and dreamed beyond the status quo as a way of reclaiming notions of competence for their children and themselves as women of color who have children with disabilities. Mothers of Color position themselves as leaders by challenging deficit-based views on parental involvement and resisting the status quo in their children's schooling. Using the FST and lens of intersectionality, inputs within this study include the intersections of disability and race, though there were additional positionalities with which families identified. Within family interactions, participants identified as mothers. Though other relationships were not explicitly addressed, some participants shared what they also identified as a grandmother. For outputs, participants offered counterstories to deficit-framing of their parenting and children. They also advocated for services by navigating the special education system, and volunteering across school events in advocacy for their children. Though there were no stated individual life changes experienced by families, a societal event that influenced families includes the recognition that young, disabled children continue to disproportionately experience pathologization and criminalization in schools. These events spurred family advocacy affecting both inputs and outputs as families repositioned their involvement in school. Applying intersectionality to FST shows how families experience and navigate systemic inequities, while also honoring ways that they demonstrate resilience and counter racist and ableist practices for themselves and their children.

DISCUSSION

Intersectionality can be approached from a systems perspective to understand how individuals' lived experiences are impacted by structures, laws, and practices that have led to certain advantages and disadvantages for certain groups (Crenshaw, 1989). By situating disability intersectionality within the sociohistorical nature and contexts, researchers can learn how disabled individuals and their families navigate intersectional discourses, experience their oppression as intersectional, and engage in meaning making of their intersecting identities through their grounded lived experiences (Hernández-Saca et al., 2018). One way of honoring those identities is to acknowledge their intersections within family inputs and how families navigate through their privileges and/or oppression to maintain equilibrium. For example, mothers from Beneke et al.'s (2021) study demonstrated a strong awareness of racism and ableism in early education, which were guided by their own inputs in values and identities as advocates, and mothers of a child with a disability. They resisted deficit-based notions of their children's abilities and their own parenting competencies as mothers of color, by advocating for their children's care, fighting exclusionary practices, and dreaming for better. These values guided their advocacy. Acknowledging the intersections also allows us to empathize and strengthen our understanding of how families make sense of and navigate systems of privilege and oppression.

An intersectional FST can also broaden the understanding of family dynamics and organization. Original family theories centered heterosexual, two-parent households, failing to account for the range of family structures children experience, including adoption, multigenerational households or blended families (Dore, 2008). These views limit how researchers and practitioners define families and understand the relationships salient for each system. Fujiura (2014) argued that there is no standard prototype family, and each household is highly variable. Additionally, families may include both biological and nonbiological members (Kiyama & Harper, 2018). Acknowledging intersectionality can open to understanding other subsystems of relationships within processes and incorporate these individuals as members of support within a family system.

An intersectional FST also highlights how families function by prioritizing various activities, needs, and experiences. For mothers of color, engaging in school advocacy was a critical activity in challenging systemic inequities for their children's schooling and negative perceptions on their parenting skills (Beneke et al., 2021). This counters the deficit-views society may place on families of color pertaining family engagement practices (Baquedano-Lopez et al., 2013; Hong, 2022; Lareau, 2000). Additionally, advocacy can also come in the form of self-care. Pyles (2020) argued the need to engage in healing justice by focusing on practices that transform the whole self, including emotional, spiritual, and mental selves. Cook and Williams (2015) identified informal networks of support through fictive kinship as a protective factor. Specifically, they highlighted the role of the church in creating safe spaces for women of color to exist. By reconceptualizing FSF to acknowledge these intersections, researchers can see how families actively engage in individualized activities that support their families functioning in their own ways.

Lastly, family life changes can also alter the family system, specifically in characteristics and functions. Transitions may shift the individual or group contexts within inputs. For example, if a child qualifies for special education services for the first time or receives a disability diagnosis, families may adapt or adjust as they make meaning of the change. It may also influence outputs and the activities that families engage in or needs they experience, such as navigating new systems and services, accessing resources, or shifting activities they engage in to support individual and family functions. Beneke et al's (2021) study included how mothers aimed to disrupt deficit-based assumptions by sharing their stories and advocating within existing structures that are inequitable.

A funds of knowledge approach can be applied to knowledge gained from applying the FST to acknowledge the intersectional experiences and assets families bring into early learning settings. Funds of knowledge are defined as "historically accumulated and culturally developed bodies of knowledge and skills essential for household or individual functioning and well-being" (Moll et al., 1992, p. 133). Families develop social networks in their environments, allowing for the development and exchange of resources including knowledge, skills, and labor that allow for households to survive or thrive (Moll et al., 1992). For children who experience multiple and marginalized identities, this information can be leveraged to extend learning from their home to the classroom. Educators can draw on the strengths and resources from children's cultural backgrounds and family practices by acknowledging children's active participation in their homes and community activities (González et al., 2005). Learning can be extended in a way that is relevant to children and families, honoring the various activities and lived experiences of their intersectional identities.

Funds of knowledge can also allow for families and teachers to coconstruct new ways of family engagement that acknowledges and responds to the needs of the family system. McWayne et al. (2022) conducted a study with Head Start to develop a home-to-school approach of family engagement. Programs partnered with their families across linguistic, socioeconomic, and ethnic/racial backgrounds to develop new family engagement strategies and curriculum, centering children's lived experiences in the home. They built on the principles that "parents are equal partners," "culture is what we do every day," and "learning builds on familiar knowledge" (p. 447). By utilizing a funds knowledge approach, perceptions of how families can be involved in schools can be expanded to ensure that families with intersectional identities are engaging in ways that are meaningful to them. Additionally, teachers can begin acknowledging families as experts in their own children's learning and, therefore, partners in establishing family school partnerships.

RECOMMENDATIONS FOR PRACTICE

Reflective Practice

Teachers play a critical role in partnering with families and need spaces to engage in critical reflection of their practice. Teachers bring with them their own experiences, backgrounds, and perspectives into their teaching and it can be challenging for educators from dominant backgrounds to teach in a culturally responsive manner if they do not first understand their own culture and the cultural practices of others (Gay, 2015). Reflective practice is an iterative process of continuous learning aimed to improve one's own practice (Fook, 2015; Schön, 1987). It includes identifying a problem, gathering information to deepen understanding, examining its implications, and reflecting on action items and next steps (Fook, 2015; Heffron & Murch, 2010).

Within teaching, this can mean pausing to identify a problem, such as lack of engagement of children in the classroom. Teachers may gather information through classroom observations and conversations with children, families, and staff and learn children are disconnected from the curriculum because learning experiences are not connected to their backgrounds, experiences or ways of knowing. As a response, teachers utilize this knowledge to plan and implement more culturally-responsive materials in their classrooms and lessons tied to children's interests, intersectional identities, and backgrounds. They also make a plan to strengthen home-school partnerships by inviting families to share ways they want to contribute in the class community. The reflective process allows teachers to critically think about and strengthen their own teaching practices to support the engagement of children and families across identities and cultures.

Within teacher educator and leadership programs, practitioners may benefit from opportunities to develop and practice critical reflection. By providing spaces for educators to engage with an array of speakers, texts, and stories from families with intersectional identities, they can begin to reflect, hear, and learn from the experiences of those whose backgrounds may be different than their own. Reflective practice can support practitioners in challenging their own assumptions by examining sources of power and checking on one's own reflexivity (Fook, 2015). Perceptions of family partnerships from dominant culture can also bias the way teachers engage with families from marginalized backgrounds, creating power differentials (Kalyanpur & Harry, 2012). These deficit-based views of families are reinforced through engagement practices (Baquedano-Lopez et al., 2013; Lareau, 2000). By acknowledging their own positionality and biases, practitioners can develop deeper understanding and proactively respond towards those different from them (Derman-Sparks et al., 2020; Iruka et al. 2020). Opportunities for critical reflection can begin in teacher or leadership preparation, but extend into continued professional growth once practitioners are in the workforce.

Culturally Responsive Teaching

Culturally responsive teaching can also deepen relationships with children and families. Culturally responsive teaching is defined as the recognition of and response to children's cultural displays of learning that utilize children's cultural knowledge to connect and teach (Hammond, 2015). In the classroom, this can mean teaching to and through cultural diversity as a way to provide differentiated and meaningful learning experiences, inclusive of children's backgrounds (Gay, 2010). As part of culturally responsive teaching, educators acknowledge the larger sociopolitical contexts influencing schools (Hammond, 2015). This encompasses the impacts systemic inequities have on communities, including those who are marginalized due to their disability, race, language, socioeconomic status, and more (DEC, 2022). Culturally responsive teaching can be another strategy utilized to support and honor children and families' overlapping identities.

Culturally responsive teaching in early childhood settings can also support families across identity groups by honoring and incorporating their lived experiences into the classroom. Yuan and Jiang (2019) examined culturally responsive teaching literacy practices for low-income immigrant families of children with disabilities. They found that, when teachers were able to engage content from children's heritage language by encouraging their oral and written narrations by cocreating with families, teachers could build on what children already know and differentiate learning. Additionally, culturally responsive teaching can also support planning, instruction, and reflection for young children with significant disabilities (Rivera et al., 2022). Teachers can plan for meaningful instruction through culturally responsive materials, technology, systematic instruction, family engagement, and honoring the learner (2022).

Lastly, culturally responsive teaching can be embedded into field experiences of teaching preparation programs as a framework to embed children and families' identities in learning. Chu M. (2014) examined elements that support teachers in developing culturally responsive practices. They found key characteristics of fieldwork placements include diverse field experiences with community-based partners, observation of culturally responsive teacher interactions, and social justice-centered practices centering children and families. This approach can provide and scaffold intentional opportunities for educators to learn with and from children and families within their communities.

CONCLUSION

Within this chapter, the authors advocated for the explicit acknowledgement of intersecting identities within family inputs as a way to strengthen understanding of families who hold multiple, marginalized identities. This includes recognizing the multifaceted identities of children and families and understanding how the family ecosystem, including processes, functions, and life changes may impact or be impacted by these intersections. By reconceptualizing the FST with an intersectional lens, researchers can deepen understanding of a family system and examine the complexities across inputs, processes and functions, for families who hold multiple, marginalized identities. They can begin to understand and respond by utilizing more equitable and inclusive practices of family engagement, honoring families' funds of knowledge, and engaging in ongoing reflection and learning when working with children and their families.

Future research should examine other dimensions of identity within intersectionality, as this chapter primarily focused on race and disability when looking at the navigation of special education systems for families. Additionally, the author explicitly examined intersectionality when applied to inputs in the FST in this chapter. There could be deeper exploration and interrogation on how intersectionality can be more explicitly addressed across processes, outputs, and changes.

REFERENCES

Altman, B. M., & Blackwell, D. L. (2014). Disability in U.S. households, 2000-2010: Findings from the National Health Interview Survey. *Family Relations*, 63(1), 20–38. 10.1111/fare.1204426962270

Annamma, S. B., Connor, D., & Ferri, B. (2013). Dis/ability critical race studies (DisCrit): Theorizing at the intersections of race and dis/ability. *Race, Ethnicity and Education*, 16(1), 1–31. 10.1080/13613324.2012.730511

Baquedano-López, P., Alexander, R. A., & Hernandez, S. J. (2013). Equity issues in parental and community involvement in schools: What teacher educators need to know. *Review of Research in Education*, 37(1), 149–182. 10.3102/0091732X12459718

Beneke, M. R., & Cheatham, G. A. (2020). Teacher candidates talking (but not talking) about dis/ability and race in preschool. *Journal of Literacy Research*, 52(3), 245–268. 10.1177/1086296X20939561

Beneke, M. R., Collins, S., & Powell, S. (2021). Who may be competent? Mothering young children of color with disabilities and the politics of care. *Equity & Excellence in Education*, 54(3), 328–344. 10.1080/10665684.2021.1992604

Bronfenbrenner, U. (1986). Ecology of the family as a context for human development: Research perspectives. *Developmental Psychology*, 22(6), 723–742. 10.1037/0012-1649.22.6.723

Buren, M. K., Maggin, D. M., & Brown, C. (2018). Metasynthesis on the experiences of families from nondominant communities and special education collaboration. *Exceptionality*, 28(4), 259–278. 10.1080/09362835.2018.1480953

Burke, M. M., & Goldman, S. E. (2018). Special education advocacy among culturally and linguistically diverse families. *Journal of Research in Special Educational Needs*, 18(S1), 3–14. 10.1111/1471-3802.12413

Cavendish, W., & Connor, D. (2018). Toward authentic IEPs and transition plans: Student, parent, and teacher perspectives. *Learning Disability Quarterly*, 41(1), 32–43. 10.1177/0731948716684680

Cho, S., Crenshaw, K. W., & McCall, L. (2013). Toward a field of intersectionality studies: Theory, applications, and praxis. *Signs (Chicago, Ill.)*, 38(4), 785–810. 10.1086/669608

Chu, M. (2014). Preparing tomorrow's early childhood educators: Observe and reflect about culturally responsive teachers. *YC Young Children, 69(2)*, 82–87. https://www.jstor.org/stable/ycyoungchildren.69.2.82

Chu, S. (2014). Perspectives of teachers and parents of Chinese American students with disabilities about their home–school communication. *Preventing School Failure*, 58(4), 237–248. 10.1080/1045988X.2013.809685

Cioè-Peña, M. (2020). Planning inclusion: The need to formalize parental participation in individual education plans (and meetings). *The Educational Forum*, 84(4), 377–390. 10.1080/00131725.2020.1812970

Coates, R. D., Ferber, A. L., & Brunsma, D. L. (2022). *The matrix of race: Social construction, intersectionality, and inequality* (2nd ed.). Sage.

Cook, D. A., & Williams, J. T. (2015). Expanding Intersectionality: Fictive kinship networks as supports for the educational aspirations of Black women. *The Western Journal of Black Studies*, 39(2), 157–166.

Crenshaw, K. (1989). Demarginalizing the intersection of race and sex: A Black feminist critique of antidiscrimination doctrine, feminist theory, and antiracist politics. *University of Chicago Legal Forum*, 139.

Degener, T., & de Castro, M. G. C. (2022). Toward inclusive equality: Ten years of the human rights model of disability in the work of the UN committee on the rights of persons with disabilities. In Felder, F., Davy, L., & Kayess, R. (Eds.), *Disability law and human rights*. Palgrave Macmillan Cham., 10.1007/978-3-030-86545-0_2

Derman-Sparks, L., Edwards, J. O., & Goins, C. M. (2020). *Antibias education for young children and ourselves* (2nd ed.). National Association for the Education of Young Children.

Division for Early Childhood. (2022). *Position statement on ethical practice* [Position statement]. https://divisionearlychildhood.egnyte.com/dl/KAh4cOFBZ8

Division for Early Childhood & National Association for the Education of Young Children. (2009). *Early childhood inclusion: A joint position statement of the Division for Early Childhood (DEC) and the National Association for the Education of Young Children (NAEYC)*. The University of North Carolina, FPG Child Development Institute Division for Early Childhood. (2014). https://www.dec-sped.org/dec-recommended-practices

Dore, M. M. (2008). Family systems theory. In B. A. Thyer, K. M. Sowers, & C. N. Dulmus (Eds.), *Comprehensive handbook of social work and social welfare*, (pp. 431–462). John Wiley & Sons Inc. 10.1002/9780470373705.chsw002018

Dunst, C. J. (2017). Family systems early childhood intervention. In H. Sukkar, C. J. Dunst, & J. Kirkby (Eds.), *Early childhood intervention: Working with families of young children with special needs* (pp. 36–58). Routledge/Taylor & Francis Group.

Fook, J. (2015). Reflective practice and critical reflection. In Lishman, J. (Ed.), *Handbook for practice learning in social work and social care* (3rd ed.). Jessica Kingsley Publishers.

Friedman-Krauss, A. H., & Barnett, W. S. (2023). *The state(s) of early intervention and early childhood special education: Looking at equity*. National Institute for Early Education Research.

Fujiura, G. T. (2014). The political arithmetic of disability and the American family: A demographic perspective. *Family Relations*, 63(1), 7–19. 10.1111/fare.12051

Gay, G. (2015). The what, why, and how of culturally responsive teaching: International mandates, challenges, and opportunities. *Multicultural Education Review*, 7(3), 123–139. 10.1080/2005615X.2015.1072079

Gerzel-Short, L., Kiru, E. W., Hsiao, Y. J., Hovey, K. A., Wei, Y., & Miller, R. D. (2019). Engaging culturally and linguistically diverse families of children with disabilities. *Intervention in School and Clinic*, 55(2), 120–126. 10.1177/1053451219837637

Gilliam, W. S., Maupin, A. N., Reyes, C. R., Accavitti, M., & Shic, F. (2016). Do early educators' implicit biases regarding sex and race relate to behavior expectations and recommendations of preschool expulsions and suspensions? *Yale University Child Study Center*, 9(28), 1–16.

González, N., Moll, L. C., & Amanti, C. (2005). *Funds of knowledge: Theorizing practices in household communities, and classrooms*. Lawrence Erlbaum.

Grindal, T., Schifter, L., Schwartz, G., & Hehir, T. (2019). Racial differences in special education identification and placement: Evidence across three states. *Harvard Educational Review*, 89(4), 525–553. 10.17763/1943-5045-89.4.525

Haines, S. J., Summers, J. A., Turnbull, A. P., Turnbull, H. R.III, & Palmer, S. (2015). Fostering Habib's engagement and self-regulation: A case study of a child from a refugee family at home and preschool. *Topics in Early Childhood Special Education*, 35(1), 28–39. 10.1177/0271121414552905

Hammond, Z. (2015). *Culturally responsive teaching and the brain: Promoting authentic engagement and rigor among culturally and linguistically diverse students*. Corwin.

Heffron, M. C., & Murch, T. (2010). *Reflective supervision and leadership in early childhood programs*. Zero to Three Press.

Hernández-Saca, D. I., Gutmann Kahn, L., & Cannon, M. A. (2018). Intersectionality dis/ability research: How dis/ability research in education engages intersectionality to uncover the multidimensional construction of dis/abled experiences. *Review of Research in Education*, 42(1), 286–311. 10.3102/0091732X18762439

Hong, S., Baloch, M. H., Conklin, K. H., & Warren, H. W. (2022). Teacher-Family Solidarity as Culturally Sustaining Pedagogy and Practice. *Urban Education*, 0(0). 10.1177/00420859221131809

Individuals with Disabilities Education Act, 20 U.S.C. § 1400 (2004). Iruka, I. U., Curenton, S. M., Durden, T. R., & Escayg, K. (2020). *Don't look away: Embracing antibias classrooms.* Gryphon House, Inc.

Kalyanpur, M., & Harry, B. (2012). *Cultural reciprocity in special education: Building reciprocal family-professional relationships.* Brookes.

Kayser, A., Kayser, B., Holmstrom, L., & Brazil Keys, B. (2021). We appreciate what you are doing, but you are doing it wrong: Two schools address school-family tensions through culturally responsive family partnerships. *Taboo: The Journal of Culture and Education, 20*(2). https://digitalscholarship.unlv.edu/taboo/vol20/iss2/2

Kiyama, J. M., & Harper, C. E. (2018). Beyond hovering: A conceptual argument for an inclusive model of family engagement in higher education. *Review of Higher Education*, 41(3), 365–385. 10.1353/rhe.2018.0012

Ladau, E. (2021). *Demystifying disability: what to know, what to say, and how to be an ally* (1st ed.). Ten Speed Press.

Maxwell, J. A. (2013). *Qualitative research design: An interactive approach* (3rd ed.). Sage Publications, Inc.

McBride, S. L., & Brotherson, M. J. (1997). Guiding practitioners toward valuing and implementing family centered practices. In Winton, P., McCollum, J., & Catlett, C. (Eds.), *Reforming personnel preparation in early intervention.* Paul H. Brookes Publishing Co.

McWayne, C., Sunah, H., Diez, V., & Jayanthi, M. (2022). "We feel connected… and like we belong:" A parent-led, staff-supported model of family engagement in early childhood. *Early Childhood Education Journal*, 50(3), 445–457. 10.1007/s10643-021-01160-x

Moll, L. C., Amanti, C., Neff, D., & Gonzalez, N. (1992). Funds of knowledge for teaching: Using a qualitative approach to connect homes and classrooms. *Theory into Practice*, 31(2), 132–141. 10.1080/00405849209543534

National Association for the Education of Young Children. (2019). *Advancing equity in early childhood education* [Position statement]. NAEYC. https://www.naeyc.org/sites/default/files/globally-shared/downloads/pdfs/resources/position-statements/advancingequitypositionstatement.pdf

Nieto, S., & Bode, P. (2018). *Affirming diversity: The sociopolitical context of multicultural education* (7th ed.). Pearson.

Ortega, L. (2014). Ways forward for a bi/multilingual turn for SLA. In May, S. (Ed.), *The multilingual turn: Implications for SLA, TESOL, and bilingual education* (pp. 32–52). Routledge.

Peshkin, A. (1988). In search of subjectivity: One's own. *Educational Researcher*, 17(7), 17–21.

Pyles, L. (2020). Healing justice, transformative justice, and holistic self-care for social workers. *Social Work*, 65(2), 178–187. 10.1093/sw/swaa01332236450

Rios, K., & Tu, W.-M. (2023). Navigating IEP meetings: Effective approaches for supporting Asian families of children with IDD in special education. *The Journal of Special Education Apprenticeship*, 12(3), 27–38. 10.58729/2167-3454.1179

Rios-Aguilar, C., & Kiyama, J. M. (2012). Funds of knowledge: An approach to studying Latina(o) students' transition to college. *Journal of Latinos and Education*, 11(1), 2–16. 10.1080/15348431.2012.631430

Rivera, C. J., Haughney, K. L., Clark, K. A., & Werunga, R. (2022). Culturally responsive planning, instruction, and reflection for young children with significant disabilities. *Young Exceptional Children*, 25(2), 74–87. 10.1177/1096250620951767

Rossetti, Z., Redash, A., Sauer, J. S., Bui, O., Wen, Y., & Regensburger, D. (2020). Access, accountability, and advocacy: Culturally and linguistically diverse families' participation in IEP meetings. *Exceptionality*, 28(4), 243–258. 10.1080/09362835.2018.1480948

Schön, D. A. (1987). *Educating the reflective practitioner*. Jossey-Bass.

Turnbull, A. P., Summers, J. A., & Brotherson, M. J. (1984). Working with families with disabled members: A family systems approach. Research & Training Center on Independent Living, University of Kansas.

Turnbull, A. P., Turnbull, R., Erwin, E. J., Soodak, L. C., & Shogren, K. A. (2015). *Families, professionals, and exceptionality: Positive outcomes through partnerships and trust* (7th ed.). Pearson.

United Nations. (2006). *Convention on the rights of persons with disabilities*. UN.

U.S. Department of Education, Office of Special Education and Rehabilitative Services, Office of Special Education Programs. (2021). *42nd annual report to Congress on the implementation of the Individuals With Disabilities Education Act, 2020.*

Vélez-Agosto, N. M., Soto-Crespo, J. G., Vizcarrondo-Oppenheimer, M., Vega-Molina, S., & García Coll, C. (2017). Bronfenbrenner's bioecological theory revision: Moving culture from the macro into the micro. *Perspectives on Psychological Science*, 12(5), 900–910. 10.1177/174569161770439728972838

Vygotsky, L. S. (1978). *Mind in society: The development of higher psychological processes*. Harvard University Press.

World Health Organization. (2011). *World report on disability*. WHO. https://www.who.int/disabilities/world_report/2011/en/

Yuan, T., & Jiang, H. (2019). Culturally responsive teaching for children from low-income, immigrant families. *Young Exceptional Children, 22*(3), 150—161. h 10.1177/1096250618756897

Yull, D., Blitz, L., Thompson, T., & Murray, C. (2014). Can we talk? Using community-based participatory action research to build family and school partnerships with families of color. *School Community Journal*, 24(9).

Zack, N. (2023). Social Construction and Racial Identities. In *Philosophy of Race*. Palgrave Philosophy Today. Palgrave Macmillan., 10.1007/978-3-031-27374-2_6

KEY TERMS AND DEFINITIONS

Culturally Responsive Teaching: An approach to learning that builds trust and relationships with children by connecting their cultures, languages, and experiences into school experiences.

Disability: Individual contexts or conditions that in conjunction with societal barriers, create difficulties for individuals to access and participate in daily living experiences and tasks.

Family Systems Theory: A framework for understanding a child with a disability within the context of their family unit by acknowledging the dynamic relationships between family characteristics, interactions, functions, and life cycle changes.

Funds of Knowledge: An approach to embedding cultural practices and other knowledge acquired from daily living tasks and experiences to learning.

Individualized Education Program: A legal document developed in partnership with families and children around special education services for children ages three to twenty one, which includes present levels, assessments, goals, and services.

Individualized Family Service Plan: A legal document developed for infants and toddlers with developmental delays or disabilities around early intervention services for young children birth to three and their families.

Individuals With Disabilities Education Act: Federal legislation that guarantees the educational rights of children with disabilities from birth through twenty one and their families to access special education and early intervention services.

Intersectionality: How multiple identities interact to exacerbate patterns of oppression.

Race: A socially constructed concept used to classify groups of people based on perceived differences, leading to various forms of power in society that systemically advantages some and disadvantages others. Each group may identify with their own set of shared values, norms, or culture.

Reflective Practice: A process of engaging in a cycle of self-inquiry to reflect on one's own actions to deepen understanding around beliefs, biases, and actions.

Chapter 5
Participatory Help–Giving AAC Practices:
Bridging the Equity Gap in Family Centered AAC Services in Early Intervention

John Kim

https://orcid.org/0009-0000-0253-7272

San Francisco State University, USA & University of California, Berkeley, USA

ABSTRACT

This chapter addresses an equity-centered approach to family-professional partnerships on augmentative and alternative communication (AAC) service delivery for young children with complex communication needs (CCN). Despite the recognition of family-centered practices as best practices, families often voice their frustrations when attempting to implement AAC in their homes, especially for families with culturally and linguistically diverse backgrounds. The aims of this chapter are (a) to discuss the current state of the field in family-centered AAC practices; (b) to describe family perspectives of AAC implementation in the home; and (c) to describe how "participatory help-giving AAC practices" can bridge the equity gap in AAC service delivery. Moreover, this chapter aims to discuss the foundational principle of participatory help-giving AAC practices as a form of equity between practitioners and families across the assessment, recommendation, and intervention phases in clinical practice.

DOI: 10.4018/979-8-3693-0924-7.ch005

INTRODUCTION

Early intervention (EI) services in the United States are publicly mandated under Part C of the Individuals with Disabilities Education Improvement Act (IDEIA, 2004) for children with developmental disabilities from birth to three. These services are designed, delivered, and monitored via the Individualized Family Service Plan (IFSP). Under the IFSP, augmentative and alternative communication (AAC) services are provided for children with complex communication needs (CCN) where speech and language are compromised (Lin & Gold, 2017). AAC systems consist of both unaided (e.g., gestures, manual signs, facial expressions) and aided (e.g., speech-generating devices, voice output communication aids, communication books, communication boards, or written words) communication modalities to improve communicative success (Barbosa et al., 2018; Bondy & Frost, 1994; Crowe et al., 2021). The combination of the two (e.g., aided and unaided) is to augment and be an alternative form of communication modality.

Young children with CCN are in the early stages of communication development by acquiring the rudimentary skills to participate in daily life (Beukelman & Light, 2020). Without appropriate intervention and support, children with significant communication disabilities are at risk of educational and social isolation, with vital repercussions across most aspects of development (Light et al., 2004; Light et al., 2007; Sevcik et al., 2004). The use of AAC in EI is to support language development by (a) augmenting existing speech, (b) providing a communication output mode, (c) serving as both language input and output modality, and (d) utilizing as a form of speech and language intervention (Lorang et al., 2022; Romski & Sevcik, 2005).

Although some families are hesitant to introduce AAC to their children with the concern that it will inhibit their speech and language development, numerous studies have suggested otherwise. Using AAC in EI supported language development for children from ages one to three (Branson & Demchak, 2009; Solomon-Rice & Soto, 2014), increased conversational turns and expressive utterances (Romski et al., 2010; Wright et al., 2013; Yoder & Stone, 2006), and promoted morpho-syntactic development in their expressive language repertoire (Binger & Light, 2007; Brady 2000; Drager et al., 2006; Kasari et al., 2014). Due to its visual modality (e.g., pictures, graphic symbols, scene-based, etc.), AAC has also shown evidence to aid receptive language skills (Dada et al., 2020). Overall, evidence has repeatedly suggested that using AAC does not adversely impact the development of natural speech (Hustad & Shapley, 2003; Johnson et al., 2009; Light et al., 2002). To expect this outcome, family involvement is a vital element in the process. Collaborative teaming with families throughout the decision-making process, the AAC system selection, and the introduction process have a significant impact on the prognosis of AAC intervention (Goldbart & Marshall, 2004; Hunt et al., 2002; Robinson & Solomon-Rice, 2009).

The purpose of this chapter is to address service providers who works with AAC in early intervention to implement an equity centered approach when working with families (e.g., participatory help-giving practices).

FAMILY INVOLVEMENT IN EARLY INTERVENTION

Most EI services are conducted in the family's *natural environment* consisting of the home and the community. The *natural environment* in this case is to create an authentic learning experience within familiar routines (e.g., mealtime, bath time, bedtime) which offers realistic and ecologically valid engagements (e.g., real-life contexts), to acquire language and communication with others (Bernheimer & Weismer, 2007; Roper & Dunst, 2003; Roth & Worthington, 2023). Thus, service providers are situated to offer family-centered approaches such as honoring the home language, culturally affirming practices, and centering the family's priorities in various family routines. As a result, caregiver and service providers partnerships are essential to developing a therapy plan and ultimately for caregiver-implemented communication and language intervention (Kashinath et al., 2006; Wetherby & Woods, 2006).

AAC in the Natural Environment

For families requiring AAC support, service providers need to embed the aided AAC system in the *natural environment*. This task requires service providers to not only know the family and their routines, but to incorporate the AAC into the family. This task is done by selecting and personalizing the AAC system to meet the unique needs, capabilities, experiences, interests, languages, and identities of the family and the user (Beukleman & Light, 2020). The challenge here is to find an appropriate fit that addresses the overall family's needs (e.g., culture, language, identity, accessibility, and flexibility) where the system is used with ease and flexibility across the daily routines of the child (Light et al., 2019). This becomes a complex clinical process from assessment, system requirement, feature matching, system trials, AAC selection, and personalization (Light & McNaughton, 2013). Although having families involved in these steps are the gold standard, service providers are recommending AAC based on prior clinical experiences and familiarity where the connection to the natural environment is questionable (Johnson et al., 2009).

The Intersecting Barriers in Families

As AAC systems are introduced, service providers frequently underestimate the long-term effects of the intersecting barriers that families encounter. Caregivers are often underusing or abandoning AAC systems altogether (De Leon et al., 2023; Johnson et al., 2009; Moorecroft et al., 2020; Pope et al. 2022). A recent scoping review by Kim & Soto (2024) illustrated how families face barriers to AAC in the home related to the family unit, the service providers (e.g., IFSP teams), and the AAC system itself.

In the family unit, caregivers are faced with multiple competing demands (Bailey et al., 2006; Doak, 2021; O'Neil & Wilkerson, 2020), unaddressed communication needs of the home (Marshall& Goldbart, 2008; Stuart & Parette, 2002), and a sense of isolation, shame, confusion, and grief when raising a child with a disability (Moorcroft et al., 2021; Parette et al., 2000). Within the domain of family unit, Kim and Soto (2024) identified that caregivers were having to juggle multiple responsibilities where using the AAC system were not feasible and had minimal time to learn how to use it. Additionally, parents were confused especially when to introduce the device, especially those who wanted to "wait and see" if their child woud talk (Johnston et al., 2022; O'Neill & Wilkinson, 2020; Park, 2021; Schladant & Dowling, 2020) and expressing a sense of isolation and shame just by intersecting identities of having a child with a disability and with a communication system (Crisp et al., 2014; Marshall & Goldbart, 2008; Moorcroft et al., 2021; Parette et al., 2000). Families who are currently using an AAC system report that the vocabulary available in the AAC device was most appropriate for school and that the words and phrases that family members valued, such as emotions and feelings, were missing or cumbersome to find (Marshall & Goldbart, 2008; Stuart & Parette, 2002).

Within the aspect of service providers, caregivers report the feelings of frustration experienced with the disjointed form of service delivery (Moorcroft et al., 2020), the lack of AAC knowledge from service providers (Crisp et al., 2014; Glacken et al., 2019; McNaughton et al., 2008), and the evaluation process for AAC devices (Anderson et al., 2014; Berenguer et al., 2022). Delving further into this domain, caregivers voiced their frustration on the delay in the entire process of obtaining the AAC system as well as maintaining with the upkeep of the system (Crisp et al., 2014; Glacken et al., 2019; Johnston et al., 2022; Marshall & Goldbart, 2008; McNaughton et al., 2008; Moorcroft et al., 2020; Parette et al., 2000; Schladant & Dowling, 2020). In addition, service providers are not knowledgeable of various AAC supports, systems, and intervention that it makes caregivers concerned about the overall services being provided (Anderson et al., 2014; Bailey et al., 2006; McNaughton et al., 2008; Muttiah et al., 2022; Schladant & Dowling, 2020). Most importantly, caregivers expressed that their input was not valued in the AAC assessment process, this resulted with an AAC recommendation where caregivers disagreed on (Marshall & Goldbart, 2008; McNaughton et al., 2008; Pickl, 2011).

Regarding the AAC systems, families expressed a lack of knowledge about the systems and devices (Hettirarchchi et al., 2020; Johnston et al., 2022; Romano & Chun, 2018), concerns about the cost (Crisp et al., 2014; Marshall & Goldbart, 2008; Moorcroft et al., 2021), and a lack of cultural and linguistic representation (McCord & Soto, 2004; Pickl, 2011; Stuart & Parette, 2002). Specifically, a study conducted by McCord and Soto (2004) conveyed the idea that caregivers did not have the skills use to the program, repair, or maintain the equipment. Others have also reported not knowing enough about the software or hardware to support its use and not understanding how the language on the device was organized (Crisp et al., 2014; O'Neill & Wilkinson, 2020; Park, 2021; Schladant & Dowling, 2020). Due to the lack of personalization and programming, the AAC system did not portray the language of the AAC user and the family. Specifically, Stuart and Parette (2002) documented that AAC systems were inadequate to program certain languages, such as Navajo, making their use within the family impossible. Moreover, the appropriate voice output features that create effective communication in the users' home language was lacking (Huer et al., 2001). Not only that, the cost was also an additional concern for families who had to self-fund to obtain an AAC system (Marshall & Goldbart, 2008; Moorcroft et al., 2021). See Table 1 for a summary of the Intersecting Barriers.

Table 1. The intersecting barriers in families

Domain	Barriers
The family unit	Multiple demands on parents Parental emotions Disconnect of communication needs
The service providers	Lack of continuation of services Lack of Knowledge of professionals AAC assessment process
The AAC system	Caregivers' knowledge of the AAC system Language Identity Cost of AAC system

Note: Adapted from Kim, J., & Soto, G. (2024). A comprehensive scoping review of barriers to parental-professional partnerships in AAC for school-aged children. Language, Speech, and Hearing Services in Schools.

FAMILY-CENTERED PRACTICES IN AAC SERVICES

The findings from Kim and Soto (2024) emphasize the need to address the barriers to implementing AAC systems at home. It is plausible that the intersecting barriers of AAC implementation emerged from the lack of collaboration between EI teams and the families. Mandak et al., (2017) proposed that families are a system (e.g., family systems theory) where all family members are interdependent and integrally linked. Changes in any part of the family will affect all members. Applying this concept to the ecological systems model (Bronfenbrenner, 1979), families function and interact within and across settings and contexts, such as schools and places of employment. In this case, having an external AAC system implies that family members have multiple roles across the social domains. Combining the two theoretical frameworks (i.e., family systems theory and ecological systems model), family systems affect and can be affected by broader social circumstances. To extend this concept, Coburn et al. (2021) added that the interaction between the family systems (microsystems) with their surrounding environment is not consistent and is always in flux depending on the age of the AAC user, the nuclear family, the extended family, and the life outside of the family. Therefore, any new changes such as an AAC system may have a major impact on families and EI teams. The outcome of an AAC intervention is mostly determined by how well the AAC fits into the family systems, not just the AAC user (Granlund et al., 2008; Simmons-Mackie et al., 2013).

To address this gap, one of the solutions is family-centered practices. The existing literature describes family-centered practices as a way of interacting, treating, and including caregivers and other family members in various services relating to their child (Mas et al., 2022). By centering families, service providers are naturally considering the communication strengths as well as the needs of specific communication of the child. By identifying the two, the service providers are designing the EI services where AAC can bridge authentic communication experiences in the natural environment (Light & McNaughton. 2015). This very concept of family-centered practices is still considered an abstract concept by many service providers. Families express that their input was not taken into consideration during the assessment and the selection of the AAC system (Marshall & Goldbart, 2008; McNaughton et al., 2008; Pickl, 2011). Caregivers have felt disempowered ever since the AAC assessment process (Anderson et al., 2014). Thus, families strongly expressed the need for service providers to connect with their child and the family, (Johnston et al., 2022; Parette et al., 2000). When including families especially when working with AAC, we are able address specific discourse and language practices that represents the family and the identity relating to culture, traditions, and intimacy between the child and other family members (McCord & Soto, 2004; Soto & Yu, 2014).

From this notion, family-centered practices are considered as 'help-giving' practices. Existing literature on family-centered practices proposes two different 'help-giving' models: (a) relationship-building practices and (b) participatory help-giving practices (Dunst et al., 2007). Relational building practices include the skills necessary when communicating with families (e.g., active and reflective listening, empathy, practitioner beliefs about family strengths, and practitioner sensitivity to personal and cultural values and practices) (Hill. 2001). Participatory help-giving practices on the other hand, pertain to practitioners' behavior of involving the family members in informed decision-making, building on the strengths of the family, supporting new skills and abilities, and active caregiver involvement with caregiver coaching and resources (Dunst & Trivette, 2009). Outcomes on both models of family-centered practices show improvements in caregiver-child relationships, and child development outcomes (Dempsey & Keen, 2008; King et al., 2004; Kuhlthau et al., 2011). Upon an implementation study, participatory practices have shown more robust outcomes, but this method of family-centered approach is less practiced by service providers (Dunst et al., 2019; Dunst et al., 2020).

PARTICIPATORY HELP-GIVING AAC PRACTICES

Service providers working with young children need to go beyond relational practices of active listening, respect, and holding positive beliefs and attitudes. Participatory practices are necessary, which involve inviting the families and their children to voice their needs and concerns during their decision-making processes, building on family strengths, and creating opportunities for families to be involved in the assessment, device recommendation, and intervention process (Dunst, 2002; Dunst et al., 2007). When AAC is involved in early intervention, this clinical strategy is now Participatory help-giving AAC practices. The addition of the word "AAC" in the title indicates that service providers now must incorporate the AAC systems within the *natural environment*. This implies that planning an AAC assessment and subsequent implementation require collaborative involvement between the family and the service providers (Coghlan & Brannick, 2010; Guy et al., 2020; Walker, 1993). In other words, AAC assessment is co-constructed with the family. Therefore, obtaining input and suggestions from the family is the very first step to designing the assessment and intervention. Choosing which assessment tool to use, interpreting the results, recommending an AAC system, and creating a treatment plan should involve consistent feedback between the service providers and caregivers. This approach may be viewed as an equity-centered service delivery where there are no power differentials between the service providers and the families. Engaging in this practice empowers families to make informed decisions as well as build the capacity to implement AAC independently (Coogle & Hanline, 2016).

Bridging the Equity Gap

Participatory help-giving AAC practices view caregivers as equal participants in making AAC decisions and designing intervention plans. The nature of this approach eradicates the hidden dichotomy between the service provider and the family. Typically, caregivers view service providers as the experts which asserts service providers at a top-down perspective when providing EI services (Dunst et al., 2002). This is evident, especially for families with culturally and linguistically diverse backgrounds (Groce & Zola, 1993). Certain cultural norms in families place caregivers to accept and adhere to service providers' recommendations since it is the expert's suggestion even when family members internally disagree (De Leon et al., 2023). The very nature of participatory help-giving AAC practices disrupts the top-down hierarchy and the balance of power shifts towards the family by strengthening family members' capabilities, and new competencies are mastered, and mobilizing the desired resources and supports (Dunst et al., 2002). By disrupting the hierarchy between the service provider and the family, access to communication can truly be supported in across both the heritage language as well as the English language. By doing so, the language and the socialization practices at home pertaining to certain vocabulary words specific to the family (e.g., familylect) and certain family members (e.g., idiolect) can also be utilized and honored with the use of AAC (Otheguy et al., 2015; Van Mensel, 2018).

Foundational Principles

To conceptualize equity in participatory help-giving AAC practices, service providers are encouraged to create space for caregivers in a co-constructive process. This clinical procedure alone closely represents equity-centered AAC services via the social constructivism framework. The social constructivism perspective is a philosophical paradigm that analyzes how knowledge is formed through interacting with others in a given society and within one's cultural identity (Creswell & Poth, 2018). Combining clinical expertise with firsthand lived experiences from families, the AAC therapeutic design and implementation is the outcome of this equity-centered AAC service. To further investigate this clinical practices, three foundational principles are proposed. These principles are the following: (a) family and service provider interaction, (b) lived experiences informing AAC intervention, and (c) synergizing family values and AAC practices. With these principles, the priorities and the values of AAC intervention design synergize both the lived experiences of families and the service providers' expertise.

Family and Service Provider Interaction

The nature of participatory help-giving practices conceptualizes that AAC decisions and interventions are co-constructed with the family and the practitioner. This implies that families are involved in almost all clinical decisions (e.g., assessment, recommendation, and intervention). To invite families to partake in the clinical process, service providers must empower the caregivers to become collaborative partners (Dunst et al., 2002; Klatte et al., 2023). In addition, the service provider also has an ethical responsibility to inform the clinical rationale of the families based on the inputs shared. When the interaction between the service provider and family becomes transparent, caregivers are capable of making informed decisions and actively implementing therapeutic approaches (Kruijsen-Terpstra et al., 2016).

Lived Experiences Informing AAC Intervention

When service providers work alongside with the families, the assumption is that the lived experiences of using AAC and its barriers are guiding the service provider in designing the intervention. Caregivers are now considered as a resource for service providers to understand how AAC systems are used and perceived by the families. This will not only identify the pressing AAC issues from the caregivers, but also reveal the long-term emotional needs of the family (Brassart et al., 2017).

Synergizing Family Values With AAC Practices

The third principle examines how individual values are honored and negotiated amongst others (Creswell & Poth, 2018). In the context of AAC in EI, this would appear as how family values and priorities with AAC practices are synergized in the overall clinical practices. This domain would be a vital element as it aims to merge the caregivers' input and clinical expertise into one clinical practice.

Combing all three principles set up the tone for families to be empowered, create a space for caregivers to share their lived experiences, synergize caregivers' priorities and values from their lived experiences with service provider recommendations. Although the outcome will vary on a case-by-case basis, one concrete factor is how the AAC systems are personalized to support that individualized need. The synergy of the two parties (e.g., family and service provider) is balanced as the home language, family traditions, and cultural values are preserved within the AAC language system while addressing the clinical outcomes (e.g., to use AAC across all settings).

EQUITY IN AACTION: FROM PRINCIPLE TO PRACTICE

The three foundational principles of participatory help giving AAC practices are the components that construct a unified clinical process. The three principles are interwoven as the service provider conducts the (a) AAC assessment, (b) AAC system recommendation, and (c) AAC intervention to integrate AAC in the *natural environment*. Under this model, families are consistently consulted from the initial assessment, service providers honor the caregivers' concerns within the AAC recommendation, and the AAC system is appropriately programmed. The following will analyze how Participatory Help-Giving AAC Practices are conducted in the following clinical phases.

AAC Assessment

During the AAC assessment phase, service providers need to get to know the family. By *starting with a conversation*, the family will ideally provide information about the AAC user, communication styles, and the priority of the caregivers. Within the conversation, the use of an *ethnographic interview* will engender vital information as a part of the AAC assessment. From the conversations, the service providers have multiple opportunities to be transparent about the clinical process as well as provide appropriate resources regarding the use of an AAC system. As caregivers become informed, the families can also provide suggestions concerning language programming and home vocabulary for the service providers to consider in the AAC system altogether.

Starting With a Conversation.

Starting with simple a conversation, both families and practitioners are in a vulnerable position to learn from each other. This process usually starts with the assessment and intake process (Dean, 1993). Service providers should listen to the needs of the families first (Akamoglu et al., 2018). The caregivers' needs then assist the service providers to equip them with appropriate information. In addition, it also gives insights to service providers on what the families are not aware of regarding AAC. It is also advisable to have multiple modalities to share information via written notes and communication logs, audio and video files, and follow-up conversations (Blue-Banning et al., 2004). Thus, this interaction informs the service providers to be mindful about using technical vocabulary, providing concrete examples, or coordinating various resources to provide appropriate information. For the service provider to create a space for caregivers to share, one must ask appropriate questions. Although these questions may change depending on the family, situating the scene for families to share their stories is vital. One way to initiate this conversation is through ethnographic interviewing (Westby et al., 2003).

Ethnographic Interviewing

The goal of the ethnographic interview is for caregivers and AAC users to provide a vivid description of their life experiences (Westby et al., 2003). While a typical interview aims to probe more about the symptomatic characteristics and the diagnosis of the AAC user, ethnographic interviewing yields crucial family-specific information that remarkably shapes the communication dynamic occurring in the home and of the child with CCN (Hassey, 2022). By conducting this type, of interview, the service provider offers the family to describe their experiences, their daily activities, and objects and people in their lives (Westby et al., 2003). To conduct an ethnographic interview, there are four distinct types of interview questions (Spradley, 1979). These questions are the following: (a) grand tour questions, (b) details through questions, (c) experience questions, and (d) native-like questions. The *grand tour questions* are comprised of asking the family members to share broad experiences (e.g., Tell me about a typical day using AAC for your child). The *details through questions* are further probing about a specific event from the grand tour questions (e.g., In that day, could you tell me how your child understood you?). The *experience questions* specifically center around a given experience (e.g., What does playtime look like for you and your child?). The *native-like questions* ask specific family members to share their personal experiences (e.g., How do you communicate with your child compared to others?). See Table 2 for Ethnographic Interview Questions Specific to Communication and AAC.

Table 2. Ethnographic interview questions specific for communication and AAC

Question Types	Definition	Examples
Grand Tour Questions	Asking the family to share about broad experiences.	• Tell me about a typical day using AAC with your child? • How does your child communicate with you throughout the day?
Details Through Questions	Asking the family follow-up questions about a certain event, act, or category.	• Could you tell me more about how your child understands you? • How does your child tell you "no"? • Could you give me an example of how your child tells you "yes"?

continued on following page

Table 2. Continued

Question Types	Definition	Examples
Experience Questions	Asking the family about a general experience.	• What does playtime look like for you and your child? • Could you tell me some places you go the most with you child? • How does your child communicate with you in your home language?
Native-like Questions	Asking specific family members to share their own experiences	• How do you communicate with your child? • How does your child engage with you during mealtime? • How does the extended family members communicate with your child?

AAC System Recommendation

In the recommendation phase, service providers are encouraged to reflect on what the families have shared in the ethnographic interview. The families' lived experiences, beliefs, and values will be taken into consideration as the practitioner is making the AAC recommendations and its intervention plan. In this phase, it is also advisable for the service providers to consistently ask questions to the families regarding certain plans or AAC systems. By having an iterative process, the family and the service provider are co-constructing an AAC system to program an appropriate language system (e.g., *vocabulary and language selection*) while promoting the flexibility of the AAC system (e.g., *representation, organization, and layout*) for families to use for their child.

Vocabulary and Language Selection

The ethnographic interview ideally guides the service provider to identify the language(s) spoken and the socialization dynamic in the home. The practitioner may determine if a bilingual AAC system with a toggle feature is necessary or simply incorporating the core vocabulary of the home language. Both options always require the family's input to program the AAC system. Even within the home language, service providers must take into consideration the personalized vocabulary (Beukelman & Light, 2020). For example, these consist of names of specific people, locations, and activities, and individualized expressions. Within the personalized vocabulary, service providers can also center the values and priorities the families have for their child in the AAC system. In addition to the ethnographic interview, questions regarding the language and vocabulary selection of AAC user are also encouraged. This is an essential component that is strength-based and centers words and phrases that are most used by the child. See Table 3 for Questions Regarding the language and vocabulary selection of the AAC User.

Table 3. Questions regarding the AAC user

Topics	Rationale	Examples
Favorite things	Asking about the child's interest	• What is your favorite food? • What is your favorite music? • What is your favorite tv shows or movies? • What is your favorite thing to do?
Family Members	Asking about the child's family member	• Who is your favorite person to talk to? • Who do you talk to the most? • Who do you miss or talk about the most?
Dislikes	Asking the child about what they don't like.	• What is your least favorite food? • What do you not like to do? • What is your least favorite music or song?

Representation, Organization, and Layout

There is abundant evidence that AAC users can learn to use different types of symbolic representation (e.g., line drawing) to express their wants and needs, share information, and develop social closeness with others (Beukelman et al., 2011; Fried-Oken et al., 2015). However, the symbols themselves are not of importance, it is how one uses these symbols to enhance communication (Beukelman & Light, 2020). To reach this goal, the family must have ownership in AAC symbol programming so that implementing AAC systems in the home is successful. This means that caregivers are programming the symbols for the words that are used in the home in various modalities (e.g., photographs, line drawings, real items). For example, these include traditional foods, particular toys the child enjoys, participating in religious activities, and specific family traditions. The role of the service provider in this case is to assist with how each symbol and vocabulary are paired and located. Having a co-constructed process between the family and the service provider will overall design how each symbol, the vocabulary words, and the location of each word will be housed. This can be done by identifying the vocabulary that is used most frequently by the family and ha the words mostly used easily accessible (e.g., home page). Overall, this procedure will again empower families to use the AAC system across settings.

AAC Intervention

To goal of an AAC intervention in the EI is to support the communication and language development in the child's natural environment, typically these sessions occur in the clinic or in a hybrid of the home and the clinic site. Regardless of the setting, AAC intervention needs to be nested in the typical routines of the child's natural environment. Therefore, caregivers must be service provider an active member of the treatment plan. This is where the service provider and the families *check for comprehension* as well as *understanding the therapy process*. By having the caregivers involved, the execution of a bi-directional relationship is evident. For instance, the service provider coaches the family members on a certain AAC technique while the family dictates when and how it should be conducted in their daily routines. In addition, *providing consistent feedback* between the service provider and the family may elucidate the value of a certain therapeutic activity. Within this process, the families can translate the skills that are being taught in the therapeutic session to be used in real-life situations all by being active participants in the session.

Checking for Comprehension

The most valuable component within a participatory process is understanding both the practitioner and the caregiver. By checking for comprehension, both participants can establish a mutually agreed-upon plan. This is initiated by the service provider by welcoming inquiries from caregivers and asking follow-up questions (King et al., 2015). This particular skill may also identify areas of misunderstanding in terms of AAC and its specific clinical approaches. From these instances, it opens the opportunity to modify and or provide alternative solutions that satisfy both the caregiver and the service provider (Brassart et al., 2017). In closing, checking for comprehension can serve as an opportunity for service providers to check the overall caregivers' reaction as well as for families to understand how AAC systems could be incorporated into everyday routines (Meadan et al., 2018).

Understanding the Therapy Process

To collaborate with caregivers effectively, family members should be informed of all therapeutic processes (Meadan et al., 2018). These include explaining the rationale of each clinical decisions and co-constructing a therapy plan (e.g., assessment selection and therapeutic strategies) explaining the caregivers' role in each activity, and assisting caregivers link everyday activities and the therapy goals. By explaining the rationale of the assessment and treatment, caregivers may also provide insightful information that the service provider may have missed (Edwards et al., 2016). In addition, it opens up the potential to reduce cultural biases and in-corporate the home language into the assessment and treatment design. Within that process, families also have the opportunity to learn their roles in how to assist their child using the AAC. As the caregivers are involved in therapy, service providers can also demonstrate how everyday activities (e.g., routines) can be linked to the therapy goals (Klatte et al., 2019).

Providing Consistent Feedback

For caregivers to become empowered to implement AAC in the home, service providers must provide consistent feedback (Blue-Banning et al., 2004). These can be in the form of joint observation, caregiver reflection, and family expectations., Joint observation in a typical EI intervention session creates a space where caregivers and service providers observe the session together and provide real-time feedback (Di Rezze et al., 2014). As most direct services in EI are offered with a minimum of an hour per week, family reflection on how AAC is used within daily routines can provide information as to what service providers can provide and modify so the AAC is easily implemented throughout the day (Graham et al., 2018). Lastly, discussing family expectations concerning AAC and the child's communication development will center on the mutually agreed upon goals. Especially how the caregivers view AAC in terms of an augmented or an alternative form of commu-nication, the therapeutic design and trajectory are heavily influenced by how the family wants to use the AAC system (Edwards et al., 2016).

PRACTICAL IMPLICATIONS ON EQUITY AND INCLUSION

Participatory help-giving AAC practices centers the co-constructive therapeutic process between the family and the service provider. This very dynamic is evident across all clinical phases in (a) AAC assessment, (b) AAC system recommendation, and (c) AAC intervention. By having the families share their lived experiences, the service providers are inviting the families to be a part of the clinical decision-making process. With this model, there are implications for both equity and inclusion. Concerning equity, families are taking the lead in providing language intervention (e.g., caregiver-led intervention). Being transparent and inclusive of families in all phases of AAC services, caregivers are equipped to initiate communication and language intervention (Luo et al., 2019). In addition, AAC implementation in the home is significantly increased when caregivers replicate the therapeutic strategies (Gevarter et al., 2021). As EI services are conducted within the home, the use of

AAC and the exposure to the home language is maximized resulting in language and communication competency (Roberts & Kaiser, 2011).

Personalizing AAC systems with a home language represents a sense of belonging, reducing participation barriers, and valuing diversity representing inclusive practices (Cologon & Mevawalla, 2018). The AAC system becomes a mutually understood communication between the child and the family members, hence serves source for inclusion in cultural and linguistically responsive practice (Soto & Yu, 2014). From programming the home language to symbolic representation, caregivers take the lead in determining what represents the natural environment (e.g., daily routines). As the AAC system centers the family, it widens the lens for practitioners to analyze the family holistically including the frustrations, priorities, emotions, and the competing demands of the family (Doak, 2021). Although its implication may be menial as programming a vocabulary word in the AAC system, it has a deep repercussion to creating a sense of belonging for the family. Programming words or phrases mostly used in the home creates a sense of intimacy between the AAC user and the caregiver (McCord & Soto, 2004). Coordinating the home language with the appropriate symbols in the AAC system can reduce barriers to participating in cultural and religious events that are significant to the family (Stuart & Parette, 2002). Having access to a shared home language and the community can impact school and home participation (Pickl, 2011). With an equity-based approach by involving the family member, the implementation of the AAC system becomes inclusive for the user hence truly representing the *natural environment*.

CONCLUSION

This chapter unpacked the importance of participatory help-giving AAC practices for equity in EI services. Despite how the current EI service models are aimed to be conducted in the natural environment, service providers often omit the additional modifications when AAC is involved. Consequently, families are voicing various frustrations and barriers when implementing AAC in the home. To address this issue, this chapter introduced the foundational principles of participatory help-giving AAC practices across its clinical phases in AAC assessment, recommendation, and intervention. This clinical practice bridges the equity gap by centering the family values, cultures, and the heritage language(s) when AAC is involved. Implementing participatory help-giving AAC practices provides a space for caregivers to implement AAC independently and create a sense of belonging and inclusion within the family. This clinical practice not only disrupted the top-down hierarchy between the service provider and the family, but it also empower caregivers to have autonomy in providing accessible communication with AAC for their children.

REFERENCES

Akamoglu, Y., Meadan, H., Pearson, J. N., & Cummings, K. (2018). Getting connected: Speech and language pathologists' perceptions of building rapport via telepractice. *Journal of Developmental and Physical Disabilities*, 30(4), 569–585. 10.1007/s10882-018-9603-3

Anderson, K., Balandin, S., & Stancliffe, R. (2014). Australian parents' experience of speech generating device (SGD) service delivery. *Developmental Neurorehabilitation*, 17(2), 75–83. 10.3109/17518423.2013.85773524304229

Bailey, R. L., Parette, H. P.Jr, Stoner, J. B., Angell, M. E., & Carroll, K. (2006). Family members' perceptions of augmentative and alternative communication device use. *Language, Speech, and Hearing Services in Schools*, 37(1), 50–60. 10.1044/0161-1461(2006/006)16615749

Barbosa, R. T. D. A., de Oliveira, A. S. B., de Lima Antão, J. Y. F., Crocetta, T. B., Guarnieri, R., Antunes, T. P. C., Arab, C., Massetti, T., Bezerra, I. M. P., de Mello Monteiro, C. B., & de Abreu, L. C. (2018). Augmentative and alternative communication in children with Down's syndrome: A systematic review. *BMC Pediatrics*, 18(1), 1–16. 10.1186/s12887-018-1144-529751828

Berenguer, C., Martínez, E. R., De Stasio, S., & Baixauli, I. (2022). Parents' perceptions and experiences with their children's use of augmentative/alternative communication: A systematic review and qualitative meta-synthesis. *International Journal of Environmental Research and Public Health*, 19(13), 8091. 10.3390/ijerph1913809135805750

Bernheimer, L., & Weismer, T. (2007). "Let me tell you what I do all day…": The family story at the center of intervention research and practice. *Infants and Young Children*, 20(3), 192–201. 10.1097/01.IYC.0000277751.62819.9b

Beukelman, D., Fager, S., & Nordness, A. (2011). Communication support for people with ALS. *Neurology Research International*, 2011, 1–6. Advance online publication. 10.1155/2011/71469321603029

Beukelman, D. R., & Light, J. C. (2020). *Augmentative & Alternative Communication Supporting Children and adults with complex communication needs*. Paul H. Brookes Publishing Co.

Binger, C., & Light, J. (2007). The effect of aided AAC modeling on the expression of multi-symbol messages by preschoolers who use AAC. *Augmentative and Alternative Communication (Baltimore, MD: 1985), 23*(1), 30–43. 10.1080/07434610600807470

Blue-Banning, M., Summers, J. A., Frankland, H. C., Lord Nelson, L., & Beegle, G. (2004). Dimensions of family and professional partnerships: Constructive guidelines for collaboration. *Exceptional Children*, 70(2), 167–184. 10.1177/001440290407000203

Bondy, A. S., & Frost, L. A. (1994). The picture exchange communication system. *Focus on Autistic Behavior*, 9(3), 1–19. 10.1177/108835769400900301

Brady, N. C. (2000). Improved comprehension of object names following voice output communication aid use: Two case studies. *Augmentative and Alternative Communication*, 16(3), 197–204. 10.1080/07434610012331279054

Branson, D., & Demchak, M. (2009). The use of augmentative and alternative communication methods with infants and toddlers with disabilities: *A research review. Augmentative and Alternative Communication*, 25(4), 274–286. 10.3109/0743461 090338452919883287

Brassart, E., Prévost, C., Bétrisey, C., Lemieux, M., & Desmarais, C. (2017). Strategies Developed by Service Providers to Enhance Treatment Engagement by Immigrant Parents Raising a Child with a Disability. *Journal of Child and Family Studies*, 26(4), 1230–1244. 10.1007/s10826-016-0646-8

Bronfenbrenner, U. (1979). *The ecology of human development*. Harvard University Press. 10.4159/9780674028845

Coburn, K. L., Jung, S., Ousley, C. L., Sowers, D. J., Wendelken, M., & Wilkinson, K. M. (2021). Centering the family in their system: A framework to promote family-centered AAC services. *Augmentative and Alternative Communication*, 37(4), 229–240. 10.1080/07434618.2021.1991471349672773

Coghlan, D., & Brannick, T. (2010). *Doing Action Research in Your Own Organization*. Sage.

Cologon, K., & Mevawalla, Z. (2018). Increasing inclusion in early childhood: Key Word Sign as a communication partner intervention. *International Journal of Inclusive Education*, 22(8), 902–920. 10.1080/13603116.2017.1412515

Coogle, C. G., & Hanline, M. F. (2016). An exploratory study of family-centred help-giving practices in early intervention: Families of young children with autism spectrum disorder. *Child & Family Social Work*, 21(2), 249–260. 10.1111/cfs.12148

Creswell, J. W., & Poth, C. N. (2018). *Qualitative inquiry and research design: Choosing among five approaches* (4th ed.). Sage Publications.

Crisp, C., Drauker, C. B., & Cirgin Ellett, M. L. (2014). Barriers and facilitators to children's use of speech-generating devices: A descriptive qualitative study of mothers' perspectives. *Pediatric Nursing*, 14(3), 229–237. 10.1111/jspn.1207424636104

Crotty, M. (1998). *The foundation of social research: Meaning and perspectives in the research process*. Sage Publications.

Crowe, B., Machalicek, W., Wei, Q., Drew, C., & Ganz, J. (2021). Augmentative and alternative communication for children with intellectual and developmental disabilities: A mega-review of the literature. *Journal of Developmental and Physical Disabilities*, 34(1), 1–42. 10.1007/s10882-021-09790-033814873

Dada, S., Flores, C., Bastable, K., & Schlosser, R. W. (2021). The effects of augmentative and alternative communication interventions on the receptive language skills of children with developmental disabilities: A scoping review. *International Journal of Speech-Language Pathology*, 23(3), 247–257. 10.1080/17549507.2020 .179716532893695

De Leon, M., Solomon-Rice, P., & Soto, G. (2023). Perspectives and experiences of eight latina mothers of young children with augmentative and alternative communication Needs. *Perspectives of the ASHA Special Interest Groups*, 8(5), 1–14. 10.1044/2023_PERSP-23-00074

Dean, R. G. (1993). Constructivism: An approach to clinical practice. *Smith College Studies in Social Work*, 63(2), 127–146. 10.1080/00377319309517382

Dempsey, I., & Keen, D. (2008). A review of processes and outcomes in family-centered services for children with a disability. *Topics in Early Childhood Special Education*, 28(1), 42–52. 10.1177/0271121408316699

Di Rezze, B., Law, M., Eva, K., Pollock, N., & Gorter, J. W. (2014). Therapy behaviours in paediatric rehabilitation: Essential attributes for intervention with children with physical disabilities. *Disability and Rehabilitation*, 36(1), 16–23. 10 .3109/09638288.2013.77535823594052

Doak, L. (2021). Rethinking family (dis)engagement with augmentative & alternative communication. *Journal of Research in Special Educational Needs*, 21(3), 198–210. 10.1111/1471-3802.12510

Drager, K., Postal, V. J., Carrolus, L., Castellano, M., Gagliano, C., & Glynn, J. (2006). The effect of aided language modeling on symbol comprehension and production in 2 preschoolers with autism. *American Journal of Speech-Language Pathology*, 15(2), 112–125. 10.1044/1058-0360(2006/012)16782684

Dunst, C. J. (2002). Family-centered practices: Birth through high school. *The Journal of Special Education*, 36(3), 141–149. 10.1177/00224669020360030401

Dunst, C. J., Bruder, M. B., Maude, S. P., Schnurr, M., Van Polen, A., Clark, G. F., Winslow, A., & Gethmann, D. (2020). Predictors of practitioners' use of recommended early childhood intervention practices. *International Education Studies*, 13(9), 36. 10.5539/ies.v13n9p36

Dunst, C.J., Espe-Sherwindt, M., & Hamby, D. (2019). Does capacity-building professional development engender practitioners' use of capacity-building family-centered practices? *European Journal of Educational Research*, 8(2), 515–526. 10.12973/eu-jer.8.2.513

Dunst, C. J., & Trivette, C. M. (2009). Capacity-building family-systems intervention practices. *Journal of Family Social Work*, 12(2), 119–143. 10.1080/10522150802713322

Dunst, C.J., Trivette, C. M., & Hamby, D. W. (2007). Meta-analysis of family-centered help giving practices research. *Mental Retardation and Developmental Disabilities Research Reviews*, 13(4), 370–378. 10.1002/mrdd.2017617979208

Edwards, A., Brebner, C., McCormack, P. F., & McDougall, C. (2016). More than blowing bubbles: What parents want from therapists working with children with autism spectrum disorder. *International Journal of Speech-Language Pathology*, 18(5), 493–505. 10.3109/17549507.2015.111283527063689

Fried-Oken, M., Mooney, A., & Peters, B. (2015). Supporting communication for patients with neurodegenerative disease. *NeuroRehabilitation*, 37(1), 69–87. 10.3233/NRE-15124126409694

Gevarter, C., Groll, M., Stone, E., & Medina Najar, A. (2021). A parent-implemented embedded AAC intervention for teaching navigational requests and other communicative functions to children with autism spectrum disorder. *Augmentative and Alternative Communication*, 37(3), 180–193. 10.1080/07434618.2021.194684634669532

Glacken, M., Healy, D., Gilrane, U., Gowan, S. H.-M., Dolan, S., Walsh-Gallagher, D., & Jennings, C. (2018). Key word signing: Parents' experiences of an unaided form of augmentative and alternative communication (LÁMH). *Journal of Intellectual Disabilities*, 23(3), 327–343. 10.1177/17446295187908253012292

Goldbart, J., & Marshall, J. (2004). Pushes and pulls on the parents of children who use AAC. *Augmentative and Alternative Communication*, 22(4), 194–208. 10.1080/07434610400010960

Graham, F., Boland, P., Ziviani, J., & Rodger, S. (2018). Occupational therapists' and physiotherapists' perceptions of implementing occupational performance coaching. *Disability and Rehabilitation*, 40(12), 1386–1392. 10.1080/09638288. 2017.129547428288531

Granlund, M., Bjorck-Akesson, E., Wilder, J., & Ylven, R. (2008). AAC interventions for children in a family environment: Implementing evidence in practice. *Augmentative and Alternative Communication*, 24(3), 207–219. 10.1080/0899022 080238793518830910

Groce, N. E., & Zola, I. K. (1993). Multiculturalism, chronic illness, and disability. *Pediatrics*, 91(5), 1048–1055. 10.1542/peds.91.5.10488479830

Guy, B., Feldman, T., Cain, C., Leesman, L., & Hood, C. (2020). Defining and navigating 'action' in a Participatory Action Research project. *Educational Action Research*, 28(1), 142–153. 10.1080/09650792.2019.1675524

Hassey, J. T. (2022). *Time Trials: Ethnographic Interviewing Within Health Care System Constraints*. Leader Live., 10.1044/leader.FTR1.27072022. ethnographic-interviews.40

Hettiarachchi, S., Kitnasamy, G., & Gopi, D. (2020). "Now I am a techie too" – parental perceptions of using mobile technology for communication by children with complex communication needs in the Global South. *Disability and Rehabilitation. Assistive Technology*, 15(2), 183–194. 10.1080/17483107.2018.155471330735067

Hill, C. E. (2001). *Helping Skills: The Empirical Foundation*. American Psychological Association., 10.1037/10412-000

Hunt, p., Soto, G., Maier, J., Müller, E., & Goetz, L. (2002). Collaborative teaming to support students with augmentative and alternative communication needs in general education classrooms. *Augmentative & Alternative Communication, 18*, 20–35. 10.1080/aac.18.1.20.35

Hustad, K. C., & Shapley, K. L. (2003). Communicative Competence for Individuals who use AAC. In Light, J., Beukelman, D. R., & Reichle, J. (Eds.), *Communicative Competence for Individuals who use AAC* (pp. 147–162). Paul H. Brookes Publishing.

Individuals with Disabilities Education Improvement Act (IDEIA) of 2004, PL 108-446, 20 U.S.C. §§ 1400 *et esq.*

Johnson, J. M., Inglebret, E., Jones, C., & Ray, J. (2009). Perspectives of speech language pathologists regarding success versus abandonment of AAC. *Augmentative and Alternative Communication*, 22(2), 85–99. 10.1080/0743461050048358817114167

Johnston, S. S., Blue, C. W., & Stegenga, S. M. (2022). AAC barriers and facilitators for children with Koolen de Vries syndrome and childhood apraxia of speech: Parent perceptions. *Augmentative and Alternative Communication*, 38(3), 1–13. 10.1080/07434618.2022.208562635726705

Kasari, C., Kaiser, A., Goods, K., Nietfeld, J., Mathy, P., Landa, R., Murphy, S., & Almirall, D. (2014). Communication interventions for minimally verbal children with autism: Sequential multiple assignment randomized trial. *Journal of the American Academy of Child and Adolescent Psychiatry*, 53(6), 635–646. 10.1016/j.jaac.2014.01.01924839882

Kashinath, S., Woods, J., & Goldstein, H. (2006). Enhancing generalized teaching strategy use in daily routines by parents of children with autism. *Journal of Speech, Language, and Hearing Research: JSLHR*, 49(3), 466–485. 10.1044/1092-4388(2006/036)16787891

Kim, J., & Soto, G. (2024). A comprehensive scoping review of caregivers' experiences with Augmentative and Alternative Communication and their collaboration with school professionals. *Language, Speech, and Hearing Services in Schools*, 55(2), 607–627. Advance online publication. 10.1044/2024_LSHSS-23-0011738324385

King, G., Desmarais, C., Lindsay, S., Piérart, G., & Tétreault, S. (2015). The roles of effective communication and client engagement in delivering culturally sensitive care to immigrant parents of children with disabilities. *Disability and Rehabilitation*, 37(15), 1372–1381. 10.3109/09638288.2014.97258025323397

King, S., Teplicky, R., King, G., & Rosenbaum, P. (2004). Family-centered service for children with cerebral palsy and their families: A review of the literature. *Seminars in Pediatric Neurology*, 11(1), 78–86. 10.1016/j.spen.2004.01.00915132256

Klatte, I. S., Harding, S., & Roulstone, S. (2019). Speech and language therapists' views on parents' engagement in Parent-Child Interaction Therapy (PCIT). *International Journal of Language & Communication Disorders*, 54(4), 553–564. 10.1111/1460-6984.1245930729613

Klatte, I. S., Ketelaar, M., de Groot, A., Bloemen, M., & Gerrits, E. (2024, January). (2023). Collaboration: How does it work according to therapists and parents of young children? A systematic review. *Child: Care, Health and Development*, 50(1), e13167. 10.1111/cch.1316737724049

Kruijsen-Terpstra, A. J., Verschuren, O., Ketelaar, M., Riedijk, L., Gorter, J. W., Jongmans, M. J., & Boeije, H. (2016). Parents' experiences and needs regarding physical and occupational therapy for their young children with cerebral palsy. *Research in Developmental Disabilities*, 53-54, 314–322. 10.1016/j.ridd.2016.02.01226970858

Kuhlthau, K. A., Bloom, S., Van Cleave, J., Knapp, A. A., Romm, D., Klatka, K., Homer, C. J., Newacheck, P. W., & Perrin, J. M. (2011). Evidence for family-centered care for children with Special Health Care Needs: A systematic review. *Academic Pediatrics*, 11(2), 136–143.e8. 10.1016/j.acap.2010.12.01421396616

Light, J., & Drager, K. (2007). AAC technologies for young children with complex communication needs: State of the science and future research directions. *Augmentative and Alternative Communication*, 23(3), 204–216. 10.1080/074346107 0155363517701740

Light, J., Drager, K., McCarthy, J., Mellott, S., Millar, D., Parrish, C., Parsons, A., Rhoads, S., Ward, M., & Welliver, M. (2004). Performance of typically developing four- and five-year-old children with AAC systems using different language organization techniques. *Augmentative and Alternative Communication*, 20(2), 63–88. 10.1080/07434610410001655553

Light, J., & McNaughton, D. (2013). Putting people first: Re-thinking the role of technology in augmentative and alternative communication intervention. *Augmentative and Alternative Communication*, 29(4), 299–309. 10.3109/07434618.2013. 84893524229334

Light, J., Wilkinson, K. M., Thiessen, A., Beukelman, D. R., & Fager, S. K. (2019). Designing effective AAC displays for individuals with developmental or acquired disabilities: State of the science and future research directions. *Augmentative and Alternative Communication*, 35(1), 42–55. 10.1080/07434618.2018.155828330648896

Light, J. C., Parsons, A. R., & Drager, K. (2002). "There's more to life than cookies," Developing interactions for social closeness with beginning communicators who use AAC. In J. Reichle, D. Beukelman, & J. Light *Eds)., *Exemplary practices for beginning communicators: Implications for AAC* (pp. 187--218). Paul H. Brookes.

Lin, S. C., & Gold, R. S. (2017). Assistive technology needs, functional difficulties, and services utilization and coordination of children with developmental disabilities in the United States. *Assistive Technology*, 30(2), 100–106. 10.1080/10400435.20 16.126502328140832

Lorang, E., Maltman, N., Venker, C., Eith, A., & Sterling, A. (2022). Speech-language pathologists' practices in augmentative and alternative communication during early intervention. *Augmentative and Alternative Communication*, 38(1), 41–52. 10.108 0/07434618.2022.204685335422176

Luo, R., Alper, R. M., Hirsh-Pasek, K., Mogul, M., Chen, Y., Masek, L. R., Paterson, S., Pace, A., Adamson, L. B., Bakeman, R., Golinkoff, R. M., & Owen, M. T. (2019). Community-Based, Caregiver-Implemented Early Language Intervention in High-Risk Families: Lessons Learned. *Progress in Community Health Partnerships*, 13(3), 283–291. 10.1353/cpr.2019.005631564669

Mandak, K., O'Neill, T., Light, J., & Fosco, G. M. (2017). Bridging the gap from values to actions: A family systems framework for family-centered AAC services. *Augmentative and Alternative Communication*, 33(1), 32–41. 10.1080/07434618. 2016.127145328081651

Marshall, J., & Goldbart, J. (2008). 'Communication is everything I think.' parenting A child who needs augmentative and alternative communication (AAC). *International Journal of Language & Communication Disorders*, 43(1), 77–98. 10.1080/ 1368282070126744417852533

Mas, J. M., Dunst, C. J., Hamby, D. W., Balcells-Balcells, A., García-Ventura, S., Baqués, N., & Giné, C. (2020). Relationships between family-centred practices and parent involvement in early childhood intervention. *European Journal of Special Needs Education*, 37(1), 1–13. 10.1080/08856257.2020.1823165

McCord, M. S., & Soto, G. (2004). Perceptions of AAC: An ethnographic investigation of Mexican-American families. *Augmentative and Alternative Communication*, 20(4), 209–227. 10.1080/07434610400005648

McNaughton, D., Rackensperger, T., Benedek-Wood, E., Kerzman, C., Williams, M. B., & Light, J. (2008). "A child needs to be given a chance to succeed": Parents of individuals who use AAC describe the benefits and challenges of learning AAC technologies. *Augmentative and Alternative Communication*, 24(1), 43–55. 10.10 80/0743461070142100718256963

Meadan, H., Douglas, S. N., Kammes, R., & Schraml-Block, K. (2018). "I'm a different coach with every family": Early interventionists' beliefs and practices. *Infants and Young Children*, 31(3), 200–214. 10.1097/IYC.0000000000000118

Moorcroft, A., Scarinci, N., & Meyer, C. (2020). 'We were just kind of handed it and then it was smoke bombed by everyone': How do external stakeholders contribute to parent rejection and the abandonment of AAC systems? *International Journal of Language &amp. International Journal of Language & Communication Disorders*, 55(1), 59–69. 10.1111/1460-6984.1250231553126

Moorcroft, A., Scarinci, N., & Meyer, C. (2021). "I've had a love-hate, I mean mostly hate relationship with these PODD books": Parent perceptions of how they and their child contributed to AAC rejection and abandonment. *Disability and Rehabilitation. Assistive Technology*, 16(1), 72–82. 10.1080/17483107.2019.163294431250678

Muttiah, N., Seneviratne, A., Drager, K. D., & Panterliyon, N. A. (2022). Parent perspectives on augmentative and alternative com-munication in Sri Lanka. *Augmentative and Alternative Commu-nication,38*(3), 173–183. https://doi.org/.212194010.1080/07434618.2022

O'Neill, T., & Wilkinson, K. M. (2020). Preliminary investigation of the perspectives of parents of children with cerebral palsy on the supports, challenges, and realities of integrating augmentative and alternative communication into Everyday Life. *American Journal of Speech-Language Pathology*, 29(1), 238–254. 10.1044/2019_AJSLP-19-0010331961702

Otheguy, R., García, O., & Reid, W. (2015). Clarifying translanguaging and deconstructing named languages: A perspective from linguistics. *Applied Linguistics Review*, 6(3), 281–307. 10.1515/applirev-2015-0014

Parette, H. P.Jr, Brotherson, M. J., & Huer, M. B. (2000). Giving families a voice in augmentative and alternative communication decision-making. *Education and Training in Mental Retardation and Developmental Disabilities*, 177–190.

Park, H. (2021). "I kept questioning it in the first 6th months": The process of AAC acceptance in parents of children with complex communication needs. *Communication Sciences & Disorders (Seoul, Korea)*, 26(1), 120–136. 10.12963/csd.21801

Pickl, G. (2011). Communication intervention in children with severe disabilities and multilingual backgrounds: Perceptions of pedagogues and parents. *Augmentative and Alternative Communication*, 27(4), 229–244. 10.3109/07434618.2011.63002122136362

Pope, L., Light, J., & Franklin, A. (2022). Black Children with Developmental Disabilities Receive Less AAC Intervention than their White Peers: Preliminary Evidence of Racial Disparities from a Secondary Data Analysis. *American Journal of Speech-Language Pathology*, 31(5), 2159. 10.1044/2022_AJSLP-22-0007936044883

Roberts, M. Y., & Kaiser, A. P. (2011). The Effectiveness of Parent-Implemented Language Interventions: A Meta-Analysis. *American Journal of Speech-Language Pathology*, 20(3), 180–199. 10.1044/1058-0360(2011/10-0055)21478280

Robinson, N. B., & Solomon-Rice, P. L. (2009). Supporting collaborative teams and families. In G. Soto & C. Zangari (Eds)., *Practically speaking: Language, literacy, and academic development for students with AAC needs.* (pp. 289–312). Paul H. Brooks Publishing.

Romano, N., & Chun, R. Y. (2018). Augmentative and alternative communication use: Family and professionals' perceptions of facilitators and barriers. *CoDAS*, 30(4), 1–9. 10.1590/2317-1782/2016201713830043827

Romski, M., & Sevcik, R. A. (2005). Augmentative communication and early intervention: Myths and realities. *Infants and Young Children*, 18(3), 174–185. 10.1 097/00001163-200507000-00002

Romski, M., Sevcik, R. A., Adamson, L. B., Cheslock, M., Smith, A., Barker, R. M., & Bakeman, R. (2010). Randomized comparison of augmented and nonaugmented language interventions for toddlers with developmental delays and their parents. *Journal of Speech, Language, and Hearing Research: JSLHR*, 53(2), 350–364. 10 .1044/1092-4388(2009/08-0156)20360461

Roper, N., & Dunst, C. J. (2003). Communication intervention in natural environments. *Infants and Young Children*, 16(3), 215–225. 10.1097/00001163-200307000-00004

Roth, F. P., & Worthington, C. K. (2023). *Treatment resource manual for speech-language pathology.* Plural Publishing.

Schladant, M., & Dowling, M. (2020). Parent perspectives on augmentative and alternative communication integration for children with fragile X syndrome: It starts in the home. *Intellectual and Developmental Disabilities*, 58(5), 409–421. 10.135 2/1934-9556-58.5.40933032315

Sevcik, R. A., Romski, M. A., & Adamson, L. B. (2004). Research directions in augmentative and alternative communication for preschool children. *Disability and Rehabilitation*, 26(21-22), 1323–1329. 10.1080/0963828041233128035215513732

Simmons-Mackie, N., King, J. M., & Beukelman, D. (2013). *Supporting communication for adults with acute and chronic aphasia.* Paul H. Brookes Publishing Co.

Solomon-Rice, P. L., & Soto, G. (2014). Facilitating vocabulary in toddlers using AAC: A preliminary study comparing focused stimulation and augmented input. *Communication Disorders Quarterly*, 35(4), 204–215. 10.1177/1525740114522856

Solomon-Rice, P. L., & Soto, G. (2014). Facilitating vocabulary in toddlers using AAC: A preliminary study comparing focused stimulation and augmented input. *Communication Disorders Quarterly*, 35(4), 204–215. 10.1177/1525740114522856

Soto, G., & Yu, B. (2014). Considerations for the provision of services to bilingual children who use augmentative and alternative communication. *Augmentative and Alternative Communication*, 30(1), 83–92. 10.3109/07434618.2013.87875124471987

Spradley, J. P. (1979). *The Ethnographic Interview*. Harcourt Brace Jovanovich College Publishers.

Stuart, S. A., & Parette, H. P.Jr. (2002). Native americans and augmentative and alternative communication issues. *Multiple Voices for Ethnically Diverse Exceptional Learners*, 5(1), 38–53. 10.56829/muvo.5.1.p8006861217m5414

Van Mensel, L. (2018). 'Quiere koffie? 'The multilingual familylect of transcultural families. *International Journal of Multilingualism*, 15(3), 233–248. 10.1080/14790718.2018.1477096

Walker, M. L. (1993). Participatory action research. *Rehabilitation Counseling Bulletin*, 37, 2–2.

Westby, C., Burda, A., & Mehta, Z. (2003). Asking the right questions in the right ways: Strategies for ethnographic interviewing. *ASHA Leader*, 8(8), 4–17. 10.1044/leader.FTR3.08082003.4

Wetherby, A. M., & Woods, J. J. (2006). Early social interaction project for children with autism spectrum disorders beginning in the second year of life: A preliminary study. *Topics in Early Childhood Special Education*, 26(2), 67–82. 10.1177/02711214060260020201

Wright, C. A., Kaiser, A. P., Reikowsky, D. I., & Roberts, M. Y. (2013). Effects of a naturalistic sign intervention on expressive language of toddlers with down syndrome. *Journal of Speech, Language, and Hearing Research: JSLHR*, 56(3), 994–1008. 10.1044/1092-4388(2012/12-0060)23275419

Yoder, P., & Stone, W. L. (2006). A randomized comparison of the effect of two prelinguistic communication interventions on the acquisition of spoken communication in preschoolers with ASD. *Journal of Speech, Language, and Hearing Research: JSLHR*, 49(4), 698–711. 10.1044/1092-4388(2006/051)16908870

Chapter 6
Teachers Are Allowed to Be Human Starting With Trauma–Informed Care of Educators Who Care for Youth

Erica J. Bosque
San Francisco State University, USA

ABSTRACT

This chapter explores the experiences and integration of approaches and selfcare techniques of teachers in their TK–12 credential programs and human service workers in providing trauma-informed care or teaching. Focus groups and interviews were used to collect the data from human service providers and TK–12 teachers currently enrolled in credential programs or working in care systems in California. Content analysis of the rich data elevated the voices of these teachers and service providers and the massive gaps in skill development, preparedness, and care to provide heart work and trauma informed care in their classrooms, care systems and communities. The results suggested that the abusive and toxic relationship of working in the education or care systems is a foundational element that impacts and harms both teachers, providers and their students or clients—which stifles the access and effectiveness of trauma informed practices. These stories of adults doing heart work in care systems shows equitable, inclusive care for the adults is where to start.

DOI: 10.4018/979-8-3693-0924-7.ch006

WELCOME: THE IMPORTANCE OF OUR CARE AND HUMANIZING HEART WORK

As a school social worker, I have had the privilege of being a member of the many care and learning systems, and also being a lonely department and glue that holds many resources together for students, families, and staff. For 20 years, I believed and trusted the rhetoric with which most people are indoctrinated while working in schools: "The struggle" of this work is "just the way it is" (NEA, 2022, para. 4) I have experienced repeated work days that included death; I have seen horrific acts committed on children and families; I have met with members of legal prosecution teams; I have served as a grassroots developer of resources; and I have been the voice elevator for the students, families, and staff I serve. Starting in 2017 in Sonoma County, California, parts of the community were burned to the ground by wildfires for 5 subsequent years, which also included 2 years of flooding that destroyed two towns. Then, as reinforced the organization Trauma Transformed (2023), and people's shared experiences of the COVID-19 global pandemic and resulting shelter-in-place mandates; protests and vandalism connected to Black Lives Matter; distance learning; and skyrocketing numbers of homelessness, domestic violence, and child abuse. In addition to the "normal" elements of working in schools, I carried the load of these experiences with my teacher peers into the classroom and was asked by educational and human services system administrators to use a trauma-informed approach with students—without a trauma-informed approach being applied to us. There cannot be one without the other. Working in schools means being a human and working with one's heart; yet, there is only so much the heart can take before it breaks without equitable, inclusive, encompassing maintained care for the adults, first. Early childhood educators and providers are not shielded for these types of challenging experiences. Early childhood teachers and support providers actually have the opportunity to potentially see and experience the challenges faced by youth and families early on in a child's development; in some ways making their heart work more intense as these adults are providing prevention and early intervention. As a school based social worker my early childhood colleagues and I would consistently carry the worry of "what can we do before things get worse and harder for everyone involved".

"Can I talk to you for a minute?"

This question is how conversations have often started with many of the teachers I have collaborated with, trained, and mentored for over 20 years. I have sat across and looked into the eyes of compassionate, dedicated teachers and care providers, who realized they were not adequately trained nor cared for by the education system to do the job they were expected to perform. In my current role working in Preschool–12th grade school districts, I have listened to these teachers' countless stories of how their students were suffering in their classrooms, trying to manage their lives and development while attempting to learn. The phrases I have heard weekly at my job, and which I have struggled to answer, include: "How am I supposed to help them learn if they have so much going on?"; "My heart breaks listening to what my students go through every day"; "I cannot fix what happens outside of my class"; "What is happening to my students is real and in my face . . . what do I say?"; "I am so tired, stressed, overwhelmed . . . I don't know if I can do this . . . who can help me?"; "This stuff is not my job. I am here to teach the standards"; and "I am not ok, and other parts of my life are being impacted by my job."

These quotes could go on and on. I have remained in the trenches of this work and these experiences as schools have continued to slowly move into the realities of the layered, complex traumas of students, teachers and care providers. Administrators tell school staff to engage in self-care. Administrators say, "Remember, you have to put your oxygen mask on first before you help someone else," and "You can only do what you can do." These condescending brush offs of the daily trauma consumption teachers experience are the equivalent of an abuser telling the victim the beating they just endured was their fault. One may ask what is worse than being beaten down: feeling betrayed by the system to which one goes for support and protection. Student support and protection are mandated at school, and macro-educational systems and policies have a continuous commitment to expand resources in practice; however, teachers and providers are the heart that creates the conduit nexus of what is "pulsed" to students. Early childhood educators and providers is where this "pulse" begins. The care, resources, and learning opportunities students receive will only be as good as the support, training, and care that teachers and providers receive from the educational system in which they do their heart work, day in and day out.

PROBLEMS OF THE HEART

Teachers and their classrooms are vital to care, learning, and long-term student outcomes; however, the common practice of teaching credential and induction programs for now Preschool–12th grade, is to train new teachers and providers to be less human and more focused on standards, class content, classroom management, and relationship building in an academic context. The irony rests in the fact that trauma-informed practices, role clarity, and wraparound care for teachers are currently not part of the required standards for the California Commission on Teacher Credentialing (2020). Students' academic standards, testing, grades, and traumas come before discussing the many roles of teachers, trauma-informed teaching practices, and trauma-informed well-being of the teachers and providers devoting themselves to this work. Student and induction teachers are put through grueling circumstances to earn and clear their credentials. Prospective teachers are required to earn a bachelor's degree, apply to credential programs, pay for their classes, take a full load of classes while sometimes teaching in the classroom, pass state-mandated tests, and then continue to teach full-time while attending monthly classes and supervision to complete credential requirements (California Commission on Teacher Credentialing, 2020). Even once they finish clearing these credentials, the teachers are most likely have not yet earned a master's degree and will start at the bottom of a school district's pay scale. Early childhood educators and providers are going to be new to this credentialing system. However, the maltreatment of early childhood educators and providers is not a new experience to this community of adults. Early childhood education, preschool, is currently still a luxury for many families, where is contrast the teachers and providers have been undervalued and under supported for decades. Early childhood educators and providers entering the credentialing system have an opportunity to center care and equity on the adults who are doing this foundational, early development, nurturing heart work. This prioritizing of adult care will enable and foster the early childhood educators and providers ability to sustainable prioritize their personal trauma-informed care, so that the educators can sustain their trauma-informed practices in their classrooms.

Trauma-informed care broadly refers to a set of principles that guide and direct how individuals view the impact of severe harm on young people's mental, physical, and emotional health. Trauma-informed care encourages support and treatment for the whole person rather than focusing on only treating individual symptoms or specific behaviors (Ginwright, 2018). The craft of providing a trauma-informed teaching approach is a mixture of nuanced experiences, connections, and feelings, combined with direct lines of communication and shared information to meet outcomes established between individuals and care providers—which, in the school environment, is the teacher (Venet, 2021). A trauma-informed educator care provider (TIECP) experience includes, but is not limited to, (a) access to the resources and services connected to all three care systems (i.e., medical, educational, social services); (b) ongoing, trauma-informed approach training on cultural and human behavior development competency and nonjudgmental verbal and nonverbal communication interactions; and (c) consistent educational provider supervision/evaluation process mandated during their paid time, along with required teacher participation in personal mental health and wellness services to manage trauma and stress consumption that impact the quality, experience, and access to the care offered to the students and communities teachers serve.

These intensive and enriching training components to become a TIECP begin in all credential programs and could include continued training in induction programs and throughout a teacher and provider's career (Venet, 2021). After teachers participate in the introductory educational training experience, consistent TIECP supervision and evaluation would foster and expand the TIECPs' tools and approaches in their practice. TIECPs would also receive personal mental health and wellness services to manage trauma and stress consumption mandated during the TIECPs' paid time. These services would be ongoing throughout their careers to ensure safe, high-quality classroom experiences and potentially increase students' necessary access to the care offered during the school day outside the scope of the TIECPs' roles in the classroom. There have been attempts, strategies, and policies established to provide broader care and wellness to students with some success; however, the lack of training and wellness services offered and applied to teachers as "care providers" and their continued practice development has consequently harmed teachers personally and professionally (Lizana & Lera, 2022).

This intense level of harm is evident in the increasing number of educators leaving the profession: "According to the U.S. Bureau of Labor Statistics, there were approximately 10.6 million educators working in public education in January 2020; today there are 10.0 million, a net loss of around 600,000" (National Educator Association [NEA], 2022, para. 8). This metric is seemingly just the beginning of the teacher shortage crisis, as "a staggering 55% of educators are thinking about leaving the profession earlier than they had planned" (NEA, 2022, para. 1). In addition, this uncoordinated professional care approach for the adults working in all levels of education, is reflective of an increased number of barriers to justify the need for providing a broader amount of care for teachers and students throughout the school year, during the school day, and on school campuses. The NEA (2022) reported:

91% of educators say that the pandemic-related stress is a serious problem for educators and 90% say feeling burned out is a serious problem . . . when asked about potential ways to address the issue, respondents pointed to higher salaries, providing additional mental supports for students, hiring more teachers and less paperwork. (para. 18)

Even in a survey completed by the NEA, mental support for teachers was not an option within the survey questions to address this critical crisis in the education system.

The 1990s brought (a) increased classroom task demands on teachers to implement standardized testing; (b) the use of highly structured federal and state education methodologies; (c) school shootings; and (d) heightened numbers of teen suicide, pregnancy, and drug use. In response, the goals of integrating mental health and wellness services into the school day for students gained momentum as biological and social science research studies also formalized the concept of adverse childhood experiences (ACEs; Green et al., 2015) and the development of trauma-informed care approaches. As Sarason (1996) stated, "Unfortunately, many child advocates and researchers, despite their good intentions, have proposed fragmented initiatives to address problems without an adequate understanding of the mission, priorities, and culture of schools" (p. 14). The early studies Sarason mentioned did not acknowledge that teachers also have an ACE score, nor that the job of teaching includes massive amounts of trauma consumption, which impacts teachers' abilities to care for students because they also need to care for themselves first and foremost. Greenberg et al. (2003) stated, "The demands on schools to implement effective educational approaches that promote academic success, enhance health, and prevent problem behaviors have grown" (p. 467). The same and additional challenges continued through the COVID-19 global pandemic, shelter-in-place mandates, and return to in-person school in Fall 2021, with the unrelenting demands predominantly placed on teachers (NEA, 2022).

Educators in their first 5 years of professional development and teaching are vulnerable to initial exposure to abuse, trauma consumption and fatigue, and overloaded expectations of the educational system to be everything for their students (Venet, 2021). The shift from teachers just teaching to teachers serving as trauma-informed educational providers due to the current credential program standards reflects a massive leap that lacks ongoing training and care practices applied to teachers. Integrating a human-focused heart work (i.e., trauma-informed approach as the foundation and framework for teaching credential and induction programs and for the continued development of the teacher) destigmatizes the challenges of being an educator. In turn, this change in foundation and framework (a) supports the well-being of the teacher, (b) decreases the number of teachers leaving the profession, (c) enriches the human development of students—which expands points of access to assist in treating generational community trauma to promote healing—and learning, and (d) positively impacts the outcomes of students.

Heart work for teachers involves the innate actions, communication, facilitation, collaboration, and expression of showing and feeling compassion, empathy, humility, trust, and love for themselves, their students, and their community in their roles as educators (Hooks, 2000). The complex layers of heart work and care teachers give are delivered through human interactions and relationships with students. Training educational providers to implement and maintain trauma-informed experiences from the beginning of their practice cultivation is also key to developing the transformational leadership elements required to shift the lens, scope, and quality of care and services provided to teachers first and students second. During the COVID-19 global pandemic, transformational leadership models attempted to improve the current funding and implementation structures of teacher training to support teachers as vital and intentional providers of student systems of care (NEA, 2022).

However, maintaining the practice of shaming the victim still looms from the longstanding history of abusive power and White supremacy in education (Ginwright, 2018). In this practice, the teacher and/or student is the problem, and their social and emotional deficits are external to the education system. The abusive power dynamics of distancing and othering of teachers and students has normalized feeling guilt and weakness if people are dependent on or need the systems of care (Giroux, 1997). These dehumanizing experiences and perspectives in teaching are cycles of abuse and social injustice commonly draped in the polite, digestible approaches of transformative leadership by placating these experiences as simply a part of working in schools. Early childhood educators and providers are people who come to work to LOVE and teach young, small, children. These trauma-informed practices and leading from their hearts in a common component of how they do their job. There is a need for recognition and understanding that equitable, love and care for youth is a deep-rooted value in early childhood education. As these loving adults "officially" enter the education system through the credentialing system, there is a need to heed warning and begin focusing on the care of the adults first. In order, to capture and learn from the experiences of credentialed teachers, and my positionality as a school social worker, I examined this problem of the heart and using qualitative data I collected in Spring 2022 to create care services for teachers, training curricula, wellness tools, and influences to expand teaching credential programs and the longitudinal care of teachers and care providers. As we make our transition into the story sharing of educators and providers, we will look at the culture of humane practices for the adults working in the education system and how people's "purpose" within the work can be part of how they keep going.

TEACHERS ARE NOT ALLOWED TO BE HUMAN

Teachers' job duties and roles revolve around teaching students what is required to become educated and contributing members of society. At the beginning of the U.S. education system, schools had an understated need to keep children and adult learners alive, safe, healthy, and supervised (Venet, 2019). These elements of an educational system of care are possible due to the human heart work, dedication, and sacrifices of educators who make these vital elements come to fruition in their classrooms. As teachers and the U.S. educational system continue moving through current societal challenges, role clarity and boundaries of trauma-informed practices will remain necessary; moreover, TK–12 credential and induction programs must equip and train new teachers coming into the profession with a clearer understanding of their jobs, roles, and the impact this work will have on their hearts, personal well-being, and everyday lives (Venet, 2019). Kennedy (2016) stated:

From the beginning of a student teacher's professional development, they are continuously balancing among multiple and conflicting goals and ideals, some self-imposed and some externally imposed. As a society, we expect teachers to treat all students equally, yet respond to each person's unique needs; to be strict yet forgiving; and to be intellectually demanding yet leave no one behind. (p. 11)

The noise of these conflicting messages about teachers' responsibilities to their students has drowned out the needs and responsibilities teachers have to care for and support themselves first before they attempt the management of a job. No one uses a megaphone to say the current teaching role is *impossible* within the current educational system.

Human beings in education and human services work can only consider attempting the impossible because the drive comes from their love for this heart work. Such focus also needs to move toward teachers using self-love as a political act to demand the reprioritization of teacher care. Gibbs (2020) stated:

Love is an important part of both teaching and learning-the love of the self and the love of others . . . and the resulting agency they uncover through understanding how their contributions matter to the world fosters a love of self. Simultaneously, we understand a trauma-informed framework to hinge on the idea of care. Thus, if we engage our students[—and teachers—] in ways that foster the love of others as they uncover ways to love themselves. (p. 102)

A deeper and expansive individual and systematic understanding of how to teach and care in trauma-informed frameworks and classroom practices is possible.

The educational system that trains and credentials teachers does not value them as humans who deserve trauma-informed care when they choose to dedicate their lives to the profession of teaching—thus, one may ask how these new teachers would know how to integrate trauma-informed practices into their classrooms. Additionally, one may wonder how they would know how to care for themselves from a trauma-informed approach. The disconnect between teachers experiencing trauma-informed learning and work environments for themselves as they attempt to cultivate trauma-informed practices in their classrooms is the main reason countless articles, social media postings, and news reporters have discussed the mass exodus of teachers from the profession every day. The crucial shift of supporting teachers must first begin with remembering these adults are human, and continue during the credential and induction programs. Consistent foundational awareness is needed for any chance of acknowledging and repairing the trauma that has been inflicted on teachers.

The practice of remembering the purposefulness of these jobs and roles helps sustain the daily dehumanizing elements of being an educator or care provider. Just like youth, adults need a purpose in their contributions to their communities. Next is an activity to reconnect and reflect on the purpose within one's job or roles. The practice of coming back to the purpose of one's work can return focus to what they are or are not receiving to support their capacity to prioritize their care needs, which can support their purpose. The purpose circle image (see Figure 1) is based on the dominant Western culture and values of purpose. Multiple cultures have images and definitions of purpose; for this activity, I use the dominant Western culture definition to be in alignment with how we as educators are valued within education and care systems to find and use our purpose. Purposeful connection to heart work is a reasonable need for teachers and caregivers for their care and well-being.

Activity One: Your Purpose and Whys for Being in This Work

Activity Invitation for the Reader: Using the Venn diagram (see Figure 1) or the image with question prompts (see Figure 2), take as much time as necessary to reconnect and reflect on your purpose and/or whys for being in your jobs and roles. There are no right answers. The continued practice of understanding why you do this work is imperative to advocating and maintaining your visibility as a human being whose purposeful work requires purposeful care.

Figure 1. Purpose circle venn diagram

(Adapted from "What Consumes Me," by B. Caddell, 2023, www.whatconsumesme.com)

Figure 2. Purpose circle question prompts

 😊	What are you good at?	How do you use or see what you are good at in your job or roles?
 ♡	What or who do you love?	How do you use or see what or who you love in your job or roles?
 ☆	What jobs or professions do you or could you get paid for?	How do you use or see what you can get paid for in your job or roles?
 ☮	What do you wish you could change about the world?	How do you use or see what you would change in the world in your job or roles?

A Humane and Honest Research Story: Care for Us First—Experiences of New TK–12 Teachers Performing Heart Work and Providing Trauma-Informed Teaching

Awareness Opportunity for the Reader: In the culture of academia and higher education, research is valued as a way to prove or validate research questions and find areas that need more research. In the following research story, there are deeply raw and compelling lived experiences of new teachers. While reading through their voices, I offer prompts to make personal connections to your lived experiences as an educator or care provider. Universal human connection to storytelling or "research" is a communal resource to remind us of our strength, power, and love for ourselves and our heart work.

Whose Story am I Sharing?

Participants in this research story were students and teachers during the Spring 2022 semester of the Be a Teacher intern credential and teacher induction programs at the North Coast School of Education (NCSOE) in Santa Rosa, California. These participants were in Year 1, Year 2, or Year 3 of earning or clearing a single, secondary, or special education credential as part of these programs. All participants in the classes I attended for data collection were invited—not required—to participate in the data collection process. All participants completed an informed consent and were reminded of their participant options at the beginning of our time together. The instructors of the classes I attended for data collection were also asked—not required—to have me come to their class and use 1.5 hours of their class time for data collection. The instructors also completed an informed consent because most of them participated in the focus group component of the data collection process, and they watched and listened to what the new teachers shared.

The teachers who participated in my research had been through 5 years of California's wildfire seasons and were in Year 3 of the COVID-19 global pandemic and shelter-in-place mandates. They were teaching in the classroom, continuing to manage their personal lives, and attending graduate school—all while trying to care for themselves and their students. These teachers were the daily trailblazers and evolving heart of the trauma-informed education system as local, state, national, and global leaders attempted to survive the new landscape of day-to-day life during this generation's "war." These realities only further reinforced the need for teachers' time and energy during this data collection period to be resourceful; empathetic; compassionate; safe; and offer some level of processing and self-care as they unpacked their experiences and geared-up for another day in the complex, trauma-inducing, relationship-driven, heart work job of teaching.

To prompt the participating educator care providers to share their personal experiences of not being given trauma-informed care first and not being prioritized as humans to do trauma-informed teaching, I developed three research questions. These questions resulted from my daily exposure to these new teachers working themselves into selfless exhaustion to care for and be trauma-informed teachers to their students at the high cost to their personal well-being:

- What are the experiences of teachers in their TK–12 credential and induction programs in providing trauma-informed teaching?
- How are teachers in their TK–12 credential and induction programs integrating trauma-informed teaching into their classrooms?
- How do the teachers in TK–12 credential and induction programs cope and care for themselves while doing trauma-informed teaching?

Getting people in care professions to talk about their needs and values without them first talking about the populations for whom they care is a challenge. New teachers are an example of how, from the very beginning of entering this work, a disconnecting from identities and emotions is required to do the job.

Reflection Invitation for the reader: How and when do you feel the need to disconnect from yourself to stay in your job or role? What do you gain and/or lose from decreasing your awareness of your needs and value?

Research Sample

NCSOE gave me the honor of spending 5 months with their cohort of student teachers who were all in their first 5 years of teaching, earning their credentials or completing induction. Data were gathered though focus groups and writing activities and then analyzed through in-depth manifest and latent content analysis from the voices of 20 participants (see Table 1).

continued on following page

Table 1. Continued

Table 1. Research sample

Participant identifier	Age range	Gender	Ethnicity	Years working in education	Current role in education system	Type of credential
Cindy	20–29	Female	Latinx/Hispanic	1–5	Student teacher, currently in credential program	Special education
Alli	40–49	Female	White/Caucasian Black, African American	1–5	Student teacher, currently in credential program	Special education
Danielle	20–29	Female	Indigenous People/ Native American	1–5	Student teacher, currently in credential program	Special education
Veronica	20–29	Male	Latinx/Hispanic	1–5	Teacher, induction program status	Special education
Jaquin	30–39	Male	Latinx/Hispanic	1–5	Student teacher, currently in credential program	Special education
Sarah	30–39	Female	White/Caucasian Indigenous People/ Native American	1–5	Student teacher, currently in credential program	Special education
Lisa	50–59	Female	Asian	1–5	Teacher, induction program status	Multiple subject
Jon	40–49	Female	Indigenous People/ Native American	1–5	Student teacher, currently in credential program	Special education
Georgia	20–29	Nonbinary/third gender	Latinx/Hispanic	1–5	Student teacher, currently in credential program	Single subject
Leslie	20–29	Female	White/Caucasian Latinx/Hispanic	1–5	Teacher, induction program status	Multiple subject
Ellen	20–29	Female	Asian	1–5	Student teacher, currently in credential program	Single subject
Rachel	20–29	Female	Latinx/Hispanic	1–5	Student teacher, currently in credential program	Single subject
James	40–49	Male	Latinx/Hispanic	1–5	Student teacher, currently in credential program	Single subject
Vera	30–39	Female	Indigenous People/ Native American	1–5	Student teacher, currently in credential program	Single subject
Jose	20–29	Male	Latinx/Hispanic	1–5	Student teacher, currently in credential program	Single subject
Cassy	20–29	Female	Latinx/Hispanic	1–5	Student teacher, currently in credential program	Single subject

continued on following page

Table 1. Continued

Participant identifier	Age range	Gender	Ethnicity	Years working in education	Current role in education system	Type of credential
Melissa	40–49	Female	White/Caucasian	1–5	Student teacher, currently in credential program	Special education
Chad	50–59	Male	White/Caucasian	1–5	Student teacher, currently in credential program	Multiple subject
David	30–39	Male	White/Caucasian	6–10	Teacher, induction program status	Single subject
Nicole	40–49	Female	White/Caucasian	11–15	Teacher, induction program status	Special education
Megan	40–49	Female	White/Caucasian	1–5	Student teacher, currently in credential program	Special education

Note. Participant demographics. Data were gathered though focus groups and writing activities and then analyzed through in-depth manifest and latent content analysis from the voices of 20 participants.

Reflection Invitation for the Reader: When you started in your job or role, what was your why for wanting to work in education or care systems? Are any of those early whys still present for you?

Research Story Results and Elevating Teacher Voices

The 20 participants described in Table 1 shared their experiences, feelings, and stories, which were developed into the results shared in this section. Content analysis of the focus group discussions and written group activities I completed with these 20 participants uncovered four major interrelated themes; each major theme had two or three subthemes, as shown in Table 2.

Table 2. Themes

Major themes	Subthemes
Self-Care Practices for Doing Selfless Heart Work	Intentional Self-Love Rituals for Survival Reciprocal Loving Connection Moments Family and Colleague Life Raft
Harm and Opportunity	The Impossible Job Beat Down Pouring From an Empty Cup Hypocrisy of Expectations
Get a Little but Give A LOT	Creating and Facilitating Toxic Overwhelm The Weight of Holding the Safe Space

continued on following page

Table 2. Continued

Major themes	Subthemes
Struggling With Dehumanizing Practices	Care for the Student Versus Demonstration of Compliance and Learning
	Suppressing the Instincts of LOVE and HOPE

Note. Themes based on content analysis from focus group discussions and written group activities with 20 participants.

Reflection Invitation for the Reader: Which major and/or subthemes in Table 2 speak to you the most, and why? Where do you feel the reaction or resonation to a theme in your body?

WHAT DOES HARM AND OPPORTUNITY LOOK AND FEEL LIKE?

Even with the wide range of age groups, school campuses, student needs, and self-care practices addressed, all 20 participants spoke in some way about the harm trauma-informed teaching practices have had on teachers and their students. They all discussed torn or injured feelings when learning or implementing trauma-informed practices in their classrooms due to the nature of what students shared or expressed, thereby creating a traumatic process environment without the teacher knowing what to do next. Participants noted that students and teachers alike experience high amounts of vicarious trauma; as such, there is an opportunity to have teachers use their facilitation, love, and care skills to create space for exploration and healing in the classroom, so long as teachers can access and implement their personal and professional capacity resources. In addition to needed decompression, teachers must complete the processing support needed after this deep emotional in-class work to aid in sustaining and rebooting their abilities to continue with trauma-informed care practices for their students.

As early childhood educators and providers, the recognition and awareness to how these experiences are similar and different is required, as equitable care practices are implemented for the adults, so equitable care practices are provided to youth. Without time to reboot or "refill their cups," teachers' self-trust may become damaged, which can impact new teachers in building a safe and loving environment with their students. Due to the instability or stress of uncertainty that can exude from a new teacher's self-doubt, there is also a potential of students not trusting the teacher. While crying, Cassy openly asked, "If I don't trust what I am doing, why would my students?" This loss of confidence and self-trust can also increase as these new teachers begin the process of lesson planning. Participants discussed realizing quickly there is not enough time in the school day to fit everything a student "needs." The new teachers' time crunch realization then led to decisions of what to keep and what to do later, or not at all. The participants realized the priorities were grades and standards instead of teachers and students being loved and well in the educational system.

At the beginning of every class I attended for data collection, I noticed a heaviness and depletion of energy and spirit from the teachers. The classes participating in this research project were held Monday through Thursday from 4:00 p.m.–8:00 p.m. on Zoom after students had completed a full day of teaching. It was the 1st year back to in-person teaching after shelter-in-place protocols due to the COVID-19 global pandemic. The immediate honesty I experienced from Day 1 of data collection from all 20 participants was shocking. One vital element of a trauma-informed practice approach is the ability to recognize and regulate what is happening personally in one's environment, body, mind, and soul before attempting to support the regulation care of someone else. In a mocking, laughing tone, Veronica stated, "This is the commonly under explained as the oxygen mask comment said to teachers repeatedly when they are told in a condescending tone reminded about 'self-care.'" Absent a crucial personal pause, reflection, insight, and love of the self first comes a continuous reciprocal creation and facilitation of the toxic level of overwhelm the teacher and care provider is trying to mitigate. During a reflection, Ellen shouted, "The care provider is the teacher [in the classroom]." If the teacher exercises their own continuous, reciprocal creation and facilitates their own toxic overwhelm, they can become the deregulating pulse that ripples through the environment and interactions in the classroom.

Out of safety, trust, and love, students feel the energy, see and hear tones of emotions, look to the teacher for modeling, and ride the waves of the day their teacher is having. Due to this daily submersion in the layers of churning human feelings and connections—and without the initial community allowance of sustainable capacity building and practice of fostering self-love—teachers are potentially feeding themselves and their students harm. Such harm can unravel the trauma-informed practices the teachers intentionally or unintentionally offer in their classrooms, impacting students' abilities to feel safe, trust, and love, and access learning. This weight of responsibility can be worth it throughout an enriching career. However, the weight can simultaneously be an anchor that pulls down the teachers' abilities to care for themselves as well, which can have life-changing consequences for teachers that can deplete their overall professional and personal wellness.

Teaching credential and induction programs place massive amounts of attention on classroom management strategies and approaches that will aid in teachers having control over their classroom, respect from their students, and the ability to maximize their learning experiences. In a few ways, this concept contradicts a trauma-informed teacher care provider approach and the creation of a classroom where students feel seen, heard, accepted, and loved by their teacher and peers. Eleven participants asked a question like Lisa asked: "What is the right thing to do for the student?" Many said such questions kept them up during the night. The education system is engaged in a very internal and external battle with Nicole opining the "school districts, teaching pedagogies, and trauma-informed teaching practices that do not align to meet the needs of ALL students." Nicole had worked in education the longest out of the group of participants.

The conflicting academic exposure and training of new teachers, in addition to their experiences in the classroom, could lead teachers to the practice of detaching from and dehumanizing their students as a self-preservation practice because they quickly learn they cannot save everyone as a teacher. As a way to keep showing up to their jobs, new teachers often fall into the generational habits of educators to, as Nicole continued, "label, blame, and punish the students for the failures and mistakes of the system, while also holding the guilt and wishing there was more they could do as a teacher for their students." All participants shared statements such as:

- "I feel like I am never doing enough."
- "How am I going to get everything into the school day?"
- "No matter what I do, the lives of my students is so hard outside of school and it all is in my classroom, what I am supposed to do?"
- "Some days I cannot even look at them knowing what is going to happen at home or what they have already been through."

After shelter-in-place protocols due to the COVID-19 global pandemic, classrooms reopened and contained all of the challenges and joys that was there before the students went home in March 2020—in addition "to many behaviors, emotions, developmental gaps, betrayal, and unimaginable stories that will be shared over time in one way or another," as Nicole added. New teachers have had to decide how to protect themselves as they physically stood before students and bore witness to the consequences of not being in person for 18 months; similar to how soldiers who are sent to the front lines cope, at some point, teachers cope by no longer viewing students as humans.

In addition to being exposed to or implementing trauma-informed care teaching practices, participants discussed being given a presentation by their school districts about the multitiered system of support (MTSS) model (see Figure 3). I shared the image in Figure 3 with all students and induction teachers who participated in data collection. All participants referenced this model as the "intervention and prevention plan" used by their districts to support students. The image in Figure 3 is the first page of the packet given to them to show the essential domains of the whole child in the education system of learning and care. The participants, like Melissa, quickly realized most of these domains were to be "effectively implemented with fidelity" by teachers in their classrooms. The priority of these domains also started with academic instruction; then behavior support and management; and lastly, social–emotional instruction and mental health. These new teachers noticed their levels of care and support to implement these domains were not even on this first page. Melissa asked, "How can we support the development of whole children if we are not whole?" Her colleague, Danielle, followed her and stated, "If this was an inclusive plan, it would include the domains of the teachers first, since we are the ones mainly responsible to make this all happen." All participants extensively shared the frustration of knowing trauma-informed teaching includes social–emotional learning lessons, and the mental health of the student has become the main priority in post-shelter-in-place school years. To this point, many participants yelled and expressed anger. Danielle yelled even in this figure:

[The] state did not make mental health the priority in the first orange box on the page and no recognition of the demands on teachers being the facilitators of this balance between care, compliance, productivity and bridging that "gap" in students' learning.

Figure 3. Care for teacher and student versus demonstration of compliance and learning

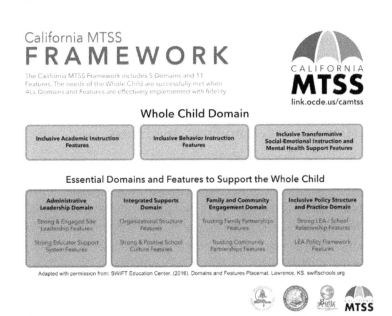

("California MTSS Framework," n.d., Orange County Department of Education (https://ocde.us/MTSS/Pages/CA-MTSS.aspx)

Entering the teaching profession begins with this systematic, physical, mental, and emotional conflict of seeing multiple images illustrating the complex expectations of the teacher to have so many different types of roles and resources in the classroom community. The model outlined in Figure 3 also assumed safety, trust, and love were already established on some intermediate level for these domains to be understood and considered by all humans involved in this MTSS model of care. The MTSS model is covered in a multitude of trauma-informed teaching languages without actually addressing one of the foundational components of the model. This murky delivery of a robust, expansive, trauma-informed, state and districtwide-implemented, student-centered model forces new teachers to, as David stated, "tag or label who is eligible or worthy of getting these care services first, who will wait, and who will not get them at all due to the teachers and schools' capacity to fund and implement services."

Such triaging of the teachers' care of their students requires educators to use various means to numb and detach from some of their students, knowing more students and teachers are highly likely to be direct and collateral damage in the current societal circumstances—resulting in high-stakes consequences of low school attendance, low graduation rates, poor physical and mental health, and incarceration or death. This list of circumstances was provided by seven districts where teacher participants worked to underscore why the MTSS model was crucial for implementation. For new teachers to go to work every day and attempt to use the MTSS model during a layered societal, systematic war, they have to turn down or off their hearts, detach from there emotions, to make life-or-death decisions for their lives and the lives of their students. This practice of unplugging from love is the very opposite of what is encouraged in a trauma-informed teaching practice.

Consequences of Teaching From the Heart

The teachers attending NCSOE were not only students earning their elementary, secondary, or special education teaching credentials, but were also full-time teachers. The dual workload and responsibility of being full-time students while working as new, full-time teachers was a challenging scenario even amid best-possible circumstances of support, time management, self-care, financial means, and professional development—and all of these circumstances would be for the teacher! In addition, students' and families' needs, school campus culture, colleague collaboration, administration leadership, and the daily realities of everyday life were layered into this complex experience for new teachers. As stated by Megan:

NCSOE was developed to help with the teacher shortage due to "high workload and low pay" in the North Bay to entice people to enter the profession so they could earn a salary while being a teacher and going to school.

Based on the volume of work, level of sacrifice, and quality of life that could be experienced during these first years of the program and teaching, NCSOE staff and administrators have done everything they could to build recruitment into the program and retention of the student teachers to survive the process of entering the profession of education.

From my professional and personal experiences of being a school-based social worker who has supported these new teachers in their educator development journey, I began my research questions by asking how these new teachers were prepared for their role and experiences as a trauma-informed care practitioner in the NCSOE program, their school district, their classroom, and in themselves to emphatically and compassionately care for themselves first before caring for their students. The need to conduct this research was only further ignited by the 5 years of California wildfire seasons; the COVID-19 global pandemic and shelter-in-place mandates. Through these history making experiences the emerging need to sift through the current and future consequences of these generational, universal traumatic events as they show up in teachers and students is mandatory for the reimaging of equitable care for everyone.

Activity Invitation Two: Know Your WORTH

Activity Invitation: Looking at the WORTH graphic (see Table 4), take as much time as you need to place words, phrases, and drawings into the boxes that express what you are feeling. For example, for a Worry you have, you could draw a clock because there is never enough time; for Realization, you could write, "I am doing the best I can with what I have," and so on, with each of the words that can provide some concise encompassing of your WORTH as a human doing this heart work.

Table 3. WORTH

W	O	R	T	H
Worry:	Obstacle:	Reality:	Truth:	Help:
Wish:	Opportunity:	Realization:	Thankful:	Hope:

Note. Readers can use this table as a guide to complete the suggested activity to highlight their worth.

Teaching is an act of love and a vocation of hope building for current and future generations. These two core essential human virtues are continually suppressed by the systems and infrastructures of education by a systemic practice of adults resisting their instincts to love children and adults in the intimate and capitalistic systems of care in schools. As Ginwright (2018) stated, "After all 'love' as a program strategy doesn't fit nicely into theory of change models, evaluation protocols, and outcome metrics" (p. 9). Schools continue to be a place of workforce development, but there has emerged a demand for standards about how students will be seen, cared for, and elevated to the workforce of their choice versus the previous history of caste workforce determination. Such a demand to humanize the school systems and experiences of students requires a continuous understanding of development and practice of connecting to student backgrounds, life experiences, and hopes for their future through healing and exposure to opportunities. These types of acts, behaviors, and choices are those of love woven into trauma-informed teaching practices that most human beings and teachers already have in their essences, souls, and hearts, which is why most of them entered the profession in the first place.

Initiation into the teaching profession includes intentional and unintentional training for new teachers that love for themselves and their students is, as Jose shared, "not a practical or sustainable way to be a teacher . . . [they] will burnout"—as if loving people is a set of behaviors and practices that will distract, disrupt, cloud, and endanger the productivity of teaching and learning; as if loving is not professional nor evidenced-based in meeting standards for grade levels; or as if loving is not at the root of healing trauma-informed teaching. Teachers must have love of self to be able to love their students. If this communal educational love were acknowledged and ignited, system leaders would have to ask, "Why do we hurt people that we love?" "Why do we not feel safe in schools?" "Why do we have feelings of hopelessness?" "How will we love with authenticity and honesty?" and "How do we love BIGGER?"

If love and hope are first stifled and then shoved deep down to be forgotten, then denial first provides comfort and then becomes guilt, covering the fear of knowing the truth. This process starts at the beginning of school orientation as a child student and only continues as children become adults; it is reinforced as new teachers learn how not to allow themselves to love their students and to forget loving themselves as all being "part of the job." New teachers are allowed to (a) celebrate small and large wins, (b) share meeting numerical outcomes, (c) share what is going well in their classrooms, (d) trust the process dictated by their credential programs and school districts, (e) only provide feedback or opinions when asked by those in power, (f) remember someone always has it worse than them, (g) push themselves to do all they can for their students, and (h) squeeze in self-care when they can.

If there is a relationship that honors love and sustains hope, the educational and human services systems practices of minimal care for the adults doing these jobs is not good enough. The key to a loving, hope-filled relationship is a reciprocal relationship. New teachers learn quickly they are not in a reciprocal, loving, hope-filled relationship with the education system, and they, as Jose said, "should be grateful for what they get and not ask for more." This relationship is the type of unhealthy relationship new teachers try to shield their students from at the beginning of their careers. Part of this shielding is using what teachers instinctually know in their hearts and what they learn about in doing trauma-informed teaching through direct training and first-hand experiences. However, this shielding that new teachers do is exhausting and is a contributing factor to the decline in their mental and physical health and quality of life. Cindy shared:

I just wish I could shut the classroom door and hold them. I don't care how old you get students want to be held and know their teacher is going to teach them how to learn and get through life. That is why I became a teacher. I had a teacher who loved me.

The combination of withholding love, having realistic hope, if any, and teaching from a trauma-informed approach were three of the major daily habits these new teachers used to survive their first 5 years of teaching. Similar to being in a toxic, romantic relationship, all participants were "staying in it for the kids" at the cost of harming themselves over time. New teachers said, "I love most of my students," "I know most of my students care about me," and "What is happening right now will get better." However, this standard of love and hope is not good enough for the movement from surviving to thriving, trauma informed to healing centered, wanted by the current teachers working, hoping, and loving in the current school system.

Listening, observing, and reading the intense experiential stories of these individuals served as a powerful, brutal, and compelling experience as researcher and only reinforced what I already knew in my heart—teachers do this heart work for the LOVE, CARE, and OPPORTUNITY they provide to their students. Trauma-informed teaching practices are rooted in these relationship-driven emotions, experiences, and evolutionary moments that happen between teachers and students. The challenge and consequences exist in the compounding and conflicting mandates of the education system focused on standards and numerical outcomes versus the vital human necessities of love, trust, and safety. Teachers who have self-love, personal care resources, communal support, and capacity for a life outside the classroom shoulder holding these learning and healing experiences of students and families without harming students or themselves in the process of the school year in an environment that fosters growth, mistakes, repair, healing identity development, and compassionate communication and community.

Data from these 20 NCSOE participants illuminated education systems of care have not found this balance between love and learning. Based on the participants' voices, current circumstances have only aided in fewer people being teachers or sustaining people as teachers due to the trauma they have experienced and consumed by learning and doing trauma-informed teaching practices without sustainable healing care for teachers. Participants' shared guilt for what they wanted for themselves, which spoke to the speed at which the manipulation of them owing the system of education happens. They did not see the opposite is actually true: the United States could not survive without teachers. Even with the COVID-19 global pandemic and serial natural disasters illustrating how this point was continuously true, there was still doubt in the participants' body languages, tones, and words regarding their value in the profession and as individuals.

The tension of these decisions connected to the hypocrisy new teachers have faced trying to teach from a trauma-informed practice. To have a trauma-informed classroom, teachers must prioritize the love, trust, safety, and overall well-being of teachers and students, not on the grading or ranking of meeting academic standards, which are tied to the current definition of school performance and success. Conflicting teacher emotions impact teachers' mental health while working under these goals and environmental conditions of what is more important: (a) the supportive trauma-informed healthcare of teachers and students or (b) the systematic assimilation of students into the societal norms of achievement through cerebral academic requirements. The hypocritical expectations go a step further with the massive amounts of information accessible to educators about the impact trauma has on the brain's ability to learn. This impact is compounded by the very slow progress of the school system, making this reparative information the foundational and fundamental starting point of teaching practices in an effort to decrease and stop the toxic ruptures of blaming teachers and students for their lack of ability to thrive as humans and professionals in an abusive relationship with the educational and care systems.

Activity Three: Internal and External Accomplishments and Appreciations

Sometimes, we forget all we do in an hour, day, week, month, or year—we are capable and stronger than we think! By completing this activity, we can bring awareness and appreciation to our internal and external experiences, sensations, emotions, and connection to our, bodies, identities, cultures, relationships and needs.

*   On the outside of the Gingerbread figure (see Figure 4), write, draw, or make symbols of what you have externally accomplished or appreciate about what you have done in the many aspects of your life over the past 6 months. Examples of external: work, school, COVID, the election, trips, self-care, experiences, etc. Also, place a goal or a hope for the external aspects of your life for the next 6 months.
*   On the inside of the Gingerbread figure, write, draw, or make symbols of what you have internally accomplished or appreciate about what you have done in the many aspects of your life over the past 6 months. Internal examples may include identity, relationships, knowledge, friends, family, emotional experiences, feelings, physical and somatic body sensations, and changes in thoughts or beliefs. Also, place a goal or a hope for the internal aspects of your life for the next 6 months.
*   This activity is for you. There is no right way to do it, and you could share two external and two internal items of your choice that you put down with someone you trust as an opportunity to be heard and seen for all you do.

Figure 4. Internal and external awareness and appreciations

Note. Awareness and Appreciation Activity Figure

What Is Next for the Care and Love of Teachers?

The possible next steps based on the stories shared by these amazing educators could take this coalition of love and heart work into teachers' of all levels and providers, current and future care so they can thrive as human beings and as the trauma-informed care providers they are every day. This research story can provide a deeper acknowledgement, useful awareness resource for early childhood educators and providers, of the harm inflicted on educators and recommendations of where repairing, healing, and loving can live within school communities, credential programs, union contracts, and policies, to elevate the care of teachers to the first priority; without teachers, we will not have an educational care system and their value as heart work crusaders must be urgently respected on multiple levels even to attempt to address the multilayered challenges in need of immediate change in the trauma-informed care system of education by rehumanizing the adults who care for the youth.

Appreciation to the Reader: I have never read anything that has thanked me for reading and engaging with the content, so I thought I would thank you, the reader, for your time, energy, trust, and heart space for giving this chapter a chance. The writing of this chapter is an honor and privilege to share these stories, questions, ideas, and LOVE with humans like you, who are some of the most important people in the lives of individuals, families, and communities. I am grateful to be in this heart work with you all.

REFERENCES

Caddell, B. (2023). *3-Cricle Venn Diagram.*https://www.whatconsumesme.com

Gibbs, B. (2020). Threading the needle: On balancing trauma and critical teaching. *Occasional Paper Series, 2020*(43), Article 10. 10.58295/2375-3668.1350

Ginwright, S. (2018, May 31). *The future of healing: Shifting from trauma-informed care to healing centered engagement.* Medium. https://ginwright.medium.com/the-future-of-healing-shifting-from-trauma-informed-care-to-healing-centered-engagement-634f557ce69c

Giroux, H. A. (1997). Authority, intellectuals, and the politics of practical learning. In Giroux, H. A. (Ed.), *Pedagogy and the politics of hope* (1st ed., pp. 95–116). Routledge. 10.4324/9780429498428-4

Green, B. L., Saunders, P. A., Power, E., Dass-Brailsford, P., Schelbert, K. B., Giller, E., Wissow, L., Hurtado-de-Mendoza, A., & Mete, M. (2015). Trauma-informed medical care: CME communication training for primary care providers. *Family Medicine*, 47(1), 7–14. 10.22454/FamMed.2022.19748625646872

Greenberg, M. T., Weissberg, R. P., O'Brien, M. U., Zins, J. E., Fredericks, L., Resnik, H., & Elias, M. J. (2003). Enhancing school-based prevention and youth development through coordinated social, emotional, and academic learning. *The American Psychologist*, 58(6/7), 466–474. 10.1037/0003-066X.58.6-7.46612971193

Kennedy, M. M. (2016). How does professional development improve teaching? *Review of Educational Research*, 86(4), 945–980. 10.3102/0034654315626800

Lizana, P. A., & Lera, L. (2022). Depression, anxiety, and stress among teachers during the second COVID-19 wave. *International Journal of Environmental Research and Public Health*, 19(10), 5968. 10.3390/ijerph1910596835627505

Orange County Department of Education. (n.d.). *California MTSS framework.* OCDE. https://ocde.us/MTSS/Pages/CA-MTSS.aspx

Sarason, S. B. (1996). *Revisting "The Culture of the School and the Problem of Change.".* Teachers College Press.

Trauma Transformed. (n.d.). *Trauma informed systems.*https://traumatransformed.org/communities-of-practice/communities-of-practice-tis.asp

Venet, A. S. (2019). *Role-clarity and boundaries for trauma-informed teachers* (EJ1206249). ERIC. https://files.eric.ed.gov/fulltext/EJ1206249.pdf

Venet, A. S. (2021). *Equity-centered trauma-informed education (equity and social justice in education)*. W. W. Norton & Company.

ADDITIONAL READING

Braman, L. (2022, July 28). *Illustration: Rupture & repair are key to attachment in health relationships.* Lindsay Braman. https://lindsaybraman.com/rupture-repair -attachment/

Bronfenbrenner, U. (1994). Ecological models of human development. In M. Gauvain & M. Cole (Eds.), *Readings on the development of children* (pp. 37–43). Freeman.

Brown, A. M. (2017). *Emergent strategy: Shaping change, changing worlds.* AK Press.

California Commission on Teacher Credentialing. (2020). *Credential requirements.* CTA. https://www.ctc.ca.gov/credentials/req-credentials

Camera, L. (2022, September 27). New federal data: Too few applicants in K-12 School. *U.S. News & World Report.* https://www.usnews.com/news/education-news/ articles/2022-09-27/new-federal-data-too-few-applicants-in-k-12-schools

Capstone Counseling Centers. (2016, October 4). *Cycle of abuse.* Capstone Coun- seling Centers. https://www.capstonecounselingcenters.com/blog/cycle-of-abuse

Domestic Abuse Prevention Programs. (n.d.). *Wheel library.* https://www .theduluthmodel.org/wheel-gallery/

McIntosh, M. L. (2019). *Compound fractures: Healing the intersectionality of racism, classism and trauma in schools with a trauma-informed approach as part of a social justice framework* (EJ226938). ERIC. https://files.eric.ed.gov/fulltext/ EJ1226938.pdf

Noonoo, S. (2022, May 2). *The mental health crisis causing teachers to quit.* Ed- Surge. https://www.edsurge.com/news/2022-05-02-the-mental-health-crisis-causing -teachers-to-quit

Penner, J. (2022, August 12). *Words that work: Rupture and repair for cofounders and teams.* Medium. https://juliepenner.medium.com/words-that-work-rupture-and -repair-for-cofounders-and-teams-abb2bf43110

Smithgall, C., Cusick, G., & Griffin, G. (2013). Responding to students affected by trauma: Collaboration across public systems. *Family Court Review, 51*(3), 401–408. doi:10.1111/fcre.1203610.1111/fcre.12036

Walker, T. (2022, February 1). *Survey: Alarming number of educators may soon leave the profession.* NEA News. https://www.nea.org/advocating-for-change/new -from-nea/survey-alarming-number-educators-may-soon-leave-profession

KEY TERMS AND DEFINITIONS

Buddy System: A reference to an activity used when working with youth in schools or on field trips that everyone should "have a buddy" to stay safe and supported.

Designated Subjects Credential Program: A program of classes required to earn a single, secondary, or special education teaching credential in the state of California. The Designated Subjects Credential is completed during the first 2 years of the program where the student teachers earn the credential and then begin the teacher induction program phase. The Teacher induction program consists of the postteaching credential program classes required to clear a single, secondary, or special education teaching credential in the state of California. Teachers during the induction phase are teaching classes and attending additional professional development and are mentored by a veteran teachers to support the new teachers skill development.

Heart Work: For teachers, this is the innate actions, communication, facilitation, collaboration, and expression of showing and feeling compassion, empathy, humility, trust, and love for themselves, their students, and their community within their role as an educator. The complex layers of heart work care that teachers give is delivered through human interactions and relationships with students.

Life Raft: A metaphor used with the imagery description of what or who can keep people "afloat."

Multi-Tiered Systems of Support (MTSS): This model is used for intervention and prevention plans used by school districts to support students. The priority of these domains includes academic instruction, behavior support and management, and lastly social emotional instruction and mental health.

Practice Purposefulness: This happens within our jobs and roles and helps sustain the daily dehumanizing elements of being an educator or care provider. Just like youth, adults need a purpose in their contributions to their communities. The practice of coming back to the purpose of one's work can return focus to what they are or are not receiving to support their capacity to prioritize their care needs, which can support their purpose. Purposeful connection to heart work is a reasonable need for teachers and caregivers for their care and well-being.

TK-12: These are the grade levels that students go through within the education system in the United States of America. These are also the grade levels that can be taught by educators and are housed within elementary and secondary school locations.

Trauma-Informed Educator Care Provider (TIECP): Experience includes, but is not limited to (a) access to the resources and services connected to all three care systems (i.e., medical, educational, social services); (b) ongoing trauma-informed approach training on cultural/human behavior development competency and non-judgmental verbal/nonverbal communication interactions; and (c) consistent educational provider supervision/evaluation process mandated during their paid time and required teacher participation in personal mental health and wellness services to manage trauma/stress consumption that impact the quality, experience, and access to the care offered to students and communities teachers serve.

Chapter 7
Preparing a New Generation of Practitioners:
An Equity- and Inclusion-Focused ECSE and SW Personnel Preparation Program

Maryssa Kucskar Mitsch
https://orcid.org/0000-0002-9285-3478
San Francisco State University, USA

Prince Estanislao
San Francisco State University, USA & University of California, Berkeley, USA

Hadas Arbit
San Francisco State University, USA & University of California, Berkeley, USA

ABSTRACT

Project Adversity and Resiliency Interventions for Social Emotional Development in Early Childhood (Project ARISE) is a preservice personnel preparation program training Early Childhood Special Educators and Social Workers to serve young children with disabilities with high intensity needs social emotional needs, specifically children with early childhood mental health (ECMH) needs in inclusive learning environments. Project ARISE seeks to address the state and nationwide shortage of high-quality ECSE and SW personnel whose diversity and identities are reflective of the communities in which they serve. The chapter discusses issues related to the rationale for the interdisciplinary program, a roadmap for the program, reflections

DOI: 10.4018/979-8-3693-0924-7.ch007

and lessons learned, and considerations for others interested in developing similar programs in their communities.

INTRODUCTION

In their early years, it is vital young children have enriching learning experiences and supportive, nurturing adults to support them in acknowledging and valuing differences in others. Early childhood experiences and interactions impact overall development, including but not limited to cognitive, social, emotional, physical and mental health outcomes of young children (Center on the Developing Child at Harvard University [CDCHU], 2016). Specifically, an infant's first relationships with their primary caregivers, starting in the first minutes after birth, serve as the infant's buffer through which to regulate their emotions. This regulation teaches the infants about emotions and relationships. The quality of the environment and the quality of the experiences an infant is exposed to early in life will have a significant influence on them as they grow up and interact with their outside world (Gerhardt, 2015). The primary relationship an infant has with their caregiver is attuned and available to minimize negative affect, such as fear, and maximize positive affect, such as joy. Feeling the range of emotions while feeling safe and secure from a caregiver is essential for their future mental health and the infant's ability to build relationships in the future (Schore, 2003).

There are many things that can solely or collectively impact an infant or young child's development. The initial 3 years of a child's life mark a critical phase for brain development, characterized by remarkable plasticity and adaptability. During this period, the brain undergoes substantial growth and sets the foundation for emotional understanding and regulation (Gerhardt, 2015). However, early brain development is negatively impacted when adversity and/or when young learners are stripped of sensory, emotional, and social experiences. More recently, research has indicated the COVID-19 global pandemic increased the likelihood of children being subjected to maltreatment and experiencing interpersonal trauma (Cénat et al., 2020). Additional elements that have become more centered in discussions are adverse childhood experiences (ACEs), or 10 potentially traumatic events or experiences that occur during childhood. These adversities are experiences to which a developing infant or child must notably adapt socially, developmentally, and psychologically (McLaughlin, 2014). When compounded with systemic racism and inequities, young children who are Black, Indigenous, and/or people of color (BIPOC) face even more dire negative impacts in accessing early intervention and special education services (Division for Early Childhood of the Council for Exceptional Children [DEC], 2023) and on their overall well-being (CDCHU, n.d.; Heard-Garris et al., 2018; U.S. Department of

Education [DOE], 2016; U.S. Department of Health and Human Services [DHHS] & DOE, 2015b).

With 9%–14% of infants and young children experiencing emotional or early childhood mental health (ECMH) issues with enough intensity to interfere with their development and learning, practitioners must be trained to intensely, accurately, and quickly respond (WestEd, 2012). In this chapter, the term "practitioners" refers to professionals who support the learning, development, care, and overall well-being of young children identified as being at-risk, delayed, or having disabilities and their families. These practitioners include early childhood special educators (ECSE), early interventionists (i.e., developmental specialists), early childhood educators, social workers (SW), occupational therapist, speech language therapists, physical therapists, and other service providers.

Early childhood is defined as the education of young children from birth through age 8 (National Association for the Education of Young Children [NAEYC], 2020a). As a pillar of early childhood education for all young children, developmentally appropriate practice (DAP) recognizes children as part of families and their communities, where young children begin to develop a sense of self, identity, and belonging while beginning to construct ideas of differences (Derman-Sparks et al., 2020; NAEYC, 2020a). It is in these early learning experiences and environments where antibias and equity work begins, with practitioners cultivating children's sense of identity and honoring all dimensions of human diversity while also acknowledging the *whole child* (Learning Policy Institute, 2022).

Every child should be acknowledged, valued, and given opportunities to reach their full potential (Derman-Sparks et al., 2020). In particular, practitioners should acknowledge and value the differing abilities and support needs of all children, including young children with high-intensity social–emotional needs. Equity can be achieved when individuals fare the same way regardless of race, class, gender, language, disability and/or other social/cultural characteristics and all children and families receive the necessary supports to develop their full intellectual and social potential (NAEYC, 2019).

PURPOSE OF THE CHAPTER

First, the authors discuss issues related to children and families that demonstrate need, including the importance of early childhood development, partnerships with families, and inclusive learning opportunities for young children. Next, the shortages of an effective workforce and the potential impact they have on children's development and learning are presented. Later, the authors share the details of an interdisciplinary personnel preparation program, Project Adversity and Resiliency

Interventions for Social Emotional Development in Early Childhood (Project ARISE) at San Francisco State University, designed to address these issues. Details of the exemplar program include the program's competencies, strategies for recruitment and retention of diverse scholars, and coursework and experiences. Last, lessons learned, considerations for others interested in developing a similar training program, and how the program could be adapted to meet the needs of other communities are shared.

CRITICAL ISSUES FOR YOUNG CHILDREN WITH DISABILITIES AND THEIR FAMILIES

Young children with disabilities and delays and their families face a multitude of issues on a recurring basis. As outlined by state and professional standards and organizations guiding the field, personnel preparation programs must embed opportunities for understanding, applying, reflecting on, and receiving feedback about their programs. Likewise, practitioners in the field who support young children with disabilities and families must understand these key issues as a means to combat systemic impacts and advocate for stronger child and family outcomes.

Partnerships With Families

At the heart of DAP is understanding children within the context of their environments, which includes their families (NAEYC, 2020a). Families are critical to their child's overall growth and development and play a vital role on their child's interdisciplinary team (Weglarz-Ward et al., 2024). The growth and development of a young child occurs within the family, community, and culture in which they live. Family engagement goes beyond being an after-thought or supplemental to supporting a child–family engagement is an essential component to children's development (DHHS/DOE, 2015a). Families who develop strong relationships with professionals are more likely to be involved in their child's education services, and these children have a higher likelihood of experiencing enhanced short- and long-term development across all domains of learning (DHHS & DOE, 2016).

One way to consider the ways in which disability can impact the roles, interactions, and functions of a family can be explained by the family systems framework, coined by Turnbull and colleagues (1984, 2014). It is important for practitioners to take the time to understand the experiences of families and support their capacity to foster children's development. Celebrating the uniqueness of every child situated in the context of their family, overcoming biases, and creating caring partnerships provides space for families to have confidence in practitioners and programs, feel respected and cared for, and develop a sense of partnership with their child's team of supports. These considerations for the family systems framework, and specifically a two-generational approach, are especially important for families experiencing challenges (e.g., children and parents with disabilities, multilingual families, families experiencing trauma, families living in poverty; Mosle & Sims, 2021). Using strengths-based family practices and strategies to promote families' decision-making skills can help families attain their individualized family goals (Bruder et al., 2019; DEC, 2014).

Moreover, partnerships and engagement with families is vital for equitable and inclusive early childhood experiences (NAEYC, 2019). Collectively, the integration of inclusive instructional strategies in early childhood programs and involving families further support equity and inclusion for young children (DHHS & DOE, 2015a, b, DEC, 2023; DOE, 2016). This is reflected in NAEYC's (2019) recommendations for equity and DAP (NAEYC, 2020) by establishing reciprocal relationships with families and advocating on behalf of young children, families, and the early childhood professionals. For families of children with disabilities and delays, reciprocal relationships includes recognizing and honoring the central role of the family in their child's learning and development.

Trauma and Toxic Stress

Research has indicated racism has detrimental impacts on child health, mental health, and overall well-being. Children who are exposed to racism, whether as targets or bystanders, experience adverse effects on their physical and mental health (Trent et al., 2019). Studies have shown racism can lead to disparities in educational opportunities, mental health disorders, and social determinants of health among BIPOC children (Farquharson & Thornton, 2020). The effects of racism on child health are pervasive and can manifest in various forms, including internalized behaviors, mental health problems, and disparities in healthcare access (Osborne et al., 2021). Though much of these effects is outside of practitioners' control, it is imperative practitioners are aware of, seek to understand, and refute patterns of injustice.

ACEs include abuse, violence, mental illness, and family substance abuse and can lead to toxic stress which negatively impacts brain development (Centers for Disease Control and Prevention [CDC], 2021). ACEs are more common in the United States than previously thought, as more than six out of 10 individuals have experienced one or more ACEs, and one in six have experienced four or more ACEs (Bhushan et al., 2020). However, not all adversities rise to the level of trauma, and these adversities can be counterbalanced with targeted interventions, social interactions, and supportive learning environments (CDCHU, 2016). Positive and responsive relationships from adults, positive early experiences, and early acquisition of adaptive skills, can build strong brain architecture for resiliency in the face of adversity (CDCHU, 2016). Protective factors such as positive relationships play a leading role in creating a sense of safety and security and mitigate the harmful effects of toxic stress and trauma (Harris, 2018; Perry & Szalavitz, 2006; van der Kolk, 2014). These positive relationships can be with family members or practitioners in early learning environments.

Negative effects of ACEs and other traumatic events hinder children's overall development, learning, and capacity to establish relationships with peers and caregivers (National Child Traumatic Stress Network, n.d.; van der Kolk, 2014). These harmful effects reach into the educational domain, wherein trauma-exposed children frequently find themselves at risk of special education eligibility and subsequent disability diagnoses, emphasizing the disabling nature of trauma. For instance, Miller (2018) reported children who have experienced trauma are 4 times more likely to receive a learning disability diagnosis and are overrepresented in special education. Similarly, Jones and colleagues (2012) found children with disabilities are more likely to experience trauma than nondisabled children. This problem is further exacerbated by the clear inadequacy in teacher preparedness to address the needs of students affected by trauma (see Chudzik et al., 2023; McClain, 2021; Miller, 2018). The aforementioned relationship between early childhood special education and trauma underscores the need for integrating trauma-informed approaches in special education settings and practitioner preparation programs.

Implementing trauma-informed care (TIC) is one way to mitigate the adverse effects of trauma among individuals. TIC is an approach that acknowledges and responds to the impact of trauma on individuals, with the goal of establishing a secure and nurturing environment to facilitate healing and rehabilitation (Purtle, 2018). In education, TIC involves integrating knowledge about trauma and its consequences into every facet of the educational setting, such as policies, procedures, and interactions with students and families (Branson et al., 2017). Additionally, TIC allows educators to cater to children with identified traumas, children whose traumas remain unrecognized, and children affected by their peers' traumas (Cole et al., 2013). According to Substance Abuse and Mental Health Services Administration (2014), the four components of TIC are: (a) realizing the impact of trauma; (b) recognizing the signs and symptoms of trauma; (c) responding by fully integrating the signs and symptoms of trauma into policies, procedures, and practices; and (d) actively resist retraumatization.

Early Childhood Mental Health

At birth, infants lack the capacity to manage emotions effectively, but through interactions with their environment, caregivers, and social experiences, they gradually develop these essential skills (Gerhardt, 2015). The primary function of the human brain is survival—adapting to various conditions and stimuli to ensure individual well-being. Unlike other species, in which brain development occurs primarily before birth, the human brain undergoes significant growth outside the womb, emphasizing the crucial role of environmental and social interactions in shaping its development. Importantly, the formation of a human infant's brain occurs within the context of relationships with caregivers, which highlights the profound impact of social connections on neural growth and emotional development (Schore, 2003).

Infant and ECMH (hereby collectively referred to as ECMH) is profoundly influenced by early experiences, which play a crucial role in shaping the development of an infant's right brain and their ability to regulate and comprehend their emotional world (Schore, 2003). These early experiences have long-term implications and impact an infant's understanding of relationships as they grow older. Additionally, these formative experiences shape not only an infant's physical health but also their social–emotional well-being throughout their lives. Moreover, early experiences have a significant impact on the biochemical processes in the infant's brain.

When an infant does not have a secure relationship with an attuned caregiver or experiences neglect, abuse, or unstable relationships, the infant is in danger of significant health, emotional, and brain development delays. Maltreatment (i.e., physical abuse, sexual abuse, or medical neglect) in childhood creates long-lasting biological changes in stress response systems that do not go away (Shonkoff & Garner, 2012). The body does not forget maltreatment that happens during infancy and early childhood, even if an infant does not remember or have a distinct memory of it. Biological memory and toxic stress cause excessive and persistent activation of the stress system in the absence of the buffering protection provided by caring relationships with adults. The body and mind are linked. Things that affect the body affect individuals' emotional world and vice versa (Shonkoff & Garner, 2012).

Families and caregivers of children with or at risk for developmental delays are more prone to experiencing anxiety and depression (Delahooke, 2017). This emotional burden is compounded for families lacking a stable support system of friends and family, as they must navigate the challenges of caring for their child's needs alone. The way caregivers perceive their children and their children's diagnoses profoundly influence a child's future outcomes and well-being. Therefore, it is crucial for ECSE and early childhood educators are adequately trained to address the developmental needs of the child and the emotional well-being of caregivers. According to Delahooke (2017), prioritizing caregivers' emotional health alongside ECMH is essential for providing comprehensive support to families in these circumstances. As displayed in Figure 1, the role of early intervention and ECMH intersect regarding personnel responsibilities and roles to support social–emotional development and the dyadic relationship of caregiver–child.

Figure 1. Intersection of early intervention and ECMH

Inclusive Learning Opportunities for Young Children

For children with disabilities, inclusion in early childhood programs refers to placement alongside peers without disabilities; promotion of high expectations and intentional participation in all learning and social activities, facilitated by accommodations; and the use of evidence-based services and supports to foster their development (i.e., cognitive, language, communication, physical, behavioral, and social–emotional), friendships with peers, and sense of belonging (DEC & NAEYC, 2009). Opportunities for inclusion should be available to *all* children with disabilities, including the youngest of children as well as those with the mildest disabilities to those with the most significant disabilities (DHHS & DOE, 2015a). Children with and without disabilities benefit from inclusive education for a multitude of reasons (Lawrence et al., 2016). For children with disabilities demonstrating a higher levels of understanding, tolerance, friendships, and peer acceptance (Kart & Kart, 2021; Lawrence et al., 2016; Odom et al., 2004). For young children with disabilities to access and participate meaningfully in inclusive learning environments, the team of professionals supporting them must have had adequate preservice and/or in-service training (Steed et al., 2023).

Despite legislation mandating education in the least restrictive environment and professional development and training to bolster these regulations, almost a quarter of young children ages 3–5 receive all their early education opportunities in separate settings with limited access to interactions with nondisabled peers. Young children from marginalized populations continue to be placed in special education disproportionately, especially in preschool Part B Section 619 programs (Aratani et al., 2011; Meek et al., 2020). Practitioners must commit to nurturing children's sense of identity and to creating learning communities that embrace all dimensions of human diversity, including acknowledging and valuing differing abilities to support the needs of all children. The advancement of equity in early childhood education hinge on the belief that every child should be acknowledged, valued, and given opportunities to reach their full potential (Derman-Sparks et al., 2020). Likewise, the DHHS and DOE's (2015a) recommendations in using ECMH consultation strategies to support inclusion reduces practitioner stress, burnout, and attrition.

Workforce Shortages

Special Educator Shortages

A growing number of students receive special education under the Individuals with Disabilities Education Act (IDEA, 2004), with 14% or 7.3 million students ages 3–21 receiving special education services in 2019–2020 (DOE, 2021). Additionally, there are over 800,000 children with diagnosed disabilities, ages 3–5, receiving special education services in the United States (DOE, 2021). However, the effectiveness of these services is challenged by a national shortage of highly qualified personnel in early intervention and special education (Bruder, 2010; DOE, 2017; U.S. Bureau of Labor Statistics, 2021b), with 98% of school districts reporting a special educator shortage (U.S. Bureau of Labor Statistics, 2021b).

For instance, the special educator shortage is vividly seen in schools across the state of California, the nation's most populated and diverse state. Enrollment in California's educator preparation programs has dropped by more than 70% over the last decade (Education Policy at AIR, 2016). Emergency-style credentials administered in California have increased seven-fold since 2012–2013 (Carver-Thomas et al., 2020). Two out of every three special educators have a substandard credential—they are not yet qualified per state requirements but are teaching in classrooms and doing everything expected of fully qualified and credentialed special educators, including implementing individual education programs (Ondrasek et al., 2020). California's special educator shortage numbers rose in recent years due to resignations, retirements, and fewer teachers joining the profession (Carver-Thomas et al., 2021). It is estimated special educators would comprise nearly 50% of new teacher hires in

2021–2022, indicating a need for more than 8,500 new special educators in one year alone (California Department of Education [CDE], n.d.-d).

In addition to shortages of candidates entering the field, attrition and retention of special educators have short- and long-term implications for child and family outcomes. When compounded with a dwindling veteran special educator pool available for mentoring new and non-credentialed special educators, the impact on child and family outcomes is more dire. With high-poverty schools having a higher percentage of special educator turnover, children with disabilities in these schools are less likely to be taught by a highly-qualified or credentialed teacher. In turn, attrition exacerbates the shortage (Billingsley & Bettini, 2019), leaving educators who remain in the field stretched even more thin. By understanding the factors contributing to teacher burnout, plans to address special education teacher shortages and attrition can be developed. Unfortunately, addressing contributing factors of burnout is multifaceted and cannot be addressed solely by one entity. Discussed later in this chapter are elements of a special education teacher preparation program that sought to embed burnout prevention measures in its program.

Social Worker Shortages

School social workers (SWs) are often the primary or only counseling professionals available to public school students and their families to initially identify challenges they face and provide appropriate interventions. Child, family, and school SWs are projected to grow 12% from 2019 to 2029, which reflects faster growth than the average occupation (U.S. Bureau of Labor Statistics (2021a). More than 181,000 SWs will be needed through 2029 (U.S. Bureau of Labor Statistics, 2021a). California faces a shortage of BIPOC behavioral health providers from culturally and linguistically diverse (CLD) backgrounds, including at the pre-K–12 level, with pre-K being the point of contact for detection and early intervention. The California Future Health Workforce Commission (2019) recommended prioritizing diversity in health/mental health professions and educational pipelines. In turn, this prioritization could potentially produce approximately 30,000 workers from underrepresented communities and supporting over 60,000 students in health/mental health careers. Similar to the shared special educator shortages, California's projected SW shortage by 2030 was given a letter score of "D" when accounting for an aging population and ratio of need (Lin et al., 2016). This rating indicates a need to recruit, retain, and graduate more highly qualified SWs to serve diverse students and their families.

Shortage of Personnel From Diverse Cultural and Linguistic Backgrounds

There is a need to recruit and retain highly qualified credentialed personnel who are prepared to serve young CLD children with disabilities and their families. The current landscape of ECSE and SWs do not reflect the diversity of the communities they serve, limiting students' access to the rich racial, ethnic, cultural, and linguistic diversity in the state. In 2019–2020, the ethnic demographics in California's public schools included: 54.9% Hispanic/Latino, 22.4% Caucasian, 9.3% Asian, 5.3% African American, 2.4% Filipino, 0.5% American Indian, 0.4% Pacific Islander, and 3.9% two or more races not Hispanic (CDE, n.d.-a). With 74 different language groups represented throughout the state (CDE, n.d.-c) and 18% of students officially designated as English learners (CDE, n.d.-b), personnel must reflect these demographics. The reality is currently there is a misalignment in BIPOC identification between California's educators (35%) and SWs (31%) to students (74%; CDE, 2024). Nine percent of school districts in the state have no teachers of color, and 58% of districts have less than 20% teachers of color (Carver-Thomas et al., 2020). These data make evident the urgency to enhance diversity recruitment and retention efforts for personnel supporting students with disabilities, including ECSE and SW.

State and national data requires stakeholders to face the disproportionality of children from marginalized populations in special education, and the higher likelihood these children may experience discipline and/or expulsion, including in preschools (Aratani et al., 2011; DHHS, 2015b). The need for culturally responsive ECSE and SW in high-needs schools is apparent given their disproportionate lack of resources, higher teacher turnover, and lower testing scores. All individuals and programs, including practitioners, institutions of higher education, and governing bodies, involved in supporting young children with delays and disabilities and their families share a responsibility to prioritize and promote high-quality early childhood education for all young children, regardless of race, ethnicity, native language, gender, ability, socioeconomic, and other characteristics (Power to the Profession Task Force, 2020). In particular, receiving appropriate early intervention and special education services has long been a critical issue for children with disabilities who have high-intensity social–emotional needs and live in poverty (Brunelle et al., 2019). Personnel, specifically ECSE and SW, who are diverse, culturally responsive, and justice-driven are in high demand in the state and across the country (DHHS, 2015b; Love & Beneke, 2021).

Need for Interdisciplinary and Collaborative Personnel Preparation

The intersection of ECSE and SW responsibilities include conducting assessment, providing intervention, supporting inclusion, promoting child welfare, and establishing partnerships with families. Although these critical responsibilities and daily tasks overlap, there is a lack of formal and regular interaction between preservice preparation programs. In preservice preparation programs, faculty shared their preservice practitioners regularly reported feelings of inadequacy in managing issues outside their preservice training area. Practice-related challenges for preservice special educators have led to a widening of the research-to-practice gap (Teasley, 2016). Practitioners attempting interdisciplinary services often fall short and default to a multidisciplinary approach, in which professionals from different disciplines have minimal to no interaction among team members and implement their plans independently (Little, 2020). Barriers to effective collaboration are multifaceted and can include external constraints like lack of time; however, research has shown fundamental barriers include the absence of a shared theoretical orientation to the purpose and ethics of teaming, lack of knowledge about roles, and shared goals (Bricker et al., 2020; DEC, 2020). Preservice training is an ideal time to address these competencies because disciplinary identities and boundaries begin to form during this time. Practitioners must have the opportunity to learn, practice, and reflect on the knowledge, skills, and dispositions needed to support the holistic, interrelated development of young CLD children with disabilities and their families (Bruder et al., 2019). Practitioners must have opportunities to learn with and about individuals of different personal (e.g., disability, race) and professional backgrounds (e.g., training field, experiences) to provide cohesive, equitable, and positive early learning experiences for young CLD children with disabilities and their families (NAEYC, 2019).

Without opportunities for practice and feedback in a preservice program, it is illogical to expect practitioners to know key characteristics of other fields (e.g., professional organizations, requirements, best practices). Likewise, it is irrational to expect preservice professionals to implement effective and efficient integrated, interdisciplinary practices to once licensed to work in the field. Disciplinary silos that currently exist in institutions of higher education and in the field must be diminished so both interdisciplinary preparation and collaboration in the field become the norm. Understanding the philosophical, preservice, and professional developmental differences between disciplines allows for opportunities in which individuals can identify and discuss misconceptions when presented and create a common understanding. It will be difficult for practitioners to partner with families without first partnering with other practitioners directly to support a family. Moreover, collaborative endeavors must shift to a more equity-empowered and interdisciplinary focus to improve the outcomes of young children with disabilities and their families (Blanchard et al., 2021; NAEYC, 2019; Steed et al., 2023). Presented next is the description of an exemplar interdisciplinary program designed to respond to the identified critical issues related to young children with disabilities and their families.

PROJECT ADVERSITY AND RESILIENCY INTERVENTIONS FOR SOCIAL EMOTIONAL DEVELOPMENT IN EARLY CHILDHOOD

The Project Adversity and Resiliency Interventions for Social Emotional Development in Early Childhood (Project ARISE) at San Francisco State University is a 325K personnel preparation program funded through the Office of Special Education Programs in the DOE. The purpose of Project ARISE is to provide interdisciplinary preservice training for 36 university students (18 ECSE and 18 SW) seeking to become ECSE and SW and serve young children with disabilities who have high-intensity social–emotional needs, specifically children with ECMH needs in inclusive learning environments. Project ARISE seeks to address state and nationwide shortages of high-quality ECSE and SW personnel whose diversity and identities are reflective of the communities they serve. Specifically, Project ARISE programming is centered on ensuring personnel will deliver family centered, racially and culturally responsive, and child welfare-focused services to young CLD children with disabilities and their families. Project ARISE is committed to a social justice framework that requires individuals to continuously seek to understand and uproot patterns of injustice and to hold one another accountable (Mitsch et al., 2023).

To do this, Project ARISE includes: (a) recruitment and graduation of a diverse pool of high-quality scholars, including recruiting scholars from nontraditional (e.g., career switchers, para-educators) and unrepresented backgrounds (e.g., race, ethnicity, native language); (b) preparation of well-trained ECSE and SW professionals who are able to provide high-quality services to young children with disabilities who have high intensity social–emotional needs and their families, specifically providing shared coursework, shared learning experiences (e.g., institutes/conferences), coordinated field experiences; and (c) ongoing support so scholars feel confident in their skillset as they transition to the workplace (e.g., PLC meetings, one-on-one support).

By providing interdisciplinary training and stipends to scholars, Project ARISE projects to add high-qualified and -trained ECSE and SW to the field. Research has suggested student stipends, scholarships, and/or loan forgiveness programs attract high-quality individuals to the teaching profession. Because students from low-income backgrounds perceive student loans as a greater burden than students from other income backgrounds who earn similar salaries in the field (Baum &

O'Malley, 2003), stipends, such as ones offered in Project ARISE (i.e., stipend in exchange for service obligation), may be effective for recruiting scholars from low-income and minority backgrounds (Podolsky & Kini, 2016).

Through Project ARISE, scholars develop their knowledge, skills, and dispositions by participating in enriching experiences they may not otherwise have exposure to in a preservice program. Project ARISE scholars work to meet ARISE-specific competencies by completing additional required coursework and coordinated field experiences. They also participate in shared supplemental learning opportunities and an ongoing professional learning community (PLC). The combination of these supports were designed to facilitate mastery of the competency areas over the course of scholars' time in Project ARISE. Beginning in Fall 2021, the 5-year scholarship opportunity sought to be the first cross-college collaboration at the university, breaking barriers and building new collaborations for years to come.

Project ARISE is a new cross-college collaboration bringing together the expertise between the Master of Social Work (MSW), Pupil Personnel Services Credential (PPSC), and the Master of Arts (MA) and credential program in ECSE. Scholars also earn a graduate certificate as part of their participation. In all, it would take social work scholars four semesters and early childhood special education scholars five semesters to graduate. By the end of the program, Project ARISE scholars are equipped with the knowledge, skills, and dispositions to work as part of interdisciplinary teams providing high-quality services for young CLD children with disabilities who have high-intensity social–emotional needs and their families (Bruder et al., 2019). The elements of Project ARISE are designed to provide a more fluid and adaptable experience and training for equity-driven service providers. One way Project ARISE remains centered on its core values is through its six competencies and indicators.

Overview of Project ARISE's Competencies

The demands placed on personnel preparation programs present challenges to ensure coursework is applied to fieldwork and that preservice practitioners have opportunities to demonstrate research-to-practice skills in their work with young children and their families. The six Project ARISE competencies were developed in an effort to interconnect and ground coursework, supplemental learning opportunities, and field experiences. The competency areas were selected based on the early childhood special education and social work programs' shared philosophies, best practices from professional organizations, and interdisciplinary teaming to meet the needs of young CLD children with disabilities who have high-intensity social–emotional needs and their families in inclusive settings. Moreover, the underlying foundation for Project ARISE competencies include the family systems framework (Turnbull et al., 1984,

2014), ACEs and toxic stress (CDC, 2021), ECMH systems of care (CDC, 2021; Lieberman & Horn, 2005), social justice and antioppressive practices (Healy, 2014; Love & Beneke, 2021), and antibias education (Derman-Sparks & Edwards, 2019).

Developing the Competencies

Competencies were identified based on recommendations from governing bodies, state standards, interdisciplinary preparation, and evidence-based practices in early childhood special education and social work. To meet the project's goals of preparing well-trained personnel to work with young CLD children with disabilities who have high-intensity social–emotional needs, Project ARISE emphasizes six key competency areas with 76 indicators. Though the six competency areas were developed in the grant proposal stage (e.g., before Project ARISE's acceptance and funding), the 76 indicators were developed during Project ARISE's Year 1. Having over a year to discuss and cultivate the final competencies and indicators allowed project personnel to feel confident in the final outcome.

The competency development process included several rounds of completing crosswalk or alignment tables to envision where and how the two fields intersected and where integration of other competencies should be included. The discussions and final decisions of the competencies and indicators included personnel from both the early childhood special education and social work fields, an expert on infant–family and ECMH, and consultation with Project ARISE's advisory board. To determine the competencies, professional materials were gathered and discussed by Project ARISE personnel. The core guiding documents used in developing the six competency areas and 76 indicators included: early childhood special education recommended practices (DEC, 2014), California's early childhood special education preparation standards, national initial practice-based preparation standards (DEC, 2020), a crosswalk of national and California social work standards (Council on Social Work Education, 2015), California's infant–family ECMH competencies (2016), and cross-disciplinary competencies (Bruder et al., 2019). In addition to this is an expansive list, other documents guided this process, including cultural competencies (National Association of Social Work, 2015), position statement on advancing equity (NAEYC, 2019), and national quality online teaching standards. Project ARISE's shared coursework, shared supplemental learning opportunities, coordinated field experiences, and PLC were then tailored and/or designed to facilitate mastery of the competency areas over the course of the program.

Project ARISE's Six Competencies

The six competencies consist of core knowledge, skills, and dispositions scholars should master by the end of the program: (a) assessment; (b) natural environments and inclusive settings; (c) supports to facilitate interactions; (d) teaming and collaboration; (e) professional development and leadership; and (f) equity, social justice, and honoring diversity. As part of Project ARISE's evaluation, scholars complete a self-assessment on these competencies at three points in their program (i.e., beginning, middle, end) as project outcome measures. Through facilitated reflective practice (Heffron & Murch, 2010; NAEYC, 2020b) scholars self-identify learning gaps via the competencies and adapt their individualized learning goals as such.

Assessment

The purpose of assessment depends on the needs of the child and family, the service delivery model, and characteristics of the intervention program (Pretti-Frontczak & Grisham, 2022). There are six purposes for assessment, including developmental and behavioral screening, eligibility for IDEA, planning instruction, revising instruction (e.g., progress monitoring), program evaluation, and accountability. Scholars are expected to demonstrate an understanding of and use a wide range of methods (e.g., authentic, play-based) and use critical thinking to interpret assessment data and make individualized intervention plans. They also use reflective practice and consultation to develop and maintain awareness of the impact of assessment on relationships and to understand how one's own personal experiences and affective reactions may affect assessment and decision making.

Natural Environments and Inclusive Settings

Early childhood inclusion embodies the values, policies, and practices that support the right of every infant and young child and their family, regardless of ability, to participate in a broad range of activities and contexts as full members of families, communities, and society. Infants and toddlers learn best through everyday experiences and interactions with familiar people in familiar contexts found in the natural environment (Raver & Childress, 2015). The desired results of inclusive experiences for children with and without disabilities and their families include a sense of belonging and membership, positive social relationships and friendships, and development and learning to reach their full potential. The defining features of inclusion used to identify high-quality early childhood programs and services are access, participation, and supports (DEC & NAEYC, 2009). Scholars are expected to demonstrate a comprehensive understanding of state/local standards for young children (i.e., paying particular attention to understanding how development is interrelated and where social–emotional skills are embedded), use strategies and accommodations/modifications that support inclusion, and integrate Universal Design for Learning principles (CAST, 2018). Likewise, scholars provide caring and supportive relationships, establish high expectations, and create innovative opportunities for individuals, families, and communities to practice and promote social–emotional inclusion.

Supports to Facilitate Interactions

For early childhood special education and social work scholars, interactions include all individuals part of the intervention and supports process, including but not limited to infants, toddlers, young children, families, other professionals, and stakeholders. These should be meaningful interactions that embrace differences and are culturally and individually responsive. For infants, toddlers, and young children, the role of the instructor/interventionist should be decentralized to promote child-led social interaction with other children and adults in their natural environments (Johnson et al., 2015). Peer-mediated interactions and interventions should be promoted in the learning spaces. Scholars facilitate the continuation of young children's social–emotional learning progress across multiple contexts and transitions, including a variety of environments (e.g., home, school, community, hospital), and people (e.g., peers, service providers, family, community).

Teaming and Collaboration

Engaging in team-based and interdisciplinary collaboration supports reflective practitioners in the field who are equipped with the knowledge, skills, and dispositions to celebrate the successes and problem solve the challenges of young children with disabilities who have high-intensity social–emotional needs and their families (Bruder et al., 2019). Practitioners' expertise are used to enhance communication, interaction, and cooperation among team members, further promoting interdisciplinary collaboration (Bricker et al., 2020; Steed et al., 2023).

Professional Development and Leadership

The leadership process entails the social influence of individuals and groups to maximize the efforts of others to achieve specific goals (DEC, 2014; Nicholson et al., 2020). Although there is an expectation to understand professional ethics and make decisions using relevant laws and regulations (i.e., FERPA, HIPPA, IDEA) and models for ethical decision making, scholars also need to both understand there are multiple ways of knowing and use critical thinking skills and recognize their professional limitations regarding when to seek a referral/support. A survey of early childhood teacher preparation programs found professional knowledge/skills connected to leadership were minimally covered (Buettner et al., 2016). Consequently, both experiences and mentorship in leadership is vital for practitioners to view themselves as leaders open to evolving and gaining needed skills for a changing field (Mitsch et al., 2022).

Equity, Social Justice, and Honoring Diversity

In Project ARISE, equity includes equitable access, services, and supports for children with disabilities and their families that result in positive outcomes not correlated with race, ethnicity, language, income, or other demographics. This competency includes scholars understanding and combating the adverse effects of poverty, ableism, racism and other forms of oppression via ECMH services. The competency also expects scholars to acknowledge and advocate for change to structural inequities and their impact over time and identify and seek to manage the influence of personal or implicit biases (e.g., Staats, 2016). Ableism and racism are deeply embedded in special education, and, historically, there has been oversight of intersectional identities of families (Harry & Ocasio-Stoutenburg, 2020), urging the need for individuals to examine how they are advocating for an equitable and inclusive service delivery model. In other words, practitioners have had to weigh whether they are part of the problem or part of the solution. Understanding how social identity, intersectionality, socioeconomic status, citizenship status, resiliency, human development, community-based factors, and ecological factors are related to individual and group diversity are topics covered within coursework and are embedded within this competency strand. Scholars' knowledge, skills, and dispositions of these topics inform on-going reflective practice (Heffron & Murch, 2010) to promote culturally responsive practices in early ECMH.

Four Key Elements

Project ARISE is comprised of four key elements: (a) shared coursework, (b) shared supplemental learning opportunities, (c) coordinated field experiences, and (d) a PLC (see Figure 2). Research has suggested practitioners are rarely given the opportunity or instruction to develop the skills necessary for successful interdisciplinary collaboration (Herrenkohl et al., 2021). While also completing their own programmatic requirements (either early childhood special education and social work), scholars engage in these additional elements to acquire the knowledge, skills, and dispositions in the six Project ARISE competencies. Project ARISE personnel strive for these key elements of the program to embody Universal Design for Learning (CAST, 2018) so both coursework and experiences allow scholars to represent, engage, and provide a means of expression aligned to what they need. Each cohort's programming requires unique tailoring to ensure all scholars can capitalize on applying their past experiences to filling in knowledge, skills, and dispositions in other competency areas.

Figure 2. Key elements of project ARISE

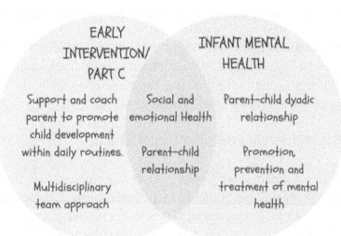

A shared value of both the early childhood special education and social work programs is intentionality around whose voices are elevated. Project ARISE embodies this intentionality by ensuring individuals with diverse, intersecting identities and lived experiences are included in coursework, guest speaking, shared supplemental learning opportunities (e.g., annual conference), PLCs, and mentoring. It is important for scholars to hear diverse perspectives outside of an echo chamber. Subsequently, Project ARISE commits to ensuring the equity-focused, interdisciplinary program is integrated, intensive, and collaborative and includes applications with multiple opportunities for feedback from others in the field of early childhood special education and social work.

Shared Coursework

There are four shared courses early childhood special education and social work scholars enroll in throughout their time in Project ARISE. The shared courses from each program were revised to ensure they are aligned with the six competencies, which are reflective of evidence-based practices, guiding documents, professional organizations, and state credential requirements. An outcome of the shared coursework includes scholars earning one of two graduate certificates. early childhood special education scholars complete a newly created trauma-informed social work practices graduate certificate that focuses on child welfare practices with young children and families, social work practices in education and natural environments, understanding ACEs, and systemic ECMH strategies to enhance the positive impact of collaboration. Social work scholars complete the previously established inclusive early childhood practices graduate certificate, an initiative between the early childhood special education and early childhood education programs. This graduate certificate focuses on inclusive practices for all children, child development and assessment, and family–community partnerships.

Shared Supplemental Learning Opportunities

Three shared supplemental learning opportunities were identified to support the interdisciplinary training of scholars together. Each year, these experiences are curated to either provide opportunities for scholars to strengthen their understanding of the competencies or to fill gaps in the competencies. Understanding each scholar and cohort is going to have unique needs, these three experiences allow for adaptability and flexibility when needed. Two of the three opportunities were events that long-existed in the early childhood special education program, whereas one opportunity was developed specifically for Project ARISE. All three supplemental learning opportunities are embedded in shared coursework, making it feasible for scholars to balance their responsibilities. These experiences increase the frequency of interactions and provide opportunities for scholars to build rapport with one another, strengthen their relationships over time with one another, and further connect their fields and work supporting children and families.

First, the Meaningful Collaborations in Early Childhood Annual Conference is a long-standing event in the early childhood special education program. Since Spring 2014, the annual conference has brought together scholars, students, alums, and community partners. The event includes a keynote speaker and interactive workshops led by practitioners, alumni, community partners, and, occasionally, current university students. In an effort to grow collaboration across university programs, the event evolved to include other programs on campus, including early childhood education, speech language hearing sciences, and SW. By expanding to include other programs, more students are impacted and provided the opportunity for interdisciplinary collaboration. Past conferences have focused on topics including antiracism, social–emotional curriculum, intersectionality, culturally relevant content and pedagogy, equitable representation, and authenticity while re(finding) joy in one's work.

Second, the early childhood special education program hosts a Partnering with Families Institute in the fall. A series of guest speakers are invited to share their lived experiences being a practitioner (e.g., occupational therapist), program leader, community partner, family member, advocate, person with a disability, and/or multiple identities. Each year a new group of speakers is invited, and scholars and students alike are invited to ask questions and reflect on the discussions.

At the time of publication, the third supplemental learning opportunity is in preparation but has not yet been held. This third event is the inaugural Integrated Social Work Research Symposium in the Spring. The hope for this event is twofold – to invite targeted guest speakers who are SW leaders in the community, as well as have students present their action research. While the presenters of the inaugural event will be from the School of Social Work, in future years the hope is to open the event to students from other related programs, including early childhood special education.

Complementary guest speakers may present on topics such as partnerships with families, macro/microlevel systems change, empowerment, and social change for those who have been marginalized, disenfranchised, and oppressed.

Project ARISE scholars are asked to reflect and provide feedback via verbal and written evaluation forms individually, in small groups, and as a large group after each event. Previously in person, the events have been maintained virtually following the COVID-19 global pandemic. As part of past evaluations, participants (both scholars and other university students) shared how virtual events provided access to individuals who typically would not have been able to participate (e.g., disability, health, work, childcare responsibilities). Likewise, recording the events allow space for current and future scholars, stakeholders, and partners to view the event as a whole or in parts at a later time, increasing accessibility and participation for Project ARISE scholars, students, alumni, and stakeholders for years to come. Event recordings are added to the early childhood special education program's student resources (i.e., university learning management site, early childhood special education program's YouTube channel) as a way to build professional development resources that serve as a living history of the program.

Coordinated Field Experiences

The early childhood special education and social work programs each have two extensive field experience requirements grounded in ECMH and inclusion practices. In Project ARISE, scholars complete some required hours (i.e., student teaching, internship) in settings that provide opportunities to apply knowledge, skills, and dispositions gained or evolved from time spent in Project ARISE. Specifically, these experiences provide time and an immediate feedback space to further their skills related to supporting young children with disabilities who have high-intensity social–emotional needs requiring ECMH support in inclusive settings. The field experience requirements pair hours in the field with a seminar. In each of these field experiences, scholars are provided opportunities to practice newly learned instructional skills, evidence–based practices, and intervention strategies to further close the research-to-practice gap (Teasley, 2016).

A strength of the early childhood special education and social work programs involved in Project ARISE are their community partnerships. In one of their two field experience settings, scholars have the opportunity to apply the competencies—specifically working with young children with disabilities who have high-intensity social–emotional needs requiring ECMH supports in an inclusive setting. When available, scholars are paired together at their field work placement sites. The coordinated field experiences include the completion of individual portfolios and ongoing reflective practice (Heffron & Murch, 2010; see also Mitsch et al., 2023). Examples of items in the portfolios include a welcome letter to families in the program, scholar-created intervention guides and individualized activities for target students, and data analysis. For one of their field experiences, the portfolio is centered on ECMH and inclusive practices for young children with disabilities and their families.

Professional Learning Community, Advising, and Mentoring

To promote equity and inclusion, Project ARISE targets the recruitment of scholars from underrepresented and nontraditional backgrounds. Project ARISE has a multifaceted approach to supporting scholars in the hopes of being a successful program. The principal investigator (PI), co-PI, and graduate assistant of the Project ARISE support the retention and continued success of all scholars. Having multiple and ongoing supports for scholars allows for flexible advising and mentorship to scholars who are identified as at risk of failing or leaving the program. This process includes the following elements: (a) recruitment, (b) orientation, (c) induction period, (c) ongoing PLC meetings, (d) ongoing advising, (e) and mentoring (i.e., individualized and group). These elements are informed by ongoing meetings between Project ARISE personnel and the scholar's self-evaluation on Project ARISE's competencies.

If scholars demonstrate they need additional support, advising and mentorship is individualized to meet their needs. Recruitment provides opportunities for dissemination of information about the scholarship opportunity ensures the elements of Project ARISE (e.g., topics and ages covered in coursework for their credential) and the DOE service obligations after graduation can be met by their future career choices. Some potential scholars find the goals, outcomes, and postgraduation requirements are not a good fit for the work they hope to do after graduation.

During the induction period, scholars register for classes and attend early childhood special education and social work required orientations. They also review and sign paperwork, agreements, and commit to the expectations of being a Project ARISE scholar, such as understanding the need to complete shared coursework, supplemental learning opportunities, coordinated field experiences, and participate in ongoing PLC meetings. Scholars are informed of available wrap-around supports, which are imperative to getting the most out of their time at the university and the program and, ultimately, to their success.

Scholars and their advisors have meetings each semester. Scholars are advised by respective Project ARISE personnel in their early childhood special education or social work program. Project ARISE personnel also teach many, if not all, of the shared courses. This structure provides regular opportunities to check in with scholars. As needed, an individualized plan is developed to support scholars who require further support. Individualized mentorship has included weekly or biweekly text messaging, video conferences, and/or on campus check-ins.

The PLC is the most dynamic and fluid element of Project ARISE as it is ever changing to meet the needs of scholars and the field. The PLC was created as a way to embed social resources and collegiality in the field (Bettini et al., 2020), a dependable community individuals can rely on when their workplaces may not be as consistent or reliable. This differentiation allows for vibrant programming to better prepare scholars as they transition into practitioners in the field. PLCs are regularly attended by Project ARISE personnel, scholars, and the graduate student who supports the program. On-site mentors, university supervisors, Project ARISE's advisory board members, and related faculty are invited and, on occasion, attend. PLC meetings formally take place three or four times per semester in a combination of face-to-face and synchronous virtual meetings.

PLC agenda items are derived from competencies and needs of scholars. For instance, a board member joined a PLC meeting to share about their expertise regarding California's endorsement for reflective practice facilitators and infant–family and ECMH specialists (see https://cacenter-ecmh.org/wp/professional-development/professional-endorsement-defining-a-standard-of-excellence/). Having invited speakers in the PLC allows additional dedicated space for individuals with diverse intersecting identities and lived experiences to share their stories with Project ARISE scholars throughout their duration in the program.

For scholars, PLC meetings provide space for emotional support and mutual empathy—strengthening resilience and connection between scholars in and across cohorts— bolstering connections to professional communities of ECSE, SW, and interdisciplinary collaboration (Gu & Day, 2007). Likewise, an aim of the PLC is to form a community while in the program and once they are in the field. There are high rates of practitioner burnout specific to special education and SW (Lloyd et al., 2009; Nelson et al., 2020; Park & Shin, 2020). In turn, prevention, awareness, and consultation models must be considered in recruitment and retention of practitioners to prevent burnout. Project ARISE's mission of interdisciplinary training of preservice ECSE and SW, specifically the components of ECMH consultation, aligns with DHHS and DOE's (2015a) recommendations for reducing practitioner stress, burnout, and turnover.

STRENGTHS AND LESSONS LEARNED

As a cross-college collaboration, the first year was a planning year. The first cohort began in the program's second year. Per federal guidelines, program personnel submit a formal evaluation each year. This evaluation provides an opportunity for personnel to reflect on the past and adjust, as needed, for future programming. Specifically, "continuous reflection brings possibilities for new ways of thinking, acting, and teaching" (Urbani et al., 2022, p. 98). Throughout Project ARISE, the program has been able to capitalize on expertise and knowledge from program personnel, instructors, supervisors, and advisory board members across early childhood special education, social work, and related disciplines at San Francisco State University and the broader San Francisco Bay Area community. The project's coordinated and collaborative efforts model interdisciplinary teaming and provide a diversity of perspectives to support scholars' learning.

Based on the limited observations and feedback from advisory board members, course instructors, and program personnel, there is excitement around Project ARISE and the potential to make a positive community impact. Project ARISE personnel look forward to feedback from other practitioners, supervisors, family members, and program leaders/administrators. Formal and informal evaluation tools will be used to gain feedback from each of these groups to support the evolution of Project ARISE programming for future cohorts and sustain programming at the university.

Strengths of Project ARISE have included differentiation of instruction and experiences between the two graduate programs and the varying backgrounds and levels of expertise of Project ARISE scholars. As Project ARISE has attracted strong candidates who reflect the diverse communities they serve (i.e., San Francisco Bay Area), many scholars have entered the program with a wealth of prior related experience. For instance, scholars join the program with experiences in early intervention, elementary education, case work, childcare, and more. These past experiences are invaluable to scholars' development and essential to collaborative efforts devised as part of the project.

Project ARISE personnel made several adjustments to improve interdisciplinary teaming, collaboration, and experiences thus far in the program. Both the early childhood special education and social work programs are intensive in different ways. The master's programming in each program has requirements including high credit loads of coursework. As social work has a required internship each year resulting in 3 full days a week in the field, scholars take more coursework and fieldwork units each semester. In early childhood special education, nearly all students in the master's and credential program are working full-time in the field in some capacity (e.g., ECSE teacher, paraprofessional, early interventionist). These varied yet intensive responsibilities have left students in each program and Project ARISE scholars strained for time. Regular opportunities for reflection and discussion (e.g., PLC, advising meetings) provide space to problem solve around individual and cohort challenges. Each program's learning modalities for course offerings are also different (e.g., online virtual or face to face). Therefore, cross program scheduling for shared coursework has been a challenge that must be addressed by the PI and co-PI in collaboration with their respective programs and colleges.

One recurring theme that has grounded the Project ARISE program is the shared mutual importance with a clear goal and vision. In turn, this collective disposition of *wanting* to work together to create something that had never been done before at the university, resulted in Project ARISE, an innovative interdisciplinary personnel preparation program focused on training preservice ECSE and SW. There was acknowledgment that Project ARISE was bringing together two existing programs. Yet, the intrinsic motivation of project personnel was essential to take Project ARISE from an idea to a submitted program proposal to an active and evolving program on campus. It took the support of a small group of dedicated ECSE and SW faculty to ensure each college, department chair/director, and program coordinators were in support of and regularly considered Project ARISE in larger college-wide planning. Regularly scheduled meetings between project personnel is recommended. Similar to what often times are part of group projects, personnel entered the project by setting the norms, expectations, and providing space for humanizing experiences to strengthen the personal experience for those involved and to translate and model this process for scholars. Project personnel also showed a collective effort and feelings of gratitude because they knew the amount of time, energy, and problem solving needed to implement Project ARISE. Project ARISE personnel have adopted the "loving kindness" (Magee, 2019) mindset to show grace and humility in this process. Project personnel strive to be mindful that underrepresented individuals may be overburdened with service responsibilities (Wood et al., 2015) and that discussions around time, balance, and responsibilities are necessary to ensure equitable workload for those involved (Branch et al., 2021).

CONCLUSION

Research continues to direct early childhood special education, social work, and related fields to support the ECMH of young children and their families. Infants and young children and their families who are experiencing poverty, sustained adversities, and are impacted by systemic inequities and racism, discrimination, and oppression have compounded factors when also attributing to diagnosed disabilities and/or delays (CDCHU, n.d.; DHHS & DOE, 2015b; DOE, 2016; Tomlinson, 2015). The interdisciplinary program aspires to be intensive, collaborative, and responsive to the community's needs and includes real world application with multiple opportunities for feedback and growth. Developing and implementing a cross-college program has been demanding, resulting in deeper discussions, creativity around problem solving, and an openness to persist through the barriers. Future interdisciplinary programs would benefit from addressing soft skills needed for working on teams. Additionally, future teams would benefit from continuing to respond to needs in the field while considering individualizing scholar supports in a way that does not overburden scholars with more tasks yet prepares them for work that likely includes high-stress environments.

Project ARISE has provided one example for increasing interdisciplinary opportunities in graduate preservice programs, specifically in early childhood special education and social work. The project aims to deliver coursework, supplemental shared learning opportunities, coordinated field experiences, and PLCs for future ECSE and SW practitioners committed to equity-focused learning and development for young children with disabilities who have high-intensity social–emotional needs requiring ECMH in inclusive learning environments and their families. The hope in sharing the key elements, competencies, reflections, and lessons learned from Project ARISE is that other programs around the country will feel confident and have more tools to build and implement their own interdisciplinary programs supporting preservice ECSE and SW to become collaborative colleagues. In Project ARISE's aim of developing ECSE and SW who are well-prepared and committed to support equity-focused ECMH, inclusive learning opportunities, and seek to understand, uproot patterns of injustice, and hold themselves and one another accountable, inter-disciplinary teams in the field will be met with collaborative and focused colleagues.

REFERENCES

Aratani, Y., Wright, V. R., & Cooper, J. L. (2011). *Racial gaps in early childhood: Socio-emotional health, development, and educational outcomes among African American boys* (ED522681). ERIC. https://files.eric.ed.gov/fulltext/ED522681.pdf

Baum, S., & O'Malley, M. (2003). College on credit: How borrowers perceive their education debt. *Journal of Student Financial Aid, 33*(3), 1. 10.55504/0884-9153.1068

Bettini, E., Gilmour, A. F., Williams, T. O., & Billingsley, B. (2020). Predicting special and general educators' intent to continue teaching using conservation of resources theory. *Exceptional Children, 86*(3), 310–329. 10.1177/0014402919870464

Billingsley, B., & Bettini, E. (2019). Special education teacher attrition and retention: A review of the literature. *Review of Educational Research, 89*(5), 697–744. 10.3102/0034654319862495

Blanchard, S. B., Newton, J. R., Diderickson, K. W., Daniels, M., & Glosson, K. (2021). Confronting racism and bias within early intervention: The responsibility of systems and individuals to influence change and advance equity. *Topics in Early Childhood Special Education, 41*(1), 1–12. 10.1177/0271121421992470

Branch, J., Chapman, M., & Gomez, M. (2021). Investigating the interplay between institution, spousal, parental, and personal demands in tenure track faculty everyday life. *Community Work & Family, 24*(2), 143–154. 10.1080/13668803.2020.1727414

Branson, C. E., Baetz, C. L., Horwitz, S. M., & Hoagwood, K. (2017). Trauma-informed juvenile justice systems: A systematic review of definitions and core components. *Psychological Trauma: Theory, Research, Practice, and Policy, 9*(6), 635–646. 10.1037/tra000025528165266

Bricker, D. D., Felimban, H. S., Lin, F. Y., Stegenga, S. M., & Storie, S. O. (2020). A proposed framework for enhancing collaboration in early intervention/early childhood special education. *Topics in Early Childhood Special Education, 41*(4), 240–252. 10.1177/0271121419890683

Bruder, M. B. (2010). Early childhood intervention: A promise to children and families for their future. *Exceptional Children, 76*(3), 339–355. 10.1177/001440291007600306

Bruder, M. B., Catalino, T., Chiarello, L. A., Cox Mitchell, M., Deppe, J., Gundler, D., Kemp, P., LeMoine, S., Long, T., Muhlenhaupt, M., Prelock, P., Schefkind, S., Stayton, V., & Ziegler, D. (2019). Finding a common lens: Competencies across professional disciplines providing early childhood intervention. *Infants and Young Children, 32*(4), 280–293. 10.1097/IYC.0000000000000153

Buettner, C. K., Hur, E. H., Jeon, L., & Andrews, D. W. (2016). What are we teaching the teachers? Child development curricula in U.S. higher education. *Child and Youth Care Forum*, 45(1), 155–175. 10.1007/s10566-015-9323-0

California Department of Education. (2024, April 4). *Fingertip facts on education in California*. CDE. https://www.cde.ca.gov/ds/ad/ceffingertipfacts.asp

California Department of Education. (n.d.-a). *2018–19 enrollment by ethnicity and grade: State report*. CDE. https://data1.cde.ca.gov/dataquest/dqcensus/EnrEthGrd.aspx?cds=00&agglevel=state&year=2018-19

California Department of Education. (n.d.-b). *2020–2021 enrollment by English language acquisition status (ELAS) (with county data): Statewide report*. CDE. https://dq.cde.ca.gov/dataquest/longtermel/ELASLevels.aspx?Cds=00&agglevel=State&year=2020-21

California Department of Education. (n.d.-c). *English learner students by language by grade: State of California 202021*. CDE. https://dq.cde.ca.gov/dataquest/SpringData/StudentsByLanguage.aspx?Level=State&TheYear=202021&SubGroup=All&ShortYear=2021&GenderGroup=B&CDSCode=00000000000000&RecordType=EL

Carver-Thomas, D., Kini, T., & Burns, D. (2020). *Sharpening the divide: How California's teacher shortages expand inequality* (research brief). Palo Alto, CA: Learning Policy Institute.

Carver-Thomas, D., Leung, M., & Burns, D. (2021). *California teachers and COVID-19: How the pandemic is impacting the teacher workforce*. Learning Policy Institute.

CAST. (2018). *Universal design for learning guidelines version 2.2*. CAST. http://udlguidelines.cast.org

Cénat, J. M., Dalexis, R. D., Kokou-Kpolou, C. K., Mukunzi, J. N., & Rousseau, C. (2020). Social inequalities and collateral damages of the COVID-19 pandemic: When basic needs challenge mental health care. *International Journal of Public Health*, 65(6), 717–718. https://www.ncbi.nlm.nih.gov/pmc/articles/PMC7348102/. 10.1007/s00038-020-01426-y32651593

Center for Disease Control and Prevention. (2021, August 23). *Adverse childhood experiences (ACEs): Preventing early trauma to improve adult health*. CDC. https://www.cdc.gov/vitalsigns/aces/index.html

Center on the Developing Child at Harvard University. (2016). *From best practices to breakthrough impacts: A science-based approach to building more promising future for young children and families.* Center on the Developing Child at Harvard University. https://developingchild.harvard.edu/resources/from-best-practices-to -breakthrough-impacts/

Center on the Developing Child at Harvard University. (n.d.). *How racism can affect child development.* Center on the Developing Child at Harvard University. https:// developingchild.harvard.edu/resources/racism-and-ecd/

Chudzik, M., Corr, C., & Wolowiec-Fisher, K. (2023). Trauma: Early childhood special education teachers' attitudes and experiences. *Early Childhood Education Journal*, 51(1), 189–200. 10.1007/s10643-021-01302-1

Cole, S. F., Eisner, A., Gregory, M., & Ristuccia, J. (2013). *Helping traumatized children learn: Creating and advocating for trauma-sensitive schools(Vol. 2).* Massachusetts Advocates for Children. https://traumasensitiveschools.org/tlpi-publications/ download-a-free-copy-of-a-guide-to-creating-trauma-sensitive-schools/

Council on Social Work Education. (2015). *2015 Educational policy and accreditation standards for baccalaureate and master's social work programs.* https:// www.cswe.org/getmedia/23a35a39-78c7-453f-b805-b67f1dca2ee5/2015-epas-and -glossary.pdf

Delahooke, M. (2017). *Social and emotional development.* PSESI Publications & Media.

Derman-Sparks, L., & Edwards, J. O. (2019). Understanding anti-bias education: Bringing the four core goals to every facet of your curriculum. *Young Children*, 74(5), 6–13. https://www.jstor.org/stable/26842300

Derman-Sparks, L., Edwards, J. O., & Goins, C. M. (2020). *Anti-bias education for young children and ourselves* (2nd ed.). National Association for the Education of Young Children.

Division for Early Childhood of the Council for Exceptional Children. (2014). *DEC recommended practices.* DEC. http://www.dec-sped.org/recommendedpractices

Division for Early Childhood of the Council for Exceptional Children. (2020). *Initial practice based professional preparation standards for early interventionist/early childhood special educators (EI/ECSE; Initial birth through age 8).* Division for Early Childhood. https://www.dec-sped.org/_files/ugd/95f212_4d9c51a4b6e5 4e67a2ba1df3541903da.pdf?index=true

Division for Early Childhood of the Council for Exceptional Children. (2023). *Racial equity point of view*. https://divisionearlychildhood.egnyte.com/dl/GPVEY6LbYW

Division for Early Childhood of the Council for Exceptional Children, & National Association for the Education of Young Children. (2009). *Early childhood inclusion: A joint position statement of the Division for the Early Childhood (DEC) and the National Association for the Education of Young Children (NAEYC)*. The University of North Carolina at Chapel Hill; FPG Child Development Institute. https://www.naeyc.org/sites/default/files/globally-shared/downloads/PDFs/resources/position-statements/ps_inclusion_dec_naeyc_ec.pdf

Education Policy at AIR. (2016). *California's emerging teacher shortage: New evidence and policy responses*. AIR. https://www.air.org/sites/default/files/Program%20-%20final.pdf

Farquharson, W., & Thornton, C. J. (2020). Debate: Exposing the most serious infirmity—Racism's impact on health in the era of COVID-19. *Child and Adolescent Mental Health*, 25(3), 182–183. 10.1111/camh.1240732686292

Gerhardt, S. (2015). *Why love matters: How affection shapes a baby's brain*. Routledge.

Gu, Q., & Day, C. (2007). Teachers resilience: A necessary condition for effectiveness. *Teaching and Teacher Education*, 23(8), 1302–1316. 10.1016/j.tate.2006.06.006

Harris, N. B. (2018). *The deepest well: Healing the long-term effects of childhood adversity*. Houghton Mifflin Harcourt.

Harry, B., & Ocasio-Stoutenburg, L. (2020). *Meeting families where they are: Building equity through advocacy with diverse schools and communities*. Teachers College Press.

Healy, K. (2014). *Social work theories in context: Creating frameworks for practice*. Bloomsbury Academic. 10.1007/978-1-137-02425-1

Heard-Garris, N. J., Cale, M., Camaj, L., Hamati, M. C., & Dominguez, T. P. (2018). Transmitting trauma: A systematic review of vicarious racism and child health. *Social Science & Medicine*, 199, 230–240. 10.1016/j.socscimed.2017.04.01828456418

Heffron, M. C., & Murch, T. (2010). Reflective supervision and leadership in infant and early childhood programs. *Zero to Three*.

Herrenkohl, T. I., Scott, D., Higgins, D. J., Klika, J. B., & Lonne, B. (2021). How COVID-19 is placing vulnerable children at risk and why we need a different approach to child welfare. *Child Maltreatment*, 26(1), 9–16. 10.1177/107755952096391633025825

Individuals With Disabilities Education Act, 20 U.S.C. § 1400 (2004). https://www.congress.gov/108/plaws/publ446/PLAW-108publ446.pdf

Johnson, J., Rahn, N. L., & Bricker, D. (2015). *An activity-based approach to early intervention* (4th ed.). Brookes Publishing.

Jones, L., Bellis, M. A., Wood, S., Hughes, K., McCoy, E., Eckley, L., Bates, G., Mikton, C., Shakespeare, T., & Officer, A. (2012). Prevalence and risk of violence against children with disabilities: A systematic review and meta-analysis of observational studies. *Lancet*, 380(9845), 899–907. 10.1016/S0140-6736(12)60692-822795511

Kart, A., & Kart, M. (2021). Academic and social effects of inclusion on students without disabilities: A review of the literature. *Education Sciences*, 11(16), 1–13. 10.3390/educsci11010016

Lawrence, S., Smith, S., & Banerjee, R. (2016). *Preschool inclusion: Key findings from research and implications for policy*. Child Care & Early Education Research Connections. https://www.nccp.org/wp-content/uploads/2020/05/text_1154.pdf

Learning Policy Institute. (2022). *Whole child policy toolkit*. Learning Policy Institute. https://www.wholechildpolicy.org/rkdl-page/full/whole-child-policy-toolkit.pdf

Lieberman, A. F., & Van Horn, P. (2005). Don't hit my mommy!: A manual for child-parent psychotherapy with young witnesses of family violence. *Zero to Three*.

Lin, V. W., Lin, J., & Zhang, X. (2016). U.S. social workforce report card: Forecasting nationwide shortages. *Social Work*, 61(1), 7–15. 10.1093/sw/swv04726897994

Little, C. (2020). Collaboration. In Spandagou, I., Little, C., Evans, D., & Bonati, M. L. (Eds.), *Inclusive education in schools and early childhood settings* (pp. 85–92). Springer. 10.1007/978-981-15-2541-4_8

Lloyd, C., King, R., & Chenoweth, L. (2009). Social work, stress, and burnout: A review. *Journal of Mental Health (Abingdon, England)*, 11(3), 255–265. 10.1080/09638230020023642

Love, H. R., & Beneke, M. R. (2021). Pursuing justice-driven inclusive education research: Disability critical race theory (DisCrit) in early childhood. *Topics in Early Childhood Special Education*, 41(1), 31–44. 10.1177/0271121421990833

Magee, R. V. (2019). *The inner work of racial justice: Healing ourselves and transforming our communities through mindfulness*. TarcherPerigee.

McClain, M. P. (2021). Teacher candidates' perceptions of preparedness of teaching students who experience trauma. *Journal of Teacher Education and Educators*, 10(1), 5–23. https://files.eric.ed.gov/fulltext/EJ1310243.pdf

Meek, S., Smith, L., Allen, R., Catherine, E., Edyburn, K., Williams, C., Fabes, R., McIntosh, K., Garica, E., Takanishi, R., Gordon, L., Jimenez-Castellanos, O., Hemmeter, M. L., Gilliam, W., & Pontier, R. (2020). *Start with equity: From the early years to the early grades*. Children's Equity Project; Bipartisan Policy Center. https://bipartisanpolicy.org/download/?file=/wp-content/uploads/2020/07/cep-report-071320-final.pdf

Miller, D. (2018). *The space between: Current practices and perceptions regarding trauma-informed supports and special education services* [Doctoral dissertation, University of Illinois at Urbana-Champaign]. Graduate Dissertations and Theses at Illinois. http://hdl.handle.net/2142/102769

Mitsch, M. K., Collins, B., Friesen, A., & Hermoso, J. C. R. (2023). Social emotional development and mental health: Special education and social work interdisciplinary collaboration. In Slanda, D., & Pike, L. (Eds.), *Handbook of research on interdisciplinary preparation for equitable special education* (pp. 468–494). IGI Global. 10.4018/978-1-6684-6438-0.ch023

Mitsch, M. K., Weglarz-Ward, J., & Branch, J. (2022). "I'm new here": Leveraging responsibilities, relationships, and resources for new faculty leaders. *Young Exceptional Children*, 26(4), 193–206. 10.1177/10962506221111362

Mosle, A., & Sims, M. (2021). *State of the field: Two-generation approaches to family well-being*. Aspen Institute.

National Association for the Education of Young Children. (2019). *Advancing equity in early childhood education A position statement of the National Association of the Education of Young Children*. NAEYC. https://www.naeyc.org/sites/default/files/globally-shared/downloads/PDFs/resources/position-statements/advancingequitypositionstatement.pdf

National Association for the Education of Young Children. (2020a). *Developmentally appropriate practice: A position statement of the National Association of the Education of Young Children*. NAEYC. https://www.naeyc.org/sites/default/files/globally-shared/downloads/pdfs/resources/position-statements/dap-statement_0.pdf

National Association for the Education of Young Children. (2020b). *Professional standards and competencies for early childhood educators*. NAEYC. https://www.naeyc.org/sites/default/files/globally-shared/downloads/pdfs/resources/position-statements/standards_and_competencies_ps.pdf

National Association of Social Work. (2015). *Standards and indicators for cultural competence*. NASW. https://www.socialworkers.org/linkclick.aspx?fileticket=7dvckzayumk%3d&portali=0

National Child Traumatic Stress Network. (n.d.). *About child trauma*. NCTSN. https://www.nctsn.org/what-is-child-trauma/about-child-trauma

Nelson, C. A., Scott, R. D., Bhutta, Z. A., Harris, N. B., Danese, A., & Samara, M. (2020). Adversity in childhood is linked to mental and physical health throughout life. *BMJ (Clinical Research Ed.)*, 371, m3048. 10.1136/bmj.m304833115717

Nicholson, J., Kuhl, K., Maniates, H., Lin, B., & Bonetti, S. (2020). A review of the literature on leadership in early childhood: Examining epistemological foundation and considerations of social justice. *Early Child Development and Care*, 190(2), 91–122. 10.1080/03004430.2018.1455036

Odom, S. L., Vitztum, J., Wolery, R., Lieber, J., Sandall, S., Hanson, M. J., Beckman, P., Schwartz, I., & Horn, E. (2004). Preschool inclusion in the United States: A review of research from an ecological systems perspective. *Journal of Research in Special Educational Needs*, 4(1), 17–49. 10.1111/J.1471-3802.2004.00016.x

Ondrasek, N., Carver-Thomas, D., Scott, C., & Darling-Hammond, L. (2020). *California's special education teacher shortage* (report). Palo Alto, CA: Policy Analysis for California Education.

Osborne, K. R., Caughy, M. O., Oshri, A., Smith, E. P., & Owen, M. T. (2021). Racism and preparation for bias within African American families. *Cultural Diversity & Ethnic Minority Psychology*, 27(2), 269–279. 10.1037/cdp000033932297761

Park, E.-Y., & Shin, M. (2020). A meta-analysis of special education teachers' burnout. *SAGE Open*, 10(2). Advance online publication. 10.1177/2158244020918297

Perry, B. D., & Szalavitz, M. (2006). *The boy who was raised as a dog: And other stories from a child psychiatrist's notebook—What traumatized children can teach us about loss, love, and healing*. Basic.

Podolsky, A., & Kini, T. (2016). *How effective are loan forgiveness and service scholarships for recruiting teachers?* [Policy brief]. Learning Policy Institute. https://learningpolicyinstitute.org/media/185/download?inline&file=how_effective_are-loan_forgiveness_and_service-scholarships_recruiting_teachers.pdf

Power to the Profession Task Force. (2020). *Unifying framework for the early childhood profession*. Power to the Profession Task Force. https://powertotheprofession.org/wp-content/uploads/2020/03/power-to-profession-framework-03312020-web.pdf

Pretti-Frontczak, K., & Grisham, J. (2022). *Assessing young children in inclusive settings* (2nd ed.). Brookes Publishing.

Purtle, J. (2018). Systematic review of evaluations of trauma-informed organizational interventions that include staff trainings. *Trauma, Violence & Abuse*, 21(4), 725–740. 10.1177/15248380187913043007982

Raver, S. A., & Childress, D. C. (2015). *Family-centered early intervention*. Brookes Publishing.

Schore, A. N. (2003). *Affect regulation and the repair of the self*. W.W. Norton & Company.

Shonkoff, J. P., Garner, A. S., Siegel, B. S., Dobbins, M. I., Earls, M. F., Garner, A. S., McGuinn, L., Pascoe, J., & Wood, D. L. (2012). The lifelong effects of early childhood adversity and toxic stress. *Pediatrics*, 129(1), e232–e246. 10.1542/peds.2011-266322201156

Staats, C. (2016). Understanding implicit bias: What educators should know. *American Educator*, 39(4), 29–33, 43. https://files.eric.ed.gov/fulltext/EJ1086492.pdf

Steed, E. A., Rausch, A., Strain, P. S., Bold, E., & Leech, N. (2023). High-quality inclusion in preschool settings: A survey of early childhood personnel. *Topics in Early Childhood Special Education*, 43(2), 142–155. 10.1177/02711214211063921

Substance Abuse and Mental Health Services Administration. (2014). *SAMHSA's concept of trauma and guidance for a trauma-informed approach* (HHS Publication No. [SMA] 14-4884). SAMHSA. https://store.samhsa.gov/sites/default/files/sma14-4884.pdf

Teasley, M. L. (2016). Related services personnel and evidence-based practice: Past and present challenges. *Children & Schools*, 38(1), 5–8. 10.1093/cs/cdv039

Tomlinson, M. (2015). Infant mental health in the next decade: A call for action. *Infant Mental Health Journal*, 36(6), 538–541. 10.1002/imhj.2153726514552

Trent, M., Dooley, D. G., Dougé, J., Cavanaugh, R. M.Jr, Lacroix, A. E., Fanburg, J., Rahmandar, M. H., Hornberger, L. L., Schneider, M. B., Yen, S., Chilton, L. A., Green, A. E., Dilley, K. J., Gutierrez, J. R., Duffee, J. H., Keane, V. A., Krugman, S. D., McKelvey, C. D., Linton, J. M., & Wallace, S. B. (2019). The impact of racism on child and adolescent health. *Pediatrics*, 144(2), e20191765. 10.1542/peds.2019-176531358665

Turnbull, A. P., Summers, J. A., & Brotherson, M. J. (1984). *Working with families with disabled members: A family systems approach*. University of Kansas.

Turnbull, A. P., Turnbull, H. R., Erwin, E., Soodak, L., & Shogren, K. (2014). *Families, professionals, and exceptionality: Positive outcomes through partnerships and trust* (7th ed.). Pearson.

Urbani, J. M., Collado, C., Manalo, A., & Gonzalez, N. (2022). Building the on-ramp to inclusion: Developing critical consciousness in future early childhood educators. *Issues in Teacher Education*, 31(2), 91–121. https://www.itejournal.org/wp-content/pdfs-issues/summer-2022/09urbanietal.pdf

U.S. Bureau of Labor Statistics. (2021a). *Social workers*. BLS. https://www.bls.gov/ooh/community-and-social-service/social-workers.htm

U.S. Bureau of Labor Statistics. (2021b). *Special education teachers*. BLS. https://www.bls.gov/ooh/education-training-and-library/special-education-teachers.htm

U.S. Department of Education. (2016). *Racial and ethnic disparities in special education: A multi-year disproportionality analysis by state, analysis category, and race/ethnicity*. USDoE. https://www2.ed.gov/programs/osepidea/618-data/LEA-racial-ethnic-disparities-tables/disproportionality-analysis-by-state-analysis-category.pdf

U.S. Department of Education. (2017). *Teacher shortage areas nationwide: Listing 1990–1991 through 2017–2018*. USDoE. https://www2.ed.gov/about/offices/list/ope/pol/ateachershortageareasreport2017-18.pdf

U.S. Department of Education. (2021). *Individuals with Disabilities Education Act (IDEA) database: Digest of Education Statistics 2020*. Office of Special Education Programs. https://data.ed.gov/dataset/idea-section-618-data-products-state-level-data-files

U.S. Department of Health and Human Services. (2022). *Protective factors and adverse childhood experiences*. USDoE. https://www.childwelfare.gov/topics/preventing/preventionmonth/about/protective-factors-aces/

U.S. Department of Health and Human Services, & U.S. Department of Education. (2015a). *Policy statement on inclusion of children with disabilities in early childhood programs*. USDoE. https://www2.ed.gov/policy/speced/guid/earlylearning/joint-statement-full-text.pdf

U.S. Department of Health and Human Services, & U.S. Department of Education. (2015b). *Policy statement on expulsion and suspension policies in early childhood settings*. OESE. https://oese.ed.gov/files/2020/07/policy-statement-ece-expulsions-suspensions.pdf

van der Kolk, B. (2014). *The body keeps the score: Brain, mind, and body in the healing of trauma*. Penguin Books.

Weglarz-Ward, J., Mitsch, M. K., Branch, J., Yarczower, M. B., & Anang, C. (2024). Family practices in educator licensure: A content analysis of U.S. state requirements. *Journal of Early Childhood Teacher Education*, 1–19. 10.1080/10901027.2024.2314290

WestEd. (2012). *Early childhood mental health: Raising awareness, taking action. R & D Alert, 13*(3), 1–3. https://www.wested.org/wp-content/uploads/2016/11/1372730177article_earlychildhoodmentalhealth_2012-3.pdf

Wood, J. L., Hilton, A. A., & Nevarez, C. (2015). Faculty of color and white faculty: An analysis of service in colleges of education in Arizona public university system. *Journal of the Professoriate*, 8(1), 85–109. https://caarpweb.org/wp-content/uploads/2015/06/8-1_Wood_p85.pdf

Chapter 8
Mathematics for Social Justice:
Building on Students' Agency, Empathy, and Mathematics Ingenuity

Maria del Rosario Zavala
San Francisco State University, USA

Jennifer Ward
https://orcid.org/0000-0002-7068-3826
Kennesaw State University, USA

Courtney Koestler
Ohio University, USA

Tonya Bartell
https://orcid.org/0000-0002-0820-9699
Michigan State University, USA

ABSTRACT

Early childhood mathematics instruction is child-centered and play-based, supporting children to learn foundational mathematical concepts like counting, quantity, and pattern through hands-on experiences. Recent work in ethnic studies and social justice shows that young children are keenly aware of their own identities, empathic, and ready to take action in the world in age-appropriate ways. How might this research inform our understanding of mathematics instruction in early childhood inclusion spaces? Mathematics for social justice is a way to support identity development and mathematics learning, while challenging the medical models of mathematics

DOI: 10.4018/979-8-3693-0924-7.ch008

that dominate special education discourses. In this chapter, the authors introduce principles for social justice mathematics for early childhood. They build on Learning for Justice's social justice standards and illustrate them through a classroom vignette. They conclude with advice to educators about engaging with social justice mathematics through attention to context, content, and the "who, when, and how" of social justice mathematics lessons.

INTRODUCTION

Young children make sense of the world using everything they know– their whole selves– including critical and quantitative reasoning. When teaching young children mathematics, dominant arguments in the field center on developmentally appropriate strategies and allowing exploration and play. Some go further to include connections to lived experiences and using familiar objects in instruction. Children certainly benefit from these strategies. However, research has shown that young children also are keenly aware of their own identities, are learning how to name and express empathy, and are able to act as agents for social change in age-appropriate ways (Derman-Sparks & Edwards, 2009; Souto-Manning, 2013, Souto-Manning & Rabadi-Raol, 2018; Zermeño, 2022).

Early childhood educators interested in equity and expanding opportunities in mathematics might ask the question, *how do we bridge what we know about the capacity for empathy and agency development in young children with the ingenuity they bring to mathematics learning, and to what end?* Mathematics for social justice offers a way to understand and design learning experiences for young children, in ways that account for mathematical idea development, identity development, and cultivating a sense of having responsibility and ability to respond to issues in the world. As we argue in this chapter, mathematics instruction that takes a social justice perspective is an avenue for inclusion and equity through principles and instructional strategies that humanize mathematics and de-pathologize traditional discourses of special education. In this chapter, we introduce principles for social justice mathematics instruction for early childhood contexts. We build on 4 domains of Learning for Justice's Social Justice Standards, to offer a mathematical interpretation, and illustrate them in action through a classroom vignette. We conclude with some advice to teachers and researchers about the ways such principles can inform our everyday instruction, and our understanding of the nature of learning and teaching mathematics to young children.

Why Social Justice Math in Early Childhood Inclusion Spaces?

Children from an early age begin to construct knowledge from their experiences within the world (Rogoff, 2008). Widely shared ideas centered on the children's learning in mathematics, such as learning trajectories, (Clements & Sarama, 2014) are often taken up in early childhood classrooms, however reliance solely on development is largely reflective of the norms in western culture (Woodhead, 2006). Strong mathematics curriculum in the early years emphasizes connections between concrete and abstract thinking about concepts, problem solving, and play-based experiences (NAEYC, 2010), however where these resources fall short is often on the connection to real-world experiences, situating mathematics learned in school as different from mathematics learned at homes and in communities. Early childhood mathematics should be centered on topics that children care about, integrated in meaningful, thoughtful ways (NAEYC, 2020).

Mathematics itself cannot be disembedded from social context, as connections between mathematics and knowledge of the world become entangled as children transform their mathematical knowledge into meaningful thinking during problem-based experiences that draw upon their world (Gonzalez et. al, 2001). Thoughtful and purposeful integration of social justice concepts and standards within the early childhood mathematics classroom compliments these student-centered approaches and is essential for children to understand life, power, and social issues (Gonzalez, 2009, Koestler et. al, 2023). Where many adults may underestimate the abilities of young children to talk about justice centered topics (e.g., Sullivan et. al, 2021) teachers often recognize these conversations as impactful for young children's growth as change-agents (Nieto, 2000). We are advocating for children to experience math that is relevant, engaging, and applicable to their school lives. Moreso, we are positioning children as capable of engaging in this type of mathematics learning.

Further, it is crucial for early childhood educators to foster a learning (mathematics) environment that supports children in developing their social and cultural identities. Teachers must also be mindful of their own biases that shape their practices and interactions with the children in their classrooms and their families, especially of those who have different social, cultural, and linguistic backgrounds from themselves (NAEYC, 2020; Koestler et al, 2023).

Mathematics for social justice is fundamentally an orientation to teaching mathematics that embraces human-centered instruction, relevant contexts for problem posing and problem solving, and supports the connection between mathematical exploration and real-life action on social issues. Children are supported to *read* the world with mathematics (i.e., understand how mathematics shows up in their lives), as well as *write* the world with mathematics (i.e., use mathematical reasoning to think through and even take action to make change for the better) (Gutstein, 2006).

In their book on early elementary mathematics to explore, understand, and respond to social injustice, Koestler et al (2023) describe teaching mathematics for social justice (TMSJ) as "teaching that builds mathematical literacy, supports children to use mathematics as a tool for social change, empowers children as agents of change, and rehumanizes mathematics education" (p. 10).

Readers might ask, what is dehumanizing about mathematics, especially the mathematics that young children engage in? One way mathematics is dehumanizing is through claims of objectivity and neutrality. Tate (2012) describes how people rarely count in the real world for the sake of counting itself, that we usually count with a purpose, and often the purpose is related to power somehow - to gain, to lose, to account for the order of things. In the real world, we center our experiences as we do mathematics that impacts our lives. In contrast, in mathematics classrooms we usually teach mathematics as though it was divorced from the real world (Verschaffel et al, 2000), somehow objective and neutral, introducing a level of depersonalization, or dehumanization. A deeper discussion of what it means to re-humanize mathematics can be found in the work of Goffney and Gutiérrez (2018), where they describe rehumanizing practices in mathematics education as including, among others, attention to culture and histories, broadening what counts as mathematics beyond the scope of westernized knowledge and into everyday practices, and expanding beyond a focus on the brain (e.g., "mathematical thinking") to include emotions, senses, and connections we feel as people.

The idea that children learn mathematics through relevant contexts is well established by research such as the Cognitively Guided Instruction studies, which showed that children learn about relationships between quantities and the four fundamental arithmetic operations through stories contextualized in familiar contexts and that teachers who know about the ways children think about these relationships are more effective teachers (Carpenter et al, 1996, 2000). Contextualizing mathematics should be not just about any story problems, but also social issue-oriented problems (e.g., Koestler et al, 2023), which add a connection between children's understanding of everyday situations and their sense of justice and fairness. Still, research on mathematics instruction for social justice has mostly taken place in middle and high school classrooms. Studies usually are small scale and based in classrooms where teachers are studying the impact of their instruction on their students' mathematical learning and sense of agency. Some of this research points to empowering children to use mathematics to get a deeper understanding of how social issues impact their communities, such as the many examples contained in the Rethinking Schools Publication *Rethinking Mathematics* (Gutstein & Peterson, 2012).

Harper (2019) undertook a metasynthesis of classroom social justice mathematics implementation and found that social justice lessons provided opportunities for students to discuss racism and other forms of injustice, but with variation into how and whether racism was explicitly addressed. But she also found that social issues did not detract from the mathematics, rather the mathematics was rigorous: "for the most part, students engaged in deep, substantial, and authentic mathematical analysis of social justice issues." (p. 292).

However, Kokka (2017) also found that the impact of social justice mathematics is not singular, rather one's background and experiences matter. For example, she compared the learning experiences of students in two distinct sixth grade classrooms, one with more affluence than the other. The more affluent students learned to be increasingly empathetic and gained new understanding of issues, while less-affluent students (also more students of color) experienced stronger emotional responses to the social contexts, as they were usually more directly affected. These results suggest that teachers do need to be considerate of how they engage students with the contexts they choose, so that students are not left feeling there is no hope. Such considerations are also reminiscent of recent work on climate justice, such as Sisk-Hilton's (2024), which advocates for ways to teach children climate change science while also teaching practical steps they can take to not lose hope when faced with the size of the problem.

Social justice mathematics lessons rely on 4 domains from Learning for Justice's Social Justice Standards: Identity, Diversity, Justice, and Action. In our work (e.g., Koestler et al 2023), we draw on Yeh's (2021) and Learning for Justice's *Toolkit for 'Mathematics in Context: The Pedagogy of Liberation"* that adapts the social justice standards specifically for mathematics. Each domain is described more in the table below, along with examples of what it means that teachers do and what children do when these domains are in action.

Table 1. Learning for justice (2021) domains from the social justice standards, adapted for mathematics

Domain	Teachers	Children
Identity exploring who we are and where we are from	● Re-center identities, perspectives, and knowledge traditions that have often been silenced. ● Attend to and honor students' multiple social identities in curricular design and its implementation. ● View students as competent mathematical beings in which their lived experiences and community and cultural ways of knowing are leveraged during mathematics instruction. ● Deconstruct negative stereotypes about children' mathematical identities and about who can and cannot do mathematics.	● Recognize that people's multiple identities interact and create unique and complex individuals that contribute to their learning of mathematics. ● Develop language and historical and cultural knowledge to affirm and describe their membership in multiple identity groups and their contribution to mathematics. ● Express self-love, pride, confidence, and healthy self-esteem about themselves and their community as mathematical thinkers and learners. ● Recognize the traits of the dominant culture, their own culture, and other cultures and understand how to negotiate their own identity in multiple spaces.
Diversity creating a climate of respect and empathy for differences	● Design curriculum and implementation that honor diversity in mathematical reasoning, sense-making and engagement as strengths for individual and collective learning. ● Create multidimensional classrooms, raising classmates' expectations for contributions from each and every child in their classroom. ● Deconstruct stereotypes about students' mathematical identities and who can and cannot do mathematics.	● Express comfort in working with and learning from people who are both similar to and different from them and engage respectfully in collaborative work and discussion. ● Express curiosity about the mathematical contribution and experiences of others and exchange ideas and perspectives in an open-minded way. ● Respond to diversity by building respect, understanding, connections, and empathy for different ways of knowing and being in mathematics classrooms.
Justice examining oppression and injustice, towards a more justice outcome	● Locate causes of inequalities in social conditions (e.g., tracking, ability grouping, Eurocentric curriculum) rather than believe conditions are inherent within individuals. ● Recognize inequities of the larger society are replicated in common structures and practices that perpetuate disparities in mathematics learning opportunities based on race, class, language, gender, and ability status. ● Explicitly shift the power dynamic between student-and-teacher and student-and-student by centering identities, perspectives, and knowledge traditions that have often been silenced.	● Recognize stereotypes and pervasive myths in mathematics around what mathematics is and what it means to know and be good at math. ● Recognize that power and privilege influence relationships on interpersonal, intergroup, and institutional levels and consider how they have been affected by those dynamics in their mathematics learning experiences and in the world. ● Use mathematics as a tool to identify unfairness on the individual, interpersonal, and institutional or systemic level.

continued on following page

Table 1. Continued

Domain	Teachers	Children
Action engaging agency to make change	● Engage in community- and place-based pedagogies and experiences that bridge mathematics classrooms with community and social movements. ● Understand learning can emerge from a problem-posing pedagogy, designed around the ideas, hopes, doubt, fears, joy, and questions that occur when students use mathematics to develop "generative themes" about their world. ● Provide students consistent opportunity to recognize their own responsibility to stand up to exclusion, prejudice, and injustice.	● Understand the nature and creation of social oppression and feel empowered to intervene and seek equity. ● Make principled decisions about when and how to take a stand against bias and status differences within the mathematics classroom and in their communities. ● Plan and carry out collective action using mathematics as a tool to address injustice in the world.

Adapted from Learning for Justice/Yeh & Dingle (2021), and reproduced from Koestler et al, 2023, pp. 18-22.

Historically, mathematics learning discourses of students with learning differences treat children as lacking knowledge and being in need of remediation. The research is replete with diagnosing mathematical shortcomings or problems in children, prescribing specific interventions, reassessing and repeating (Tan et al, 2022). Mathematics educators focused on special education have also called for a rehumanizing of mathematics for students identified with learning differences (Yeh et al., 2020; Lewis et al., 2018; Lambert et al., 2018; Tan et al., 2022). Alternatively, Yeh (2023) argues that a counter to such dehumanizing discourses is to view learning through a DisCrit lens. Yeh (2023) challenges us to rethink what is made to be normative in mathematics, and therefore who gets to be seen as "normal". She describes a framework to aid teachers in the work of striving towards disability justice in mathematics by repurposing teacher noticing with an intersectional lens, and provides two reasons for such work:

First, ... There is a need to attend to how racism and ableism are inter-reliant processes built into the beliefs, policies, and practices of the mathematics education systems. Second, the commitment here is to not only uncover intersecting systems of ableism and racism but to also identify ways to design classrooms as spaces of subversion and refusal. Ultimately, the goal is to take an intersectional perspective to make visible to teachers, teacher educators, and mathematics education researchers how disability is fluid and intersectional, constructed within dominant sociohistorical discourses and material realities within US society, schooling, and the mathematics classroom. (pp. 4-5).

Social justice mathematics, with its explicit embracing of diverse perspectives and ways of being, can be a central part of this "subversion". Social justice mathematics lessons elicit perspectives, feelings, and interpretations from students in such a way that their unique experiences are valued. Their communities become contexts for exploring mathematics. In a social justice mathematics lesson, teachers can broaden what counts as valued knowledge beyond just the mathematical calculations, to include often devalued community knowledge and contextual knowledge. For example, when introducing the question of "is this fair?" into a mathematics lesson with students with learning differences we begin to change the trajectory towards a more humanizing experience (Kemper & Zavala, 2014). Therefore, we argue that this pivot towards centering students' experiences and sense of justice when teaching mathematics is especially important to rehumanize mathematics for students with learning differences.

A Classroom Vignette

We offer the following vignette, written in the first person by co-author Jennifer Ward, based on her experience as a teacher in a year 4 classroom (e.g., preschool with 4-year-old children). As Jennifer recounts the vignette, she also provides insight into her own thought process along the way. We invite readers to reflect on the vignette through the domains described in Table 1. We offer a brief analysis afterwards.

Setting the Stage

Jennifer Ward, or Ms. Ward to her students, had worked in early childhood and elementary classrooms for most of her career. Prior to her work in this classroom, she had completed coursework for her doctoral degree in both early childhood and mathematics education and worked as the pedagogical liaison between the university and its lab campus preschool. As part of this role, she had spent the last year working with teachers at the preschool in thinking about their knowledge of, planning for, implementation, and documentation of children's mathematics learning. This included working with teachers in classrooms to co-plan and co-teach lessons, work in small groups with children, and support the sharing of children's assessment data during family conferences. The school itself used inquiry centered teaching and learning so that curricular design was negotiated between teachers, who made sure standards were being met, and children, who provided their interests and questions to help drive the topics to be explored. Because of these experiences, she was uniquely situated to design lessons and facilitate justice-centered conversations with children in the classroom.

Children at the school were a mix of children who lived in the local community, and children of faculty, staff, or students at the university. As part of school-wide efforts to get to know families' backgrounds and experiences better, school staff, including Jennifer, had spent time during planning meetings thinking about the ways in which families might contribute to learning experiences in the classroom, and how teachers might better leverage the knowledge of families in their instructional planning.

Launching the Lesson on Food Insecurity

Recently, in a transitional kindergarten classroom summer session, I wanted to reinforce the idea of instant number recognition, or subitizing (Clements, 1999), and comparing quantities for my youngest learners. From teaching Kindergarten and first grade, I knew the importance of subitizing and what it contributed to students' ability to count as well as general number sense. I knew using dice supported the development of this concept and anticipated that children would be able to grasp this concept quickly. This, in turn, would allow time for more emphasis on the social justice issue I was weaving into the lesson: food insecurity in our community.

My desire to focus on this particular social justice issue came from a recent project the students had completed where they were designing a classroom pizza garden, which led to studying the location of community gardens. This led to a conversation about where different supermarkets and grocery stores were located in the community. Children had access to maps and data points that showed the overall SES (represented by color) of certain areas within the county, seeing the disparity in food access in places with lower (darker) colors on the map. At one point during this exploration a child (Anthony) began to note that a narrative he had heard was that if you didn't have enough food you should "just go get a job". Other children questioned why some people had an excess of food, while others did not have enough access to food. As we progressed, students wondered about families who might not have access to community garden space. To me, the stage was set to explore the narratives and beliefs children held about food insecurity, and to use mathematics in our exploration.

Around this time, I was also involved in work with a local organization and the school system on locating food deserts in our community and thinking about how we get families in these areas access to fresh fruits and vegetables. From this work, I knew that one out of every five children in the United States was food insecure and needed to determine a way to present this ratio to the children (Feeding America, 2024). While none of the students in our classroom space were considered food insecure (as well as the school itself provided breakfast, snacks, and lunch daily through a food program), the issue was prevalent in our community and impacted children the same age as those in our classroom. I happened to stumble across some manipulatives shaped like small people that I had packed in my giant teacher tub of mathematics manipulatives. I pulled the bag out of the top of the tub, looking at the green, yellow, red and blue people in assorted sizes. *I could use these. These could help to present the one out of five ratio.* I took one yellow person and four green people from the bag and linked them together. *I think this will work. This might just be the concrete representation I need.*

Getting settled, the children circled around me and the people-shaped manipulatives that I had strategically laid on the carpet; the yellow person isolated and the four green people connected to one another, but not yet to the yellow person.

"Can we count the number of green people? Who thinks they can count them for me? You do, Andrew? Okay, count nice and loud for me. You ready?"

"One, two, three, four…." The group joined in as Andrew reached two. Natalie and Andrea continued to go onto five, before stopping mid-word, realizing there were only four green people and giggling at their error.

"What's the yellow one?" Anthony was trying to move our discussion along, noticing the yellow one off to the side.

"How many green people do we have?" I asked, reinforcing cardinality as part of our counting.

"Four!" The group responded chorally, shouting with excitement.

"Okay, how many yellow people?

"One!"

"Okay," I continued, *"We are going to put them together and see how many we have now."*

Anthony sprang forward to touch each person as he counted aloud. "Five, that means there are five. One, two, three, four, five."

"Okay, Anthony thinks there are five; that one plus four equals five. Do we agree or disagree? Let's count them all to see if he is right." The group began counting, arriving at five and determining that Anthony was correct in his thinking.

"So here is what I want you all to know about these five people. Last time we were together, we looked at maps of our community. In our community, one out of every five people don't have enough food to eat."

"Why?" Andrea sat looking at me, mouth open in shock. I paused at Andrea's question. I still felt some sense of imposter syndrome even after researching mathematics and social justice, building my knowledge of the community, designing the lessons, and working with these children and families already for some time. Was I best prepared to deliver this lesson? I was not food insecure, nor was my family. Sure, I knew families and children that were food insecure from my prior experiences in teaching, but that was all. Moreover, food insecurity did not directly impact these

children. However, this was an issue that was directly related to children. This was something happening in the community in which these children lived. They could become change agents, acting against this issue and advocating for at least aware-ness of food insecurity.

Anthony said, "So instead of that, the people that don't have enough food can, the people who have enough food can give some to the other people that don't have enough food?"

"Yeah," interjected Andrew.

"That means that it doesn't happen all enough. It means that if they can't go, if they wanted food, all the ones that don't have enough, if they want more they can just go to the store and buy some," Natalie offered.

"Well, sometimes the people don't have enough money to go to the store and buy food." Andrew inserted.

"Maybe someone can eat with the people?" Natalie offered. Wait, what? Am I understanding her words correctly? Is she trying to think about sharing food? Where is this thought process going? This was not a response I anticipated the children sharing. I do not feel prepared to address this idea. I felt at this point like I had underestimated what ideas young children would come up with.

"Teacher, what about if the other, if this yellow people doesn't have enough food, if we ask one of these people, and one of this people, and one of this people, and one of this people to give them money," She pointed to each green figure as the words came to her.

I revoiced some ideas, asking, "So Andrea what I hear you saying is that if the yellow person doesn't have enough food there should be a way for the green people to give them money. Or could the green people give the yellow person some food if they have extra?" Andrea nodded.

"No. But, but, but" Anthony was up on his knees ready to go again. "Someone that has something you can't ask them for anything else. My dad says that. So you can't do that."

Reflection and Analysis on the Planning and Launch of the Lesson

Instantly my thoughts shifted to how best to proceed at this moment. I knew my stance on the issue of child hunger and some of the societal inequities that resulted in families and children generally lacking access to their needs. *How much do I push this? It seems as if Anthony's family has other ideas. Or maybe other perceptions? I wonder why they feel this way? Does Anthony agree? Is this conversation going to go home? Am I going to be in trouble, get reprimanded for talking about this? How can I cautiously unpack more of this topic and the children's thinking without overstepping and inserting too much of my beliefs? Am I doing an injustice by not addressing this? If I do address this idea, what might be the consequences or back-lash I face from families?*

Looking back at the introduction of this concept and how the launch was facilitated, I was not fully prepared to address the topic with the children in our group. I did not prepare for the background and conceptions the children would bring to our work. Selfishly, I had only considered my own perspectives and beliefs and did not anticipate those of others, predominantly the adults in the lives of these students. As a teacher working with these students for only a short period of time, I was worried. I did not want to say something that offended their family beliefs, or to "get into trouble" or be "reported" to the school director. I used this experience to move forward later on in planning to become more transparent with families around the ways we were connecting math to justice issues in our community. In doing so, I began to better anticipate what ideas might be shared and how to facilitate a space where the children and I could actively listen to each other and respectfully disagree, but have our voices and ideas heard by others. This was done through intentional community building with the children in our classroom space, as well as purpose-fully getting to know families and communities and what issues and concerns they believed were important.

Continuing the Lesson With a Dice Game: Merging Food Insecurity With Mathematics

"Alright, let me introduce our game." Quickly, I diverted from the impending conversation, launching the learners into our game so they could more closely examine the mathematics at play. The goal was to model this 1 out of 5 ratio through dice rolls. I passed out the materials to each child and reviewed what we would be doing. In the game, each child took a turn rolling a die. I designed the game such that we used dice with the numbers one through five for some children and one through twelve for others, depending on the standards children were working towards. On each roll of the die, a child would either put five goldfish crackers in their cup, symbolizing they got to eat a meal, or not put anything in their cup, symbolizing they went without that meal. We modeled the 1 in five chance like this:

- If a child rolled a 2, 3, 4, or 5 (or 8, 9, 10, or 11 for the larger number dice), they put one item into their cup.
- If a child rolled a 1 (or 7), they did not put anything in their cup for that turn.
- If children rolled a six or twelve, they were asked to re-roll.

After one minute of free exploration time with the manipulatives and dice, we began to play. Each child rolled their dice and then, as instructed, placed their hands on their head, allowing me to circulate and see who had made sure to complete their turn that round. Moving around the circle of children, they shared the number that they had rolled out loud for all to hear. Liz, unfortunately, was the first to roll a one, and therefore did not put anything in her cup. Everyone else placed something into their cups.

"So if you put something in your cup, you got to 'eat breakfast'." I motioned with air quotes at "eat breakfast" for effect.

"Liz, you did not get to eat breakfast?" All eyes were now on Liz. Her smile began to fade. Natalie and Andrew looked at her with sympathetic eyes, as if to say sorry. "How did that make you feel?" Liz just sat and looked at her cup. After allowing a few moments in case she wanted to say something, I then prompted the class to keep going. *Okay, maybe more iterations, to get the point, or to process enough to try to explain how it feels to "not eat", and have it be out of your control.*

The children rolled again. This time Andrew and Natalie were unable to add to their cups. We continued on this way for a total of 9 rounds, moving through three hypothetical 3-meals-a-day scenarios. At some point or another, each child in the group had a time when they were not able to eat a meal. Liz by far had the most, being unable to eat five out of nine times. After regaining the children's attention, we began to talk about how Liz might be feeling in our simulation.

"So, we rolled and on each roll the dice told us if we got to have breakfast, lunch, and then dinner. Liz you did not get to have breakfast, lunch, or dinner at some points of the activity. How did that make you feel?"

Liz shook and lowered her head. Her nonverbal response demonstrated she was not up to this conversation right now. I turned to the rest of the group. "So how would you feel if this was you?"

"I had breakfast," said Natalie.

"I know you did. You were very lucky. Natalie, you said you'd feel sad?" She shook her head no. "You wouldn't feel sad if you didn't eat?" Her head shook again. Oh goodness, I wondered, Is this concrete enough for Natalie?

I asked, "So we are talking about how we would feel if we were one of those people and we couldn't eat, right?"

"We would be sad because we would be hungry." Anthony had made a connection that I was hoping others would see too. Pull more out of him, I thought, and maybe others will hear what he is saying and be able to respond to it.

I continued. "Tell me more. How would you feel if you got to eat food, but your friends didn't?" But Anthony did not continue. Andrea was ready to speak.

"Andrea?" I prompted.

"Maybe, what about, what about if, um if I share some snacks or not?" Andrea asked.

"So you are saying you might share snacks with friends who don't have any?" I love how Andrea was jumping into trying to solve the issue. But, I wish I could bring more of the children into the conversation.

I backed up for a moment, asking a big picture question: "Do you think we all need food to be strong and grow healthy?"

A resounding "yes" echoed in the room. I continued, "Is it good that some people don't have food to eat, or is that a problem?"

"NOOOOOOOOO!" came the overwhelming response from the children.

"It's a problem," rang Andrea's voice from the circle, her eyes fixed on me.

Reflection and Analysis on the Dice Game and Discussion

By the end of that discussion, I could tell they were getting there. *They are still engaged in the conversation,* I thought. *Should I stop here, and leave them intrigued and hanging a bit and then come back to this idea tomorrow?* My brain was working overtime after the simulation about what to do next. This group was so set on finding a solution to the problem. Right away, they went to the question of trying to understand what they could do to help. I kept thinking about how I might follow their lead and keep the momentum to act going, but I also questioned what they were taking away from the experience. Did they truly understand why this was a problem? Did they understand the pervasiveness of food insecurity for children just like them? Moreover, I felt a sense of imposter syndrome creep in again: *Do I have any place talking about these issues when they are not something that pertains to me?* I do not know why I could not shake this sense of worry. As my experience in planning and teaching justice-centered math lessons built over time, this worry began to fade. Spending more time listening to children and families, being in the community, reading and learning about justice issues and justice standards and conceptualizing what those looked like for our youngest learners provided me with a sense of confidence that I was doing what was best for my learners.

Looking back, the simulation may not have been the best choice for these children, but it may not have been the worst either. As time has passed, I have thought about using more literature connections to build lessons off of, finding images and using launches such as "Notice, Wonder, Feel, Act" (Kahn et al., 2022) to engage children in conversations about justice and mathematics. Moreso, I spend more time following the lead of my children and what they share with me is important. I listen - really listen - to them and their voices. Their sense of becoming change agents is alive from such a young age, but oftentimes this voice goes ignored. By deeply listening to them I have learned to position them as the experts in their lives and in their thoughts about justice, equity, and inclusion. I can serve as the person who knows more about math content and standards. When we work together to co-design mathematics experiences that center the wonderings they deem important, in ways that allow them to showcase their brilliance, it not only creates space to develop their agency, but also positions them as powerful for the world.

While this vignette highlights one small lesson, it is important to note that the work with these children around their understanding of food insecurity in general, along with the conditions which may impact one being food insecure were highlighted in other lessons. As described in the Launching the Lesson section, prior to the activity in the vignette, children had examined their county for where community gardens were located. That work had helped elicit beliefs the children held about who is food insecure, and how it works in our society, including the opportunity to trouble the belief that food insecure people just need to "get jobs." The children began to problematize the narratives they heard about why and how some people might be food insecure and develop alternative understandings rooted in data and sense-making about their world. Some of the children questioned why some people had an excess of food, while others did not have enough access to food. Moreover, they saw a problem in their local community and took action to offer their voice and perspectives by writing to local representatives to share their learning and persuade them to visit food banks and examine areas in need to ensure that food was going to those who truly needed it.

Analysis of the Vignette Through the Lens of the Four Domains

Just one classroom vignette in a single book chapter may not illustrate the depths and potential for going deep with the domains in the Social Justice Standards; however it helps us get on our way to envisioning what classroom instruction based on social justice mathematics could look like. We can identify clear illustrations of aspects of the domains, while also imagining what could be next in store for Jennifer's class of students.

First is the domain of *Identity*. This domain is defined by exploring who we are and where we are from. The way this domain shows up is in the selection of the context of the problem, the issue of food insecurity. The teacher knows this is an issue impacting this community of children - if not the children in the classroom directly, definitely others in their community. They waver in their positioning in relation to the issue – is the teacher the right person to engage this with children? This tension is instructive, and an important part of their decision making. In addition, we see in the vignette the teacher's action of "view[ing] students as competent mathematical beings," (figure 1) who could draw on their own understanding of experiences and emotions to make sense of food inequalities. Jennifer expected that the children could participate in a game that modeled unfairness, and that they could analyze it without lasting repercussions to their own sense of selves. This trust didn't come from nowhere, and yet you can also see that as the lesson goes on the teacher is concerned that she did or didn't do enough to earn that trust. This tension is real, and Jennifer represents her struggle in a relatable way. She elicits the children's perspectives and listens to how their compassion drives them to want to take action. We can imagine a future step with the students, where they do move towards taking action in the community based on what they learn in the classroom.

The domains of *Diversity* and *Justice* come through strongest in the vignette. Most notably for *Diversity*, the children engage in a mathematical activity that stokes empathy and builds connections to different ways of being. *What does it mean to go hungry?* This is a question that is posed to the children through the game they play. They experience a visceral response, perhaps evidenced in student Liz's silence when she experiences a round where nothing goes into her cup. We could imagine a future activity in which children build on their empathetic responses and offer ideas based on mathematical reasoning on how to help address food insecurity in their communities. *Justice*, as a domain, plays a role here too, as the mathematics represented in the dice game introduces students to unfairness as couched in a yet invisible system. They have not yet explored why some students are going hungry in the game, but they can see the outcome. In the activity, the roll of the dice determined who got to eat, but as they explore the issue more deeply children can start to explore, *Is food insecurity really left to chance, or is there something else going on here?* By continuing this line of reasoning in future lessons, the teacher can now take them into examining factors beyond their control, beyond the remedies of sharing their own snacks and lunches, and begin to turn their attention to hunger as a systemic issue, even if they are not quite ready to name it as such. The conclusion that it is big, and that it has a name, food insecurity, may be where the children get in an exploration at this point in their learning over days of exploration. What this lesson does is lay ground to examine the structural issue of wealth distribution, and alongside that to examine one form of societal remedy, connecting back to their explorations of food deserts, or those community gardens they learned about prior to this lesson, to move to *Action*, the one domain that is not yet present in our short vignette, and, in our experience, often comes as a culmination of studying an issue over time.

Guidance to Early Childhood Educators

For early childhood educators who are newer to teaching mathematics for social justice, we suggest starting with already developed resources, such as lessons from the *Early Elementary Mathematics to Explore, Understand, and Respond to Social Injustice* (Koestler et al., 2023), as these lessons are written by various early childhood educators, have been field tested, and can be adapted for a variety of contexts. All of these lessons integrate mathematics standards and the Learning for Justice Social Justice Standards, and offer a cross-disciplinary approach to teaching mathematics for social justice.

However, we encourage early childhood educators interested in engaging in teaching mathematics for social justice to consider this work to be bigger than simply planning and teaching lessons, but rather about setting up a classroom community and culture that positions young children as competent mathematical thinkers who enter early childhood classrooms with important knowledge and experiences that they can use to *read and write the world with mathematics*. These aspects of teaching mathematics for social justice are evident in Jennifer's classroom, as she conveys the depth and breadth of exploration and sharing that goes on in her classroom, and how she provides opportunities for children to see themselves as agents of change individually and collectively. To do this, teachers must consider broader aspects related to teaching and learning. Some questions we suggest teachers ask themselves:

- *Context*: *What topics and issues are important to the children in your classroom and how might you mathematize these topics to explore in TMSJ lessons?* In the vignette, Jennifer sees an opportunity to mathematize food insecurity as a part of a bigger theme of who has access to what kind of food, and connects to the exploration children did with maps and in-person around locations of community gardens and supermarkets.
- *Content*: *How might these TMSJ lessons support the development of "important" mathematics for your students? In what ways are your children positioned as capable and competent in these lessons and are you building on their strengths and prior experience?* In the vignette, children grapple with probability but also work on subitizing, quantity, and other aspects of counting through the hands-on modeling of food insecurity.
- *Who*: *How are children's identities explored and understood respectfully in the TMSJ lesson? Do all children have access and equitable participation in the lessons?* For example, Jennifer designs both the activity and the debrief in ways that allow all children access, and opportunities to participate in the debriefing of the activity. She uses dice rolling rules to help them experience new situations, being someone who "gets to eat" or not, to help activate their

empathy. She monitors how the activity is proceeding to ensure ample opportunity for everyone to experience the mathematics, so that they can make connections in the debrief, at one point deciding to give everyone time to do one more round of dice rolling.

- **When**: *How does this work build on or fit into your curriculum, both in terms of the mathematics or social justice goals?* Though it's hard to convey in one short vignette, Jennifer describes in the reflection section how this one mathematics lesson was situated in the longer work her class was doing exploring food insecurity in interdisciplinary ways, with field trips, maps, interactive read alouds, etc.

- **How**: *How will you attempt to engage all children in the TMSJ lessons? How will you reflect on your own biases and positionality to create justice-oriented mathematics lessons?* In the vignette, Jennifer does not reveal her own beliefs about food insecurity or its root causes, but rather she sets up the explorations to elicit children's thinking, and to support their own abilities to raise questions and trouble narratives. She describes the work they are doing as collective, and monitors how she asks questions and makes space for children to share their own beliefs with each other.

(For more information about *Context, Content, Who, When,* and *How* when planning to teach mathematics for social justice, see Koestler et al., 2023, pp. 24–40.)

An important consideration (and sometimes tension) when planning social justice mathematics lessons is centering both social justice goals and mathematics goals within lessons (e.g., Bartell, 2013). Sometimes teachers may begin with the mathematics in mind, and then connect an important social issue that fits with the content. Other times, such as in the vignette, teachers may begin by thinking about the social justice topic they wish to explore and think about how they might mathematize it to support their students' understanding. Either way, it is important in TMSJ lessons that teachers have clear goals for understanding for their students related to both mathematics and the social justice topic(s).

Another aspect that teachers need to be mindful of is how much they insert their own perspectives of the social justice issue into the lesson, especially when working with young children. As mentioned above, Jennifer monitored her contributions, putting her energy towards designing experiences where children could raise questions and draw their own conclusions. But certainly, she began from the perspective that food insecurity was an issue worth exploration with the children. While it is important that at times teachers bring alternative and non-dominant perspectives to discussions that children might be unaware of, teachers should take care to follow the lead of the children as much as possible. We see how Jennifer grappled with this, not just in the lesson planning, but in how the lesson unfolded. Remaining aware of how you step into and step back from contributing to a discussion is important, ensuring there is space for children to take the lead. Gutstein (2006) connected the need to watch one's own bias with the power teachers hold over students. He described the importance of being in a dialectic relationship with students, building on Paolo Freire's ideas of developing a pedagogy of questioning. As he notes, it was important to develop *political* relationships with students, in order to grapple with the tension of "providing students space to develop their own ideas, voice, and understanding, and on the other hand, helping them develop deeper analyses of complex social phenomena" (p. 140). The tension between supporting deeper analysis and space for students to develop their own views is where we suggest teachers need to put their efforts. With a focus on this tension, teachers have a way to ask themselves when their own biases and viewpoints might be cropping up in ways that shut down the dialog between children and teacher.

We also want to note that the teacher workforce continues to be skewed white, while the student population is more diverse; at times whole classrooms may be homogeneously distinct from the teacher. Given this context, while efforts to diversify the teacher workforce continue, white teachers, and indeed teachers who hold various dominant identities in relation to their students and families, must be cautious about how they approach teaching mathematics for social justice. Martin (2007) cautioned those who would teach urban Black students mathematics against the mentality of being a savior, raising questions about what it means to be "highly qualified" to teach Black children. No good comes out of any mindset in which the teacher purports to know better than the students and families who live within communities and contexts experiencing the issue. White teachers and teachers from other dominant positions must hold themselves and each other accountable to working *with* families, not against them.

Finally, we have found it particularly effective to connect to important stakeholders (families, ally teachers, administrators, community members, etc.) when engaging in mathematics for social justice with young children. Whether it is reaching out to families to communicate the goals of a unit before teaching it or collaborating with a local community member with knowledge about a particular issue to plan a lesson, social justice mathematics lessons are often strengthened and more supported when others are involved from the outset. Too often teachers lament that it is hard to get parents involved, or that parents are too busy to bother with questions about their experiences and mathematics. This viewpoint must be challenged, and has been by national organizations like NAEYC and, more recently specific to mathematics education, TODOS (2020), who wrote:

A step in this process is valuing the home mathematical practices of parents, in particular

BIPOC (Black, Indigenous, and People of Color) parents, and finding ways to bridge from home experiences to school knowledge, and not vice versa. (TODOS, 2020, p. 16)

CONCLUSION

Some early childhood educators who work with children don't feel confident or competent when teaching mathematics. But imagine a world in which mathematics, from the start, was embedded as an everyday activity, one that helps us to actually understand our world, one that is embodied in our experiences, one in which we felt we belonged. Our relationships with mathematics, and who we think of as mathematical, would be so much different. We might also see more mathematical brilliance shine in the world if our mathematical instruction made space for it. When we design lessons that incorporate social justice, children see mathematics as important and relevant, and they see it as a tool that they can use to explore and understand their world, as well as use it to make change. When we design such lessons in partnership with parents and communities, mathematics seems as natural as growing food. And when we do this from an early age, we normalize the integration of mathematical concepts and issues that impact us, to the point where maybe it will simply be the norm for upcoming generations.

This is the vision for mathematics that we have shared in this chapter. All young children deserve to feel like they are knowledgeable and connected to mathematics, and confident that mathematics is a part of them. Mathematics for social justice can help make that happen, and can be an essential part of our vision for inclusive early childhood spaces.

REFERENCES

Bartell, T. G. (2013). Learning to teach mathematics for social justice: Negotiating social justice and mathematical goals. *Journal for Research in Mathematics Education*, 44(1), 129–163. 10.5951/jresemath_educ.44.1.0129

Carpenter, T. P., Fennema, E., & Franke, M. L. (1996). Cognitively guided instruction: A knowledge base for reform in primary mathematics instruction. *The Elementary School Journal*, 97(1), 3–20. 10.1086/461846

Carpenter, T. P., Fennema, E., Franke, M. L., Levi, L., & Empson, S. B. (2000). Cognitively Guided Instruction: A Research-Based Teacher Professional Development Program for Elementary School Mathematics. *Research Reports (Montgomery)*.

Clements, D., & Sarama, J. (2014). *Learning and teaching math: The learning trajectories approach* (2nd ed.). Routledge. 10.4324/9780203520574

Clements, D. H. (1999). Subitizing: What Is It? Why Teach It? *Teaching Children Mathematics*, 5(7), 400–405. 10.5951/TCM.5.7.0400

Derman-Sparks, L., & Edwards, J. O. (2010). *Anti-bias education for young children and ourselves*. National Association for the Education of Young Children.

Goffney, I., & Gutiérrez, R. (2018). *Rehumanizing mathematics for Black, Indigenous, and Latinx students*. National Council of Teachers of Mathematics.

Gonzalez, L. (2009). Teaching math for social justice: Reflections on a community of practice for high school math teachers. *Journal of Urban Mathematics Education*, 2(1), 22–51. 10.21423/jume-v2i1a32

González, N., Andrade, R., Civil, M., & Moll, L. (2001). Bridging funds of distributed knowledge: Creating zones of practices in mathematics. *Journal of Education for Students Placed at Risk*, 6(1-2), 115–132. 10.1207/S15327671ESPR0601-2_7

Gutstein, E. (2006). *Reading and writing the world with mathematics: toward a pedagogy for social justice*. Routledge.

Harper, F. K. (2019). A Qualitative Metasynthesis of Teaching Mathematics for Social Justice in Action: Pitfalls and Promises of Practice. *Journal for Research in Mathematics Education*, 50(3), 268–310. Retrieved January 10, 2024, from. 10.5951/jresemath&educ.50.3.0268

Kahn, J. B., Peralta, L. M., Rubel, L. H., Lim, V. Y., Jiang, S., & Herbel-Eisenmann, B. (2022). Notice, wonder, feel, act, and reimagine as a path toward social justice in data science education. *Journal of Educational Technology & Society*, 25(4), 80–92.

Kemper, T., & Zavala, M. (2024). Culturally Responsive Mathematics Teaching in Special Education Spaces. In M. Zavala & J.M. Aguirre (Authors) *Cultivating Mathematical Hearts: Culturally Responsive Mathematics Teaching in Elementary Classrooms.* Corwin. pp. 182-195.

Koestler, C., Ward, J., Zavala, M. del R., & Bartell, T. G. (2023). *Early elementary mathematics lessons to explore, understand, and respond to social injustice.* Corwin. 10.4135/9781071880630

Kokka, K. (2017). *Social Justice Mathematics: Pedagogy of the Oppressed or Pedagogy of the Privileged? A Comparative Case Study of Students of Historically Marginalized and Privileged Backgrounds.* [Doctoral dissertation, Harvard Graduate School of Education].

Lambert, R., Tan, P., Hunt, J., & Candela, A. G. (2018). Rehumanizing the mathematics education of students with disabilities; critical perspectives on research and practice. *Investigations in Mathematics Learning*, 10(3), 129–132. 10.1080/19477503.2018.1463006

Learning for Justice & Yeh, C. (2021). *Toolkit for "Mathematics in Context": The pedagogy of liberation.* Learning for Justice. https://www.learningforjustice.org/magazine/spring-2021/toolkit-for-mathematics-in-context-the-pedagogy-of-liberation

Martin, D. B. (2007). Beyond Missionaries or Cannibals: Who Should Teach Mathematics to African American Children? *High School Journal*, 91(1), 6–28. 10.1353/hsj.2007.0023

National Association for the Education of Young Children & National Council of Teachers of Mathematics. (2010). *Early childhood mathematics: Promoting good beginnings.* Washington DC: NAEYC National Association for the Education of Young Children. (2020). Developmentally Appropriate Practice [PDF file]. https://www.naeyc.org/sites/default/files/globallyshared/downloads/PDFs/resources/position-statements/dap-statement_0.pdf

Nieto, S. (2000). Placing equity front and center: Some thoughts on transforming teacher education for a new century. *Journal of Teacher Education*, 51(3), 180–187. 10.1177/0022487100051003004

Rogoff, B. (2003). *The cultural nature of human development.* Oxford University Press.

Sisk-Hilton, S. (2024). *Teaching Climate Science in the Elementary Classroom: A Place-Based, Hope-Filled Approach to Understanding Earth's Systems.* Routledge.

Souto-Manning, M. (2013). *Multicultural teaching in the early childhood classroom: Approaches, strategies, and tools, preschool-2nd grade*. Teachers College Press.

Souto-Manning, M., & Rabadi-Raol, A. (2018). (Re)Centering Quality in Early Childhood Education: Toward Intersectional Justice for Minoritized Children. *Review of Research in Education*, 42(1), 203–225. 10.3102/0091732X18759550

Sullivan, J., Wilton, L., & Apfelbaum, E. P. (2021). Adults delay conversations about race because they underestimate children's processing of race. *Journal of Experimental Psychology. General*, 150(2), 395–400. 10.1037/xge000085132757612

Tate, W. (2012). Race, retrenchment, and the reform of school mathematics. In Gutstein, E., & Peterson, B. (Eds.), *Rethinking mathematics: teaching social justice by the numbers* (2nd ed., pp. 42–52). Rethinking Schools.

TODOS. (2020). *The Mo(ve)ment to Prioritize Antiracist Mathematics: Planning for this and every school year*. Tempe, AZ. https://www.todos-math.org/statements

Verschaffel, L., Greer, B., & De Corte, E. (2000). *Making sense of word problems*. Swets & Zeitlinger.

Woodhead, M. (2006). Changing perspectives on early childhood: Theory, research and policy. *International Journal of Equity and Innovation in Early Childhood*, 4(2), 1–43.

Yeh, C., Ellis, M., & Mahmood, D. (2020). From the margin to the center: A framework for rehumanizing mathematics education for students with dis/abilities. *The Journal of Mathematical Behavior*, 58, 100758. 10.1016/j.jmathb.2020.100758

Zermeño, B. P. (2022). I Come from Mathema*ticians and Engineers: Reclaiming Histories Towards Ethnic Studies in Early Childhood* (Publication No. 28971341) [Doctoral dissertation, Mills College]. ProQuest Dissertations & Theses Global.

Chapter 9
Promoting Self–Determination as an Emancipatory Practice in Early Childhood Inclusion

Jacqueline Anton
https://orcid.org/0000-0003-0667-6004
San Francisco State University, USA & University of California, Berkeley, USA

Sara Ucar
San Francisco State University, USA & University of California, Berkeley, USA

Mayumi Hagiwara
https://orcid.org/0000-0001-5134-5867
San Francisco State University, USA

ABSTRACT

Early intervention and early childhood special education are shifting to more inclusive and equity-empowered systems. High-quality inclusion challenges dominant norms around dis-ability and ableism to honor the strengths, preferences, and support needs of young children and their families. Equity-empowered systems promote high expectations and facilitate culturally responsive family-centered education aligned with anti-bias and anti-racist education frameworks. Research shows that promoting self-determination for children with dis-abilities can increase access to inclusive settings and enhance anti-bias and anti-racism by elevating individual and communal voices. This chapter proposes promoting self-determination as an emancipatory practice in early childhood and links high-quality inclusion with opportunities to engage in self-determined action. Further, the chapter proposes the promotion of

DOI: 10.4018/979-8-3693-0924-7.ch009

self-determination as a culturally responsive practice aligned with anti-bias and anti-racism frameworks. Recommendations for practice and implications for future research are also discussed.

BACKGROUND

Self-determination is a dispositional characteristic that enables people to act as causal agents in their lives by making choices and decisions based on their strengths and preferences and solving problems in order to achieve their goals (Shogren et al., 2015). For young children, developing an early foundation for self-determination is important to grow and strengthen more complex self-determination skills and abilities later, leading to an improved quality of life (Shogren et al., 2021). Young children require frequent and consistent routines and opportunities to engage in self-determined actions to hone these skills and abilities. However, systemic barriers, such as a lack of inclusion across the environment (e.g., education, community) or limited access to trained practitioners with beliefs and knowledge in self-determination instruction, can influence authentic opportunities to practice and strengthen their self-determination (Hagiwara et al., 2021). Previous research shows families value promoting self-determination for their young children with dis-abilities and want to establish family-school partnerships to develop a shared understanding about family and cultural influences on self-determination and how families define and operationalize self-determination based on such influences (Haines et al., 2017; Summer et al., 2014). Nonetheless, there is a dearth of recent research regarding ways to support foundational self-determination skills and abilities for young dis-abled children or those receiving special education services, focusing on inclusion and culturally responsive practices. Thus, we propose promoting self-determination in culturally responsive ways for young dis-abled children within inclusive early childhood settings.

In this chapter, we will (a) discuss the theoretical roots of self-determination; (b) synthesize the research on self-determination for young children; (c) emphasize the role of culture in self-determination and consider self-determination as a culturally-responsive practice; (d) promote self-determination in inclusive early childhood settings, as a way to strengthen equity-driven early childhood inclusion; (e) use self-determination to support high expectations for all students, and (f) explore future directions for self-determination in inclusive early childhood that align with anti-bias and anti-ableist practices. Finally, we will provide recommendations for future research concerning self-determination and early childhood. We propose that the promotion of self-determination in early childhood will simultaneously empower young children in developing their own agency and allow practitioners to celebrate children's unique identities in the classroom from equity-empowered perspectives. This can also enhance practitioners' anti-ableist practices. We also offer beliefs about developmentally appropriate practices supporting young children's agency and self-determination which build upon strengths-based and emancipatory practices and are rooted in inclusive, anti-bias, and anti-ableist pedagogies.

Additionally, we recognize the varied perspectives and intentions in using both person-first and identity-first languages when talking about dis-abled children in inclusive early childhood settings. For example, highlighting the inequitable racial disproportionality in special education, Cioè-Peña (2021) uses the language of emergent bilinguals labeled as disabled (EBLAD) to underscore how emergent bilingual students and families experience biases based on racial, ethnic, and linguistic grounds that can impact various components of their educational experiences and placements. These students can also experience further marginalization and pathologization due to dis-ability labels (Cioè-Peña, 2021). We share the intentional use of EBLADs to provide one example of many ways that various scholars and communities interpret and use both person-first and identity-first language. Regarding the use of various choices on person-first and identity-first language, "each of these terms has a history and offers problems and possibilities" (Buffington-Adams & Vaughan, 2019, p.6). This includes using the terminology of dis/ability (Annamma et al., 2013) or dis-ability (Cruz et al., 2023).

To address intersections of racism and ableism for young children and families receiving special education services and the need for inclusive educational spaces, this chapter leverages a Critical Inclusion (InCrit; Cruz et al., 2023) framework. The InCrit framework is beneficial for understanding the relationship between equity-empowered frameworks and self-determination within inclusive settings. Drawing upon the tenets from Disability Critical Race Theory (DisCrit; Annamma et al., 2013), which acknowledge the ways in which racial identities impact people with dis-abilities, InCrit claims that "a reliance on disability labels for instructional decision-making *is deeply flawed*" (Cruz et al., 2023, p. 14, emphasis added). Recognizing the need to celebrate the unique diversity among young children in culturally responsive ways, inclusive pedagogy ideally engages and honors all children's lived experiences and their dynamic, intersectional identities, rather than segregating students into groups based on dis-ability status and other marginalized identities. We believe that using the InCrit framework aligns with setting high expectations for students in inclusive settings and utilizing the promotion of self-determination as an emancipatory practice. To align with the framework, in this chapter, we intentionally use the person-first terminology of dis-ability (see Cruz et al., 2023 for more information).

SELF-DETERMINATION

Definition of Self-Determination

According to Causal Agency Theory, self-determination is defined as a dispositional characteristic "manifested as acting as the causal agent in one's life. Self-determined people (i.e., causal agents) act in service to freely chosen goals. Self-determined actions function to enable a person to be the causal agent in his or her life" (Shogren et al., 2015, p. 258). Causal Agency Theory builds upon the functional model of self-determination (Wehmeyer, 1992), provides a theoretical framework for understanding how individuals engage in self-determined actions, and identifies barriers and facilitators that exist in navigating toward their own goals in life (Mumbardó-Adam et al., 2018). Causal Agency Theory defines self-determined actions with three characteristics; *Volitional Action* (referred to as *Decide*) involves making intentional choices based on one's personal preferences and interests and is characterized by autonomy and self-initiation. *Agentic Action* (referred to as *Act*) involves overcoming barriers and taking action to accomplish goals, and is characterized by self-regulation, self-direction and pathways thinking. *Action-Control Belief* (referred to as *Believe*) involves reflection and understanding that actions lead to outcomes and is characterized by control-expectancy, psychological empowerment, and self-realization (Shogren et al., 2015). People who act as causal agents in their lives make choices based on personal preferences, act in service of their goals, and believe that self-determined actions will help them attain their goals (Parker et al., 2020; Shogren et al., 2015).

Self-determination is associated with skills and abilities such as choice-making, problem-solving, goal-setting, and self-knowledge (Hagiwara et al., 2021). Self-determination develops throughout the life course as people experience opportunities to practice, learn from mistakes, and challenge further these skills and abilities in school, home, work, and other settings (Raley et al., 2021). A long line of research shows that higher levels of self-determination are associated with positive in-school and postschool outcomes and greater life satisfaction (Erwin et al., 2016; Mazzotti et al., 2020). Furthermore, receiving self-determination instruction in inclusive settings promotes better social and academic outcomes for all students (Anton et al., in press). However, dis-abled students and adults often report lower levels of self-determination compared to students and adults without dis-abilities (Garrels & Palmer, 2020; Shogren et al., 2018). As highlighted by Burke et al. (2018), the majority of research targeting self-determination skills and abilities for dis-abled people occurs with older students (i.e., high school and transition age). Therefore, beginning in early childhood, self-determination is critical to be supported by key supporters around young dis-abled children (e.g., families, practitioners) by setting high expectations for their young children and providing supports and opportunities aligned with self-determined action. For these reasons, we propose self-determination as an emancipatory practice to empower young children with and without dis-abilities in inclusive classrooms. See Figure 1 for the Causal Agency Theory theoretical framework.

Figure 1. Causal agency theory theoretical framework

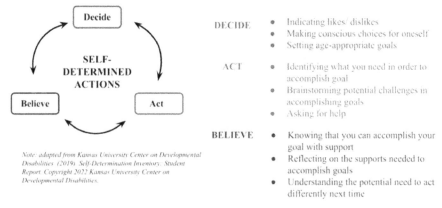

Note: adapted from Kansas University Center on Developmental Disabilities. (2019). Self-Determination Inventory: Student Report. Copyright 2022 Kansas University Center on Developmental Disabilities.

DECIDE
- Indicating likes/ dislikes
- Making conscious choices for oneself
- Setting age-appropriate goals

ACT
- Identifying what you need in order to accomplish goal
- Brainstorming potential challenges in accomplishing goals
- Asking for help

BELIEVE
- Knowing that you can accomplish your goal with support
- Reflecting on the supports needed to accomplish goals
- Understanding the potential need to act differently next time

(Ucar et al., under review; adapted with permission from Shogren, 2017)

Self-Determination in Young Children

In young children, it has been widely expected that certain foundational skills lead to the development of self-determination throughout the life course (Palmer et al., 2013; Summers et al., 2014). Summers et al (2014) define these foundational skills as (a) engaging in age-appropriate choice-making; (b) developing skills and abilities for self-regulation; and (c) engaging with a wide variety of people and activities. Families and practitioners hold unique positions to foster these foundational skills in young children, both at home and at school. It is essential that young children, especially those with dis-abilities, are exposed to environments which allow for frequent choice-making, support in self-regulation, and engagement opportunities.

Furthermore, young children may engage in self-determined actions in age- and developmentally-appropriate wasy. Following the self-determination action cycle, young children engaging in *Decide* might practice indicating their likes and dislikes, make conscious choices based on their preferences (e.g., choosing a craft activity during center time), and set age-appropriate goals (e.g., deciding what to wear for school, selecting a reading buddy). Next, they might *Act* by identifying what they need to do in order to accomplish their goals (e.g., create a picture for their parent), brainstorm potential barriers (e.g., teachers need to give the children paints), and practice asking for help (e.g., ask the teacher for paints). Finally, students engage in the *Believe* phase by reflecting on the supports needed to accomplish their goals (e.g., support from teachers to access materials), understanding that they can accomplish their goals with support (e.g., learning from experience that asking for help can lead to positive results), and acknowledging what they might do differently next time (e.g., share their goal with the teacher when asking for materials) (Ucar et al., under review). Practitioners and adults can help young children develop their emerging self-determination by explicitly naming each part of the cycle of *Decide, Act,* and *Believe* while simultaneously engaging students in reflective practice (Ucar et al., under review) to understand the outcomes of their own causal actions. Furthermore, practitioners might guide students through each step of the process by providing many opportunities for children to engage in this cycle, with support.

Self-Determination in Family-School Collaboration

Practitioners and families actively working to promote young children's foundational self-determination skills may benefit from additional support to analyze which strategies best promote self-determined action. Through community partnerships, practitioners and researchers may work with young children and their families to develop a more comprehensive understanding of ways to enhance self-determination skills and abilities in young children. This collaborative approach can elevate existing strategies that families and practitioners currently utilize to effectively strengthen foundational self-determination skills. As there is limited research on collaboration among invested stakeholders, ongoing work is necessary to develop deeper insights into how to support young children's foundational self-determination skills. Collaboration among researchers, families, and practitioners can increase awareness of the benefits of self-determination for young children and promote practices that enhance children's foundational self-determination skills.

One possible area for research collaboration among young children in a variety of settings, as practitioners and families may already be supporting foundational self-determination skills, is during activity-based interventions. For example, beginning in early intervention, practitioners and families can work together to implement activity-based interventions for young children. Activity-based intervention approaches embed child and family goals into a child's routine, daily activities, and are appropriate for young children receiving early intervention or early childhood special education (Johnson et al., 2015). This embedded approach aims to optimize the opportunities for learning and developing meaningful skills throughout daily life experiences, including play and other routines. Individualized Family Service Plans

(IFSP), which include goals that guide child and family outcomes for young children from birth to three, can include activity-based interventions to outline how young children, families, and providers will work together to meet child and family goals. Similarly, for young children receiving early childhood special education services in preschool, their Individualized Education Program (IEP) goals can also build upon activity-based interventions. Among early elementary school children, routines and activities in the classroom and at home still reflect appropriate times to promote self-determined actions and can be embedded into existing child and family goals. By recognizing these opportunities for foundational self-determination within every-day experiences, educators and families can use routine activities at home or early childhood educational settings to provide robust opportunities for young children to feel empowered to make choices or engage in the self-determination action cycle.

Self-Determination and Culture

While research has shown that self-determination is a universal construct that is honored across contexts (e.g., school, home, community), different cultures might express self-determined actions in different ways (Shogren et al., 2019a). For example, if one expression of self-determination is making choices and setting goals based on personal preferences, then we must expect personal preferences to reflect one's individual culture, family, and life experiences (Shogren et al., 2021). Conflict may arise if educational spaces do not honor different ways in which self-determination might be expressed or practiced. For example, Palmer et al. (2013) explain how problem-solving strategies are often honed at home first, amongst family members. In addition, Summers et al. (2014) found that at times, families have felt that their expectations and conceptualization of self-determination were not always shared and respected by schools. For example, although families value self-determination, how they provide self-determination opportunities, such as picking their own clothes, snacks, and free-time activities at home, may look different from how school would do, depending on the availability of options, supports, financial resources, and time as well as depending on cultural practices and beliefs. Specifically, suppose children with dis-abilities practice a choice-making skill using widely available snacks like fish crackers and popcorn in American schools, which do not reflect family preferences. In that case, the children need to re-learn choice making with snacks that family members usually buy and eat. Or, if school does not allow cultural or traditional clothing to be worn to school, the selection of clothes will limit the culturally responsive expression of self-determination. Moreover, some families indicated the need for discussion and culturally responsive guidance from school or other families with more experience promoting self-determination at home (Hagiwara et al., 2021). This indicates a need for greater professional development to understand how culture and positionality may influence how people construct self-determination and to start a conversation with families to discuss how families perceive self-determination and hope to provide supports and opportunities for their children at home and in community and how school can facilitate family-centered goals across settings. Such a professional development opportunity could invite family members who have experience promoting self-determined actions at home to brainstorm with practitioners about strategies in classrooms or hold a follow-up session to check on practitioners' progress, successes, and areas of further growth. Therefore, these authors propose strong family-school partnerships and communication to promote self-determination in a culturally responsive and affirming manner.

Self-Determination as a Culturally Responsive Practice

The development of young children's self-determination is influenced by many environmental factors, including a child's identity and culture (Shogren et al., 2018). To include and support all children in developing self-determination, practitioners can implement culturally responsive practices (Gay, 2018). Culturally responsive practices seek to honor children's natural human differences and view diversity as an asset, specifically in classroom settings. Culturally responsive pedagogy, aligned with self-determined actions, can meet the unique needs of children and their families by honoring their concerns, priorities, family language, commitment, and culture. Framing intersecting identities and dis-abilities as beneficial allows practitioners to create environments in which children are not blamed for their differences (Souto-Manning & Rabadi, 2018). Instead, culturally responsive practices may disrupt deficit mindsets surrounding dis-ability while simultaneously honoring children's and their families' cultures and setting high expectations for their academic and personal growth (Fallon et al., 2021; Obiakor & Rotatori, 2014).

Self-Determination as a Means to Facilitate Strong Family-School Partnerships

One example of culturally responsive approaches to supporting self-determination skills and abilities in early childhood can be seen from an international educator with an understanding of cultural expectations and classroom goals of greater independence. Sun (2015), a Chinese early childhood educator working in the United States, described her experience building family-professional partnerships to address differences between home culture, family goals, and the school's expectations. Regarding feeding, Sun (2015) explained that "historically, in Chinese culture and society, most adults believe that young children need to eat as much as possible to grow and be healthy" (p.65). Therefore, they spoon-fed this young boy in front of the television to ensure he was well-fed. However, in his early childhood education center, they practiced and preferred young children to feed themselves. Sun understood and respected the family's culture, and the mismatch between family and school goals. Communicating with the child's father, they came to a shared understanding that "helping Ricky eat well and become more independent was equally important. We agreed to work collaboratively to find new ways to increase Ricky's self-feeding at the dining table" (Sun, 2015, p.65). In this instance, the child's family wanted to ensure that he received adequate food and nutrition. At the same time, the early childhood center had goals related to each child's self-care, which were age-appropriate and supported the children's growing independence. Through simple routines like mealtimes, they worked together to find a way to support the child's self-care.

Self-care routines can be meaningful ways for practitioners and families to connect IFSP/IEP goals to self-determination goals. Additionally, fostering self-determination skills through self-care routines not only enhances a child's independence but also promotes a sense of agency and empowerment. By incorporating IFSP/IEP goals into daily activities like self-care practices, families and practitioners can guide children through the self-determination action cycle. This can support children's understanding of the importance of working towards their own goals for greater independence and agency, while fostering a sense of self-efficacy that extends beyond self-care skills. As families and practitioners work collaboratively to build and sustain meaningful partnerships, they can co-create spaces for children's self-determination skills to be nurtured through daily routines and interactions, such as mealtime or self-care routines. This collaborative effort can strengthen how much support children and families receive and impact IFSP/IEP goal attainment. Integrating goals into everyday activities like self-care practices or mealtimes represents one way that families and practitioners can strengthen both family-professional partnerships and foundational self-determination skills.

Reflective Practices to Facilitate Children's Self-Determination

Overall, facilitating self-determination in early childhood allows practitioners to work more effectively with families to identify and provide individualized support as needed. Children have varying abilities, social identities, and heritages. To implement culturally responsive practices, it is critical to recognize that families from diverse cultural backgrounds acknowledge the importance of self-determination for their children, while the ways that families create opportunities for self-determination are more likely to vary depending on the extent to which families feel comfortable or experienced with that. Furthermore, self-determination and culturally responsive practices share core and overlapping elements, including high expectations, strengths- and asset-based approaches, personalized supports and supporters, inclusive opportunities, and focus on in-school and postschool outcomes (Hagiwara et al., 2024). Therefore, incorporating self-determination into inclusive early childhood practices can complement a culturally responsive pedagogy and existing efforts to empower young children and their families. At the same time, practitioners should recognize that each family has a different prioritization of self-determination skills and abilities and leverage a personalized support system as an essential part of these efforts. In this way, promoting self-determination skills and abilities can empower children to be aware of their environment (e.g., classroom, school, neighborhood, cultural community) and to act as agents of change by advocating for agendas which matter to them and their unique communities.

To understand the complex intersections of family and culture on children's self-determination and to deliver culturally responsive self-determination instruction, when practitioners are planning on promoting self-determination in inclusive early childhood settings, they must first reflect on their own cultural values that they have embedded within their understanding of self-determination. Additionally, practitioners may benefit from participating in ongoing reflective practices to continuously reassess conceptions of self-determination, and how to respectfully center each family's expectations. This also aligns with anti-bias practices to ensure that expectations or expressions of self-determination skills and abilities do not align exclusively with those from only one culture. This includes those from non-dominant communities, such as racial, ethnic, and linguistic communities, as these communities are disproportionately placed in Special Education (Annamma et al., 2013). It is important to note that cultures are not monolithic, and to garner a nuanced understanding self-determination skills are culturally responsive to children's unique home cultures and languages (Palmer et al., 2013; Shogren et al., 2021). This may further strengthen family-professional partnerships when families recognize practitioners' efforts to center family values and preferences and cater anti-bias education content "based on what classroom teachers and families think is important for children to learn" (Derman-Sparks & Edwards, 2019, p. 9). In the next section, we describe the importance of inclusive early childhood educational settings for educational outcomes and self-determination skills, as well as ways to promote self-determination within inclusive classrooms.

Promoting Self-Determination in Inclusive Early Childhood Settings

Section 612(a)(5) of IDEA explains that:

"To the maximum extent appropriate, children with disabilities, including children in public or private institutions or other care facilities, must be educated with children who are not disabled. Further, special classes, separate schooling, or other removal of children with disabilities from the regular educational environment occurs only when the nature or severity of the disability of a child is such that education in regular classes with the use of supplementary aids and services cannot be achieved satisfactorily."

Therefore, dis-abled students must be educated in the general education classroom as their first and main educational setting. Additionally, national organizations like the Division for Early Childhood (DEC) and National Association for the Education of Young Children (NAEYC) support early childhood inclusion. Research indicates high-quality inclusion is associated with positive outcomes for all students, especially dis-abled students (Camilli et al., 2010; Strain & Bovey, 2011). However, young children receiving special education services are not experiencing appropriate access, participation, and support even though these are key characteristics for high-quality inclusion (Barton & Smith, 2015). Specifically, in 2021, less than half (44.6%) of dis-abled children ages 3 to 5 were educated in inclusive settings (U.S. Department of Education [USDOE] & U.S. Department of Health & Human Services [USHHS], 2023). Furthermore, social identities, including race, ethnicity, language, ability, support needs, and geographic or economic circumstances further impact young children's access to inclusive educational settings (USDOE & USHHS, 2023). Although inclusion benefits all children, and all children have rights to inclusive early education opportunities, data indicate that minoritized children often do not have equal access to inclusive early childcare settings when compared to white children (USDOE & USHHS, 2023). As early educators aim to increase equity in early childhood, equity-empowered systems must prioritize mitigating structural and systemic barriers to inclusion, including through anti-racist, anti-bias, and anti-ableist policies.

Barriers to Inclusive Early Childhood Education

Not having access to and opportunities to be educated in the general education settings not only hinders the ability of dis-abled students to engage in self-determined actions (Hagiwara et al., 2021), but also may inadvertently perpetuate inequitable mindsets about intelligence and ability, which will impact young children's educational experiences for years to come (Cruz et al., 2023). This is particularly important for early childhood because young children heavily rely on key supporters (e.g., families, early interventionists, early childhood special education practitioners) and other adults in their environment to create and deliver educational opportunities which are children's first experiences with schooling.

Nonetheless, research indicates that attitudinal barriers and deficit perspectives pose profound challenges to achieving high-quality inclusion. For example, Barton & Smith (2015) underscored the persistent problem regarding the "sluggish growth rate of preschool inclusion" (p.74) by highlighting attitudinal barriers to inclusion, including concerns regarding collaboration between general and special educators, negative impact for some children regarding a lack of support for children with or without dis-abilities due to the inclusive settings, lack of teacher preparedness, lack of awareness regarding benefits of inclusion, or lack of respect. These attitudinal barriers impact the advancement of early childhood inclusion.

Similarly, practitioners and families tend to hold deficit mindsets in terms of children's abilities when it comes to self-determination, which can be seen as further indication of ableist attitudes and beliefs or low expectations. For example, there have been various studies showing that interventions meant to promote self-determination could improve access to the general education curriculum and content (e.g., Agran et al., 2006; Lee et al., 2008; Raley et al., 2021; Shogren et al., 2012). However, teachers in these studies often expressed their surprise at how well dis-abled students could perform when provided with personalized supports. This reaction reflects their low expectations. In another study concerning interventions meant to support students' self-determination, Shogren et al. (2021) found that, when presented with a self-rating scale measuring goal-attainment, teachers rated dis-abled students far lower than the students rated themselves. Similarly, Hagiwara et al. (2021) conducted a meta-synthesis of people's perceptions toward self-determination for dis-abled children and adults and found although families of children with extensive support needs valued self-determination, they were skeptical of how effectively interventions could support their children's self-determination, especially if these interventions were not aligned with family cultures and customs. Finally, Shogren et al. (2020) found that teachers rated students' levels of self-determination drastically lower than students' self-reported levels of self-determination when students had more extensive support needs. This data is troubling for many reasons, one of which is that it reflects common deficit mindsets about dis-abled students.

As early childhood inclusion should ideally aim to cultivate a sense of belonging and membership among all children, deficit perspectives and messages that fail to thoughtfully promote a belief in a child's capabilities and capacity to learn hinder one's sense of belonging, participation, and engagement. Therefore, practitioners supporting self-determination must hold all children to high expectations and educate all children in inclusive environments. These are necessary conditions to combat attitudinal barriers and biases and to allow all young children the space and opportunity to engage in self-determined actions and develop skills and abilities to become causal agents in their lives.

Strengths-Based Approaches and Inclusion

Strengths-based approaches focus on the demands of age-appropriate, inclusive environments where young children with and without dis-abilities learn, play, and live (Shogren et al., 2017). Inclusion and self-determination are key characteristics of strengths-based approaches; therefore, when supporting self-determination for young children, practitioners must be reflective of their mindset (e.g., deficits- vs. strengths-based approaches), assess their levels of expectations toward young children with and without dis-abilities, and increase inclusive opportunities for all children. Strengths-based approaches challenge deficit-based perspectives and enable all young children to engage in self-determined actions (i.e., Decide, Act, and Believe).

Promoting self-determination for young children is a promising strengths-based approach to promote inclusion by helping students acquire skills to develop their self-knowledge, advocacy, and belief in their abilities (Ucar et al., under review). Noticeably, the promotion of self-determination in inclusive settings can lead to more positive in-school and post-school outcomes for young children. Many studies (c.f. Agran et al., 2020; Jackson et al., 2008) have found that dis-abled students who participate in inclusive settings experience higher academic and social outcomes than their peers who are educated in more restrictive settings. Specifically, there is evidence that social inclusion is linked with opportunities to engage in self-determined actions (Hagiwara et al., 2021; Walker et al., 2011). Additionally, Hughes et al. (2013) found that students who attended schools with a more inclusive culture engaged in more self-determined actions. Therefore, promoting self-determination for young children can result in inclusive spaces which honor the individual identities of each child. Also, the development of self-determination in early childhood could support greater self-advocacy and help facilitate inclusion Furthermore, inclusive placements are beneficial for all students, regardless of dis-ability status, as all children benefit from interacting with a diverse group of peers (Taylor & Sailor, 2023). As inclusive early childhood encompasses the development of meaningful social relationships that contribute to a sense of membership and belonging (Lee & Recchia, 2016), it is essential that young dis-abled children see themselves, their families, and their interests as valued and encouraged in the classroom.

Although it is critical to identify the value of early childhood inclusion and the relationship between inclusion and self-determination, inclusion is not merely a classroom placement. Tilstone et al. (1998) define inclusion as "the opportunity for persons with a dis-ability to participate fully in all the educational, employment, consumer, recreational, community, and domestic activities that typify everyday society" (p. 16). To cultivate an inclusive environment, all stakeholders must commit to the ideology of inclusion by promoting a strengths-based mindset when supporting dis-abled children.

Equity-Empowered Early Childhood Inclusion

Advancing strengths-based approaches in early childhood inclusive educational settings requires a commitment to anti-bias and anti-racist pedagogy as part of an ongoing justice-driven transformative and inclusive approach to early education (Erwin et al., 2021). For example, Beneke and Park (2019) urge early educators to provide language and context regarding diversity and identity markers, as children benefit from guidance (e.g., social justice and anti-bias perspectives) to gain an understanding of social messages regarding identity, fairness, and power. Furthermore, inclusive early childhood practitioners can center anti-ableism in their curricula (Lalvani & Bacon, 2018) to combat deficit perspectives and support high-quality inclusion. We leverage the InCrit framework to promote self-determination as a valuable component of early childhood inclusion.

The promotion of self-determination skills and abilities also aligns with anti-bias education's core goals: identity, diversity, justice, and activism (Derman-Sparks & Edwards, 2019). Within inclusive early childhood settings, anti-bias and justice-driven pedagogies aim to build awareness and resist the legacy of assessments and practices based on primarily White, non-disabled populations in ways that are not racially or culturally inclusive (Love & Beneke, 2021). Notions of normativity in early childhood have consequently perpetuated deficit-laden narratives for multiply-marginalized students, particularly as systemic racism and ableism exist within inclusive early childhood contexts (Beneke & Cheatham, 2020; Lalvani & Bacon, 2018). For example, Parker et al. (2020) found that marginalized students are more likely to have inequitable experiences in their schooling, which in turn impacts their perceived levels of self-determination. Promoting self-determination in the classroom and school community could have an emancipatory and inclusive effect on these students by challenging systems of oppression that often exist in school environments.

As ableism is persistent in society, including in cultural messages and educational spaces, it is likely that ableist attitudes and beliefs also present barriers in early childhood classrooms and inhibit opportunities to practice skills and abilities associated with self-determination. Thus, self-determination can enhance anti-ableist and anti-bias perspectives, as high expectations for all young children are critical for adults to facilitate meaningful interactions that promote the development of foundational self-determination skills in early childhood. Additionally, interventions aimed at promoting self-determination can help to establish developmentally appropriate self-determined skills and abilities for young children, such as engagement, self-regulation, choice making, problem solving, self-advocacy, and self-monitoring (Diamond, 2018; Erwin et al., 2016). This includes establishing explicit and intentional awareness of how self-determination may further support anti-bias and anti-racist education frameworks through the creation of safe and supportive learning environments where children are supported to construct their identity, build confidence, and honor human diversity (Derman-Sparks & Edwards, 2019).

Setting High Expectations Through Promoting Self-Determination

In order to promote self-determination for young children, adults must explicitly create and reinforce high expectations, as high expectations can generate natural environments where young children receive supports and opportunities to strengthen their self-determination. This may be best achieved in inclusive educational environments, considering that "self-contained learning environments have long been critiqued for high levels of student absenteeism, low rates of student engagement, and minimal evidence of the differentiated instruction such environments promise to provide (Valle & Connor, 2011)" (Baglieri & Lalvani, 2019, p.19). Baglieri and Lalvani (2019) problematize segregated, self-contained learning environments, explaining that "the climates of self-contained classrooms are further associated with watered-down curricula and low expectations for students, which impose limits on educational opportunities available to children labeled as disabled (Brantlinger, 2006; Gabel & Connor, 2014)" (p.19). Taking an inclusive approach to self-determination in early childhood, we emphasize the importance of high expectations for students to both routinely achieve goals they set for themselves and to learn in inclusive environments. To move towards equity-empowered frameworks and practices, which include setting high expectations for all young children, it is necessary to develop a deeper understanding of structural and attitudinal barriers to high expectations and to take action to combat these barriers by promoting self-determination amongst children.

While access to an inclusive classroom environment can be interpreted as setting higher expectations for young children receiving special education services, it is also important for practitioners to consider how classroom activities promote self-determined actions. Adair (2014) articulated that within early childhood education, "children's access to activities that require them to use their own agency, such as experimentation and designing projects, is in decline" (p. 218). Adair (2014) defines agency within the context of schooling as "being able to influence and make decisions about what and how something is learned in order to expand capabilities… or the agency children might use in their learning" (p. 219). Furthermore, this author makes the connection between agency and academic equity, identifying agency as central to equitable early learning given that minoritized children often learn in less resourced settings, and deficit lenses contribute to task-oriented learning experiences that do not offer young children the same opportunities to develop their agency as White, U.S. born children in well-resourced schools (Adair, 2014). Educational inequities can be compounded by limited resources and deficit perspectives, which can negatively influence young children's opportunities to be empowered agents in their own learning. However, the promotion of self-determination in culturally responsive ways can provide young children with access to learning, practicing, and growing self-determination skills and abilities that are developmentally appropriate and culturally valued (Shogren et al., 2015).

FUTURE DIRECTIONS FOR SELF-DETERMINATION WITHIN INCLUSIVE EARLY CHILDHOOD

Recommendations for Practice

This chapter has outlined the theoretical basis of self-determination, framed the promotion of self-determination as anti-bias and anti-ableist emancipatory pedagogy, and highlighted the importance of culturally responsive practice when engaging in this work. The potential uses of the chapter include informing early childhood teacher preparation programs and in-service professional development; supporting the development and implementation of programs for policymakers, administration/directors, and educators; and prompting continued research and evaluation by researchers and policymakers. In the following section, we share recommendations for various stakeholders to elevate the role of self-determination within inclusive early childhood settings.

Inclusive Early Childhood Practitioners and Educators

Practitioners and families may now be interested in strategies to promote self-determination for young children. For example, the promotion of self-determination may strengthen early educators' efforts to nurture all children's development and further advocate for more inclusive and justice-driven environments. For practitioners working with young children receiving special education services, supporting foundational self-determination skills, such as self-awareness and self-knowledge, can create space for children to identify their choices and preferences and advocate for themselves based on their individual strengths and support needs. Therefore, it is important to build upon each child's interests and strengths and empower young children as capable agents. Furthermore, it may have a positive impact on relationship building with young children and their families as young children appreciate being encouraged to share their interests and achievements, and families highly value learning about their children's active engagement at school. We encourage practitioners to support young children through the *Decide, Act, and Believe* process (see Figure 1) and share their process with children's families by offering some examples of how families can apply the process at home aligned with their family life. It is meaningful for families to hear practitioners invest time in their child's interests and preferences to partner in growing the child's ability and capability to be self-determined. This is another example of practitioners communicating high expectations with families.

Often, early intervention or early childhood special education practitioners and families are already engaging in some of these practices. However, being explicit about each stage and helping students reflect on their past experiences deciding, acting, and believing may help support their journey in developing self-determination. Being intentional about the *Decide, Act, and Believe* cycle with young children across contexts can help to strengthen family-professional partnerships by promoting collaboration and consistency across settings (refer to Table 1 or Ucar et al., under review for more details).

Table 1. Decide, act, believe and embedded self-determination skills for young children (Adapted with permission from Ucar et al., under review.)

Example Early Childhood IEP goal	Embedded Self-Determination related Skill and Ability
Student will **decide** on an activity during center time based on personal needs or interests	Students may use verbal or non-verbal communication to request, **make choices,** and **set goals** based on their likes and dislikes
Student will **act** by communicating wants in social situations with peers (e.g., I want to go first)	Students may relate the simple strategies of expressing wants to daily **goal-attainment** about their experience to promote engagement in play and learning; they may **self-advocate** by expressing wants and needs
Student will engage in back-and-forth reflective communication (**believe**) to advocate for preferences, needs, and interests	Students may engage in conversation topics that reflect their own interests based on their **self-awareness**; they may reflect on their strengths and needs to support **self-knowledge**

Promoting Student Involvement in IFSP/IEP Goals

Practitioners and families receiving early intervention or early childhood special education (EI/ECSE) services can intentionally focus on the *Decide, Act, and Believe* cycle when it comes to planning for student involvement in their IEPs (see Table 1). For example, an inclusive early childhood practitioner might consider how to write IFSP/IEP goals in ways that reflect the tenets behind *Decide, Act,* and *Believe.* Since skills and abilities associated with the *Decide* phase include choice-making, decision-making, goal-setting, problem-solving, and planning (KU Center on Developmental Disabilities, 2019), a practitioner might write an IFSP/IEP goal that centers around students' choices during free play. Next, the *Act* phase includes skills such as self-management, goal attaining, problem solving, and self-advocacy. Therefore, practitioners could write IFSP/IEP goals around advocating for wants and needs in developmentally appropriate ways. While this may appear differently for children receiving early intervention services compared to preschool or early elementary school children, practitioners may encourage decisions and actions starting in early intervention. Finally, the *Believe* phase includes skills such as self-awareness and self-knowledge. An IEP goal reflecting this stage could focus on student reflection on their identity and personal preferences. Practitioners can introduce these concepts and terms in developmentally appropriate ways using multimedia (e.g., picture books, videos) and talk about goals frequently with young children. Practitioners can collaborate with families to establish shared use of these terms to make messages consistent across settings, and practitioners and families can also help children in reflective practices by involving children in progress monitoring and celebrating student progress. In this way, young children may strengthen their awareness toward their own goals and their progress. Starting the involvement of young children with dis-abilities in the IEP process early will be better prepared for them to become more active participants and take a leadership role in their own IEPs later (Papay et al. 2015).

Early Childhood Special Education Teacher Education Programs

The promotion of self-determination skills and abilities aligns with anti-bias education's core goals: Identity, Diversity, Justice, and Activism (Derman-Sparks & Edwards, 2019). Pre-service teacher preparation programs often can and do embed anti-bias pedagogies and practices into their curricula. For example, justice-driven pedagogies strive to achieve equity through alternate forms of assessments to avoid practices that inherently support White, non-disabled students (Love & Beneke, 2021). Assessments such as these, which were designed for specific populations, may inadvertently promote notions of normativity in early childhood, set up multiply marginalized students for failure, and highlight systemic racism and ableism which exist within inclusive early childhood contexts (e.g., Beneke & Cheatham, 2020; Lalvani & Bacon, 2018). As pre-service teacher preparation programs continue to build upon the need for more equitable and justice-driven systems, they can incorporate content on how to promote self-determination for young children with dis-abilities in inclusive settings into their teacher education curricula.

There are meaningful ways to educate pre-service teachers regarding how biases and perceptions of students' abilities impact student outcomes, which are often further impacted by multiple marginalized students. For example, teachers should be made aware of the research regarding the lack of inclusive school experiences for students of color and marginalized students, which may impact students' perceived ability to engage in self-determined actions (Parker et al., 2020). By promoting self-determination, teachers may be able to challenge systemic barriers and include all students in being self-determined. One way to begin such work in pre-service teacher education programs may include examining implicit biases and developing a critical consciousness regarding how one's own identity, perspective, and experience can all contribute to implicit biases in the classroom (Urbani et al., 2022). As pre-service teachers are either already working in those environments or preparing to work in those environments and may also take leadership roles, it is essential to understand and reflect on how implicit biases impact teaching and interactions with students. Pre-service teacher educators may also provide tools and set expectations for educators to continue this work post-graduation, in addition to strategies that promote student empowerment and inclusion.

School Districts, Professional Development, and Higher Education

Even within the inclusive setting, all adults in the classroom providing support for young dis-abled children benefit from intentional and ongoing conversations about their constructs of appropriate pedagogy, as culture and ability impact embodiment and classroom experience. In inclusive early childhood settings, building awareness and commitments towards equitable and justice-driven practices requires both an understanding of how interactions with young children may empower or disempower and pedagogical resources to address inequity. Reflective conversations can support practitioners' growing awareness about the ways that they provide assistance to young children.

While assistance should be provided in culturally responsive ways and ideally promote young children's own interests and child-led behaviors, young children from marginalized backgrounds receiving special education services are too often supported in inclusive settings in ways that are restrictive, adult-centered, and based on normative expectations for behaviors of non-disabled White children (Park et al., 2021). Therefore, school districts may provide ongoing professional development to educators to raise awareness about anti-bias pedagogies and practices, and ways to implement them systematically throughout the school. To ensure that practitioners are adequately given the training and tools necessary, robust and systematic support is required. This includes dedicating resources to ensure that practitioners can complete these meaningful professional development experiences and incorporate them into the classroom over an extended period of time. One way that school personnel might implement self-determination instruction is through multi-tiered systems of supports (MTSS), which apply to all students (Matusevich et al., 2023). In this way, students who face multiple systemic barriers may receive more targeted supports.

School districts and higher education teacher preparation programs would also benefit from implementing professional development sessions around promoting self-determination in the classroom. Since many teachers already engage students in skills and abilities associated with self-determination, professional development can provide practitioners with the knowledge required to be more intentional in highlighting these skills. School leaders may also engage practitioners in identifying target self-determination skills related to current students' IEP goals (see Table 1 for examples). In this way, practitioners can begin applying this framework immediately with young students.

Young dis-abled children benefit from practitioner commitments to anti-ableist pedagogies and practices to further promote self-determination in early childhood. To move towards more equitable and inclusive early childhood systems, school districts can also consider their unique records regarding how systemic racism and ableism have intersected to possibly pathologize and further marginalize young children and families. For example, in early intervention (EI) and early childhood special education (ECSE) enrollment, disparities by race and ethnicity remain prevalent, particularly for children with multiple marginalized identities (Cycyk et al., 2022), which reflects the racially disproportionate representation in special education (Annamma et al., 2013; Yu et al., 2021). Almost 50% of children receiving EI/ECSE services "are from minoritized racial, ethnic, and relatedly, linguistic backgrounds," and there is a need to reduce biases in evaluation and service delivery for minoritized children and families (Cycyk et al., 2022, p. 451). These disparities reflect persistent social and structural inequities that further marginalize minoritized children's early educational experiences and environment. These systemic barriers in EI/ECSE also impact young children's experiences in inclusive settings.

School district personnel may consider policies and practices for practitioners, as well as district policies to address educational inequities and biases within their school districts. In this process, the role of self-determination may be introduced as a policy to combat existing inequities and move towards equity-empowered practices. To improve the quality of interactions and experiences for young children receiving special education services, it is necessary to build awareness about what is culturally responsive and inclusive for the diverse student population. To achieve this in a structured and systematic way, school districts may leverage equity-empowered practices to support educators and administrators gain an understanding of anti-racist and anti-ableist education and make actionable steps to promote strengths-based changes in their school districts.

Policymakers

There is a dearth of research regarding self-determination in inclusive early childhood settings, yet we perceive the role of self-determination as a powerful way to further anti-bias and anti-racist efforts in early childhood inclusion and to build upon existing emancipatory practices. Policymakers might see improved outcomes for students with and without dis-abilities for funding programs which promote the development of self-determination. Furthermore, teachers and practitioners could benefit from a policy that bridges the research-to-practice gap by making self-determination a key component of early childhood special education pedagogy. Finally, policymakers might use the promotion of self-determination related interventions and practices as a way to promote inclusion of young children with dis-abilities.

DIRECTIONS FOR FUTURE RESEARCH

As stated above, only limited literature on self-determination for young children with dis-abilities is currently available; there is a need for more experimental research on interventions meant to promote self-determination for young children, especially those with extensive support needs. In addition, research on assessments and interventions has not been conducted in recent years. Therefore, there is an urgent need to focus on self-determination assessment and intervention research within inclusive early childhood environments.

Self-Determination Assessments, Including SDI:SR and SDI:PTR for Younger Children

Currently, the Self-Determination Inventory: Student Report (SDI:SR) was developed aligned with Causal Agency Theory and validated for over 4,700 students ages 13–22 with and without dis-abilities in 39 states. The SDI:SR is a self-report measure containing 21 items on a sliding scale from 0–99 and provides students with a snapshot of their self-reported self-determination levels in the areas of *Decide, Act,* and *Believe.* Researchers found that dis-ability status, race and socioeconomic status highly impacted students' self-reported self-determination scores (Shogren et al., 2018). In general, they found that White students without dis-abilities rated their self-determination significantly higher than dis-abled students and/or non-White students, and that students with intersectional identities scored themselves even lower. In addition, students who received free or reduced lunch reported lower self-determination scores.

These results suggest that opportunities to express self-determined actions are impacted by systemic barriers tied to race, class, and dis-ability status. Therefore, practitioners and adults must take into account children's struggles with a lack of opportunity to exert control on their environment when promoting self-determination. Among older youth and adults with dis-abilities, people often experience more restrictive academic and living environments, which inhibit their opportunities to try new things and learn from their experiences: a key factor in developing self-determination related skills and abilities (Hagiwara et al., 2021). However, these environments can be even more restrictive for students with intersecting identities. Regardless, research indicates positive impacts and substantial benefits when older children, adolescents, and dis-abled adults develop greater self-determination skills. Considering these benefits, there is an urgent need to develop and validate a reliable tool to measure self-determination for young children like the SDI:SR.

The Self-Determination Inventory: Parent/Teacher Report (SDI:PTR) is a mirrored measure to the SDI:SR and includes the same 21 items as the SDI:SR (Shogren et al., 2022). In the SDI:PTR, parents or teachers answer questions about the self-determination of a student or child. While assessments such as these might be beneficial in early childhood, this measure is still intended for use in older students (i.e., aged 13-22), and ongoing research has found that there is often a discrepancy between how students rated their self-determination status and how parents and teachers rated their students or children (Shogren et al., 2020). Therefore, there is a need for a parent/teacher assessment intended for younger children to understand the similarities and differences between self-ratings and proxy ratings to design individualized self-determination interventions.

Self-Determination Interventions, Including the SDLMI

More research is needed on the effects of interventions meant to promote self-determination for young children. In a review of the literature concerning interventions meant to promote student self-determination, Burke et al. (2018) found that more than half of the studies conducted since the year 2000 concerned students of high school age or older. Very few of the remaining studies included elementary school children, and none of the studies included children below the age of five. One evidence-based practice targeted to promote self-determination is the Self-Determined Learning Model of Instruction (SDLMI; Shogren et al., 2019b). However, as mentioned above, the majority of the studies using the SDLMI has focused on high school age or older. Future research should consider adapting the SDLMI for young children and evaluating its efficacy for promoting self-determination for students of this age in inclusive early childhood settings.

Interpreting Self-Determination Measures and Implementing Interventions in Culturally Responsive Ways

Although previous research has shown that cultural and societal identities such as dis-ability, race/ethnicity, and socio-economic status impact how people express and engage in self-determination (e.g., Shogren et al. 2018), such research does not include participants of young children with dis-abilities. To understand how to support the development of self-determination for young children from diverse backgrounds, it is critical to conduct research on the effects of race, dis-ability, and socioeconomic status on self-reported measures of self-determination in early childhood. In addition, given the fact that self-determination develops throughout the life course, starting in early childhood (Shogren et al., 2015), future work should track how cultural and societal identities impact the development of self-determination over the course of educational stages (e.g., early childhood, elementary school, middle school, high school) by using self-determination measures such as the SDI:SR. Additionally, embedding self-determination instruction or implementing self-determination interventions such as the SDLMI aligned with children's cultural identities in collaboration with families will play an essential role in increasing and sustaining the growth of self-determination for children with dis-abilities, especially those from marginalized backgrounds. In the end, working with young children to develop their self-determination related skills and abilities can have lasting impacts throughout their lives (Palmer et al., 2017; Summers et al., 2014).

Assessing Attitudes or Knowledge of Self-Determination, Inclusion, and Culturally Responsive Practices among Practitioners, Educators, and District Personnel

As discussed above, attitudinal barriers can have a powerful impact on dis-abled students' access to quality inclusive spaces and practices. Furthermore, a lack of knowledge or awareness of the importance and power of promoting self-determination may certainly hinder children's opportunities to engage in and practice skills and abilities associated with self-determination. Some practitioners may not be aware of the interrelated effects of self-determination, inclusion, and culturally responsive practices. As the attitudinal barriers and systematic biases in early intervention and early childhood special education impact young children's learning experiences and opportunities to develop self-determination skills, more research is needed in order to understand and target key stakeholders' beliefs, attitudes, and knowledge around these issues.

In summary, this chapter proposes the promotion of self-determination as an equity-empowered emancipatory practice in inclusive early childhood settings. Currently, there is a lack of research aligning self-determination with anti-bias and inclusive practices, especially for young children. We urge early childhood stakeholders, including practitioners, district administrators, early childhood organizations, teacher preparation programs, scholars, and policymaker, to take the importance of culturally responsive ways to promote all young students' self-determination into consideration when planning for instruction, designing research, and making policy and practice decisions.

REFERENCES

Adair, J. K. (2014). Agency and expanding capabilities in early grade classrooms: What it could mean for young children. *Harvard Educational Review*, 84(2), 217–241. 10.17763/haer.84.2.y46vh546h4l12144

Agran, M., Cavin, M., Wehmeyer, M. L., & Palmer, S. (2006). Participation of students with severe disabilities in the general curriculum: The effects of the self-determined learning model of instruction. *Research and Practice for Persons with Severe Disabilities : the Journal of TASH*, 31(3), 230–241. 10.1177/154079690603100303

Agran, M., Jackson, L., Kurth, J. A., Ryndak, D., Burnette, K., Jameson, M., Zagona, A., Fitzpatrick, H., & Wehmeyer, M. (2020). Why aren't students with severe disabilities being placed in general education classrooms: Examining the relations among classroom placement, learner outcomes, and other factors. *Research and Practice for Persons with Severe Disabilities : the Journal of TASH*, 41(1), 4–13. 10.1177/1540796919878134

Annamma, S. A., Connor, D., & Ferri, B. (2013). Dis/ability critical race studies (DisCrit): Theorizing at the intersections of race and dis/ability. *Race, Ethnicity and Education*, 16(1), 1–31. 10.1080/13613324.2012.730511

Anton, J., Hagiwara, M., Raley, S. K., & Burke, K. M. (in press). Inclusion and self-determination for secondary students with disabilities: The effects of interventions and classroom placement. *Journal of the American Academy of Special Education Professionals*.

Baglieri, S., & Lalvani, P. (2019). *Undoing Ableism: Teaching About Disability in K-12 Classrooms* (1st ed.). Routledge., 10.4324/9781351002868

Barton, E. E., & Smith, B. J. (2015). Advancing high-quality preschool inclusion: A discussion and recommendations for the field. *Topics in Early Childhood Special Education*, 35(2), 69–78. 10.1177/0271121415583048

Beneke, M. R., & Cheatham, G. A. (2020). Teacher candidates talking (but not talking) about dis/ability and race in preschool. *Journal of Literacy Research*, 52(3), 245–268. 10.1177/1086296X20939561

Beneke, M. R., & Park, C. C. (2019). Introduction to the special issue: Antibias curriculum and critical praxis to advance social justice in inclusive early childhood education. *Young Exceptional Children*, 22(2), 55–61. 10.1177/1096250619833337

Bruns, D. A., & Thompson, S. D. (2014). Turning mealtimes into learning opportunities: Integrating feeding goals into IEPs. *Teaching Exceptional Children*, 46(6), 179–186. 10.1177/0040059914534619

Buffington-Adams, J., & Vaughan, K. P. (2019). Introduction: An invitation to complicated conversations. *Journal of Curriculum Theorizing*, 34(1).

Burke, K. M., Raley, S. K., Shogren, K. A., Hagiwara, M., Mumbardó-Adam, C., Uyanik, H., & Behrens, S. (2018). A meta-analysis of interventions to promote self-determination for students with disabilities. *Remedial and Special Education*, 1–13. 10.1177/0074193251880274

Camilli, G., Vargas, S., Ryan, S., & Barnett, W. S. (2010). Meta-analysis of the effects of early education interventions on cognitive and social development. *Teachers College Record*, 112(3), 579–620. 10.1177/016146811011200303

Cioè-Peña, M. (2021). Raciolinguistics and the education of emergent bilinguals labeled as disabled. *The Urban Review*, 53(3), 443–469. 10.1007/s11256-020-00581-z

Cruz, R. A., Firestone, A. R., & Love, M. (2023). Beyond a seat at the table: Imagining educational equity through critical inclusion. *Educational Review*, 1–27. 10.1080/00131911.2023.2173726

Cycyk, L. M., De Anda, S., Ramsey, K. L., Sheppard, B. S., & Zuckerman, K. (2022). Moving through the pipeline: Ethnic and linguistic disparities in special education from birth through age five. *Educational Researcher*, 51(7), 451–464. 10.3102/00 13189X22112026237032722

Derman-Sparks, L., & Edwards, J. O. (2019). Understanding anti-bias education: Bringing the four core goals to every facet of your curriculum. *YC Young Children*, 74(5), 6–13.

Diamond, L. (2018). Problem solving in the early years. *Intervention in School and Clinic*, 53(4), 220–223. 10.1177/1053451217712957

Erwin, E. J., Bacon, J. K., & Lalvani, P. (2021). It's about time! Advancing justice through joyful inquiry with young children. *Topics in Early Childhood Special Education*, 1–12. 10.1177/0271121420988890

Erwin, E. J., Maude, S. P., Palmer, S. B., Summers, J. A., Brotherson, M. J., Haines, S. J., Stroup-Rentier, V., Zheng, Y., & Peck, N. F. (2016). Fostering the foundations of self-determination in early childhood: A process for enhancing child outcomes across home and school. *Early Childhood Education Journal*, 44(4), 325–333. 10.1007/s10643-015-0710-9

Fallon, L. M., DeFouw, E. R., Berkman, T. S., Cathcart, S. C., O'Keeffe, B. V., & Sugai, G. (2021). Supports to improve academic outcomes with racially and ethnically minoritized youth: A review of research. *Remedial and Special Education*, 1–18. 10.1177/07419325211046760

Garrels, V., & Palmer, S. B. (2020). A catalyst for academic achievement and self-determination for students with intellectual disability. *Journal of Intellectual Disabilities*, 24(4), 459–473. 10.1177/17446295198405263094382

Gay, G. (2018). *Culturally Responsive Teaching: Theory, Research, and Practice* (3rd ed.). Teachers College Press.

Hagiwara, M., Raley, S. K., Shogren, K. A., & Alsaeed, A. (2024). Culturally responsive and sustaining universal design for transition and student self-determination. In Scott, L. A., & Thoma, C. A. (Eds.), *Universal design for transition: The educators' guide for equity focused transition planning*. Brookes Publishing.

Hagiwara, M., Shogren, K. A., & Turner, E. L. (2021). Examining perceptions toward self-determination of people with disabilities: A meta-synthesis. *Journal of Developmental and Physical Disabilities*, 1–21. https://www.doi.org/10.1007/s10882-021-09823-8

Haines, S. J., Summers, J. A., Palmer, S. B., Stroup-Rentier, V. L., & Chu, S. Y. (2017). Immigrant Families' Perceptions of Fostering Their Preschoolers' Foundational Skills for Self-Determination. *Inclusion (Washington, D.C.)*, 5(4), 293–305. 10.1352/2326-6988-5.4.293

Heffron, M. C., & Murch, T. (2010). Reflective supervision and leadership in infant and early childhood programs. *Zero to Three*.

Hughes, C., Cosgriff, J. C., Agran, M., & Washington, B. H. (2013). Student self-determination: A preliminary investigation of the role of participation in inclusive settings. *Education and Training in Autism and Developmental Disabilities*, 48(1), 3–17. https://www.jstor.org/stable/23879882

Individuals With Disabilities Education Act, 20 U.S.C. § 1400 (2004).

Jackson, L. B., Ryndak, D. L., & Wehmeyer, M. L. (2008). The dynamic relationship between context, curriculum, and student learning: A case for inclusive education as a research based practice. *Research and Practice for Persons with Severe Disabilities : the Journal of TASH*, 34(1), 175–195. 10.2511/rpsd.33.4.175

Johnson, J., Rahn, N. L., & Bricker, D. D. (2015). *An activity-based approach to early intervention* (4th ed.). Paul H. Brookes Publishing Co.

KU Center on Developmental Disabilities. (2019). *Self-Determination Inventory: Student Report Guide*. Author.

Lalvani, P., & Bacon, J. K. (2018). Rethinking "we are all special": Anti-ableism curricula in early childhood classrooms. *Young Exceptional Children*, 22(2), 87–100. 10.1177/1096250618810706

Lee, S.-H., Wehmeyer, M. L., Palmer, S. B., Soukup, J. H., & Little, T. D. (2008). Self-determination and access to the general education curriculum. *The Journal of Special Education*, 42(2), 91–107. 10.1177/0022466907312354

Lee, Y. J., & Recchia, S. L. (2016). Zooming in and out: Exploring teacher competencies in inclusive early childhood classrooms. *Journal of Research in Childhood Education*, 30(1), 1–14. 10.1080/02568543.2015.1105330

Love, H. R., & Beneke, M. R. (2021). Pursuing justice-driven inclusive education research: Disability critical race theory (DisCrit) in early childhood. *Topics in Early Childhood Special Education*, 41(1), 31–44. 10.1177/0271121421990833

Matusevich, H. A., Shogren, K. A., Raley, S. K., Zimmerman, K. N., Alsaeed, A., & Chapman, R. (2023). A Systematic Review of the Research: The Self-Determined Learning Model of Instruction Within MTSS. *Career Development and Transition for Exceptional Individuals*, 00(0), 1–15. 10.1177/21651434231200000

Mazzotti, V. L., Rowe, D. A., Kwiatek, S., Voggt, A., Chang, W. H., Fowler, C. H., Poppen, M., Sinclair, J., & Test, D. W. (2021). Secondary transition predictors of postschool success: An update to the research base. *Career Development and Transition for Exceptional Individuals*, 44(1), 47–64. 10.1177/2165143420959793

Mumbardó-Adam, C., Guàrdia-Olmos, J., Giné, C., Raley, S. K., & Shogren, K. A. (2018). The Spanish version of the Self-Determination Inventory Student Report: Application of item response theory to self-determination measurement. *Journal of Intellectual Disability Research*, 62(4), 303–311. 10.1111/jir.1246629282783

Obiakor, F. E., & Rotatori, A. F. (2014). *Multicultural education for learners with special needs in the twenty-first century*. Information Age Publishing.

Palmer, S. A., Wehmeyer, M. L., & Shogren, K. A. (2017). The development of self-determination during childhood. In Wehmeyer, M. L., Shogren, K. A., Little, T. D., & Lopez, S. J. (Eds.), *Development of self-determination through the life-course* (pp. 71–88). Springer. 10.1007/978-94-024-1042-6_6

Palmer, S. B., Summers, J. A., Brotherson, M. J., Erwin, E. J., Maude, S. P., Stroup-Rentier, V., Hsiang-Yi, W., Peck, N. F., Zheng, Y., Weigel, C. J., Chu, S.-Y., McGrath, G. S., & Haines, S. J. (2013). Foundations for self-determination in early childhood: An inclusive model for children with disabilities. *Topics in Early Childhood Special Education*, 33(1), 38–47. 10.1177/0271121412445288

Papay, C., Unger, D. D., Williams-Diehm, K., & Mitchell, V. (2015). Begin with the end in mind: Infusing transition planning and instruction into elementary classrooms. *Teaching Exceptional Children*, 47(6), 310–318. 10.1177/0040059915587901

Park, S., Lee, S., Alonzo, M., & Adair, J. K. (2021). Reconceptualizing assistance for young children of color with disabilities in an inclusion classroom. *Topics in Early Childhood Special Education*, 41(1), 57–68. 10.1177/0271121421992429

Parker, J. S., Garnes, J. N., Oliver, E. D., Amabile, A., & Sarathy, A. (2020). It takes a village: Understanding African American high school students' self-determination in school. *School Psychology Review*, 49(2), 111–129. 10.1080/2372966X.2020.1717371

Raley, S. K., Shogren, K. A., Rifenbark, G. G., Lane, K. L., & Pace, J. R. (2021). The impact of the self-determined learning model of instruction on student self-determination in inclusive secondary classrooms. *Remedial and Special Education*, 42(6), 363–373. 10.1177/0741932520984842

Shogren, K. A., Anderson, M. H., Raley, S. K., & Hagiwara, M. (2020). Exploring the Relationship between Student and Teacher/Proxy-Respondent Scores on the Self-Determination Inventory. *Exceptionality*, 29(1), 47–60. 10.1080/09362835.2020.1729764

Shogren, K. A., Gerasimova, D., Lachapelle, Y., Lussier-Desrochers, D., Hagiwara, M., Petitpierre, G., Fontana-Lana, B., Piazza, F., Courbois, Y., Desbiens, A., Haelewyck, M., Geurts, H., Pace, J. R. & Hicks, T. (2019a). *Preliminary reliability and validity of the self-determination inventory*. Student report (trans.).

Shogren, K. A., Palmer, S. B., Wehmeyer, M. L., Williams-Diehm, K., & Little, T. D. (2012). Effect of intervention with the self-determined learning model of instruction on access and goal attainment. *Remedial and Special Education*, 33(5), 320–330. 10.1177/0741932511410072247771963

Shogren, K. A., & Raley, S. K. (2022). Assessment of Self-Determination. In *Self-Determination and Causal Agency Theory: Integrating Research into Practice* (pp. 63–75). Springer International Publishing., 10.1007/978-3-031-04260-7_6

Shogren, K. A., Raley, S. K., Burke, K. M., & Wehmeyer, M. L. (2019b). *The self-determined learning model of instruction: Teacher's guide*. Kansas University Center on Developmental Disabilities.

Shogren, K. A., Shaw, L. A., Raley, S. K., & Wehmeyer, M. L. (2018). Exploring the effect of disability, race-ethnicity, and socioeconomic status on scores on the self-determination inventory: Student-report. *Exceptional Children*, 85(1), 10–27. 10.1177/0014402918782150

Shogren, K. A., Wehmeyer, M. L., Palmer, S. B., Forber-Pratt, A., Little, T. J., & Lopez, S. (2015). Causal agency theory: Reconceptualizing a functional model of self-determination. *Education and Training in Autism and Developmental Disabilities*, 50(3), 251–263. https://www.jstor.org/stable/24827508

Shogren, K. A., Wehmeyer, M. L., & Singh, N. N. (Eds.). (2017). *Handbook of Positive Psychology in Intellectual and Developmental Disabilities: Translating Research Into Practice*. Springer. 10.1007/978-3-319-59066-0

Shogren, K. A., Zimmerman, K. N., & Toste, J. R. (2021). The potential for developing and supporting self-determination in early childhood and elementary classrooms. *Handbook of Effective Inclusive Elementary Schools: Research and Practice*, 390-410. Taylor & Francis. 10.4324/9781003043874-19

Strain, P. S., & Bovey, E. H.II. (2011). Randomized, controlled trial of the LEAP model of early intervention for young children with autism spectrum disorders. *Topics in Early Childhood Special Education*, 31(3), 133–154. 10.1177/0271121411408740

Summers, J. A., Brotherson, M. J., Erwin, E. J., Maude, S. P., Palmer, S. B., Haines, S. J., Stroup-Rentier, V., Wu, H.-Y., Peck, N. F., & Zheng, Y. Z. (2014). Family reflections on the foundations of self-determination in early childhood. *Inclusion (Washington, D.C.)*, 2(3), 175–194. 10.1352/2326-6988-2.03.175

Sun, F. (2015). Cultural consciousness: A Chinese immigrant teacher's understanding of culture and culturally responsive teaching in the United States. In Meier, D. R., & Kroll, L. R. (Eds.), *Educational Change in International Early Childhood Contexts* (pp. 73–88). Routledge. 10.4324/9781315848945-14

Suto-Manning, M., & Rabadi, A. (2018). (Re)Centering quality in early childhood education: Toward intersectional justice in minoritized children. *Review of Research in Education*, 42(1), 203–225. 10.3102/0091732X18759550

Taylor, J. L., & Sailor, W. (2023). A case for systems change in special education. *Remedial and Special Education*, 00(0), 1–11. 10.1177/07419325231181385

Tilstone, C., Florian, L., & Rose, R. (1998). *Promoting Inclusive Practice*. Routledge; London.

Urbani, J. M., Collado, C., Manalo, A., & Gonzalez, N. (2022). Building the on-ramp to inclusion: Developing critical consciousness in future early childhood educators. *Issues in Teacher Education*, 31(2), 91–121.

U.S. Department of Education & U.S. Department of Health and Human Services. (2023). *Policy Statement on Inclusion of Children with Disabilities in Early Childhood Programs*. USDoE.

Walker, H. M., Calkins, C., Wehmeyer, M. L., Walker, L., Bacon, A., Palmer, S. B., & Johnson, D. R. (2011). A social-ecological approach to promote self-determination. *Exceptionality*, 19(1), 6–18. 10.1080/09362835.2011.537220

Wehmeyer, M. L. (1992). Self-determination and the education of students with mental retardation. *Education and Training in Mental Retardation*, 27(4), 302–314. https://www.jstor.org/stable/23878861

World Health Organization. (2020, June 30). *Self-care interventions for health*. World Health Organization. https://www.who.int/news-room/fact-sheets/detail/self-care-health-interventions#:~:text=Self%2Dcare%20interventions%20promote%20individuals,convenience%2C%20confidentiality%2C%20and%20cost

Yu, B., Epstein, L., & Tisi, V. (2021). A DisCrit-informed critique of the difference vs. disorder approach in speech-language pathology. In *Critical perspectives on social justice in speech-language pathology* (pp. 105–128). IGI Global. 10.4018/978-1-7998-7134-7.ch006

Chapter 10
Becoming Reflective Early Intervention Practitioners in an Urban Area

Angi Stone-MacDonald
https://orcid.org/0000-0001-9051-1143
California State University, San Bernardino, USA

Serra Acar
https://orcid.org/0000-0002-9111-5553
University of Massachusetts, Boston, USA

Eunsuk Kim
https://orcid.org/0000-0002-1607-9521
University of Massachusetts, Boston, USA

ABSTRACT

This chapter examines how preservice early intervention (EI) practitioners become empowered as reflective practitioners through their internship, coursework, and their real-world experiences in an urban early childhood inclusive education program where over 70% of the students are from minoritized and underrepresented groups. The authors draw on two studies about students using professional, practical, and personal experiences to make their decisions in their EI and early childhood settings and use feedback and reflective practice. They examine how the reflective practice and feedback support non-traditional students who are entering EI after other educational work. One study focuses more on their development of their reflective practice and the other study focuses more on the important role of field experiences in preparing high-quality early childhood practitioners who are ready to work with the diversity found amongst children and families in an urban area.

DOI: 10.4018/979-8-3693-0924-7.ch010

INTRODUCTION

Reflective skills are crucial for early intervention students during their practicum for several reasons. To start with, reflective skills enable students to analyze and evaluate their own experiences, actions, and plans. This self-awareness promotes continuous professional growth and development. Reflective thinking practice is interrelated with critical thinking. Early intervention providers need to critically analyze their interaction with children and their families, with their colleagues, and make data-driven decisions. Reflective practice enhances their ability to make data-driven decisions and provide individualized services to children with disabilities and their families. Practicum experiences often involve challenges and difficulties that can be considered as learning opportunities for the student. Reflective practice helps students think creatively, consider alternative ways to address a challenge, learn to use their resources efficiently, and seek supervisory feedback. As they go through their training program, these experiences support their problem-solving skills and prepare them to address real-life problems.

The need for quality <u>early intervention</u> (EI- Early intervention is a program for infants and toddlers younger than 3 years old who are diagnosed with disabilities or are at a risk of developmental delay. EI identifies and provides early support for young children with disabilities to make sure they can receive instructions around their developmental and educational needs) and inclusive early childhood (EC) education, especially for infants and toddlers with disabilities, underserved children and families, and children who are emergent bilinguals, has been well documented (Marshall et al., 2005; Moran & Sheppard, 2023; Peisner-Feinberg, et al., 2001). <u>IDEIA 2004, Part C</u> (Individuals with Disabilities Education Improvement Act, commonly known as IDEA (Individuals with Disabilities Education Act), is a United States federal law that governs how states and public agencies provide services, such as early intervention, special education, and related services to children with disabilities. Part C of IDEA focuses on early intervention services to infants and toddlers with disabilities. Young children from birth to 3 who are at risk of having developmental delays or are diagnosed with disabilities can be eligible for early intervention services under Part C of IDEA.).

It states that services provided should include an educational component that promotes school readiness and incorporates pre-literacy, language and numeracy skills. <u>High quality EI and inclusive EC programs</u> (High-quality early intervention programs are considered comprehensive and effective services provided to infants and young children who may be at risk for or have developmental delays or dis-abilities. The goal of high-quality early intervention is to address developmental needs and challenges as early as possible and promote children's positive growth and development in different domains, such as cognitive, social, emotional, language, and motor skills). High-quality early childhood programs are considered educational environments that provide developmentally appropriate experiences for young children with or without disabilities (from birth to eight). The goal of high quality early childhood programs is to support children's optimal growth and development in various domains, including cognitive, social, emotional, physical, and language skills.

EI provided by well-prepared EI/EC practitioners promote greater overall infant/child development, language development, mathematical ability, literacy skills, and socialization skills (Barnett, 2001; Buysse & Hollingsworth, 2009; NICHD Early Child Care Research Network, & Duncan, 2003; Pianta et al., 2005; Vandell & Wolfe, 2000). EI programs that serve a heterogeneous group of children, provide a structured curriculum, and target their efforts to caregivers and children together appear to be the most effective (Shonkoff & Hauser-Cram, 1987). EI practitioners (Early Intervention (EI) practitioners are professionals who work in the field of early intervention services. EI practitioners provide support and services to infants, toddlers, and young children who may be at risk for developmental delays or have been diagnosed with disabilities. EI practitioners often work collaboratively as part of interdisciplinary teams that address the diverse needs of young children and their families.)

Practitioners who utilize evidence-based practices and interventions in natural environments working with caregivers are most likely to positively impact child outcomes (Dunst & Trivette, 2009; Raab & Dunst, 2006). School-age children, ages 3-21, who participated in a high-quality early intervention program achieved higher cognitive test scores (Campbell et al., 2001; Ou, 2005). High quality EI services can improve a child's developmental trajectory and support development across cognitive, social, language, and motor domains (Bailey et al., 2005; Hebbeler et. al., 2007). EI is both a family support as well as an intervention to improve child outcomes for infants and toddlers at risk of disabilities (Bailey et al., 2011; Ziviani et al., 2011).

EARLY INTERVENTION PRACTICE

Both studies were conducted by public university faculty in inclusive early education, specifically those teaching in the EI concentration in New England. Our state's decision to require a credential and specialized training in EI was a critical step toward ensuring a positive educational start for children requiring EI services and their families (Pang & Wert, 2010). Personnel preparation programs that promote family empowerment also serve to facilitate interdisciplinary relationships (Hains et al., 2005). However, we must also ensure that there are sufficient educational opportunities and support available to current and prospective EI practitioners, and that institutions of higher education build the capacity to respond to increased demand for high quality education and training (Buysse & Hollingsworth, 2009; Whitebook et al., 2004). Personnel preparation programs in EI need to address early childhood education and child development, service delivery models in multiple settings including natural environments, team collaboration, family-centered approaches, activity-based interventions, and policies, procedures, and professionalism. Preservice practitioners should participate in embedded internship opportunities over time to observe and practice family engagement strategies and evidence-based practices for intervention (Bruder, 2010; Wesley & Buysse, 1996). The Division for Early Childhood (DEC) Recommended Practices (2014) serve as a guide to best practices for preservice and inservice early intervention practitioners and providers serving young children in inclusive settings. Since the first study was conducted, DEC has also added the Initial Practice-Based Professional Preparation Standards for Early Interventionists/Early Childhood Special Educators (The Council for Exceptional Children and the DEC, 2020) [henceforth, referred to as the EI/ECSE (Early Childhood Special Education (ECSE) is guided by federal laws, including the IDEIA, which mandates that children with disabilities from birth to eight, receive a free, appropriate public education in the least restrictive environment (LRE). The goal of ECSE is to support young children's overall development and prepare these children for school success). Standards] that guide the curriculum and practices in our inclusive early childhood and early intervention programs.

It is important to have providers who themselves draw from diverse lived experiences, who are supported by preparation programs reflective practice around these experiences and professional training, to be able to meet the diverse needs of families and to diversify the workforce in meaningful ways. Study One shows how faculty can work with students through reflective practices to understand the dynamics of these types of "knowledge." Study Two aims to explore pre-service educators' reflective practices during field work, with a focus on culturally and linguistically responsive assessment in EI/early childhood special education (ECSE).

Both studies were part of two federally funded personnel preparation programs aimed to recruit and prepare personnel, especially from groups that are underrepresented and minoritized groups in the field, in order to address state-identified needs to increase the number of culturally and linguistically diverse EI practitioners in our state and metropolitan area. By increasing the number of culturally and linguistically diverse EI practitioners in the field, they are better prepared to respond to the increasingly diverse population of children and families receiving Part C services in our area. In addition to increasing the number and diversity of EI practitioners, the studies also aim to develop strong reflective practices among practitioners.

THE PROGRAMS, STUDENT POPULATION
AND THE EDUCATIONAL EXPERIENCE

Many students in our undergraduate program, and specifically in the EI concentration, are adult learners and bring various personal, practical, and professional experiences to their education and their current and future work as EI practitioners. The inclusive early education and care undergraduate degree program was created to support early childhood practitioners working in the field to complete their bachelor's degrees, as well as to earn degrees in other areas of early childhood education such as EI or administration and supervision. The undergraduate students complete a bachelor's degree program with 39 credits in the major, focusing on early education in inclusive settings with a concentration in EI. Students learn about children with and without disabilities and child development in the required eight core classes in the major. Students take three EI-specific courses and complete two 300-hour internships in state-approved EI settings.

The second study is based on an interdisciplinary personnel preparation program of scholars across: the Early Childhood Education and Care (ECEC) and the School Psychology Programs. Faculty from the two programs collaborated to prepare personnel to serve young children with disabilities who have high-intensity needs (HIN High intensity needs are defined as young children with severe disabilities or difficulties that require intensive instructions and interventions beyond the general instructions. Children with HIN, may require a range of services, accommodations, and resources on top of significant support and instructions.), and have meaningful and effective collaborations with providers, families, and administrators, through shared coursework, field experiences, and structured joint activities. For the purpose of this chapter, we will present data from the ECEC and School Psychology programs. Both programs offer a master's degree. The scholars in the ECEC cohort complete a 150-hour internship during fall semester and 300-hour internship during spring semester. The School Psychology Program includes a specialist-level (Ed.S) degree which has been fully accredited by National Association of School Psychologists (NASP). Students demonstrate increasing levels of independence during fieldwork, culminating in a 1200 hour internship experience. The average amount of time for scholars to complete the ECEC program is 36 credit hours; and the average amount of time for scholars to complete the School Psychology program is 66 credit hours. Both programs are committed to a philosophy of social and racial justice, equity, and inclusion and belonging.

Each student has a supervising practitioner who mentors on site and a university supervisor who teaches the course. Candidates are also required to have three official observations and feedback during their internship. All internship placements are coordinated through the office of field-based experiences.

Initial fieldwork activities for school psychology courses include in person observing a school psychologist performing a variety of activities involving assessment, direct intervention, and consultation; observing meetings with parents such as pre-referral or team meetings; and conducting interviews with various school personnel. Later in the program, school psychology students are required to complete two, 125-hour practica in schools during the school day. A university supervisor (Practicum Instructor) and a licensed school psychologist at the site (Field Supervisor) work together to ensure close supervision. Field Supervisors hold weekly conferences in which they provide constructive feedback about the practicum student's performance and progress. In addition, Practicum Instructors conduct weekly seminars to discuss hands-on learning plus any issues that may arise. Each student is matched with a licensed practicing school psychologist 1.5 days per week in order to apply the skills to be practiced, particularly assessment, consultation, and intervention skills. In addition, the class seminar meets on campus weekly. For this practicum experience, the school psychology program has a partnership with the public school district. During this practicum, students participate in collaborative consultation with school personnel and parents, assessment of cognitive, academic, and social/emotional skills and behaviors, participation in a prevention program, participation in an academic or social/emotional intervention program, completion of one case study involving monitoring student progress, attendance at a policy-setting meeting (e.g., school board), and attendance at an <u>Individualized Education Program (IEP) meeting</u> (The Individualized Education Program (IEP) is a legal documentation process that is developed for each eligible public-school child with disabilities who needs special education services. The IEP document is created by the child's parents and the school professionals who are knowledgeable about the child's strengths and needs. Schools are required to inform all parents about their rights as parents in the IEP. IEP meetings provide opportunities for them to address their input on special education services and allow them to share lived experiences and insights about ways to support their children more appropriately.

The interdisciplinary program uses a clinical model of supervision and values self-reflection to establish meaningful connections across research, practice, and policy. The clinical supervision model promotes an attitude of self-inquiry and problem-solving among practicum students (Corey et al., 2020; Falender, 2018). Practicum students in the ECEC program completed their one-year internship program in various sites such as childcare settings, inclusive public kindergarten, and ABA programs for young children with autism spectrum disorder. Students in the School Psychology program completed internships in a public-school setting. The majority are working with children from culturally and/or linguistically diverse (CLD) backgrounds in a large, diverse, urban school district with a student profile that reflects 140 countries and 80 languages.

The goals of our EI program at both the undergraduate and graduate levels are that are EI developmental specialist graduates will, at a minimum, be: skilled at developing family-professional partnerships; have the ability to embed learning activities in play, use both activity-based and routines-based approaches to intervention (McWilliam, 2010; Pretti-Frontczak & Bricker, 2004) conduct and use assessment for referral, diagnostics, and planning instructions; be knowledgeable about and able to work across the EI/EC systems of care for infants, toddlers, and young children; have strong communication and consultation skills; and be culturally responsive and supportive of family cultural practice, beliefs, and values in their practice. The experience includes working with families, completing multidisciplinary assessments in teams, and working with children and families in infant, toddler, and caregiver groups. Our students are embedded in the community in EI programs and/or other early childhood settings throughout classes, which each require fieldwork hours in an early childhood or EI setting to complete various class assignments.

Several of the students in the EI concentration have worked in other parts of early childhood education prior to starting the EI program. Within the degree programs, approximately 70% of these students are identified as from racial or ethnic backgrounds other than white and/or spoke a language at home that was not English. In the undergraduate program during the study period, all students in the EI concentration identified as female. In the graduate program, the first cohort's demographics include: female (88%), and the second cohort's demographics include: female (92%) during the study period. In our grant materials and reports, we identified these students as coming from culturally and/or linguistically diverse backgrounds. In addition, at least 50% of the students are nontraditional students or students who did not attend college directly after high school, are usually at least 24 years of age, and may or may not attend college full-time, but are often working at the same time as attending college (Gilardi & Guglielmetti, 2016). Our university has a 58% minority population and that percentage is higher in our early childhood program. In addition, our university is federally recognized as Minority Serving Institution (MSI) through its designation as an Asian American and Native American Pacific Islander-Serving Institution (AANAPISI) funded by the U.S. Department of Education. All of the students are completing their internship placements in urban EI programs in or around a metropolitan city. Examining the knowledge and experiences that influence the students' teaching and work with families in EI helps us to learn more about what students bring with them to the program. This understanding can allow for more responsive program design and teaching for current and future students.

STUDY ONE

In the first study, we examined the development of undergraduate EI students as reflective practitioners by analyzing students' writing assignments. In addition, we explored the relationships between EI Specialist students' professional, practical and personal experiences and their decisions in their work settings (Grisham, 2000; Vacca et al., 2003). We also examined how the context of their work within their early childhood setting influenced their educational development. Finally, we wanted to deepen our understanding of how educators are influenced by the sociocultural aspects of their lives (Vygotsky & Cole, 1978; Wertsch, 1998).

The following research questions informed this study: 1) How do EI students use personal, practical, and professional knowledge into their classroom learning experiences? 2) How do EI students incorporate personal, practical, and professional knowledge into their internship learning experiences? 3) Do students become more reflective over time and what experiences support their reflectiveness?

THEORETICAL FRAMEWORK

Using the theoretical framework of Grisham (2000) and Vacca et al. (2003) looking at educator development from the lens of multiple types of knowledge, we examined students' work in internship and EI classes to understand the types of knowledge that permeate students' reflection about their courses and internship experiences. Vacca et al. (2003) describe the relationship between a teacher's professional, practical, and personal knowledge and their beliefs about the influences on their work in a classroom. *Professional knowledge* is defined as formal academic training, often in conjunction with a degree or certification. *Practical knowledge* includes information that is learned on the job that grows with experience. *Personal knowledge* refers to beliefs developed through individual life experiences. This framework has been applied to teachers in an early childhood context (Butera et al., 2013; Grisham, 2000; Moje & Wade, 1997; Olson & Singer, 1994; Vacca et al., 2003; Vacca et al., 2004). We believe that there are similar relationships for EI practitioners between their various types of knowledge and their beliefs about their work. These three types of knowledge inform their work in the classroom and with families, but also may be in conflict with what they are learning in preservice education programs. This conflict may exist particularly for individuals entering the EI field after several years of work in an early childhood classroom as infant, toddler, or preschool teachers.

In addition to considering types of knowledge, we also examined the depth of reflection in our students' writing across several assignments in two different courses (Early Intervention and their Internship Courses) using Hatton and Smith's four levels of reflection (1995): 1) descriptive writing, 2) descriptive reflection, 3) dialogic reflection, 4) and critical reflection. In this formulation, *Descriptive writing* is not reflective at all, but involves a pure description of an event, a situation, or an issue. *Descriptive reflection*, on the other hand, provides reasons for the events, situations or issues described, based on personal judgment, experience, and/or teacher candidates' interpretations of classroom input or readings. At the next level, *dialogic reflection* is characterized by an exploration and consideration of differing reasons. Finally, *critical reflection* includes not only possible reasons, but also consideration of the broader historical, social and political contexts of the reasoning. Hatton and Smith (1995) identified a few essential issues concerning reflection. First, reflection should be a vehicle to think through and work through complex problems from our practice. Additionally, in reviewing reflective processes, we need to use systematic methods over time to solve problems and improve practice. Finally, we need to think about the larger contextual systems, and the sociocultural framework in which we work to improve the situations we and others are in, not simply ourselves.

In this case, we are looking at how students apply their learning, reflect on their work in their internship experiences, and believe the reflection might contribute to their work as an EI practitioner.

METHODOLOGY

Participants

At the beginning of the study, 16 students consented to participate in the study out of a possible 28 students in four classes over three semesters. Some students were in more than one class and consented to allow researchers to use data from multiple classes. 15 participants were students in our bachelor degree program, one student was a graduate student, all students were working toward an EI credential, and all participants identified as female. Demographically, participants identified 44% as white, 38% as Black/African American, and 18% as Latina. Students also represented a range of experiences in the field: 31% were new to early childhood education and EI, 25% had 1-5 years of experience in early childhood education, and 44% had five or more years of experience, with two students having over 15 years of experience in early childhood education before starting the EI program. These percentages are consistent with the demographics of our early childhood bachelor's degree program regarding racial and ethnic diversity and experience in the early childhood field.

METHODS

Because this research was conducted by faculty within the program, care was taken to avoid conflict of interest and ensure informed consent of participants. At the beginning of the semester, students in Early Intervention and internship classes were informed about the research study by an independent person and given the opportunity to participate. They were informed that for the purpose of the study their assignments would be reviewed by the researcher and research assistants to understand more about what they were learning in classes and internship and how they applied different types of knowledge in their EI practice. If they wished to participate, they signed the consent form and consent forms were held by an independent person in a locked cabinet until after grades were submitted. After grades were submitted, the researcher learned who had consented and the relevant student work was placed in a file for coding. Using a qualitative coding process, predetermined codes or labels informed by our theoretical frameworks, assigned to whole documents or segments of documents (i.e., paragraphs, sentences, or words) were used to help catalog key concepts while preserving the context in which these concepts occur (Miles & Huberman, 1994). Student work and course evaluations (they were anonymously submitted through the college) were coded from the students in the initial early intervention course and the two internship courses across three semesters.

To assess EI learning across the semesters and the influences of personal, practical, and professional knowledge (Grisham, 2000; Vacca et. al, 2003), we coded students' weekly reflection journals, student papers, and semester course evaluations using qualitative methods of analysis developed by Strauss and Corbin (1998) based on the categories of personal, professional, and practical knowledge discussed above. We also coded for Hatton's levels of reflection discussed above to compare the levels of reflection with the types of knowledge applied. This method was used to test the applicability of the theoretical framework on the data set available. Initially, we only used the two sets of predetermined codes described above. After the initial round of coding, we conducted a second round of open, inductive codes and found additional codes and themes in the data (See Table 2). Coding was completed independently by three coders and then discrepancies were discussed to form consensus on the codes. All three coders coded all student work and evaluations available. Coders were the lead author and two graduate students in our master's degree program in early childhood education who had taken some research courses. One graduate student had knowledge of early intervention settings and one did not, but was familiar with other early childhood education settings.

RESULTS

Understanding the students' orientations to their new roles in relation to their knowledge sources can guide faculty to better meet their needs and the needs of the families they serve. University students, as EI practitioners, are entering families' homes to work with them to support their young children. Both the university student and the family are in a new situation where they need to work together for the well-being of the child and family. In this context, it is critical that students employ multiple types of knowledge to support families and support their child to learn and grow.

Themes

Based on the conceptual framework examining types of knowledge demonstrated by EI students in their work and their levels of reflection, the data was initially coded using the predetermined set of codes: 1) types of knowledge, and 2) levels of reflection. Table 1 shows the number of occurrences and sources of data for each code.

Table 1. Summary of codes and sources from study one

Codes	Occurrences	Sources
Professional Knowledge	67	99
Practical Knowledge	65	104
Personal Knowledge	43	61
Descriptive Writing	36	42
Descriptive Reflection	41	53
Dialogic Reflection	25	37
Critical Reflection	10	11

Note. Total Sources coded = 148 documents

Table 2. Summary of themes and codes from study one

Themes	Codes
Family	● "When I enter a family's home, I enter their life" ● Education is empowerment ● Child's Progress
Partnership or Collaboration	● Doing it together
Personal Knowledge	● Assumptions about EI ● Confidence building through internship ● Overwhelmed by new knowledge
Professional Knowledge	● Definitions of terms/regulations
New ideas learned ("When I started I didn't know…")	● "now that I know….it is so much easier" ● Things not understood about how EI works
Dissonance between learned material and observed practice	● "They don't do it that way at my site" ● "But, that is not what you taught us"

In addition to the predetermined codes related to types of knowledge and reflection, four additional thematic categories emerged through inductive coding: 1) Family; 2) Partnership or Collaboration; 3) New Ideas learned ("When I started I didn't know…"); and 4) Dissonance (between learned material and observed practice). For this chapter, the following section provides explanations and evidence through quotations of the types of knowledge and reflection and then focuses on one key additional thematic category of dissonance. The data is based on student reflections, assignments, and course evaluations.

Personal Knowledge

Among the three types of knowledge, personal knowledge was the least commonly occurring type coded in the study, occurring 43 times across sources. Personal knowledge, as articulated by Grisham (2000) and Vacca et. al (2003) refers to beliefs derived through one's own experiences. Items coded as personal knowledge fit the description of "the sum of beliefs developed in the individual over the course of his or her lifetime based upon acculturation and socialization in a given society" (from study code definitions). Items coded as personal knowledge typically include student description of personal feelings or beliefs associated with their work. For instance, one student wrote about her own understanding of the role she plays as an EI provider: "In working with children and families, I make sure to see myself as a helper or goal facilitator as I realize that I will be more beneficial to everyone." Another student reflected: "I have been teaching for 4 years now and each year is more exciting to the next. One thing I find difficult at times is getting respect in the classroom from the children and other staff members…I feel I have experience and ideas that could further the education and learning of the children." In both of these instances, the knowledge is seated in an individual's own response, pointing towards cumulative experiences and socialization.

Practical Knowledge

Practical knowledge was the second most commonly coded type of knowledge, with 65 instances. Practical knowledge describes the kind of "on-the-job" learning derived through training, apprenticeship, and observation. These instances of practical knowledge contain instructional techniques as well as the intricacies of managing relationships with colleagues learned through practicum experiences. Coded examples include instances of EI students learning through encounters with children and with other professionals. One student described a moment of revelation after a challenging lesson in a preschool classroom: "I had done an acrostic with my group one day and it failed miserably, I am not sure if it was the activity, how I introduced it, or if it just wasn't the right time. But then I tried poems and did a lesson for that. The children absolutely loved making the poems, and they knew so many rhyming words…and I tried incorporating that by mentioning words they used on their homework, and this sparked so many new words..." In several instances, EI students wrote about applying what they have read to their practical experience in the classroom. One student describes trying different strategies to support a child with communication needs who would at times throw things and rip up paper in the classroom: "I've found since then simply letting the child have some space, then talking calmly to him and giving him choices has worked to control some of the challenging behavior." The student reflected on variations in the classroom that supported and didn't support the child's needs from trying out a strategy.

Professional Knowledge

Professional knowledge appears in 67 occurrences throughout coding. Professional knowledge is defined as "that which the teacher develops within a formal academic program, such as a teacher education program at a college or university and is often the least valued" (from coding definitions). In the context of this study, this knowledge relates to course content. For instance, several quotes reference course readings and professional tools. For example, one student said, "the child that entered the classroom this morning made me think of some of the readings I've done in the CLASS manual, especially those focused on positive and negative climate." Another student wrote, "since our class on Monday I've been thinking about scheduling…" In this case and in other instances of professional knowledge, the EI students are identifying knowledge gained through their formal preparation.

Interestingly, while included in the definition of professional knowledge is that it is "least valued" it was the most frequently coded form of knowledge across all types.

Levels of Reflective Practice

Regarding levels of reflective practice, results indicate that EI students were most likely to engage in descriptive writing and descriptive reflection with 36 and 41 instances, respectively. These instances typically included an account of an experience in their early childhood work setting or an account of a thought process or planning process in which they were engaged. These instances were coded as descriptive writing if they were simply an accounting of events and descriptive reflection if they contained rational or personal judgements or opinions.

Less frequent were instances of dialogic reflection and critical reflection. In the case of the former, coding identified 25 instances of dialogic reflection, which is characterized by identification of different rationales within the reflection. One example included, "... I took this intake [as] a very real reminder as to the necessity to understand the family and to move quickly if that's what the family wants and move slowly if that's what the family wants." In this instance, the EI student points towards understanding her own goals in relation to the family's needs and how to align them.

Rarely were students engaging in critical reflection, which were coded only 10 times. This number is less than a quarter the number of descriptive reflections across codes. Critical reflection extends from dialogic as it includes not only possible reasons, but also consideration of the broader historical, social and political contexts of the reasoning" (from code definitions). While rare as compared with other levels of reflection, EI students did engage in some critical reflection that was deeply meaningful to their growth. For example, students reflected on their role and responsibility in the context of education legislation:

I did not realize that service coordination was a service specifically listed under IDEA and that it had to be provided at no cost to the family... IDEA also 'reinforces the important role service coordinators play to ensure families can get and use desired supports in a way that works for them and is effective in meeting their child and family priorities.'

In this case, the student is reflecting on their important role in the system and how they have a responsibility to the family, their agency, and to the government based on the legal requirements to support the child and family through Part C services.

Another student recognized the gravity of their involvement in a family's life and their physical presence in the family's home. She stated:

I correlated this week's readings to how I manage my own personal and professional boundaries as an early intervention clinician. I truly feel that as I enter a family's home; I have a choice to make about the type of message I relay through verbal or non-verbal forms of communication. This is not only true for the first meeting with a family but for each visit. When I enter a family's home, I am entering their life. Therefore, the type of message I deliver could either support or discourage parent empowerment.

Each of these examples show how students are connecting their learning and reflection to boarder principles in their education and their context.

Dissonance

A common code that became a theme in the data was the idea of dissonance that was coded inductively. In this case, the EI students experienced dissonance on a regular basis between what they were learning in the classroom and what they were seeing in their internships or worksites in Early Intervention and inclusive early childhood settings. Students in speaking and in writing made comments such as "but, that is not what you taught us" or "that's not how they do it at my site" in response to conversations or demonstrations in class. One area that this was particularly true was in the area of assessment. In this state, there is a standardized observational and interview-based tool used to determine eligibility, but at the time of the study the implementation of the assessment tool was poor and there was limited fidelity to the training manual due to lack of training and communication between sites and the state. Students also felt dissonance when comparing ideal circumstances sometimes depicted in texts with reality. One student described concerns she had when entering families' homes that were less clean or where caregivers needed other supports and questioning why the EI practitioner didn't do anything. In discussing the situation with her supervisor, she learned that it was important to meet the families where they were and work with them at the level of support, they were willing to accept at the time. Another student commented,

I have also been having a hard time understanding how progress is expected to be made when the only experience the children have are with the EI specialist and myself for one hour a week. I have seen improvements in some of the children we have been working with, but I guess I would like to see more family involvement with some of the children.

At this time in the state, the students were just starting to see a greater focus on triadic strategies and caregivers as the key implementers of EI, with EI practitioners serving more as facilitators.

STUDY TWO

The second study aimed to explore students' reflective practices during field work, with a focus on culturally and linguistically responsive assessment in EI/early childhood special education (ECSE). We examined students' knowledge, skills, and experiences by using a pre/post design with four-checklists originally developed by the ECTA Center. We also explored students' implementation of DEC Recommended Practices during their practicum. Finally, we studied students' understanding of culturally and linguistically responsive practices through their self-reflective practices.

The Theoretical Framework

Study two is guided by 1) the ecological framework (Bronfenbrenner, 1979), 2) Disability Critical Race Theory (Annamma et al., 2013; Collier-Meek et al., 2023) and 3) culturally and linguistically sustainable practices in the field (Cioè-Peña, 2020; Souto-Manning, 2016). The ecological framework, as articulated by Bronfenbrenner (1979), provides a foundation to explain the contextual influences that contribute to health which cannot be explained by theories of individual development. It posits five levels of external influence, ranging from the distant to immediate impact on child development: the chronosystem (changes that occur within larger systems over time, e.g., environmental or historical events), macrosystem (cultural context, e.g., social and cultural values, practices), exosystem (settings or events not directly connected to child, e.g., caregivers' employment, media, politics), mesosystem (interactions and relationships among microsystem individuals, e.g., school districts, health services), and microsystem (direct interaction with the child, e.g., family, peers, teachers; Bronfenbrenner, 1979). Each layer of the ecological system influences individuals, and the relationships within the systems generate reciprocal and ever-changing influences on a child's social, behavioral, and academic development.

DisCrit theory helps examine how social co-constructions of race and ability uphold notions of normalcy, consequences for increasing numbers of marginalized children (e.g., children of Color with dis/abilities), and ways to dismantle racism and ableism within institutional processes and discourses to advance justice (Annamma et al., 2013). DisCrit theory has been applied to our field for more equitable, effective practices on behalf of children, schools, families, and grounded in implementation science, promote strategies to elevate the voices of those most marginalized and identify dynamic practices of building trusting relationships and dismantling power structures for equity-centered services (Collier-Meek et al., 2023).

Culturally and linguistically sustainable practices are intentional and systematic pedagogies that recognize and respond to children's linguistic identities, communication cultures, and provide equitable access to class participation and engagement with their peers, practitioners, and content (Cioè-Peña, 2022; Souto-Manning, 2016). Because each child has a unique language repertoire, linguistically responsive practices can support children to reach their potential and help to facilitate inclusion and belonging (Cioè-Peña, 2022; Souto-Manning, 2016).

Methods

In Study Two, we aimed to explore students' reflective practices during field work, with a focus on culturally and linguistically responsive assessment in EI/ECSE. We focused on their understanding and implementation of evidence-based, culturally and linguistically responsive assessment practices. In order to achieve this goal, we used three ways to collect data: 1) pre-post design study by using checklists, 2) implementation of DEC Recommended Practices, and 3) students self-reflection on their overall practicum experience.

Based on the pre-post mean scores (See Table 3), students reported higher scores on four post-tests in all areas: Family Capacity-Building Practices Checklist, Family Engagement Practices Checklist, Family-Centered Practices Checklist, and Informed Family Decision-Making Practices Checklist, respectively (N= 9). Students reported that the checklists were helpful to connect research into practice. For example, one student reported, "Great idea to see their pros and cons" regarding the item "Engage family members in identifying and evaluating the pros and cons of different options for addressing family-identified concerns and priorities" in the Family Engagement Practices Checklist. Another student reported,

Table 3. Pre-post mean scores of the checklists

Checklist	Pre-test (*M*)	Post-test (*M*)
Family-Centered Practices Checklist	17.33	31
Informed Family Decision-Making Practices Checklist	18.77	26.33
Family Engagement Practices Checklist	17	22.88
Family Capacity-Building Practices Checklist	22.66	32.11

The screening tool provided a list of developmentally appropriate activities for the child in a monthly schedule, one activity per day. We shared it with one of the parents and the mother was very happy using it. She color coded the ones that they enjoyed in green and the ones that the child wasn't interested in that much in red.

The student referred to the following item, "Use an everyday activity checklist to have a parent select which activities would be easiest for the parent to use" in the Family Capacity-Building Practices Checklist.

Next, we asked each student to self-select three practices from the DEC Recommended Practices and intentionally implement them with their work with children, families, and other EI/ECSE team members during their final practicum (N=9). The DEC Recommended Practices are based on the best available empirical evidence and the wisdom and experience of the field. The practices are organized into eight topic areas: leadership; assessment; environment; family; instruction; interaction; teaming and collaboration; and transition. It should be noted that the students were taking an assessment course, which was one of their shared coursework, during their practicum. So, many of the students chose practices from Assessment (e.g., A2 and A6), Family (e.g., F1 and F3), and Teaming and Collaboration (e.g., TC1 and TC2) areas (numbers indicate the specific Recommended Practice) compared to other areas. Since, the students were also doing their practicum in different settings (e.g., inclusive public kindergarten, and ABA programs), we asked them to choose the practices that fit within their practicum settings and the age group they work with the most. Table 4 summarizes self-selected three practices and student's implementation of the practice. Two students also shared additional information about the professional organization in the field. One of them shared, "I learned that DEC recommended practices include family involvement whenever possible and a wide range of assessment practices so that the child's full abilities are included". Similarly, another one said, "I learned a lot about the DEC and its recommended practices (i.e., work with the family, as a team, assessment in all domains, use a variety of methods, information about daily routines, systematic ongoing assessment, etc."

Table 4. Students' Self-selected recommended practices with implementation examples

Student ID	DEC Recommended Practice with Implementation Example
1	A2 & TC1. We do home visits as a team and debrief information with each other. A6. We collect anecdotal observations at every visit and share a copy with parents.
2	A2. We collaborate with the early childhood teacher at each observation. We share our notes and learn about the child's progress since our last observation. A4 & A10. I use developmental screening tools.

continued on following page

Table 4. Continued

Student ID	DEC Recommended Practice with Implementation Example
3	F1 & F2. My mentor uses an app to inform parents about their child's daily activities. F7. My mentor shares information about community resources with parents.
4	A5. We have a bilingual Spanish-English interventionist who conducts assessments in both languages. A3 & A10. We use Battelle Developmental Inventory.
5	A3 & A10. I use ASQ:3rd Ed. and Battelle. A11. I am practicing writing evaluation reports.
6	F3. I use open ended questions and a general one, "How is it going?" to support the parents to share their concerns and priorities. A9 & F6. I answer parents questions and share related information based on their child's artifacts.
7	A3 & A10. I use ASQ:3rd Ed. and social emotional. INS3. My mentor uses data collection forms to capture children's monthly progress and uses the data to modify EI/ECSE strategies.
8	A10. I use Wechsler Intelligence Scale for Children-Fifth Edition (WISC-V) and Behavior Assessment System for Children, Third Edition (BASC-3). A11. I write detailed psychoeducational evaluation. F9. We inform parents about their rights.
9	A7. I observe students systematically. A10. I use Wechsler Intelligence Scale for Children-Fifth Edition (WISC-V) and Behavior Assessment System for Children, Third Edition (BASC-3). A11. I write detailed psychoeducational evaluation and a one-page infographic that summarizes the report.

Note. A = Assessment, F = Family, INS = Instruction, TC = Teaming and Collaboration

Finally, we asked students to complete a self-reflection activity based on their experiences with using culturally and linguistically responsive practices in assessment (N=9). First, we asked students to reflect on how they view their own identity by listing some prompting questions (e.g., What are the characteristics that define you to yourself and to others? Where are you from? Where are your parents from? How has your worldview been affected by qualities such as your race, ethnicity, language, religion/belief system, skin color, social class, gender expression, eating habits, sexual identity and/or orientation?). Next, we asked students about how these factors contribute to their experience and how the assessment course shaped their experience. Lastly, we asked students to discuss their experience on culturally and linguistically responsive assessment and how they can use this information with their work with children, families, and their colleagues current or future.

Students shared important insights based on their experience on working with children and their families who have diverse backgrounds than their own, especially acknowledging the cultural and linguistically responsive practices as a journey rather than an end point. For instance, one student shared,

We have learned in this program that increasing our cultural awareness/humility is an ongoing journey. I have appreciated the opportunity to engage in challenging and uncomfortable conversations with faculty and students here. I aim to continuously engage in conversations in my future school district and to learn from my colleagues, students, and families.

Another student said,

It is important that I try to learn and appreciate the differences among individuals' values in order to work effectively with people from all backgrounds. Listening, being empathetic and respecting other values will allow for building trust and commitment across cultures.

DISCUSSION

These studies attempt to understand the question of how student knowledge and reflection impact and support in their development as EI practitioners. Returning to the research questions, the results in study one indicate that EI practitioners draw on personal, practical, and professional knowledge in their actions and reflections related to both classroom learning and their internship experiences. These knowledge areas present as always in relation to each other. The student writing reflects, both implicitly and explicitly, these various sources of knowledge. For instance, students may write about practical knowledge, developed through experience, which may be confirmed, challenged, or complicated by professional knowledge derived in classroom learning or by another professional in their work setting. A student may reflect, drawing from her personal reaction to a work experience as a form of knowledge and then contrast this with professional or practical knowledge she has received. As students regularly engage knowledge across types and settings, they often identify ambiguities, discontinuities, and personal revelations. In study two, students found the checklists to be very helpful in assessing knowledge and applying skills and appreciated the opportunity to engage in difficult conversations and address uncomfortable topics to learn more about and practice cultural awareness and humility. By providing opportunities for guided practice and applied practice of DEC recommended practices and culturally and linguistically responsive practices in students' practica, they are more familiar with these practices and are more likely to apply them in their practice as in-service educators and practitioners (Bruder, 2016).

This process by which knowledge interacts through reflective practice is both enacted and documented through writing. The writing samples analyzed in study one indicate EI students are regularly acting on and revising their knowledge base through experience and reflection. According to Hatton and Smith (1995), such practices are necessary and, employed systematically over time, can strengthen one's practice. As evidenced in various written materials, students engage in reflective practices at various levels. Of these levels of reflection, descriptive reflection and descriptive writing were found to be the most common examples. This is not surprising as descriptive reflection is a common feature of practicum experiences and typically begins with a basic account of an experience or understanding. Less frequent in EI student writing were instances of dialogic and critical reflection. These forms of reflection consider multiple factors and, at the critical level, engage social, historical, and political contexts. While these forms of reflection were less common, they did occur and reflect important levels of reflection for students to be able to not only situate themselves in context, but to engage with that context towards personal and systemic changes.

It is interesting to consider the dynamics between engagement of various forms of knowledge and levels of reflection. For instance, how might incorporation of personal and practical knowledge, particularly among culturally and linguistically diverse groups of EI students, engage those higher levels of reflection which necessarily concern multiple perspectives and contexts? Analysis found that instances of professional and practical knowledge were most commonly observed in the data at nearly equal frequency. Personal knowledge, on the other hand, was identified at a level almost two thirds that of the other two types. From this distinction, one may construe that students are more likely to draw from professional and practical knowledge in understanding their role as providers. Such a conclusion may be logical, given that all students in both studies are all participating in a professional degree program. As evidenced in the quotation provided in study two, students used practical and professional knowledge to grow their skills and become more reflective as practitioners in their field and context.

LIMITATIONS

Study one has only examined 16 students in one urban university's inclusive early education and EI program. More research is needed to examine how students over time apply the Vacca et. al. types of knowledge and how they become reflective practitioners. The framework has been successfully applied in teacher education, but this is one of the first studies to apply this framework to EI practitioners and examine how they become reflective professionals. Because of the different nature of the job of EI practitioners working in a family-centered framework and with families primarily in their homes, this topic requires further study and applications different from the teacher education context.

Among the limitations, we also recognize that the nature of the material gathered, and the context in which they were generated must be considered. For instance, a student may understandably compose course assignments with the intention of demonstrating the professional knowledge goals of the course, as well as their practical work experience, centering these forms of knowledge over personal knowledge. Moreover, the level of personal knowledge shared in a class assignment may be limited due to a variety of individual contextual considerations including what they are willing and able to share. Other forms of data collection, such as observation, interviews or written reflections outside of the context of a course assignment, may reveal the multiple dimensions of student knowledge and reveal to what extent students are empowered to draw upon this knowledge in their classroom and work experiences. Additional studies would serve to further saturate our themes and/or find counterexamples for our theoretical frameworks. In addition, we did not teach or practice reflective writing skills with the students in these programs. As part of the internship experiences and classwork, we discussed and reflected, but in future studies and program design it would be important to model and guide students on reflection and reflective writing to enhance their development as reflective practitioners. Finally, a limitation of this study is that writing is not always the best or preferred way for a person to reflect and the quality of reflection or clarity of their thoughts may be impacted by how easy or difficult writing is for them. For individuals for whom English is not their first language, reflecting and writing in English may also not be the best way to demonstrate knowledge and growth. In learning from this study, future classes allowed students to share their reflections in multiple ways including as an audio or video recording and in groups with others who spoke their native language.

In study two, we experienced the COVID-19 pandemic which affected course delivery methods, practicum experience, and students' attendance. We used the shared course experience to cultivate a safe and supportive learning environment that support the social, emotional, and mental health needs of graduate students who have experienced disproportionate consequences during the pandemic to support their academic outcomes. The other limitation is that we only have data from the first cohort, and the second cohort haven't completed their coursework yet.

Implications for Practice and Future Research

The first study was an exploratory study to understand how preservice EI practitioners develop their knowledge of the field and how reflection contributes to that learning. We hope that this knowledge can add to the literature on preservice EI programs for culturally and linguistically diverse learners across the country. This data will help us to better understand how individuals transitioning from other areas of early childhood into EI work understand and reflect on their role, the transition, and the practices used to serve children with disabilities and their families. This study also demonstrated the need to implement UDL principles even in reflection modalities to allow students to reflect in a variety of ways that were not solely dependent on writing in English to support the needs of our diverse future EI practitioners and non-traditional students.

This study adds to the literature on the types of knowledge used by emerging EI practitioners to understand their roles in diverse communities with whom they interact. In the years since this study was completed, our student population has also changed from primarily individuals with early childhood experience transitioning into EI to a mixture of those students and students who have little or no experience in early childhood education and are completing their degree as traditional-aged college students. Future research would examine how these two groups may be different and may have different needs in the program to learn and apply their knowledge in the field as students and EI practitioners.

As better evidenced in study two, it is very likely these two areas are interconnected. As educational practitioners explicitly recognize areas of personal knowledge, they may engage with questions of socialization and belief, which invite dialogic and critical reflection. Such multi-perspective and contextual reflection is necessary for personal and social change to improve conditions, "not simply ourselves." Such changes to EI student preparation have implications not only for students, but for faculty, and ultimately EI systems. This point is particularly salient in regard to the need to diversify the EI field in meaningful ways towards equity and quality services for children, families, and providers. In study two, the more explicit focus on culturally responsive practices in EI demonstrated the need for guided and applied practice in this area in pre-service education programs. Finally, further research would include follow-up with EI students themselves to learn how they engaged their own knowledge and reflective practice over time as they enter the workforce professionally and how they apply culturally sustaining practices and DEC practices in their work as educators.

ACKNOWLEDGMENT

The first study was funded through personnel preparation grant number H325K110412 from the Office of Special Education Programs, U.S. Department of Education. Opinions expressed herein do not necessarily represent the Department of Education's position or policy. Project Officer: Dr. Dawn Ellis.

The second study is funded through personnel preparation grant number H325K190117 from the Office of Special Education Programs, U.S. Department of Education. Opinions expressed herein do not necessarily represent the Department of Education's position or policy. Project Officer: Dr. Sunyoung Ahn.

REFERENCES

Annamma, S. A., Connor, D., & Ferri, B. (2013). Dis/ability critical race studies (DisCrit): Theorizing at the intersections of race and dis/ability. *Race, Ethnicity and Education*, 16(1), 1–31. 10.1080/13613324.2012.730511

Bailey, D. B.Jr, Hebbeler, K., Spiker, D., Scarborough, A., Mallik, S., & Nelson, L. (2005). Thirty-six-month outcomes for families of children who have disabilities and participated in early intervention. *Pediatrics*, 116(6), 1346–1352. 10.1542/peds.2004-123916322157

Bailey, D. B., Raspa, M., & Fox, L. C. (2011). What is the future of family outcomes and family-centered services? *Topics in Early Childhood Special Education*, 31(4), 216–223. 10.1177/0271121411427077

Barnett, W. S. (2001). Preschool education for economically disadvantaged children: Effects on reading achievement and related outcomes. In Neuman, S., & Dickinson, D. (Eds.), *Handbook of early literacy research* (Vol. 1, pp. 421–443). The Guilford Press.

Bronfenbrenner, U. (1979). *The ecology of human development: Experiments by nature and design*. Harvard University Press. 10.4159/9780674028845

Bruder, M. B. (2010). Early childhood intervention: A promise to children and families for their future. *Exceptional Children*, 76(3), 339–355. 10.1177/001440291007600306

Bruder, M. B. (2016). Personnel development practices in early childhood intervention. In Reichow, B., Boyd, B., Barton, E. E., & Odom, S. L. (Eds.), *Handbook of early childhood special education* (pp. 289–333). Springer. 10.1007/978-3-319-28492-7_16

Butera, G., Friesen, A., & Stone-MacDonald, A. (2013). What you can accomplish in a year: An ethnography within a Head Start community. *National Head Start Association Dialog*, 16(4), 11–29.

Buysse, V., & Hollingsworth, H. L. (2009). Program quality and early childhood inclusion: Recommendations for professional development. *Topics in Early Childhood Special Education*, 29(2), 119–128. 10.1177/0271121409332233

Campbell, F. A., Pungello, E. P., Miller-Johnson, S., Burchinal, M., & Ramey, C. T. (2001). The development of cognitive and academic abilities: Growth curves from an early childhood educational experiment. *Developmental Psychology*, 37(2), 231–242. 10.1037/0012-1649.37.2.23111269391

Cioè-Peña, M. (2022). TrUDL, a path to full inclusion: The intersectional possibilities of translanguaging and Universal Design for Learning. *TESOL Quarterly*, 56(2), 799–812. 10.1002/tesq.3074

Collier-Meek, M. A., Kratochwill, T. R., Luh, H. J., Sanetti, L. M., & Susilo, A. (2023). Reflections on consultation: Applying a DisCrit and equitable implementation lens to help school psychologists disrupt disparities. *Journal of Educational & Psychological Consultation*, 33(1), 10–44. 10.1080/10474412.2022.2131558

Corey, G., Haynes, R. H., Moulton, P., & Muratori, M. (2020). *Clinical supervision in the helping professions: A practical guide*. John Wiley & Sons.

Division for Early Childhood. (2014). *DEC Recommended Practices in early intervention/early childhood special education 2014*. DEC. http://www.dec-sped.org/recommendedpractices

Duncan, G. J.National Institute of Child Health and Human Development Early Child Care Research Network. (2003). Modeling the impacts of child care quality on children's preschool cognitive development. *Child Development*, 74(5), 1454–1475. 10.1111/1467-8624.0061714552408

Dunst, C. J., & Trivette, C. M. (2009). Let's be PALS: An evidence-based approach to professional development. *Infants and Young Children*, 22(3), 164–176. 10.1097/IYC.0b013e3181abe169

Falender, C. A. (2018). Clinical supervision-the missing ingredient. *The American Psychologist*, 73(9), 1240–1250. 10.1037/amp000038530525811

Gilardi, S., & Guglielmetti, C. (2016). University life of non-traditional students: Engagement styles and impact on attrition. *The Journal of Higher Education*, 82(1), 33–53. 10.1080/00221546.2011.11779084

Grisham, D. L. (2000). Connecting theoretical conception of reading to practice: A longitudinal study of elementary school teachers. *Reading Psychology*, 21(2), 145–170. 10.1080/02702710050084464

Hains, A. H., Rhyner, P. M., McLean, M. E., Barnekow, K., Johnson, V., & Kennedy, B. (2005). Interdisciplinary team and diverse families: Practices in early intervention personnel preparation. *Young Exceptional Children*, 8(4), 2–10. 10.1177/109625060500800401

Hatton, N., & Smith, D. (1995). Reflection in teacher education: Towards definition and implementation. *Teaching and Teacher Education*, 11(1), 33–49. 10.1016/0742-051X(94)00012-U

Hebbeler, K., Spiker, D., Bailey, D., Scarborough, A., Mallik, S., Simeonsson, R., & Nelson, L. (2007). Early intervention for infants and toddlers with disabilities and their families: Participants, services, and outcomes. *Menlo Park, CA: SRI International, 116.*

Marshall, N. L., Dennehy, J., Starr, E., & Robeson, W. W. (2005). *Preparing the early education and care workforce: The capacity of Massachusetts institutions of higher education.* Wellesley Center for Women.

McWilliam, R. A. (2010). *Routines-based early intervention: Supporting young children and their families.* Brookes.

Miles, M. B., & Huberman, A. M. (1994). *Qualitative Data Analysis: An Expanded Sourcebook.* SAGE Publications.

Moje, E. B., & Wade, S. E. (1997). What case discussions reveal about teacher thinking. *Teaching and Teacher Education*, 13(7), 691–712. 10.1016/S0742-051X(97)00015-2

Moran, K. K., & Sheppard, M. E. (2023). Finding the on ramp: Accessing early intervention and early childhood special education in an urban setting. *Journal of Early Intervention*, 45(4), 391–407. 10.1177/10538151221137801

Olson, J. R., & Singer, M. (1994). Examining teacher beliefs, reflective change, and the teaching of reading. *Literacy Research and Instruction*, 34(2), 97–110.

Ou, S. R. (2005). Pathways of long-term effects of an early intervention program on educational attainment: Findings from the Chicago longitudinal study. *Journal of Applied Developmental Psychology*, 26(5), 578–611. 10.1016/j.appdev.2005.06.008

Pang, Y., & Wert, B. Y. (2010). Preservice teachers' attitudes towards family-centered practices in early intervention: An implication for teacher education. *Educational Research*, 1(8), 253–262.

Peisner-Feinberg, E. S., Burchinal, M. R., Clifford, R. M., Culkin, M. L., Howes, C., Kagan, S. L., & Yazejian, N. (2001). The relation of preschool childcare quality to children's cognitive and social developmental trajectories through second grade. *Child Development*, 72(5), 1534–1553. 10.1111/1467-8624.0036411699686

Pianta, R., Howes, C., Burchinal, M., Bryant, D., Clifford, R., Early, D., & Barbarin, O. (2005). Features of pre-kindergarten programs, classrooms, and teachers: Do they predict observed classroom quality and child-teacher interactions? *Applied Developmental Science*, 9(3), 144–159. 10.1207/s1532480xads0903_2

Pretti-Frontczak, K., & Bricker, D. (2004). *An activity-based approach to early intervention*. Brookes Publishing Company.

Raab, M., & Dunst, C. J. (2006). Influence of child interests on variations in child behavior and functioning. *Bridges*, 4(4), 1–22.

Shonkoff, J. P., & Hauser-Cram, P. (1987). Early intervention for disabled infants and their families: A quantitative analysis. *Pediatrics*, 80(5), 650–658. 10.1542/peds.80.5.6503313255

Souto-Manning, M. (2016). Honoring and building on the rich literacy practices of young bilingual and multilingual learners. *The Reading Teacher*, 70(3), 263–271. 10.1002/trtr.1518

Strauss, A., & Corbin, J. M. (1998). *Basics of Qualitative Research: Techniques and Procedures for Developing Grounded Theory*. SAGE Publications.

The Council for Exceptional Children and The Division for Early Childhood. (2020). *Initial practice-based professional preparation standards for early interventionists/early childhood special educators (EI/ECSE) (initial birth through age 8)*. The Council for Exceptional Children and The Division for Early Childhood. https://exceptionalchildren.org/standards/initial-practice-based-standards-early -interventionists-early-childhood-special-educators

Vacca, J. L., Vacca, R. T., Gove, M. K., Burkey, L., Lenhart, L. A., & McKeon, C. (2003). *Reading and learning to read* (5th ed.). Pearson Education, Inc.

Vacca, R. T., Vacca, J. L., & Bruneau, B. (2004). Teachers Reflecting on Practice. In *Handbook of Research on Teaching Literacy Through the Communicative and Visual Arts* (pp. 445–450). Routledge.

Vandell, D., & Wolfe, B. (2000). *Child care quality: Does it matter and does it need to be improved?* Institute for Research on Poverty.

Vygotsky, L. S., & Cole, M. (1978). *Mind in society: Development of higher psychological processes.* Harvard University Press.

Wertsch, J. V. (1998). *Mind as action.* Oxford University Press.

Wesley, P. W., & Buysse, V. (1996). Supporting early childhood inclusion: Lessons learned through a statewide technical assistance project. *Topics in Early Childhood Special Education,* 16(4), 476–499. 10.1177/027112149601600407

Whitebrook, M., Phillips, D., Bellm, D., Crowell, N., Almaraz, M., & Jo, J. Y. (2004). *Two years in early care and education: A community portrait of quality and workforce stability: Alameda County, California.* University of California.

Ziviani, J., Feeney, R., & Kahn, A. (2011). Early intervention services for children with physical disability: Parents' perceptions of family-centeredness and service satisfaction. *Infants and Young Children,* 24(4), 364–382. 10.1097/IYC.0b013e31822a6b77

Chapter 11
They Who Learn Teach:
Self-Directed Activities for Early-Childhood Educators to Deepen Their Cultural Competence

Kofi LeNiles
https://orcid.org/0000-0003-0917-849X
Towson University, USA

Katherine Orlando
https://orcid.org/0000-0002-9576-9028
Towson University, USA

ABSTRACT

This chapter offers dynamic pedagogies, reflective activities, and strategies for early childhood educators who want to deepen their cultural competence. By being culturally aware and competent, early childhood educators can better serve the needs of their young learners (birth up to age 8) and help them reach their full potential. To truly revolutionize teaching and learning in early childhood settings, it is crucial for educators to engage in intentional, continuous, and inquiry-based professional development and learning. This chapter shares both theoretical concepts and practical activities to empower early childhood educators to enhance their professionalism beyond traditional professional development and learning activities.

DOI: 10.4018/979-8-3693-0924-7.ch011

INTRODUCTION

A sense of urgency is required in early-childhood learning contexts because the daily realities of Black, Brown, and other students with marginalized identities do not appear to reflect stated equity and cultural responsiveness goals in educator-preparation programs (Harris et al., 2020). Despite the introduction of federal and state policies and laws, such as the *Improving America's Schools Act* and the *Blueprint for Maryland's Future*, inequities persist. According to Roybal-Lewis (2022), professional organizations such as the National Association for the Education of Young Children (n.d.) and the American Association of Colleges for Teacher Education (n.d.) have stated the necessity for early-childhood educators (ECEs) to learn to dismantle racism and eradicate inequalities. Our youngest learners deserve to have ECEs that are willing to disrupt the status quo to ensure that they are educated to their fullest potential.

We believe that it is essential for the reader to understand our positionality as we often reference our work and roles throughout this chapter. I, Kofi LeNiles, believe that it is crucial to acknowledge the influence of history, race, culture, and society on all perspectives and narratives. I am of African/African-American descent and have published several manuscripts focused on education. I have also served as a teacher, assistant principal, and principal of schools in the United States and Ghana, and I am currently a college professor. I passionately advocate for the eradication of White racism and the systemic racism that it engenders. I believe in the right to self-determination, regardless of race, culture, or other identity markers and work tirelessly towards creating a more just society for all.

I, Kathy Orlando, am a veteran educator and administrator of Birth-grade 12 schools. I am a White woman of European descent. I have witnessed the pedagogical and identity difference mismatch between educators and those they intend to serve. I have also experienced the benefits to students and families when differences are illuminated, celebrated, understood, and addressed explicitly. However, I have also experienced harm when the aforementioned are not celebrated and addressed. I am committed to empowering educators who want to eliminate systemic racism, dismantle the systems that promote it, and provide a meaningful education for all students.

In our work, we have found that birth to P20+ educators want to positively impact all students and be culturally competent, but often do not know how to begin. Ching (2018) credits the following reasons: (1) educators understand equity differently, (2) variance exists in how a commitment to equity is demonstrated, and (3) biases exist that presume student deficits, placing the blame on students for learning and social issues in the classroom. A review of educator-preparation programs by Aguilar (2017) revealed that although educators may complete teacher-education programs, they often have challenges with understanding and demonstrating cultural competence upon entering learning spaces. These difficulties present as one or more problematic views and inequitable practices such as (1) teaching a curriculum that does not center the student identities, (2) practicing color and other identity-difference blindness that doesn't value students holistically, or (3) tokenizing a superficial appreciation of student-identity difference such as single cultural-celebration days and events (Lenski et al., 2005). Inequities for young Black and Brown learners specifically are further exacerbated by an educational system whose established institutions already enable or inscribe racial bias (Lomotey, 1990, 2022). Lomotey (2022) calls for educators to focus on the problem of systemic White racism and not the victims. According to Lomotey (2023), the solutions for developing cultural competence involve dynamic pedagogy and mastery of content to create a more inclusive and equitable learning environment that meets the needs of all students.

The purpose of this chapter is to introduce and discuss self-directed activities for ECEs who want to deepen their cultural awareness and competence. We recognize that the phrase "early-childhood educators" (which we call ECEs) includes a range of experts, including the multitude of home-, center-, and school-based caregivers and community elders. In this chapter, we will use the term ECE to represent the range of educators supporting children's development. A foundational principle is that progress toward developing cultural competence will occur only when educators, families, and other significant members of children's lives work together to imagine, build, and sustain collaborative learning environments that educate all students. "Infants and toddlers cannot be fully known or understood unless educators have a deep and meaningful relationship with families" (Gilken et al., 2023, p. 334).

In this section that follows, we combine theoretical and practical ideas from *The Afrocentric Praxis of Teaching for Freedom* Pedagogies with some core values from the National Association for the Education of Young Children (NAEYC) for further conceptualization and to strengthen the connection between theory and practice. We also present an overview of theory and concepts that frame our understanding of race, culture, power, history, and group dynamics, factors that impact ECEs' cultural competence. Because complex challenges exist in a society where systemic White racism is deeply ingrained, this chapter offers strategies that are rooted in scholarly conceptual and theoretical frameworks that are not centered in Whiteness. Rather, the frameworks are culturally-centered and draw from Afrocentric praxis. The activities presented in this chapter are self-directed and build on the theoretical and conceptual ideas presented. In addition, the activities aim to strengthen the processes educators use to understand their students' various cultural backgrounds and experiences, resulting in the creation of more inclusive and equitable learning environments.

In this chapter, we connect educator agency, pedagogy, culturally informed practices, and early childhood educator standards and beliefs to provide connections from the child and family to learning. We describe the realities of our earliest learners and the opportunities for their ECEs to develop cultural competence in new ways.

As educators who have worked in early-childhood education and leadership for decades, we understand the importance of cultural competence in creating supportive and effective learning environments. However, before we can expect educators to make changes, we must recognize that this requires a personal transformation in mindset and praxis. Moreover, we know that developing the intellectual and pedagogical dispositions necessary to educate all students effectively is challenging work. It is not simply a matter of adding new techniques or strategies to our toolbox; it involves a fundamental shift in how we view our role as educators and our relationships with students and their families.

In this chapter we also provide broader scholarship focused on teacher cultural competence so that ECEs may engage with the following objectives: (1) understand and apply the Afrocentric praxis for teaching for freedom and emancipatory pedagogies, (2) research and reflect on their critical family history projects, and (3) conduct critical policy analyses to glean the larger early-childhood context. Lastly, we embedded intentional reflective questions throughout the chapter to enhance the reader's comprehension, agency, and critical inquiry skills around the many ideas presented.

UNDERSTANDING AND APPLYING THE AFROCENTRIC PRAXIS FOR TEACHING FOR FREEDOM AND EMANCIPATORY PEDAGOGIES

In this section, we introduce an Afrocentric praxis and ways to apply it to the early childhood context. Preparing ECEs to teach and lead with equity and cultural responsiveness to benefit the young children within their care requires educators to engage in ongoing critical consciousness and transformation (Aguilar, 2017). In the United States, the majority of public-school educators are White and female, and they often serve students with identities quite different from their own (Irwin et al., 2022). Therefore, many educators must learn about children and families that are dissimilar from them in gender, race, or culture. In these classrooms it is equally as important for teachers to consider the philosophical and cultural understandings that can help them racially and culturally affirm all their students and empower them to have a sense of agency (Hilliard, 2003). By doing so, teachers consistently and consciously construct and reconstruct learning environments that are inclusive and supportive of all students, regardless of their background or identity. The challenge for many teachers is to better understand how they can deepen their cultural competence and knowledge about their students' identities while on the job.

Chapter Reflection Question: *What strategies do you use to get to know your young learners? How do you know if you are culturally centered and/or culturally responsive as you engage with learners and their families?*

Authors King and Swartz (2016) offer conceptual grounding for ECEs and others who seek to recognize and value the diverse experiences and perspectives that each student brings to the classroom. Moreover, King and Swartz help ECEs understand how to leverage what is learned to help students grow and feel seen, heard, and valued as they reach toward their full potential. In classrooms across the country, Black and Brown students' families and histories are expected to "fit" existing curricula and pedagogies (Muhammad, 2022). King and Swartz suggest centering students' cultures and lived experiences from the beginning. Cultural concepts, if acknowledged at all, are too often disconnected from content and pedagogy, making what and how educators teach appear to be universal and conceived outside of identity and culture (King & Swartz, 2016). *The Afrocentric Praxis of Teaching for Freedom* (T4F) challenges educators to recognize the uniqueness of each child. This includes acknowledging and incorporating cultural concepts into teaching practices. From King and Swartz's perspective, directly engaging with students' cultural backgrounds and experiences opens the door for the creation of a more culturally affirming and meaningful learning environment for all. King and Swartz emphasize the necessity of utilizing these processes with ourselves and others in the learning community. This approach is particularly crucial in combating the pervasive discrepancies in schooling experiences for Black, Brown, and oppressed students.

Empirical investigations have revealed the positive outcomes of implementing an Afrocentric approach to teaching and learning. For example, Green-Gibson and Collett (2014) conducted a causal comparative two-tailed T-test between two schools to evaluate the performance levels of students in reading and mathematics. In "School A," an African-centered curriculum was implemented across all subject areas, whereas "School B" did not adopt such an approach. The results indicated that students who received the African-centered curriculum significantly outperformed their peers regarding academic achievement.

In addition to Green-Gibson's and Collett's research, Duncan (2012) conducted a four-year study comparing the academic achievements of Black and Brown children exposed to either a Eurocentric or an Afrocentric social studies curriculum. The study focused on a cohort of 217 eighth-grade students over four consecutive academic years, with a demographic composition of 97% Black or Hispanic students. Duncan's research indicated that students who received an Afrocentric curriculum exhibited significantly higher performance on the New York State Social Studies Test than their counterparts exposed to the Eurocentric curriculum. These studies illuminate the positive outcomes of using a culturally grounded pedagogical and curricular focus centered on the histories, knowledge, and epistemologies of group racial/cultural groups.

Below, we have paired T4F with core beliefs from the National Association for the Education of Young Children (NAEYC). This choice was made because NAEYC emphasizes the need to move away from assuming that monolingual children are the norm and instead recognize and support each student's diverse cultures, languages, and ways of being. Moreover, NAEYC is an organization concerned with educating the United States' early-learning educators. In agreement with King and Swartz and NAEYC, scholars have suggested that embracing culturally centered ideas and becoming more culturally competent help educators extend a sense of belonging to all students (Khalifa, 2018; Ladson-Billings, 1995; Watson-Vandiver & Wiggan, 2021). King and Swartz (2016) nuance that understanding by advancing pedagogical techniques that teachers can use to connect children to their culture. As a result, below are the combined ideas (conceptual ideas) from King and Swartz and NAEYC to further conceptualize what is possible for ECEs who pursue deeper cultural competence.

Conceptual Idea One: The Positioning of the Early-Childhood Educator Is Critical

In this T4F practical application, King and Swartz urge educators to approach all children with open hearts and minds, demonstrating critical-thinking skills while also embodying kindness, compassion, and generosity. Additionally, they encourage educators to establish a "right relationship" (p. 37) with their students, valuing and respecting each child. According to NAEYC, children who experience predictable, responsive relationships and interactions with adults are likely to demonstrate increased learning competencies and executive-functioning behaviors. Taken together, King and Swartz and NAEYC are pushing for ECEs to foster a positive and inclusive learning environment by viewing children, their ways of knowing, and their culture as assets to be valued and embraced.

Conceptual Idea Two: The Praxis of the ECE Must Be Visible

Informed by African cultural ideas, King and Swartz suggest that an ECE's praxis must be visible and rooted in the cultural ideas that reflect the children they teach. Hence, how educators interact with young children and their families is critical and should be rooted in cultural ideas and precepts that are clearly articulated to all stakeholders. This requires educators to be explicit and transparent about their praxis and how it relates to the culture of their students. NAEYC's Principles of Child

Development include: (1) a recognition of the connection and reciprocity between a child and the context, (2) the interplay between physical, cognitive, social-emotional, and linguistic developmental processes, (3) the importance of play for children birth to Grade 8, and (4) the perception of children in an asset-based frame. Taken together, King and Swartz and NAEYC suggest that it is crucial for educators to recognize and celebrate the cultural and racial diversity in their community by incorporating culturally rooted and centered pedagogies into their teaching practice. Doing so can create a safer, fairer, and welcoming environment where all children can thrive.

Conceptual Idea Three: A Specific Praxis Is Needed for Culturally Competent Early-Childhood Educators

Pedagogies play a vital role in dismantling the systemic barriers faced by marginalized populations, particularly Black and Brown communities. As argued by King and Swartz, culturally informed pedagogies are highly effective in this regard, as they are rooted in the experiences of students and their families. In addition, we believe these pedagogies are aligned with widely accepted early-childhood values and beliefs. While some educators may already be well-versed in these pedagogies, others may be encountering them for the first time. To that end, King and Swartz recommend the following six pedagogies for consideration.

1. **Eldering for inclusion**: Nurturing a sense of community and promoting respect are critical in early-childhood education. This encompasses acknowledging and collaborating with elders. In many communities, elders are held in high esteem, and their knowledge, experience, and wisdom can be imparted to young students through positive engagement. Educators of young children should welcome diversity and receptively consider various viewpoints, acknowledging the beneficial role that elders can play in shaping young minds.

2. **Locating students for representation**: As educators, it is important to recognize that students from birth to Grade 3 bring their cultures, families, and experiences with them to the classroom. King and Swartz advise that to best support these learners, it is crucial to center their identities and cultures in all aspects of teaching and learning. By doing so, we can ensure that children experience "representation" (King & Swartz, 2016, p. 39) throughout their education. This means purposefully incorporating their backgrounds into the curriculum and activities and partnering with parents and the community. It is also important to remember that young children learn best through play, so it is more effective to center their identities daily rather than through a monthly heritage celebration. By being cognizant of these developmental needs, we can create a culturally competent environment that supports all young learners.

3. **Multiple ways of knowing for accurate scholarship**: Early-childhood students benefit greatly when they are exposed to diverse epistemologies in their learning environments. According to King and Swartz, epistemologies such as imagination, intuition, reason/logic, and empathy are all relevant to people's understanding of the world. For students, their views about facts and reality are often tied to their epistemological beliefs. Therefore, it is important to consider these beliefs when considering what is considered factual in a learning environment. This idea is illuminated by Lomotey (2023) when he centered the idea of a continental breakfast. Lomotey shared that if a teacher shares the concept of a continental breakfast with their students, they might state that it includes a croissant, fruit, and coffee. He went on to share that this may be true, but mostly only for students who are from Europe or North America. Lomotey highlighted that different cultures, races, and groups eat different foods for breakfast. For example, a breakfast in parts of South America may include an empanada and fresh fruit juice, while a student from Ghana, West Africa, might eat rice, egg, and fruit. Hence, a continental breakfast depends on what continent you are on; however, in this example, the teacher presents a continental breakfast as if the typical breakfast enjoyed in Europe and North America is universally enjoyed by all people for breakfast. In this scenario, a student from South America may feel that their way of being is not valued if the teacher presents only the European/North American idea of breakfast. Moreover, some students may consider the teacher's knowledge to be inaccurate or limited. By promoting more perspectives concerning what constitutes a fact, a teacher promotes more "accurate scholarship" (King & Swartz, 2016, p. 43). ECEs must provide students with opportunities to explore different epistemologies and share their own. This helps to foster a sense of community and cultural understanding in the classroom. ECEs who are culturally proficient gather evidence from various perspectives to ensure everyone's story is heard. By doing so, they show that they value communication, cultural knowledge, and the unique experiences of every student.

4. **Question-driven pedagogy for Indigenous voice**: Young children learn more effectively when they are given opportunities to demonstrate curiosity or ask questions, rather than engaging in passive learning. Early learners experience "Indigenous voice" (King & Swartz, 2016) when they experience the power of wonder through emotions, questions, and nonverbals. Culturally competent educators in early childhood education settings can help to facilitate this process by encouraging imaginative risk-taking and challenging assumptions about individuals, groups, and cultures. By welcoming critical inquiry into content, processes, and pedagogies, students can develop their critical-thinking skills and learn that seeking to understand is important.

5. **Culturally authentic assessment for critical thinking**: For early-childhood learners' benefit, it is important to recognize the value of providing multimodal, multilingual, and multicultural opportunities for children to share their knowledge and understanding. By allowing them to present their thoughts in ways that are reflective of their developmental level, culture, and learning style, we can encourage critical thinking and promote a deeper understanding of the subject matter. To be effective in this role, it is important for ECEs to intentionally plan opportunities for visual, auditory, kinesthetic, tactile, and performance-based assessments. This approach helps ECEs better understand each child's individual strengths and needs and ultimately create a more inclusive, equitable, culturally affirming learning environment for all.

6. **Communal responsibility for collaborative relationships**: Birth–Grade 3 children experience collaborative relationships and communal responsibility when elders, family and community members, caregivers, and other young children are active in supporting each other's well-being and development. Together, the greater community is responsible for ensuring all learners succeed by creating a sense of belonging and activating each learner's competence in the learning space. Culturally competent ECEs play an essential role in working with others and committing time and effort to ensure diverse participation for the benefit of all children, not just some. It is crucial to foster a positive learning environment that encourages children to explore, learn, and grow together.

Chapter Reflection Question: *What did you notice about the pedagogies advanced by King and Swartz? What was new for you, or familiar? Which pedagogy might you explore further to apply more deeply in your learning context?*

Conceptual Idea Four: ECEs' Cultural Competence Matters

As noted by Ching (2018), a culturally minded approach to education can have a highly beneficial impact on students. For ECEs, ensuring that each young learner achieves academic and social-behavioral success is crucial. The six pedagogies presented by King and Swartz provide valuable insight into how ECEs can advance the socio-academic success of all students. By studying these pedagogies, ECEs can advance their cultural competence and better serve their students.

NEXT STEPS: TWO CULTURAL COMPETENCE
SELF-DIRECTED STRATEGIES

In addition to studying and implementing the six emancipatory pedagogies and the NAEYC core values, ECEs can further their cultural competence within the teaching and learning process by engaging in two additional activities: conducting a critical family history project and completing a critical policy analysis.

Strategy One: Research and Reflect
Critically on my Family's History

A critical family history project can serve as both an entry point and a continuation for ECEs interested in advancing their cultural competence journey. A critical family-history project, also known as a critical racial autobiography, is a valuable tool for individuals to analyze their identities within social structures (Sleeter, 2016). Simultaneously, the design of the critical family history project urges us to explore the patterns of inclusion and exclusion prevalent in a racialized society. By exploring their own family histories and learning about the diverse backgrounds of their students, ECEs gain a deeper understanding of how they can create a more inclusive and equitable learning environment for all.

In American society, race and racism impact all facets of life, including education. Recent data strongly support the notion that race still plays a pivotal role in shaping the educational landscape (Zamudio et al., 2011). It is important for ECEs to acknowledge the impact of race on their lives and the lives of those from different racial and cultural backgrounds. Culturally competent ECEs have a responsibility to examine this impact and address disparities in students' experiences and achievement based on race and culture. Some ECEs have participated in activities to learn more about their own racial group and their students' racial backgrounds. This is especially true in jurisdictions where there is political pressure to address these issues. Some educator-preparation programs have initiated social training and seminars to expose preservice educators to the broader conversation surrounding achievement, social justice, and race (Raegan & Hambacher, 2021). However, more work must be done to ensure that all educators may discuss how to strive toward developing a more just and equitable education for all students, irrespective of race. From our experience, completing a critical family-history project is a step in that direction.

WHAT IS A CRITICAL FAMILY HISTORY?

This project aids individuals in comprehending the intricacies of racism and its implications on their personal lives, learning contexts, and society at large. Moreover, taking a critical approach to understanding one's family and society promotes social justice, inclusivity, and equity by fostering empathy for different perspectives and experiences (Crass, 2010). Critical family history projects differ from traditional autobiographical activities because each person must focus on their experience of their ancestors and racial group during personally selected periods of time. A critical family history project also requires each person to learn about other racial groups, the historical context, and the sociocultural context during the same period of time. Because critical family history projects require that each person confront racism by analyzing how their ancestors benefitted or were negatively impacted by racist policies and practices, the learnings provide new perspectives for ECEs on the diverse families with whom they work. We believe that all ECEs should undertake this activity to explore issues of space, identity, and differences in society. Critically reflecting on issues related to race, culture, and identity permits people, including educators, to decide in what ways they can assist in creating a more just and equitable world for all (Zamudio et al., 2011).

HOW TO GET STARTED ON A CRITICAL FAMILY HISTORY PROJECT: AN EXAMPLE FOLLOWING SLEETER'S PROTOCOL

When embarking on a critical family history project, it is important to delve into the myths and stories that are relevant to your family. For example, in one of the author's (Dr. LeNiles) critical family history project, he focused on a set of great-great-grandparents. He shares his story, findings, and next steps:

My great-great-grandfather, whom I affectionately refer to as Papa, was born in Louisiana just two years after the Emancipation Proclamation was signed. My great-great-grandmother, whom I call Mama, was born into slavery in Mississippi. One story that has been passed down in my family is about the incredible perseverance of Mama and Papa. They saved for decades and eventually were able to purchase land. One of their first acts was to build a school on that land, which has since become a cherished part of our family's history. This story is a testament to their patience, courage, vision, and dedication to family. While I love this story and am sharing how it was often told to me as a child, it is clearly missing some important context (Kofi LeNiles, personal recollection).

288

Completing the critical family history allowed for the contextualization of the story and exploration about what it was like for a family to live in Mississippi during the late 1800s. Dr. LeNiles says, "My critical family history exposed the challenges and opportunities that existed for purchasing land for my family as well as how their experiences compared to White and Indigenous (people native to the land now called the United States) people during the same period." As a result, the next step was to explore relevant structures such as laws, policies, and societal norms during that time.

I began by looking at the Mississippi Constitution of 1821 and the impact of subsequent revisions during Mama's and Papa's life. It was eye-opening to see how racism and oppression were codified in law, and it gave me a better understanding of the context in which Mama and Papa lived and sought to raise a family. The codified system of racial practices in Mississippi was representative of more extensive racial apartheid in the American South (Kofi LeNiles, personal recollection).

After delving deeper into the history of land rights in the 1800s and comparing them to today's situation in Mississippi, there are some striking similarities in the segregationist policies from then to now. For example, House Bill No. 1020, passed in Jackson, Mississippi, in 2023, has been criticized because some feel that it unfairly targets Black communities and seeks to strip the residents of their land rights. This is a clear illustration of how certain racist and oppressive patterns tend to repeat themselves over time. It is important for educators to be aware of these issues as they work toward creating a more just and equitable society. Dr. LeNiles shared:

Recognizing these patterns helped me better understand how I might leverage my work to create a more just society. While completing the critical family history project, I also considered the experiences of Indigenous people during the same period. I was particularly moved by the story of the Choctaw Indians. While my family attempted to purchase land in Mississippi, the federal and state governments forcibly moved the Choctaw off their land and relocated them to another state. These instances serve as a clear illustration of the violence and intimidation that my ancestors and other racial/cultural groups have had to endure. By delving into my family's critical history, I have gained valuable insights and knowledge from these experiences, which have informed my praxis (Kofi LeNiles, personal recollection).

POSSIBLE IMPACTS FOR THE ECE FROM THE CRITICAL FAMILY HISTORY PROJECT

It is plausible that ECEs who embark on such a project would be better equipped to comprehend the various factors that influence and shape the lived experiences of their students and families, including the impact of laws on homeownership and inheritance and how funding has impacted schools and communities. Cultural competence is developed when assumptions and biases about young children, their families, and ways of knowing can be mitigated through understanding one's own family history. Critical family history projects have the potential to help acknowledge how historical violence and discrimination have impacted early learners' families and communities and how a more equitable and just society for all may be created.

RECOMMENDED RESOURCE FOR FURTHER EXPLORATION

For ECEs who are interested in completing a critical family history project, we recommend using Sleeter's (2016) protocol. As college professors who have assigned this project to students and fellow educators over the past two years, the authors have found Sleeter's article and accompanying workbook to be a helpful resource for students and educators engaging in this work. Sleeter provides various materials to help educators and others complete critical family histories, including videos, a workbook, manuscripts, examples from others who have completed the project, and a dedicated website to assist people who are on this journey. These resources are designed to help critical family history explorers approach the project in an organized manner and complete it with accuracy.

Chapter Reflection Question: *In what ways might a Critical Family History Project inform your praxis?*

Strategy Two: Conduct Critical Policy Analyses to Glean the Larger Early-Childhood Context

As educators who prepare and mentor ECEs, we have learned that conducting critical policy analysis (CPA) is essential to ensure that ECEs are engaged in a process to better understand the policies and practices that shape their school districts and the broader community. Apple (2019) describes CPAs as a process toward understanding "the complex connections between education and the relations of dominance and subordination in the larger society—and the movements that are trying to interrupt these relations" (p. 276). By examining both historical and contemporary policies, ECEs can gain a deeper understanding of how systemic racism and inequitable policies can limit opportunities for certain groups and the resulting marginalization and disenfranchisement of these individuals. By using critical policy analysis as a means for learning and growth, ECEs can evaluate current policies and their creation while working to develop policies that work for all children. Below we provide an example of how a group of educators, including ECEs, began working on a CPA.

WHAT ARE THE STEPS WE TEACH FOR CRITICAL POLICY ANALYSIS (CPA)?

Our CPA process is:
1. Start with a policy proximate to your early childhood context.
2. Comprehend its implications for the stakeholders in the learning community.
3. Identify community members, organizations, and activists who work on and around the policy to gain deeper insights and information.
4. Identify stakeholders who played a role in shaping and executing the policy, and discuss their objectives and goals, including the policy's content and functionality.
5. Discuss intentions for the policy, including what policy says versus what policy does, particularly in terms of power relationships in society.

Learning about policy and its impact on just schooling and social justice in education can be difficult. As we have seen in our work as college professors, ECEs often experience a range of emotions as they engage with this topic. Initially, when conducting a CPA, ECEs may feel joy as they learn more about local and national policies and begin to imagine more equitable alternatives. However, this joy is often short-lived, as ECEs become increasingly aware of how policy can limit opportunities based on race, culture, and socioeconomic status. This awareness can sometimes turn to anger, particularly when ECEs identify policies that target specific groups unfairly.

A CRITICAL POLICY ANALYSIS EXAMPLE

For example, during one semester, a group of students who were full-time educators (some were ECEs, and others were not) in a mid-Atlantic urban school district undertook a 10-year CPA investigating the local school district's discipline policy. What they found was alarming: the data revealed that African American students were almost six times more likely to be disciplined than their White peers and African American preschool students were suspended at alarming rates. The data also revealed that students who received free and reduced lunch (FRL) were 1.5 times more likely to be disciplined than non-FRL students. Additionally, boys in their district were twice as likely to be disciplined as girls, regardless of their race, socioeconomic status, or special education classification.

Considering the data uncovered, students discovered that their district employed a five-tier behavior system, wherein infractions are classified from Tiers II to V based on severity. For instance, minor infractions were classified under Tier II, while major ones fall under Tier V. With this knowledge, the students opted to further investigate how their district categorized different types of behavior within their disciplinary framework.

The students decided to use a document entitled *Guidance Regarding Select Chapter 12 Provisions, Behavior and Disciplinary (pseudonym)*, which broadly described Tier II behaviors as those that cause disruption to the academic environment, involve damage to school property, or may cause minor harm to self or others. Tier II behaviors result in school-based and administrative disciplinary responses. As they delved into the list of infractions, they noticed that something as minor as a student refusing to pull up their pants or take off a hat or headphones was included. This sparked a thoughtful conversation regarding how these behaviors are often associated with Black boys and how the policy may be designed to disproportionately impact this group. The students were incensed that the policy was implemented without considering the potential impact on a specific racial or cultural group. Moreover, students considered how they, as teachers, had carried out this policy without understanding its design and disparate impact.

IMPACT OF THE CRITICAL POLICY ANALYSIS

The ECEs and others in the class decided to change how they used the discipline policy immediately and to share what they learned with their colleagues and administration. In addition, students identified local activists and organizations who were publicly challenging the discipline policy and seeking for it to be reformed or eliminated. A couple of students contacted the activists and organizations to learn more about their efforts and how they could offer their support. This step is essential because CPA work can be "grounded in the concrete understanding of and action in and with communities, cultural activists, practicing educators at all levels of the educational system, and social movements" (Apple, 2019, p. 279). Hence, CPA work moves between the theoretical and the practical and, in many ways, the imaginary as we challenge ourselves to imagine what is possible.

The last step was for students to consider what stakeholders played a role in the policy design and implementation. To do so, students secured meetings with school district administrators and began a more extensive process. This step happened outside of class because the semester ended. It was heartening to note that even after the conclusion of the semester, they continued their diligent efforts and adhered to the process we established in class.

Policy analyses are essential for those interested in learning more about the context in which they work and the policies and practices that govern them. A critical lens is necessary to help us understand how race, culture, economics, and other factors shape and guide the work toward equity. The status quo is not okay, and we must do things differently. ECEs may not only look at the policies in place where they work, but they also may explore procedures in their learning contexts. ECEs can analyze who benefits from the decisions made and the impact of those decisions on our youngest children. In other words, what are toddlers learning about identity, ability, self-regulation, and language? It's important to question the status quo and work toward a more equitable future for all children.

CONCLUSION

This is a call to action. As educators, we want to ensure that we are responsive to the needs of all our young learners. However, sometimes we may not know where to start when it comes to enhancing our cultural competence. This chapter was designed to introduce and discuss self-directed activities for ECEs who want to deepen their cultural awareness and competence. To facilitate the introspective and reflective nature of this self-work, the chapter included self-paced activities for ECEs to explore. These activities can be revisited over a lifetime to provide continued insights and learnings.

As ECEs, it is imperative to develop an awareness of equity, emancipatory pedagogy, and collaborative teaching and learning. Joyce King (2015) cautions that the reproduction of oppression, harm, and racism can occur through dysconsciousness, where individuals and educators become complacent about inequities unless they are harmed by them. Through implementing intentional pedagogies and self-directed activities, each ECE can positively impact the minds and hearts of young people and their families by placing cultures of multiple groups at the center. The critical family history project and policy analyses conducted through this process can significantly impact the early learning contexts. This happens by developing the right mindset and engaging in specific praxes. We have also provided recommendations for getting started, recognizing that each ECE is on a different step of their journey toward cultural awareness and competence.

To quote a well-known African proverb, "By trying often, the monkey learns to jump from the tree." This image emphasizes the lifelong learning commitment ECEs must engage in to achieve a deeper level of cultural awareness and competence. It is important for ECEs to continuously reflect on their current knowledge and identify areas for growth in order to reach their aspirations. We strongly encourage all ECEs to dive into the activities outlined in this chapter and to keep in mind that they are never truly finished. It is important to consistently develop oneself and advance justice for all students. Remember that every effort made toward creating an equitable and culturally and racially affirming environment for our youngest learners will have a positive impact on their lives. We encourage you to jump now and jump often. The children are counting on you!

Chapter Reflection Question: *How will you respond to this call for action for the benefit of your young learners and learning communities?*

REFERENCES

Aguilar, I. (2017). Internal revolutions: Auto-ethnography as a method for faculty who prepare K–12 educators and leaders at Hispanic serving institutions. *Journal of Latinos and Education*, 16(4), 359–373. 10.1080/15348431.2016.1262264

American Association of Colleges for Teacher Education. (n.d.). *Diversity, equity, and inclusion.* AACTE. https://www.aacte.org/resources/dei/

Apple, M. W. (2019). On doing critical policy analysis. *Educational Policy*, 33(1), 276–287. 10.1177/0895904818807307

Blueprint for Maryland's Future Act, HB 1300, 1372 (2021). https://blueprint.m arylandpublicschools.org/

Ching, C. (2018). Confronting the equity "learning problem" through practitioner inquiry. *Review of Higher Education*, 41(3), 387–421. 10.1353/rhe.2018.0013

Cochran-Smith, M., & Lytle, S. (2009). *Inquiry as stance: Practitioner research for the next generation.* Teachers College Press.

Crass, C. (2010). Towards anti-racist politics and practice: A racial autobiography. *Reflections: Narratives of Professional Helping, 16*(1), 151–160. https://reflectionsn arrativesofprofessionalhelping.org/index.php/Reflections/article/view/815

Duncan, W. (2012). The effects of Africentric United States history curriculum on Black student achievement. *Contemporary Issues in Education Research*, 5(2), 91–96. 10.19030/cier.v5i2.6925

Fariña, C., & Kotch, L. (2008). Develop a culture for sustainable learning. In *A school leader's guide to excellence: Collaborating our way to better schools* (pp. 99–120). Heinemann.

Fu-Kiau, K. K. B., & Lukondo-Wamba, A. M. (2000). *Kindezi: The Kongo art of babysitting.* Black Classic Press.

Gay, G. (2018). *Culturally responsive teaching: Theory, research, and practice.* Teachers College Press.

Gilken, J., Longley, J., & Crosby, J. (2023). Finding space for infants and toddlers in early childhood teacher preparation programs. *Early Childhood Education Journal*, 51(2), 333–344. 10.1007/s10643-021-01299-7

Gillanders, C., & Procopio, R. (Eds.). (2019). *Spotlight on young children: Equity and diversity.* NAEYC.

Gonzalez-Mena, J. (2008). *Child, family, and community: Family-centered early care and education*. Pearson.

Green-Gibson, A., & Collett, A. (2014). A comparison of African & mainstream culture on African-American students in public elementary schools. [pdf] [ed.gov]. *Multicultural Education*, 33-37, EJ1045845.

Harris, B. G., Hayes, C., & Smith, D. T. (2020). Not a "who done it" mystery: On how Whiteness sabotages equity aims in teacher preparation programs. *The Urban Review*, 52(1), 198–213. 10.1007/s11256-019-00524-3

Hilliard, A. (2003). No mystery: Closing the achievement gap between Africans and excellence. In T. Perry, C. Steele, & A. Hilliard, *Young, gifted, and Black: Promoting high achievement among African-American students* (pp. 131–165). Beacon Press.

Improving American's Schools Act of 1994, H.R.6, 103rd Congress. (1993).

Irwin, V., De La Rosa, J., Wang, K., Hein, S., Zhang, J., Burr, R., Roberts, A., Barmer, A., Bullock Mann, F., Dilig, R., & Parker, S. (2022). *The condition of education 2022* (NCES 2022-144). U.S. Department of Education. National Center for Education Statistics. https://nces.ed.gov/pubsearch/pubsinfo.asp?pubid=2022144

Khalifa, M. (2018). *Culturally responsive school leadership*. Harvard Education Press.

King, J. E. (2015). *Dysconscious racism, Afrocentric praxis, and education for human freedom: Through the years I keep on toiling: The selected works of Joyce E. King*. Routledge. 10.4324/9781315717357

King, J. E. (2017). Who will make America great again? 'Black people, of course…'. *International Journal of Qualitative Studies in Education : QSE*, 30(10), 946–956. 10.1080/09518398.2017.1312605

King, J. E., & Swartz, E. E. (2016). *The Afrocentric praxis of teaching for freedom: Connecting culture to learning*. Routledge.

Koraleck, D., Nemeth, K. N., & Ramsey, K. (2019). *Families and educators together: Building great relationships that support young children*. NAEYC.

Ladson-Billings, G. (1995). Toward a theory of culturally relevant pedagogy. *American Educational Research Journal*, 32(3), 465–491. 10.3102/00028312032003465

Ladson-Billings, G. (2014). Culturally relevant pedagogy 2.0: Aka the remix. *Harvard Educational Review*, 84(1), 74–84. 10.17763/haer.84.1.p2rj131485484751

Lenski, S. D., Crumpler, T. P., Stallworth, C., & Crawford, K. M. (2005). Beyond awareness: Preparing culturally responsive preservice teachers. *Teacher Education Quarterly*, 32(2), 85–100.

Lomotey, K. (1990). *Going to school: The African-American experience.* State University of New York Press.

Lomotey, K. (2022). *Justice for Black students: Black principals matter.* Myers Education Press.

Lomotey, K. (2023, April 27). *A Conversation on Black education.* Invited talk, Towson University.

Marshall, T. R. (2023). *Understanding Your Instructional Power: Curriculum and Language Decisions to Support Each Student.* ASCD.

Muhammad, G. E. (2022). Cultivating genius and joy in education through historically responsive literacy. *Language Arts*, 99(3), 195–204. 10.58680/la202231623

Murphy, P. K., & Alexander, P. A. (2007). Contextualizing learner-centered principles for teachers and teaching. In Hawley, W. D. (Ed.), *The keys to effective schools: Educational reform as continuous improvement* (pp. 13–32). Corwin Press. 10.4135/9781483329512.n2

National Association for the Education of Young Children. (n.d.). *Position statements.* NAEYC. https://www.naeyc.org/resources/position-statements

Neufeld, B., & Roper, D. (2003). *Coaching: A strategy for developing instructional capacity.* The Aspen Institute.

Perry, T., & Steele, C. (2004). *Young, gifted and black: Promoting high achievement among African-American students.* Beacon Press.

Reagan, E. M., & Hambacher, E. (2021). Teacher preparation for social justice: A synthesis of the literature, 1999–2019. *Teaching and Teacher Education*, 108, 103520. 10.1016/j.tate.2021.103520

Riser-Kositsky, M. (2019, January 3). *Education statistics: Facts about American schools.* EdWeek. https://www.edweek.org/leadership/education-statistics-facts-about-american-schools/2019/01

Roybal-Lewis, A. (2022). Moving towards proficiency: A grounded theory study of early childhood teacher candidates and professional development schools. *Early Childhood Education Journal*, 50(6), 913–924. 10.1007/s10643-021-01229-7

Safir, S. (2017). *The listening leader: Creating the conditions for equitable school transformation*. John Wiley & Sons.

Safir, S., & Dugan, J. (2021). *Street data: A next-generation model for equity, pedagogy, and school transformation*. Corwin.

Sleeter, C. E. (2001). Preparing teachers for culturally diverse schools: Research and the overwhelming presence of whiteness. *Journal of Teacher Education*, 52(2), 94–106. 10.1177/0022487101052002002

Sleeter, C. E. (2016). Critical family history: Situating family within contexts of power relationships. *Journal of Multidisciplinary Research*, 8(1), 11–23.

Sleeter, C. E. (2017). Critical race theory and the whiteness of teacher education. *Urban Education*, 52(2), 155–169. 10.1177/0042085916668957

Watson-Vandiver, M. J., & Wiggan, G. (2021). *The healing power of education: Afrocentric pedagogy as a tool for restoration and liberation*. Teachers College Press.

Whitford, B. L., & Wood, D. R. (2010). *Teachers Learning in Community: Realities and Possibilities*. SUNY Press. 10.1353/book518

Yosso, T. J. (2005). Whose culture has capital? A critical race theory discussion of community cultural wealth. *Race, Ethnicity and Education*, 8(1), 69–91. 10.1080/1361332052000341006

Zamudio, M., Russell, C., Rios, F., & Bridgeman, J. L. (2011). *Critical race theory matters: Education and ideology*. Routledge. 10.4324/9780203842713

KEY TERMS AND DEFINITIONS

Critical Reflection: Analyzing and evaluating one's thoughts, actions, experiences, or beliefs thoughtfully and systematically. It requires individuals to delve into the underlying assumptions, values, and perspectives that shape their thinking and behavior.

Cultural Responsiveness: Cultural responsiveness refers to recognizing, respecting, and effectively engaging with diverse cultures.

Culture: The history, practices, languages, value systems, motifs, and worldviews that give a particular group its orientation and perspectives and guide its way of life.

Early Childhood-educators: A range of educators supporting the development of children from birth to grade three.

Educator Agency: The ability of teachers and educators to make informed and intentional decisions in their teaching practices based on their knowledge, experience, and understanding of their students' needs.

Equity: Ensuring fairness and justice in distributing resources, opportunities, and access. It is a proactive approach that recognizes and addresses the historical and systemic disparities that have created barriers to equal access and outcomes for people based on race and other identity markers.

Praxis: The practical application of theory or knowledge in action. In education, it often involves the integration of theory and practice to advance a more comprehensive understanding of the subject matter.

Race: A process of categorizing people into groups based on physical characteristics (i.e., skin color, hair texture, and facial features). Race is frequently used to create and reinforce inequities, discrimination, and prejudice against people and groups.

Compilation of References

Adair, J. K. (2014). Agency and expanding capabilities in early grade classrooms: What it could mean for young children. *Harvard Educational Review*, 84(2), 217–241. 10.17763/haer.84.2.y46vh546h4l12144

Agran, M., Cavin, M., Wehmeyer, M. L., & Palmer, S. (2006). Participation of students with severe disabilities in the general curriculum: The effects of the self-determined learning model of instruction. *Research and Practice for Persons with Severe Disabilities : the Journal of TASH*, 31(3), 230–241. 10.1177/154079690603100303

Agran, M., Jackson, L., Kurth, J. A., Ryndak, D., Burnette, K., Jameson, M., Zagona, A., Fitzpatrick, H., & Wehmeyer, M. (2020). Why aren't students with severe disabilities being placed in general education classrooms: Examining the relations among classroom placement, learner outcomes, and other factors. *Research and Practice for Persons with Severe Disabilities : the Journal of TASH*, 41(1), 4–13. 10.1177/1540796919878134

Aguilar, I. (2017). Internal revolutions: Auto-ethnography as a method for faculty who prepare K–12 educators and leaders at Hispanic serving institutions. *Journal of Latinos and Education*, 16(4), 359–373. 10.1080/15348431.2016.1262264

Akamoglu, Y., Meadan, H., Pearson, J. N., & Cummings, K. (2018). Getting connected: Speech and language pathologists' perceptions of building rapport via telepractice. *Journal of Developmental and Physical Disabilities*, 30(4), 569–585. 10.1007/s10882-018-9603-3

Ali, E., Constantino, K. M., Hussain, A., & Akhtar, Z. (2018). The effects of play-based learning on early childhood education and development. *Journal of Evolution of Medical and Dental Sciences*, 7(43), 6808–6811. 10.14260/jemds/2018/1044

Altman, B. M., & Blackwell, D. L. (2014). Disability in U.S. households, 2000-2010: Findings from the National Health Interview Survey. *Family Relations*, 63(1), 20–38. 10.1111/fare.1204426962270

American Association of Colleges for Teacher Education. (n.d.). *Diversity, equity, and inclusion*. AACTE. https://www.aacte.org/resources/dei/

Anderson, K., Balandin, S., & Stancliffe, R. (2014). Australian parents' experience of speech generating device (SGD) service delivery. *Developmental Neurorehabilitation*, 17(2), 75–83. 10 .3109/17518423.2013.85773524304229

Annamma, S. B., Connor, D., & Ferri, B. (2013). Dis/ability critical race studies (DisCrit): Theorizing at the intersections of race and dis/ability. *Race, Ethnicity and Education*, 16(1), 1–31. 10.1080/13613324.2012.730511

Ansari, A. (2018). The persistence of preschool effects from early childhood through adolescence. *Journal of Educational Psychology*, 110(7), 952–973. 10.1037/edu000025530906008

Ansari, A., Pianta, R. C., Whittaker, J. V., Vitiello, V. E., & Ruzek, E. A. (2019). Starting early: The benefits of attending early childhood education programs at age 3. *American Educational Research Journal*, 56(4), 1495–1523. 10.3102/0002831218817737

Anton, J., Hagiwara, M., Raley, S. K., & Burke, K. M. (in press). Inclusion and self-determination for secondary students with disabilities: The effects of interventions and classroom placement. *Journal of the American Academy of Special Education Professionals*.

Apple, M. W. (2019). On doing critical policy analysis. *Educational Policy*, 33(1), 276–287. 10.1177/0895904818807307

Aratani, Y., Wright, V. R., & Cooper, J. L. (2011). *Racial gaps in early childhood: Socio-emotional health, development, and educational outcomes among African American boys* (ED522681). ERIC. https://files.eric.ed.gov/fulltext/ED522681.pdf

Baglieri, S., & Lalvani, P. (2019). *Undoing Ableism: Teaching About Disability in K-12 Classrooms* (1st ed.). Routledge., 10.4324/9781351002868

Bailey, D. B.Jr, Hebbeler, K., Spiker, D., Scarborough, A., Mallik, S., & Nelson, L. (2005). Thirty-six-month outcomes for families of children who have disabilities and participated in early intervention. *Pediatrics*, 116(6), 1346–1352. 10.1542/peds.2004-123916322157

Bailey, D. B., Raspa, M., & Fox, L. C. (2011). What is the future of family outcomes and family-centered services? *Topics in Early Childhood Special Education*, 31(4), 216–223. 10.1177/0271121411427077

Bailey, R. L., Parette, H. P.Jr, Stoner, J. B., Angell, M. E., & Carroll, K. (2006). Family members' perceptions of augmentative and alternative communication device use. *Language, Speech, and Hearing Services in Schools*, 37(1), 50–60. 10.1044/0161-1461(2006/006)16615749

Baquedano-López, P., Alexander, R. A., & Hernandez, S. J. (2013). Equity issues in parental and community involvement in schools: What teacher educators need to know. *Review of Research in Education*, 37(1), 149–182. 10.3102/0091732X12459718

Barbosa, R. T. D. A., de Oliveira, A. S. B., de Lima Antão, J. Y. F., Crocetta, T. B., Guarnieri, R., Antunes, T. P. C., Arab, C., Massetti, T., Bezerra, I. M. P., de Mello Monteiro, C. B., & de Abreu, L. C. (2018). Augmentative and alternative communication in children with Down's syndrome: A systematic review. *BMC Pediatrics*, 18(1), 1–16. 10.1186/s12887-018-1144-529751828

Barnard-Brac, L., Morales-Alerman, M. M., Toment, K., & McWilliam, R. A. (2021). Rural and racial/ethnic differences in children receiving early intervention services. *Family & Community Health*, 44(1), 52–58. 10.1097/FCH.0000000000000028533214410

Barnett, S., Carolan, M., & Johns, D. (2013). *Equity and Excellence: African-American Children's Access to Quality Preschool*. Center on Enhancing Early Learning Outcomes. http://ceelo.org/wp-content/uploads/2013/11/CEELO-NIEERequityExcellence-2013.pdf

Barnett, W. S. (2001). Preschool education for economically disadvantaged children: Effects on reading achievement and related outcomes. In Neuman, S., & Dickinson, D. (Eds.), *Handbook of early literacy research* (Vol. 1, pp. 421–443). The Guilford Press.

Bartell, T. G. (2013). Learning to teach mathematics for social justice: Negotiating social justice and mathematical goals. *Journal for Research in Mathematics Education*, 44(1), 129–163. 10.5951/jresematheduc.44.1.0129

Barton, E. E., Gossett, S., Waters, M. C., Murray, R., & Francis, R. (2019). Increasing play complexity in a young child with autism. *Focus on Autism and Other Developmental Disabilities*, 34(2), 81–90. 10.1177/1088357618800493

Barton, E. E., & Smith, B. J. (2015). Advancing high-quality preschool inclusion: A discussion and recommendations for the field. *Topics in Early Childhood Special Education*, 35(2), 69–78. 10.1177/0271121415583048

Barton, E., Pribble, L., & Joseph, J. (2015). Evidenced-based practices for successful inclusion. In Barton, E., & Smith, B. (Eds.), *The preschool inclusion toolbox: How to build and lead a high-quality program* (pp. 113–132). Brookes.

Bassok, D., & Galdo, E. (2016). Inequality in preschool quality? Community-level disparities in access to high-quality learning environments. *Early Education and Development*, 27(1), 128–144. 10.1080/10409289.2015.1057463

Baum, S., & O'Malley, M. (2003). College on credit: How borrowers perceive their education debt. *Journal of Student Financial Aid*, 33(3), 1. 10.55504/0884-9153.1068

Beneke, M. R., & Cheatham, G. A. (2020). Teacher candidates talking (but not talking) about dis/ability and race in preschool. *Journal of Literacy Research*, 52(3), 245–268. 10.1177/1086296X20939561

Beneke, M. R., Collins, S., & Powell, S. (2021). Who may be competent? Mothering young children of color with disabilities and the politics of care. *Equity & Excellence in Education*, 54(3), 328–344. 10.1080/10665684.2021.1992604

Beneke, M. R., & Park, C. C. (2019). Introduction to the special issue: Antibias curriculum and critical praxis to advance social justice in inclusive early childhood education. *Young Exceptional Children*, 22(2), 55–61. 10.1177/1096250619833337

Berenguer, C., Martínez, E. R., De Stasio, S., & Baixauli, I. (2022). Parents' perceptions and experiences with their children's use of augmentative/alternative communication: A systematic review and qualitative meta-synthesis. *International Journal of Environmental Research and Public Health*, 19(13), 8091. 10.3390/ijerph1913809135805750

Bernheimer, L., & Weismer, T. (2007). "Let me tell you what I do all day…": The family story at the center of intervention research and practice. *Infants and Young Children*, 20(3), 192–201. 10.1097/01.IYC.0000277751.62819.9b

Bettini, E., Gilmour, A. F., Williams, T. O., & Billingsley, B. (2020). Predicting special and general educators' intent to continue teaching using conservation of resources theory. *Exceptional Children*, 86(3), 310–329. 10.1177/0014402919870464

Beukelman, D. R., & Light, J. C. (2020). *Augmentative & Alternative Communication Supporting Children and adults with complex communication needs*. Paul H. Brookes Publishing Co.

Beukelman, D., Fager, S., & Nordness, A. (2011). Communication support for people with ALS. *Neurology Research International*, 2011, 1–6. Advance online publication. 10.1155/2011/71469321603029

Biermeier, M. A. (2015). Inspired by Reggio Emilia: Emergent curriculum in relationship-driven learning environments. *Young Children*, 70(5), 72–79.

Billingsley, B., & Bettini, E. (2019). Special education teacher attrition and retention: A review of the literature. *Review of Educational Research*, 89(5), 697–744. 10.3102/0034654319862495

Binger, C., & Light, J. (2007). The effect of aided AAC modeling on the expression of multi-symbol messages by preschoolers who use AAC. *Augmentative and Alternative Communication (Baltimore, MD: 1985), 23*(1), 30–43. 10.1080/07434610600807470

Blanchard, S. B., Newton, J. R., Didericksen, K. W., Daniels, M., & Glosson, K. (2021). Confronting racism and bias within early intervention: The responsibility of systems and individuals to influence change and advance equity. *Topics in Early Childhood Special Education*, 41(1), 1–12. 10.1177/0271121421992470

Bloch, M. (1992). Critical perspectives on the historical relationship between child development and early childhood education research. In Kessler, S., & Swadener, E. B. (Eds.), *Reconceptualizing the early childhood curriculum: Beginning the dialogue* (pp. 3–20). Teachers College Press.

Blue-Banning, M., Summers, J. A., Frankland, H. C., Lord Nelson, L., & Beegle, G. (2004). Dimensions of family and professional partnerships: Constructive guidelines for collaboration. *Exceptional Children*, 70(2), 167–184. 10.1177/001440290407000203

Blueprint for Maryland's Future Act, HB 1300, 1372 (2021). https://blueprint.marylandpublicschools.org/

Bondy, A. S., & Frost, L. A. (1994). The picture exchange communication system. *Focus on Autistic Behavior*, 9(3), 1–19. 10.1177/108835769400900301

Boutte, G., & Bryan, N. (2021). When will Black children be well? Interrupting anti-black violence in early childhood classrooms and schools. *Contemporary Issues in Early Childhood*, 22(3), 232–243. 10.1177/1463949119890598

Brady, N. C. (2000). Improved comprehension of object names following voice output communication aid use: Two case studies. *Augmentative and Alternative Communication*, 16(3), 197–204. 10.1080/07434610012331279054

Branch, J., Chapman, M., & Gomez, M. (2021). Investigating the interplay between institution, spousal, parental, and personal demands in tenure track faculty everyday life. *Community Work & Family*, 24(2), 143–154. 10.1080/13668803.2020.1727414

Branson, C. E., Baetz, C. L., Horwitz, S. M., & Hoagwood, K. (2017). Trauma-informed juvenile justice systems: A systematic review of definitions and core components. *Psychological Trauma: Theory, Research, Practice, and Policy*, 9(6), 635–646. 10.1037/tra000025528165266

Branson, D., & Demchak, M. (2009). The use of augmentative and alternative communication methods with infants and toddlers with disabilities: *A research review.Augmentative and Alternative Communication*, 25(4), 274–286. 10.3109/07434610903384529191883287

Brassart, E., Prévost, C., Bétrisey, C., Lemieux, M., & Desmarais, C. (2017). Strategies Developed by Service Providers to Enhance Treatment Engagement by Immigrant Parents Raising a Child with a Disability. *Journal of Child and Family Studies*, 26(4), 1230–1244. 10.1007/s10826-016-0646-8

Bricker, D. D., Felimban, H. S., Lin, F. Y., Stegenga, S. M., & Storie, S. O. (2020). A proposed framework for enhancing collaboration in early intervention/early childhood special education. *Topics in Early Childhood Special Education*, 41(4), 240–252. 10.1177/0271121419890683

Bronfenbrenner, U. (1979). *The ecology of human development*. Harvard University Press. 10.4159/9780674028845

Bronfenbrenner, U. (1986). Ecology of the family as a context for human development: Research perspectives. *Developmental Psychology*, 22(6), 723–742. 10.1037/0012-1649.22.6.723

Brown, M. A., Jirard, S. A., Beemyn, G., & Ansara, G. (2021). *How to decolonize and decisnormatize curricula* [Webinar]. Sage. https://www.socialsciencespace.com/2021/04/watch-the-webinar-decolonizing-and-decisnormatizing-curricula/

Bruder, M. B. (2010). Early childhood intervention: A promise to children and families for their future. *Exceptional Children*, 76(3), 339–355. 10.1177/001440291007600306

Bruder, M. B. (2016). Personnel development practices in early childhood intervention. In Reichow, B., Boyd, B., Barton, E. E., & Odom, S. L. (Eds.), *Handbook of early childhood special education* (pp. 289–333). Springer. 10.1007/978-3-319-28492-7_16

Bruder, M. B., Catalino, T., Chiarello, L. A., Cox Mitchell, M., Deppe, J., Gundler, D., Kemp, P., LeMoine, S., Long, T., Muhlenhaupt, M., Prelock, P., Schefkind, S., Stayton, V., & Ziegler, D. (2019). Finding a common lens: Competencies across professional disciplines providing early childhood intervention. *Infants and Young Children*, 32(4), 280–293. 10.1097/IYC.0000000000000153

Bruns, D. A., & Thompson, S. D. (2014). Turning mealtimes into learning opportunities: Integrating feeding goals into IEPs. *Teaching Exceptional Children*, 46(6), 179–186. 10.1177/0040059914534619

Buettner, C. K., Hur, E. H., Jeon, L., & Andrews, D. W. (2016). What are we teaching the teachers? Child development curricula in U.S. higher education. *Child and Youth Care Forum*, 45(1), 155–175. 10.1007/s10566-015-9323-0

Buffington-Adams, J., & Vaughan, K. P. (2019). Introduction: An invitation to complicated conversations. *Journal of Curriculum Theorizing*, 34(1).

Buren, M. K., Maggin, D. M., & Brown, C. (2018). Metasynthesis on the experiences of families from nondominant communities and special education collaboration. *Exceptionality*, 28(4), 259–278. 10.1080/09362835.2018.1480953

Burgos-Debray, E. (2009). *I, Rigoberta Menchú: An Indian woman in Guatemala* (Wright, A., Trans.). Verso.

Burke, K. M., Raley, S. K., Shogren, K. A., Hagiwara, M., Mumbardó-Adam, C., Uyanik, H., & Behrens, S. (2018). A meta-analysis of interventions to promote self-determination for students with disabilities. *Remedial and Special Education*, 1–13. 10.1177/0074193251880274

Burke, M. M., & Goldman, S. E. (2018). Special education advocacy among culturally and linguistically diverse families. *Journal of Research in Special Educational Needs*, 18(S1), 3–14. 10.1111/1471-3802.12413

Butera, G., Friesen, A., & Stone-MacDonald, A. (2013). What you can accomplish in a year: An ethnography within a Head Start community. *National Head Start Association Dialog*, 16(4), 11–29.

Buysse, V., & Hollingsworth, H. L. (2009). Program quality and early childhood inclusion: Recommendations for professional development. *Topics in Early Childhood Special Education*, 29(2), 119–128. 10.1177/0271121409332233

Caddell, B. (2023). *3-Cricle Venn Diagram.* https://www.whatconsumesme.com

Calarco, J. M. (2018). *Negotiating opportunities: How the middle class secures advantages in school.* Oxford University Press.

Calarco, J. M. (2020). *A field guide to grad school: Uncovering the hidden curriculum.* Princeton University Press.

California Department of Education. (2024, April 4). *Fingertip facts on education in California.* CDE. https://www.cde.ca.gov/ds/ad/ceffingertipfacts.asp

California Department of Education. (n.d.-a). *2018–19 enrollment by ethnicity and grade: State report*. CDE. https://data1.cde.ca.gov/dataquest/dqcensus/EnrEthGrd.aspx?cds=00&agglevel= state&year=2018-19

California Department of Education. (n.d.-b). *2020–2021 enrollment by English language acqui- sition status (ELAS) (with county data): Statewide report*. CDE. https://dq.cde.ca.gov/dataquest/ longtermel/ELASLevels.aspx?Cds=00&agglevel=State&year=2020-21

California Department of Education. (n.d.-c). *English learner students by language by grade: State of California 202021*. CDE. https://dq.cde.ca.gov/dataquest/SpringData/StudentsByLanguage .aspx?Level=State&TheYear=202021&SubGroup=All&ShortYear=2021&GenderGroup=B &CDSCode=00000000000000&RecordType=EL

Camilli, G., Vargas, S., Ryan, S., & Barnett, W. S. (2010). Meta-analysis of the effects of early education interventions on cognitive and social development. *Teachers College Record*, 112(3), 579–620. 10.1177/016146811011200303

Campbell, F. A., Pungello, E. P., Miller-Johnson, S., Burchinal, M., & Ramey, C. T. (2001). The development of cognitive and academic abilities: Growth curves from an early childhood educational experiment. *Developmental Psychology*, 37(2), 231–242. 10.1037/0012-1649.37 .2.23111269391

Cannella, G. S. (1997). *Deconstructing early childhood education: Social justice and revolu- tion*. Peter Lang.

Cannella, G. S., & Viruru, R. (2004). *Childhood and postcolonization: Power, education, and contemporary practice* (1st ed.). Routledge., 10.4324/9780203463536

Carpenter, T. P., Fennema, E., & Franke, M. L. (1996). Cognitively guided instruction: A knowl- edge base for reform in primary mathematics instruction. *The Elementary School Journal*, 97(1), 3–20. 10.1086/461846

Carpenter, T. P., Fennema, E., Franke, M. L., Levi, L., & Empson, S. B. (2000). Cognitively Guided Instruction: A Research-Based Teacher Professional Development Program for Elementary School Mathematics. *Research Reports (Montgomery)*.

Carter, M., & Curtis, D. (2017). *Learning together with young children: A curriculum framework for reflective teachers*. Redleaf Press.

Carver-Thomas, D., Kini, T., & Burns, D. (2020). *Sharpening the divide: How California's teacher shortages expand inequality* (research brief). Palo Alto, CA: Learning Policy Institute.

Carver-Thomas, D., Leung, M., & Burns, D. (2021). *California teachers and COVID-19: How the pandemic is impacting the teacher workforce*. Learning Policy Institute.

Cascio, E. U. (2021). *Covid-19, early care and education, and child development*. Dartmouth College and National Bureau of Economic Development. https://www.nber.org/sites/default/files/ 2021-10/cascio_seanWP_oct2021_revised.pdf

CAST. (2018). *Universal design for learning guidelines version 2.2*. CAST. http://udlguidelines .cast.org

Causton, J., & Tracy-Bronson, C. P. (2015). *The educator's handbook to inclusive school practices*. Brookes.

Cavendish, W., & Connor, D. (2018). Toward authentic IEPs and transition plans: Student, parent, and teacher perspectives. *Learning Disability Quarterly*, 41(1), 32–43. 10.1177/0731948716684680

Cénat, J. M., Dalexis, R. D., Kokou-Kpolou, C. K., Mukunzi, J. N., & Rousseau, C. (2020). Social inequalities and collateral damages of the COVID-19 pandemic: When basic needs challenge mental health care. *International Journal of Public Health*, 65(6), 717–718. https://www.ncbi .nlm.nih.gov/pmc/articles/PMC7348102/. 10.1007/s00038-020-01426-y32651593

Center for Disease Control and Prevention. (2021, August 23). *Adverse childhood experiences (ACEs): Preventing early trauma to improve adult health*. CDC. https://www.cdc.gov/vitalsigns/ aces/index.html

Center for Service-Learning and Civic Engagement. (n.d.). *Social identity wheel*. MSU. https:// communityengagedlearning.msu.edu/upload/toolkits/Social-Identity-Wheel.pdf

Center on the Developing Child at Harvard University. (2016). *From best practices to breakthrough impacts: A science-based approach to building more promising future for young children and families*. Center on the Developing Child at Harvard University. https://developingchild.harvard .edu/resources/from-best-practices-to-breakthrough-impacts/

Center on the Developing Child at Harvard University. (n.d.). *How racism can affect child development*. Center on the Developing Child at Harvard University. https://developingchild.harvard .edu/resources/racism-and-ecd/

Chau, L., Yuen, M., Chan, P., Liu, S., Chan, K., Lee, D., & Hsieh, W. Y. (2022). Play-based parent training programme supporting Hong Kong kindergarten children in social competence development. *British Journal of Guidance & Counselling*, 50(3), 386–399. 10.1080/03069885.2022.2030464

Ching, C. (2018). Confronting the equity "learning problem" through practitioner inquiry. *Review of Higher Education*, 41(3), 387–421. 10.1353/rhe.2018.0013

Cho, S., Crenshaw, K. W., & McCall, L. (2013). Toward a field of intersectionality studies: Theory, applications, and praxis. *Signs (Chicago, Ill.)*, 38(4), 785–810. 10.1086/669608

Chu, M. (2014). Preparing tomorrow's early childhood educators: Observe and reflect about culturally responsive teachers. *YC Young Children, 6*9(2), 82–87. https://www.jstor.org/stable/ ycyoungchildren.69.2.82

Chudzik, M., Corr, C., & Wolowiec-Fisher, K. (2023). Trauma: Early childhood special education teachers' attitudes and experiences. *Early Childhood Education Journal*, 51(1), 189–200. 10.1007/s10643-021-01302-1

Chu, S. (2014). Perspectives of teachers and parents of Chinese American students with disabilities about their home–school communication. *Preventing School Failure*, 58(4), 237–248. 10.1080/1045988X.2013.809685

Cioè-Peña, M. (2020). Planning inclusion: The need to formalize parental participation in individual education plans (and meetings). *The Educational Forum*, 84(4), 377–390. 10.1080/00131725.2020.1812970

Cioè-Peña, M. (2021). Raciolinguistics and the education of emergent bilinguals labeled as disabled. *The Urban Review*, 53(3), 443–469. 10.1007/s11256-020-00581-z

Cioè-Peña, M. (2022). TrUDL, a path to full inclusion: The intersectional possibilities of translanguaging and Universal Design for Learning. *TESOL Quarterly*, 56(2), 799–812. 10.1002/tesq.3074

Clements, D. H. (1999). Subitizing: What Is It? Why Teach It? *Teaching Children Mathematics*, 5(7), 400–405. 10.5951/TCM.5.7.0400

Clements, D., & Sarama, J. (2014). *Learning and teaching math: The learning trajectories approach* (2nd ed.). Routledge. 10.4324/9780203520574

Coates, R. D., Ferber, A. L., & Brunsma, D. L. (2022). *The matrix of race: Social construction, intersectionality, and inequality* (2nd ed.). Sage.

Coburn, K. L., Jung, S., Ousley, C. L., Sowers, D. J., Wendelken, M., & Wilkinson, K. M. (2021). Centering the family in their system: A framework to promote family-centered AAC services. *Augmentative and Alternative Communication*, 37(4), 229–240. 10.1080/07434618.2021.199147134967273

Cochran-Smith, M., & Lytle, S. (2009). *Inquiry as stance: Practitioner research for the next generation*. Teachers College Press.

Coghlan, D., & Brannick, T. (2010). *Doing Action Research in Your Own Organization*. Sage.

Cole, S. F., Eisner, A., Gregory, M., & Ristuccia, J. (2013). *Helping traumatized children learn: Creating and advocating for trauma-sensitive schools(Vol. 2)*. Massachusetts Advocates for Children. https://traumasensitiveschools.org/tlpi-publications/download-a-free-copy-of-a-guide-to-creating-trauma-sensitive-schools/

Collier-Meek, M. A., Kratochwill, T. R., Luh, H. J., Sanetti, L. M., & Susilo, A. (2023). Reflections on consultation: Applying a DisCrit and equitable implementation lens to help school psychologists disrupt disparities. *Journal of Educational & Psychological Consultation*, 33(1), 10–44. 10.1080/10474412.2022.2131558

Cologon, K., & Mevawalla, Z. (2018). Increasing inclusion in early childhood: Key Word Sign as a communication partner intervention. *International Journal of Inclusive Education*, 22(8), 902–920. 10.1080/13603116.2017.1412515

Conine, D. E., & Vollmer, T. R. (2019). Relative preferences for edible and leisure stimuli in children with autism. *Journal of Applied Behavior Analysis*, 52(2), 557–573. 10.1002/jaba.52530468244

Coogle, C. G., & Hanline, M. F. (2016). An exploratory study of family-centred help-giving practices in early intervention: Families of young children with autism spectrum disorder. *Child & Family Social Work*, 21(2), 249–260. 10.1111/cfs.12148

Coogle, C. G., Lakey, E. R., Ottley, J. R., Brown, J. A., & Romano, M. K. (2021). Embedded learning opportunities for children with and without disabilities. *Young Children*, 76(4), 8–15.

Cook, D. A., & Williams, J. T. (2015). Expanding Intersectionality: Fictive kinship networks as supports for the educational aspirations of Black women. *The Western Journal of Black Studies*, 39(2), 157–166.

Corey, G., Haynes, R. H., Moulton, P., & Muratori, M. (2020). *Clinical supervision in the helping professions: A practical guide*. John Wiley & Sons.

Council on Social Work Education. (2015). *2015 Educational policy and accreditation standards for baccalaureate and master's social work programs*. https://www.cswe.org/getmedia/23a35a39 -78c7-453f-b805-b67f1dca2ee5/2015-epas-and-glossary.pdf

Crass, C. (2010). Towards anti-racist politics and practice: A racial autobiography. *Reflections: Narratives of Professional Helping, 16*(1), 151–160. https://reflectionsnarrativesofprofessio nalhelping.org/index.php/Reflections/article/view/815

Crenshaw, K. (1989). Demarginalizing the intersection of race and sex: A Black feminist critique of antidiscrimination doctrine, feminist theory, and antiracist politics. *University of Chicago Legal Forum*, 139.

Creswell, J. W., & Poth, C. N. (2018). *Qualitative inquiry and research design: Choosing among five approaches* (4th ed.). Sage Publications.

Crisp, C., Drauker, C. B., & Cirgin Ellett, M. L. (2014). Barriers and facilitators to children's use of speech-generating devices: A descriptive qualitative study of mothers' perspectives. *Pediatric Nursing*, 14(3), 229–237. 10.1111/jspn.1207424636104

Crotty, M. (1998). *The foundation of social research: Meaning and perspectives in the research process*. Sage Publications.

Crowe, B., Machalicek, W., Wei, Q., Drew, C., & Ganz, J. (2021). Augmentative and alternative communication for children with intellectual and developmental disabilities: A mega-review of the literature. *Journal of Developmental and Physical Disabilities*, 34(1), 1–42. 10.1007/ s10882-021-09790-033814873

Cruz, R. A., Firestone, A. R., & Love, M. (2023). Beyond a seat at the table: Imagining educational equity through critical inclusion. *Educational Review*, 1–27. 10.1080/00131911.2023.2173726

Cycyk, L. M., De Anda, S., Ramsey, K. L., Sheppard, B. S., & Zuckerman, K. (2022). Moving through the pipeline: Ethnic and linguistic disparities in special education from birth through age five. *Educational Researcher*, 51(7), 451–464. 10.3102/0013189X22112026237032722

Dada, S., Flores, C., Bastable, K., & Schlosser, R. W. (2021). The effects of augmentative and alternative communication interventions on the receptive language skills of children with developmental disabilities: A scoping review. *International Journal of Speech-Language Pathology*, 23(3), 247–257. 10.1080/17549507.2020.179716532893695

Davis-Temple, J., Jung, S., & Sainato, D. M. (2014). Teaching young children with special needs and their peers to play board games: Effects of a least to most prompting procedure to increase independent performance. *Behavior Analysis in Practice*, 7(1), 21–30. 10.1007/s40617-014-0001-827019792

De Leon, M., Solomon-Rice, P., & Soto, G. (2023). Perspectives and experiences of eight latina mothers of young children with augmentative and alternative communication Needs. *Perspectives of the ASHA Special Interest Groups*, 8(5), 1–14. 10.1044/2023_PERSP-23-00074

Dean, R. G. (1993). Constructivism: An approach to clinical practice. *Smith College Studies in Social Work*, 63(2), 127–146. 10.1080/00377319309517382

Degener, T., & de Castro, M. G. C. (2022). Toward inclusive equality: Ten years of the human rights model of disability in the work of the UN committee on the rights of persons with disabilities. In Felder, F., Davy, L., & Kayess, R. (Eds.), *Disability law and human rights*. Palgrave Macmillan Cham., 10.1007/978-3-030-86545-0_2

Delahooke, M. (2017). *Social and emotional development*. PSESI Publications & Media.

Dempsey, I., & Keen, D. (2008). A review of processes and outcomes in family-centered services for children with a disability. *Topics in Early Childhood Special Education*, 28(1), 42–52. 10.1177/0271121408316699

Derman-Sparks, L., & Edwards, J. O. (2019). Understanding anti-bias education: Bringing the four core goals to every facet of your curriculum. *YC Young Children*, 74(5), 6–13.

Derman-Sparks, L., & Edwards, J. O. (2019). Understanding anti-bias education: Bringing the four core goals to every facet of your curriculum. *Young Children*, 74(5), 6–13. https://www.jstor.org/stable/26842300

Derman-Sparks, L., Edwards, J. O., & Goins, C. M. (2020). *Antibias education for young children and ourselves* (2nd ed.). National Association for the Education of Young Children.

Derman-Sparks, L., Edwards, J. O., & Goins, C. M. (2020). *Anti-bias education for young children and ourselves* (2nd ed.). National Association for the Education of Young Children.

Di Rezze, B., Law, M., Eva, K., Pollock, N., & Gorter, J. W. (2014). Therapy behaviours in paediatric rehabilitation: Essential attributes for intervention with children with physical disabilities. *Disability and Rehabilitation*, 36(1), 16–23. 10.3109/09638288.2013.77535823594052

Diamond, L. (2018). Problem solving in the early years. *Intervention in School and Clinic*, 53(4), 220–223. 10.1177/1053451217712957

Dignath, C., Rimm-Kaufman, S., van Ewijk, R., & Kunter, M. (2022). Teachers' Beliefs About Inclusive Education and Insights on What Contributes to Those Beliefs: A Meta-analytical Study. *Educational Psychology Review*, 34(4), 2609–2660. 10.1007/s10648-022-09695-0

Division for Early Childhood & National Association for the Education of Young Children. (2009). *Early childhood inclusion: A joint position statement of the Division for Early Childhood (DEC) and the National Association for the Education of Young Children (NAEYC)*. The University of North Carolina, FPG Child Development Institute Division for Early Childhood. (2014). https://www.dec-sped.org/dec-recommended-practices

Division for Early Childhood of the Council for Exceptional Children, & National Association for the Education of Young Children. (2009). *Early childhood inclusion: A joint position statement of the Division for the Early Childhood (DEC) and the National Association for the Education of Young Children (NAEYC)*. The University of North Carolina at Chapel Hill; FPG Child Development Institute. https://www.naeyc.org/sites/default/files/globally-shared/downloads/PDFs/resources/position-statements/ps_inclusion_dec_naeyc_ec.pdf

Division for Early Childhood of the Council for Exceptional Children. (2014). *DEC recommended practices*. DEC. http://www.dec-sped.org/recommendedpractices

Division for Early Childhood of the Council for Exceptional Children. (2020). *Initial practice based professional preparation standards for early interventionist/early childhood special educators (EI/ECSE; Initial birth through age 8)*. Division for Early Childhood. https://www.dec-sped.org/_files/ugd/95f212_4d9c51a4b6e54e67a2ba1df3541903da.pdf?index=true

Division for Early Childhood of the Council for Exceptional Children. (2023). *Racial equity point of view*. https://divisionearlychildhood.egnyte.com/dl/GPVEY6LbYW

Division for Early Childhood. (2014). *DEC Recommended Practices in early intervention/early childhood special education 2014*. DEC. http://www.dec-sped.org/recommendedpractices

Division for Early Childhood. (2022). *Position statement on ethical practice* [Position statement]. https://divisionearlychildhood.egnyte.com/dl/KAh4cOFBZ8

Doak, L. (2021). Rethinking family (dis)engagement with augmentative & alternative communication. *Journal of Research in Special Educational Needs*, 21(3), 198–210. 10.1111/1471-3802.12510

Dobbins, D., McCready, M., Rackas, L., & Child Care Aware of America. (2016). *Unequal access: Barriers to early childhood education for boys of color [Issue Brief]*. Robert Wood Johnson Foundation. https://www.childcareaware.org/wp-content/uploads/2016/10/UnequalAccess_BoysOfColor.pdf

Dore, M. M. (2008). Family systems theory. In B. A. Thyer, K. M. Sowers, & C. N. Dulmus (Eds.), *Comprehensive handbook of social work and social welfare,* (pp. 431–462). John Wiley & Sons Inc. 10.1002/9780470373705.chsw002018

Drager, K., Postal, V. J., Carrolus, L., Castellano, M., Gagliano, C., & Glynn, J. (2006). The effect of aided language modeling on symbol comprehension and production in 2 preschoolers with autism. *American Journal of Speech-Language Pathology*, 15(2), 112–125. 10.1044/105 8-0360(2006/012)16782684

Dudley-Marling, C., & Lucas, K. (2009). Pathologizing the language and culture of poor children. *Language Arts*, 86(5), 362–370.

Dueñas, A. D., D'Agostino, S. R., & Plavnick, J. B. (2021). Teaching Young Children to Make Bids to Play to Peers With Autism Spectrum Disorder. *Focus on Autism and Other Developmental Disabilities*, 36(4), 201–212. 10.1177/10883576211023326

Duncan, G. J.National Institute of Child Health and Human Development Early Child Care Research Network. (2003). Modeling the impacts of child care quality on children's preschool cognitive development. *Child Development*, 74(5), 1454–1475. 10.1111/1467-8624.0061714552408

Duncan, W. (2012). The effects of Africentric United States history curriculum on Black student achievement. *Contemporary Issues in Education Research*, 5(2), 91–96. 10.19030/cier.v5i2.6925

Dunst, C. J. (2017). Family systems early childhood intervention. In H. Sukkar, C. J. Dunst, & J. Kirkby (Eds.), *Early childhood intervention: Working with families of young children with special needs* (pp. 36–58). Routledge/Taylor & Francis Group.

Dunst, C. J. (2002). Family-centered practices: Birth through high school. *The Journal of Special Education*, 36(3), 141–149. 10.1177/00224669020360030401

Dunst, C. J., Bruder, M. B., Maude, S. P., Schnurr, M., Van Polen, A., Clark, G. F., Winslow, A., & Gethmann, D. (2020). Predictors of practitioners' use of recommended early childhood intervention practices. *International Education Studies*, 13(9), 36. 10.5539/ies.v13n9p36

Dunst, C. J., Espe-Sherwindt, M., & Hamby, D. (2019). Does capacity-building professional development engender practitioners' use of capacity-building family-centered practices? *European Journal of Educational Research*, 8(2), 515–526. 10.12973/eu-jer.8.2.513

Dunst, C. J., & Trivette, C. M. (2009). Capacity-building family-systems intervention practices. *Journal of Family Social Work*, 12(2), 119–143. 10.1080/10522150802713322

Dunst, C. J., & Trivette, C. M. (2009). Let's be PALS: An evidence-based approach to professional development. *Infants and Young Children*, 22(3), 164–176. 10.1097/IYC.0b013e3181abe169

Dunst, C. J., Trivette, C. M., & Hamby, D. W. (2007). Meta-analysis of family-centered help giving practices research. *Mental Retardation and Developmental Disabilities Research Reviews*, 13(4), 370–378. 10.1002/mrdd.2017617979208

Durden, T. R., & Curenton, S. M. (2017). Pathways to excellence – what we know works for nurturing Black children's success. In Iruka, I. U., Cureton, S. M., & Durden, T. R. (Eds.), *African American Children in Early Childhood Education: Making the case for policy investments in families, schools, and communities* (Vol. 5, pp. 35–55). Emerald Group Publishing. 10.1108/ S2051-231720170000005003

Education Policy at AIR. (2016). *California's emerging teacher shortage: New evidence and policy responses*. AIR. https://www.air.org/sites/default/files/Program%20-%20final.pdf

Edwards, C. (2011). The Hundred Languages of Children: *The Reggio Emilia Experience in Transformation*. ProQuest Ebook Central, https://ebookcentral.proquest.com/lib/cudenver/detail.action?docID=820317

Edwards, A., Brebner, C., McCormack, P. F., & McDougall, C. (2016). More than blowing bubbles: What parents want from therapists working with children with autism spectrum disorder. *International Journal of Speech-Language Pathology*, 18(5), 493–505. 10.3109/17549507.2015.111283527063689

Eggum, N. D., Eisenberg, N., Kao, K., Spinrad, T. L., Bolnick, R., Hofer, C., Kupfer, A. S., & Fabricius, W. V. (2011). Emotion understanding, theory of mind, and prosocial orientation: Relations over time in early childhood. *The Journal of Positive Psychology*, 6(1), 4–16. 10.1080/17439760.2010.53677622518196

Elliott, S. N., Frey, J. R., & Davies, M. (2015). Systems for assessing and improving students' social skills to achieve academic competence. In Durlak, J. A., Domitrovich, C. E., Weissberg, R. P., & Gullotta, T. P. (Eds.), *Handbook of social and emotional learning: Research and practice* (pp. 301–319). The Guilford Press.

Ercis, S., Sirinkan, A., & Önal, L. (2021). Investigation of the Effect of Inclusive Play and Special Movement Education to Social Communication in Disadvantaged and Peer Children in Preschool (Erzurum Sample). *Journal of Educational Issues*, 7(3), 1–9. 10.5296/jei.v7i3.19155

Erwin, E. J., Bacon, J. K., & Lalvani, P. (2021). It's about time! Advancing justice through joyful inquiry with young children. *Topics in Early Childhood Special Education*, 1–12. 10.1177/0271121420988890

Erwin, E. J., Maude, S. P., Palmer, S. B., Summers, J. A., Brotherson, M. J., Haines, S. J., Stroup-Rentier, V., Zheng, Y., & Peck, N. F. (2016). Fostering the foundations of self-determination in early childhood: A process for enhancing child outcomes across home and school. *Early Childhood Education Journal*, 44(4), 325–333. 10.1007/s10643-015-0710-9

Escayg, K. A. (2019). "Who's got the power?": A critical examination of the anti-bias curriculum. *International Journal of Child Care and Education Policy*, 13(1), 1–18.

Evans, D. L., Feit, M. D., & Trent, T. (2016). African American parents and attitudes about child disability and early intervention services. *Journal of Social Service Research*, 42(1), 96–112. 10.1080/01488376.2015.1081118

Faculty Center for Ignatian Pedagogy. (2024). *Decolonizing your syllabus*. LUC. https://www.luc.edu/fcip/anti-racistpedagogy/anti-racistpedagogyresources/decolonizingyoursyllabus/#:~:text=Overall%2C%20it%20means%20shifting%20your,of%20Color%20(BIPOC)%20people%20are

Falender, C. A. (2018). Clinical supervision-the missing ingredient. *The American Psychologist*, 73(9), 1240–1250. 10.1037/amp000038530525811

Fallon, L. M., DeFouw, E. R., Berkman, T. S., Cathcart, S. C., O'Keeffe, B. V., & Sugai, G. (2021). Supports to improve academic outcomes with racially and ethnically minoritized youth: A review of research. *Remedial and Special Education*, 1–18. 10.1177/07419325211046760

Fariña, C., & Kotch, L. (2008). Develop a culture for sustainable learning. In *A school leader's guide to excellence: Collaborating our way to better schools* (pp. 99–120). Heinemann.

Farquharson, W., & Thornton, C. J. (2020). Debate: Exposing the most serious infirmity—Racism's impact on health in the era of COVID-19. *Child and Adolescent Mental Health*, 25(3), 182–183. 10.1111/camh.1240732686292

Ferrette, T. (2021). *Roots of discipline-induced trauma for Black children in early childhood settings*. The Center for Law and Social Policy. https://www.clasp.org/publications/fact-sheet/roots-discipline-induced-trauma-black-children-early-childhood-settings/

Ferri, B. A., & Bacon, J. (2011). Beyond inclusion: Disability studies in early childhood teacher education. *Promoting Social Justice for Young Children*, 137-146.

Fischberg, J. (2017). *The crisis in Black education: Early disparities*. Rubicon Programs. https://rubiconprograms.org/news/blog/the-crisis-in-black-education-early-disparities

Fook, J. (2015). Reflective practice and critical reflection. In Lishman, J. (Ed.), *Handbook for practice learning in social work and social care* (3rd ed.). Jessica Kingsley Publishers.

Ford, D. Y. (2020, September 14). *Miseducating Black students as a form of educational malpractice and professional betrayal.* https://www.diverseeducation.com/demographics/african-american/article/15107747/miseducating-black-students-as-a-form-of-educational-malpractice-and-professional-betrayal

Fraser, S., & Gestwicki, C. (2002). *Authentic Childhood: Exploring Reggio Emilia in the Classroom*. Delmar/Thomson Learning.

Freire, P. (2000). *Pedagogy of the oppressed* (30th anniversary edition). [Original work published in English 1970]. *Continuum*.

Friedman -Krauss. A., & Barnett, S. (2020). Access to high-quality early education and racial equity. Rutgers Graduate School of Education. *National Institute for Early Education Research*, 1-3. https://nieer.org/wp-content/uploads/2021/02/Special-Report-Access-to-High-Quality-Early-Education-and-Racial-Equity.pdf

Friedman-Krauss, A. H., & Barnett, W. S. (2023). *The state(s) of early intervention and early childhood special education: Looking at equity*. National Institute for Early Education Research.

Fried-Oken, M., Mooney, A., & Peters, B. (2015). Supporting communication for patients with neurodegenerative disease. *NeuroRehabilitation*, 37(1), 69–87. 10.3233/NRE-15124126409694

Fujiura, G. T. (2014). The political arithmetic of disability and the American family: A demographic perspective. *Family Relations*, 63(1), 7–19. 10.1111/fare.12051

Fu-Kiau, K. K. B., & Lukondo-Wamba, A. M. (2000). *Kindezi: The Kongo art of babysitting.* Black Classic Press.

Gannon, K. (2016, October 28). What goes into a syllabus. *The Chronicle of Higher Education*, 63(9), A40.

Gargiulo, R. M., & Kilgo, J. L. (2011). *An introduction to young children with special needs.* Birth Through Age Eight.

Garrels, V., & Palmer, S. B. (2020). A catalyst for academic achievement and self-determination for students with intellectual disability. *Journal of Intellectual Disabilities*, 24(4), 459–473. 10.1177/1744629519840526309438426

Gauvreau, A. N., & Schwartz, I. S. (2013). Using visual supports to promote appropriate behavior in young children with Autism and related disorders. *Young Exceptional Children Monograph Series*, 15, 29–44.

Gay, G. (2015). The what, why, and how of culturally responsive teaching: International mandates, challenges, and opportunities. *Multicultural Education Review*, 7(3), 123–139. 10.1080/2005615X.2015.1072079

Gay, G. (2018). *Culturally Responsive Teaching: Theory, Research, and Practice* (3rd ed.). Teachers College Press.

Gay, G. (2018). *Culturally responsive teaching: Theory, research, and practice.* Teachers College Press.

Gerhardt, S. (2015). *Why love matters: How affection shapes a baby's brain.* Routledge.

Gerzel-Short, L., Kiru, E. W., Hsiao, Y. J., Hovey, K. A., Wei, Y., & Miller, R. D. (2019). Engaging culturally and linguistically diverse families of children with disabilities. *Intervention in School and Clinic*, 55(2), 120–126. 10.1177/1053451219837637

Gevarter, C., Groll, M., Stone, E., & Medina Najar, A. (2021). A parent-implemented embedded AAC intervention for teaching navigational requests and other communicative functions to children with autism spectrum disorder. *Augmentative and Alternative Communication*, 37(3), 180–193. 10.1080/07434618.2021.194684634669532

Gibbs, B. (2020). Threading the needle: On balancing trauma and critical teaching. *Occasional Paper Series, 2020*(43), Article 10. 10.58295/2375-3668.1350

Gilardi, S., & Guglielmetti, C. (2016). University life of non-traditional students: Engagement styles and impact on attrition. *The Journal of Higher Education*, 82(1), 33–53. 10.1080/00221546.2011.11779084

Gilken, J., Longley, J., & Crosby, J. (2023). Finding space for infants and toddlers in early childhood teacher preparation programs. *Early Childhood Education Journal*, 51(2), 333–344. 10.1007/s10643-021-01299-7

Gillanders, C., & Procopio, R. (Eds.). (2019). *Spotlight on young children: Equity and diversity*. NAEYC.

Gilliam, W. S., Maupin, A. N., Reyes, C. R., Accavitti, M., & Shic, F. (2016). Do early educators' implicit biases regarding sex and race relate to behavior expectations and recommendations of preschool expulsions and suspensions? *Yale University Child Study Center*, 9(28), 1–16.

Gillispie, C. (2021). *Our youngest learners: Increasing equity in early intervention*. The Education Trust. https://edtrust.org/wp-content/uploads/2014/09/Increasing-Equity-in-Early-Intervention-May-2021.pdf

Gilovich, T., & Savitsky, K. (2012). Like goes with like: The role of representativeness in erroneous and pseudo-scientific beliefs. In Gilovich, T., Griffin, D., & Kahneman, D. (Eds.), *Heuristics and biases: The psychology of intuitive judgment* (pp. 617–624)., 10.1017/CBO9780511808098.036

Ginsburg, K. R. (2007). The importance of play in promoting healthy child development and maintaining strong parent-child bonds. *Pediatrics*, 119(1), 182–191. 10.1542/peds.2006-269717200287

Ginwright, S. (2018, May 31). *The future of healing: Shifting from trauma-informed care to healing centered engagement*. Medium. https://ginwright.medium.com/the-future-of-healing-shifting-from-trauma-informed-care-to-healing-centered-engagement-634f557ce69c

Giroux, H. A. (1997). Authority, intellectuals, and the politics of practical learning. In Giroux, H. A. (Ed.), *Pedagogy and the politics of hope* (1st ed., pp. 95–116). Routledge. 10.4324/9780429498428-4

Glacken, M., Healy, D., Gilrane, U., Gowan, S. H.-M., Dolan, S., Walsh-Gallagher, D., & Jennings, C. (2018). Key word signing: Parents' experiences of an unaided form of augmentative and alternative communication (LÁMH). *Journal of Intellectual Disabilities*, 23(3), 327–343. 10.1177/1744629518790825301220092

Goffney, I., & Gutiérrez, R. (2018). *Rehumanizing mathematics for Black, Indigenous, and Latinx students*. National Council of Teachers of Mathematics.

Goldbart, J., & Marshall, J. (2004). Pushes and pulls on the parents of children who use AAC. *Augmentative and Alternative Communication*, 22(4), 194–208. 10.1080/07434610400010960

Gonzalez, L. (2009). Teaching math for social justice: Reflections on a community of practice for high school math teachers. *Journal of Urban Mathematics Education*, 2(1), 22–51. 10.21423/jume-v2i1a32

Gonzalez-Mena, J. (2008). *Child, family, and community: Family-centered early care and education*. Pearson.

González, N., Andrade, R., Civil, M., & Moll, L. (2001). Bridging funds of distributed knowledge: Creating zones of practices in mathematics. *Journal of Education for Students Placed at Risk*, 6(1-2), 115–132. 10.1207/S15327671ESPR0601-2_7

González, N., Moll, L. C., & Amanti, C. (2005). *Funds of knowledge: Theorizing practices in household communities, and classrooms*. Lawrence Erlbaum.

Gorski, P. C. (2012). Teaching against essentialism and the "culture of poverty". In *Cultivating social justice teachers* (pp. 84–107). Routledge.

Graham, F., Boland, P., Ziviani, J., & Rodger, S. (2018). Occupational therapists' and physiotherapists' perceptions of implementing occupational performance coaching. *Disability and Rehabilitation*, 40(12), 1386–1392. 10.1080/09638288.2017.129547428288531

Granlund, M., Bjorck-Akesson, E., Wilder, J., & Ylven, R. (2008). AAC interventions for children in a family environment: Implementing evidence in practice. *Augmentative and Alternative Communication*, 24(3), 207–219. 10.1080/08990220802387935188830910

Green, B. L., Saunders, P. A., Power, E., Dass-Brailsford, P., Schelbert, K. B., Giller, E., Wissow, L., Hurtado-de-Mendoza, A., & Mete, M. (2015). Trauma-informed medical care: CME communication training for primary care providers. *Family Medicine*, 47(1), 7–14. 10.22454/FamMed.2022.19748625646872

Greenberg, M. T., Weissberg, R. P., O'Brien, M. U., Zins, J. E., Fredericks, L., Resnik, H., & Elias, M. J. (2003). Enhancing school-based prevention and youth development through coordinated social, emotional, and academic learning. *The American Psychologist*, 58(6/7), 466–474. 10.1037/0003-066X.58.6-7.46612971193

Green-Gibson, A., & Collett, A. (2014). A comparison of African & mainstream culture on African-American students in public elementary schools. [pdf] [ed.gov]. *Multicultural Education*, 33-37, EJ1045845.

Grindal, T., Schifter, L. A., Schwartz, G., & Hehir, T. (2019). Racial differences in special education identification and placement: Evidence across three states. *Harvard Educational Review*, 89(4), 525–553. 10.17763/1943-5045-89.4.525

Grisham, D. L. (2000). Connecting theoretical conception of reading to practice: A longitudinal study of elementary school teachers. *Reading Psychology*, 21(2), 145–170. 10.1080/02702710050084464

Groce, N. E., & Zola, I. K. (1993). Multiculturalism, chronic illness, and disability. *Pediatrics*, 91(5), 1048–1055. 10.1542/peds.91.5.10488479830

Gu, Q., & Day, C. (2007). Teachers resilience: A necessary condition for effectiveness. *Teaching and Teacher Education*, 23(8), 1302–1316. 10.1016/j.tate.2006.06.006

Gutierrez, R. (2009). Framing equity: Helping students "play the game" and "change the game". *Teaching for Excellence and Equity in Mathematics*, 1(1), 5–7.

Gutstein, E. (2006). *Reading and writing the world with mathematics: toward a pedagogy for social justice*. Routledge.

Guy, B., Feldman, T., Cain, C., Leesman, L., & Hood, C. (2020). Defining and navigating 'action' in a Participatory Action Research project. *Educational Action Research*, 28(1), 142–153. 10.1080/09650792.2019.1675524

Hagiwara, M., Raley, S. K., Shogren, K. A., & Alsaeed, A. (2024). Culturally responsive and sustaining universal design for transition and student self-determination. In Scott, L. A., & Thoma, C. A. (Eds.), *Universal design for transition: The educators' guide for equity focused transition planning*. Brookes Publishing.

Hagiwara, M., Shogren, K. A., & Turner, E. L. (2021). Examining perceptions toward self-determination of people with disabilities: A meta-synthesis. *Journal of Developmental and Physical Disabilities*, 1–21. https://www.doi.org/10.1007/s10882-021-09823-8

Haines, S. J., Summers, J. A., Palmer, S. B., Stroup-Rentier, V. L., & Chu, S. Y. (2017). Immigrant Families' Perceptions of Fostering Their Preschoolers' Foundational Skills for Self-Determination. *Inclusion (Washington, D.C.)*, 5(4), 293–305. 10.1352/2326-6988-5.4.293

Haines, S. J., Summers, J. A., Turnbull, A. P., Turnbull, H. R.III, & Palmer, S. (2015). Fostering Habib's engagement and self-regulation: A case study of a child from a refugee family at home and preschool. *Topics in Early Childhood Special Education*, 35(1), 28–39. 10.1177/0271121414552905

Hains, A. H., Rhyner, P. M., McLean, M. E., Barnekow, K., Johnson, V., & Kennedy, B. (2005). Interdisciplinary team and diverse families: Practices in early intervention personnel preparation. *Young Exceptional Children*, 8(4), 2–10. 10.1177/109625060500800401

Hakkarainen, P., & Bredikyte, M. (2010). Strong foundation through play-based learning. *Psychological Science and Education*, 3, 58–64.

Hammond, Z. (2015). *Culturally responsive teaching and the brain: Promoting authentic engagement and rigor among culturally and linguistically diverse students*. Corwin.

Harper, F. K. (2019). A Qualitative Metasynthesis of Teaching Mathematics for Social Justice in Action: Pitfalls and Promises of Practice. *Journal for Research in Mathematics Education*, 50(3), 268–310. Retrieved January 10, 2024, from. 10.5951/jresematheduc.50.3.0268

Harris, B. G., Hayes, C., & Smith, D. T. (2020). Not a "who done it" mystery: On how Whiteness sabotages equity aims in teacher preparation programs. *The Urban Review*, 52(1), 198–213. 10.1007/s11256-019-00524-3

Harris, N. B. (2018). *The deepest well: Healing the long-term effects of childhood adversity*. Houghton Mifflin Harcourt.

Harry, B., & Ocasio-Stoutenburg, L. (2020). *Meeting families where they are: Building equity through advocacy with diverse schools and communities*. Teachers College Press.

Hassey, J. T. (2022). *Time Trials: Ethnographic Interviewing Within Health Care System Constraints*. Leader Live., 10.1044/leader.FTR1.27072022.ethnographic-interviews.40

Hatton, N., & Smith, D. (1995). Reflection in teacher education: Towards definition and implementation. *Teaching and Teacher Education*, 11(1), 33–49. 10.1016/0742-051X(94)00012-U

Healy, K. (2014). *Social work theories in context: Creating frameworks for practice*. Bloomsbury Academic. 10.1007/978-1-137-02425-1

Heard-Garris, N. J., Cale, M., Camaj, L., Hamati, M. C., & Dominguez, T. P. (2018). Transmitting trauma: A systematic review of vicarious racism and child health. *Social Science & Medicine*, 199, 230–240. 10.1016/j.socscimed.2017.04.01828456418

Hebbeler, K., Spiker, D., Bailey, D., Scarborough, A., Mallik, S., Simeonsson, R., & Nelson, L. (2007). Early intervention for infants and toddlers with disabilities and their families: Participants, services, and outcomes. *Menlo Park, CA: SRI International, 116.*

Heffernan, T. (2021). Sexism, racism, prejudice, and bias: A literature review and synthesis of research surrounding student evaluations of courses and teaching. *Assessment & Evaluation in Higher Education*, 47(1), 144–154.

Heffron, M. C., & Murch, T. (2010). *Reflective supervision and leadership in early childhood programs*. Zero to Three Press.

Heffron, M. C., & Murch, T. (2010). Reflective supervision and leadership in infant and early childhood programs. *Zero to Three.*

Hemmeter, M. L., Ostrosky, M., & Fox, L. (2006). Social and emotional foundations for early learning: A conceptual model for intervention. *School Psychology Review*, 35(4), 583–601. 10.1080/02796015.2006.12087963

Henrich, J., Heine, S. J., & Norenzayan, A. (2010). Most people are not WEIRD. *Nature*, 466, 29. 10.1038/466029a20595995

Hernández-Saca, D. I., Gutmann Kahn, L., & Cannon, M. A. (2018). Intersectionality dis/ability research: How dis/ability research in education engages intersectionality to uncover the multidimensional construction of dis/abled experiences. *Review of Research in Education*, 42(1), 286–311. 10.3102/0091732X18762439

Herrenkohl, T. I., Scott, D., Higgins, D. J., Klika, J. B., & Lonne, B. (2021). How COVID-19 is placing vulnerable children at risk and why we need a different approach to child welfare. *Child Maltreatment*, 26(1), 9–16. 10.1177/10775595209639163302582.5

Hettiarachchi, S., Kitnasamy, G., & Gopi, D. (2020). "Now I am a techie too" – parental perceptions of using mobile technology for communication by children with complex communication needs in the Global South. *Disability and Rehabilitation. Assistive Technology*, 15(2), 183–194. 10.1080/17483107.2018.155471330735067

Hill, C. E. (2001). *Helping Skills: The Empirical Foundation*. American Psychological Association., 10.1037/10412-000

Hilliard, A. (2003). No mystery: Closing the achievement gap between Africans and excellence. In T. Perry, C. Steele, & A. Hilliard, *Young, gifted, and Black: Promoting high achievement among African-American students* (pp. 131–165). Beacon Press.

Hong, S., Baloch, M. H., Conklin, K. H., & Warren, H. W. (2022). Teacher-Family Solidarity as Culturally Sustaining Pedagogy and Practice. *Urban Education*, 0(0). 10.1177/00420859221131809 hooks, b. (2010). *Teaching critical thinking: Practical wisdom*. Routledge.

Hughes, C., Cosgriff, J. C., Agran, M., & Washington, B. H. (2013). Student self-determination: A preliminary investigation of the role of participation in inclusive settings. *Education and Training in Autism and Developmental Disabilities*, 48(1), 3–17. https://www.jstor.org/stable/23879882

Hunt, p., Soto, G., Maier, J., Müller, E., & Goetz, L. (2002). Collaborative teaming to support students with augmentative and alternative communication needs in general education classrooms. *Augmentative & Alternative Communication, 18,* 20–35. 10.1080/aac.18.1.20.35

Hustad, K. C., & Shapley, K. L. (2003). Communicative Competence for Individuals who use AAC. In Light, J., Beukelman, D. R., & Reichle, J. (Eds.), *Communicative Competence for Individuals who use AAC* (pp. 147–162). Paul H. Brookes Publishing.

Improving American's Schools Act of 1994, H.R.6, 103rd Congress. (1993).

Individuals with Disabilities Education Act, 20 U.S.C. § 1400 (2004).

Individuals With Disabilities Education Act, 20 U.S.C. § 1400 (2004).

Individuals With Disabilities Education Act, 20 U.S.C. § 1400 (2004). https://www.congress.gov/108/plaws/publ446/PLAW-108publ446.pdf

Individuals with Disabilities Education Act, 20 U.S.C. § 1400 (2004). Iruka, I. U., Curenton, S. M., Durden, T. R., & Escayg, K. (2020). *Don't look away: Embracing antibias classrooms*. Gryphon House, Inc.

Individuals with Disabilities Education Improvement Act (IDEIA) of 2004, PL 108-446, 20 U.S.C. §§ 1400 *et esq.*

Iruka, I. U., Gardner-Neblett, N., Telfer, N. A., Ibekwe-Okafor, N., Curenton, S. M., Sims, J., Sansbury, A. B., & Neblett, E. W. (2022). Effects of racism on child development: Advancing antiracist developmental science. *Annual Review of Developmental Psychology*, 4(1), 109–132. 10.1146/annurev-devpsych-121020-031339

Iruka, I. U., James, C., Reaves, C., & Forte, A. (2021). *Black child national agenda: America must deliver on its promise*. Equity Research Action Coalition, Frank Porter Graham Child Development Institute, The University of North Carolina at Chapel Hill. https://equity-coalition.fpg.unc.edu/resource/black-child-national-agenda-america-must-deliver-on-its-promise/

Iruka, I. U., & Morgan, J. (2014). Patterns of quality experienced by African American children in early education programs: Predictors and links to children's preschool and kindergarten academic outcomes. *The Journal of Negro Education*, 83(3), 235–255. 10.7709/jnegroeducation.83.3.0235

Irwin, V., De La Rosa, J., Wang, K., Hein, S., Zhang, J., Burr, R., Roberts, A., Barmer, A., Bullock Mann, F., Dilig, R., & Parker, S. (2022). *The condition of education 2022* (NCES 2022-144). U.S. Department of Education. National Center for Education Statistics. https://nces.ed.gov/pubsearch/pubsinfo.asp?pubid=2022144

Jackson, L. B., Ryndak, D. L., & Wehmeyer, M. L. (2008). The dynamic relationship between context, curriculum, and student learning: A case for inclusive education as a research based practice. *Research and Practice for Persons with Severe Disabilities: the Journal of TASH*, 34(1), 175–195. 10.2511/rpsd.33.4.175

Johnson, J. M., Inglebret, E., Jones, C., & Ray, J. (2009). Perspectives of speech language pathologists regarding success versus abandonment of AAC. *Augmentative and Alternative Communication*, 22(2), 85–99. 10.1080/0743461050048358817114167

Johnson, J., Rahn, N., & Bricker, D. (2015). *An activity-based approach to early intervention* (4th ed.). Brookes.

Johnston, S. S., Blue, C. W., & Stegenga, S. M. (2022). AAC barriers and facilitators for children with Koolen de Vries syndrome and childhood apraxia of speech: Parent perceptions. *Augmentative and Alternative Communication*, 38(3), 1–13. 10.1080/07434618.2022.208562635726705

Jones, E. (2012). The emergence of emergent curriculum. *Young Children*, 67(2), 66–73.

Jones, L., Bellis, M. A., Wood, S., Hughes, K., McCoy, E., Eckley, L., Bates, G., Mikton, C., Shakespeare, T., & Officer, A. (2012). Prevalence and risk of violence against children with disabilities: A systematic review and meta-analysis of observational studies. *Lancet*, 380(9845), 899–907. 10.1016/S0140-6736(12)60692-822795511

Joseph, G., & Strain, P. (2010). *Module 2 handout 2.3: Social emotional teaching strategies - You've got to have friends.* The Center on the Social and Emotional Foundations for Early Learning. http://csefel.vanderbilt.edu/modules/module2/handout3.pdf

Jung, S., & Sainato, D. M. (2013). Teaching play skills to young children with autism. *Journal of Intellectual & Developmental Disability*, 38(1), 74–90. 10.3109/13668250.2012.73222023157647

Kahn, J. B., Peralta, L. M., Rubel, L. H., Lim, V. Y., Jiang, S., & Herbel-Eisenmann, B. (2022). Notice, wonder, feel, act, and reimagine as a path toward social justice in data science education. *Journal of Educational Technology & Society*, 25(4), 80–92.

Kalil, A. (2015). Inequality begins at home: The role of parenting in the diverging destinies of rich and poor children. In Amato, P., Booth, A., McHale, S., & Van Hook, J. (Eds.), *Diverging destinies: Families in an era of increasing inequality* (pp. 63–82). Springer. 10.1007/978-3-319-08308-7_5

Kalyanpur, M., & Harry, B. (2012). *Cultural reciprocity in special education: Building reciprocal family-professional relationships.* Brookes.

Kantawala, A. (2022). Action and reflection as "living theory and practice" (hooks, 2013). *Art Education*, 75(2), 4–7.

Kart, A., & Kart, M. (2021). Academic and social effects of inclusion on students without disabilities: A review of the literature. *Education Sciences*, 11(16), 1–13. 10.3390/educsci11010016

Kasari, C., Kaiser, A., Goods, K., Nietfeld, J., Mathy, P., Landa, R., Murphy, S., & Almirall, D. (2014). Communication interventions for minimally verbal children with autism: Sequential multiple assignment randomized trial. *Journal of the American Academy of Child and Adolescent Psychiatry*, 53(6), 635–646. 10.1016/j.jaac.2014.01.01924839882

Kashinath, S., Woods, J., & Goldstein, H. (2006). Enhancing generalized teaching strategy use in daily routines by parents of children with autism. *Journal of Speech, Language, and Hearing Research: JSLHR*, 49(3), 466–485. 10.1044/1092-4388(2006/036)16787891

Kayser, A., Kayser, B., Holmstrom, L., & Brazil Keys, B. (2021). We appreciate what you are doing, but you are doing it wrong: Two schools address school-family tensions through culturally responsive family partnerships. *Taboo: The Journal of Culture and Education, 20*(2). https://digitalscholarship.unlv.edu/taboo/vol20/iss2/2

Kemper, T., & Zavala, M. (2024). Culturally Responsive Mathematics Teaching in Special Education Spaces. In M. Zavala & J.M. Aguirre (Authors) *Cultivating Mathematical Hearts: Culturally Responsive Mathematics Teaching in Elementary Classrooms*. Corwin. pp. 182-195.

Kenly, A., & Klein, A. (2020). Early childhood experiences of black children in a diverse midwestern suburb. *Journal of African American Studies*, 24(1), 129–148. 10.1007/s12111-020-09461-y

Kennedy, M. M. (2016). How does professional development improve teaching? *Review of Educational Research*, 86(4), 945–980. 10.3102/0034654315626800

Kessler, S. A., & Swadener, B. B. (1992). *Reconceptualizing the early childhood curriculum: Beginning the dialog*. Teachers College Press.

Khalifa, M. (2018). *Culturally responsive school leadership*. Harvard Education Press.

Kim, J., & Soto, G. (2024). A comprehensive scoping review of caregivers' experiences with Augmentative and Alternative Communication and their collaboration with school professionals. *Language, Speech, and Hearing Services in Schools*, 55(2), 607–627. Advance online publication. 10.1044/2024_LSHSS-23-0011738324385

King, G., Desmarais, C., Lindsay, S., Piérart, G., & Tétreault, S. (2015). The roles of effective communication and client engagement in delivering culturally sensitive care to immigrant parents of children with disabilities. *Disability and Rehabilitation*, 37(15), 1372–1381. 10.3109/09638288.2014.97258025323397

King, J. E. (2015). *Dysconscious racism, Afrocentric praxis, and education for human freedom: Through the years I keep on toiling: The selected works of Joyce E. King*. Routledge. 10.4324/9781315717357

King, J. E. (2017). Who will make America great again? 'Black people, of course…'. *International Journal of Qualitative Studies in Education : QSE*, 30(10), 946–956. 10.1080/09518398.2017.1312605

King, J. E., & Swartz, E. E. (2016). *The Afrocentric praxis of teaching for freedom: Connecting culture to learning*. Routledge.

King, S., Teplicky, R., King, G., & Rosenbaum, P. (2004). Family-centered service for children with cerebral palsy and their families: A review of the literature. *Seminars in Pediatric Neurology*, 11(1), 78–86. 10.1016/j.spen.2004.01.00915132256

Kiyama, J. M., & Harper, C. E. (2018). Beyond hovering: A conceptual argument for an inclusive model of family engagement in higher education. *Review of Higher Education*, 41(3), 365–385. 10.1353/rhe.2018.0012

Klatte, I. S., Harding, S., & Roulstone, S. (2019). Speech and language therapists' views on parents' engagement in Parent-Child Interaction Therapy (PCIT). *International Journal of Language & Communication Disorders*, 54(4), 553–564. 10.1111/1460-6984.1245930729613

Klatte, I. S., Ketelaar, M., de Groot, A., Bloemen, M., & Gerrits, E. (2024, January). (2023). Collaboration: How does it work according to therapists and parents of young children? A systematic review. *Child: Care, Health and Development*, 50(1), e13167. 10.1111/cch.1316737724049

Koegel, R. L., O'dell, M. C., & Koegel, L. K. (1987). A natural language teaching paradigm for nonverbal autistic children. *Journal of Autism and Developmental Disorders*, 17(2), 187–200. 10.1007/BF014950553610995

Koestler, C., Ward, J., Zavala, M. del R., & Bartell, T. G. (2023). *Early elementary mathematics lessons to explore, understand, and respond to social injustice*. Corwin. 10.4135/9781071880630

Kokka, K. (2017). *Social Justice Mathematics: Pedagogy of the Oppressed or Pedagogy of the Privileged? A Comparative Case Study of Students of Historically Marginalized and Privileged Backgrounds*. [Doctoral dissertation, Harvard Graduate School of Education].

Koraleck, D., Nemeth, K. N., & Ramsey, K. (2019). *Families and educators together: Building great relationships that support young children*. NAEYC.

Kruijsen-Terpstra, A. J., Verschuren, O., Ketelaar, M., Riedijk, L., Gorter, J. W., Jongmans, M. J., & Boeije, H. (2016). Parents' experiences and needs regarding physical and occupational therapy for their young children with cerebral palsy. *Research in Developmental Disabilities*, 53-54, 314–322. 10.1016/j.ridd.2016.02.01226970858

KU Center on Developmental Disabilities. (2019). *Self-Determination Inventory: Student Report Guide*. Author.

Kuhlthau, K. A., Bloom, S., Van Cleave, J., Knapp, A. A., Romm, D., Klatka, K., Homer, C. J., Newacheck, P. W., & Perrin, J. M. (2011). Evidence for family-centered care for children with Special Health Care Needs: A systematic review. *Academic Pediatrics*, 11(2), 136–143.e8. 10.1016/j.acap.2010.12.01421396616

Kwon, K. A., Hong, S. Y., & Jeon, H. J. (2017). Classroom readiness for successful inclusion: Teacher factors and preschool children's experience with and attitudes toward peers with disabilities. *Journal of Research in Childhood Education*, 31(3), 360–378. 10.1080/02568543.2017.1309480

Ladau, E. (2021). *Demystifying disability: what to know, what to say, and how to be an ally* (1st ed.). Ten Speed Press.

Ladson-Billings, G. (1995). Toward a theory of culturally relevant pedagogy. *American Educational Research Journal*, 32(3), 465–491. 10.3102/00028312032003465

Ladson-Billings, G. (2014). Culturally relevant pedagogy 2.0: Aka the remix. *Harvard Educational Review*, 84(1), 74–84. 10.17763/haer.84.1.p2rj131485484751

Ladson-Billings, G. (2021). I'm here for the hard re-set: Post pandemic pedagogy to preserve our culture. *Equity & Excellence in Education*, 54(1), 68–78. 10.1080/10665684.2020.1863883

Lalvani, P., & Bacon, J. K. (2018). Rethinking "we are all special": Anti-ableism curricula in early childhood classrooms. *Young Exceptional Children*, 22(2), 87–100. 10.1177/1096250618810706

Lambert, R., Tan, P., Hunt, J., & Candela, A. G. (2018). Rehumanizing the mathematics education of students with disabilities; critical perspectives on research and practice. *Investigations in Mathematics Learning*, 10(3), 129–132. 10.1080/19477503.2018.1463006

Land, N., & Frankowski, A. (2022). (Un)finding childhoods in citational practices with postdevelopmental pedagogies. *Contemporary Issues in Early Childhood*, 23(4), 452–466. 10.1177/14639491221106500

Land, N., Vintimilla, C. D., & Pacini-Ketchabaw, V. (2020). Propositions toward educating pedagogists: Decentering the child. *Contemporary Issues in Early Childhood*, 23(2), 109–121.

Lantz, J. (n.d.). *Play time: An examination of play intervention strategies in children with Autism Spectrum Disorders.* IIDC. https://www.iidc.indiana.edu/pages/Play-Time-An-Examination-Of-Play-Intervention-Strategies-for-Children-with-Autism-Spectrum-Disorders>

Lawrence, D., Smith, S., & Banerjee, R. (2016). Preschool inclusion: Key findings from research and implications for policy. *Child Care and Early Education Research Connections*, 1-15.

Lawrence, S., Smith, S., & Banerjee, R. (2016). *Preschool inclusion: Key findings from research and implications for policy.* Child Care & Early Education Research Connections. https://www.nccp.org/wp-content/uploads/2020/05/text_1154.pdf

Learning for Justice & Yeh, C. (2021). *Toolkit for "Mathematics in Context": The pedagogy of liberation.* Learning for Justice. https://www.learningforjustice.org/magazine/spring-2021/toolkit-for-mathematics-in-context-the-pedagogy-of-liberation

Learning Policy Institute. (2022). *Whole child policy toolkit.* Learning Policy Institute. https://www.wholechildpolicy.org/rkdl-page/full/whole-child-policy-toolkit.pdf

Lee, S.-H., Wehmeyer, M. L., Palmer, S. B., Soukup, J. H., & Little, T. D. (2008). Self-determination and access to the general education curriculum. *The Journal of Special Education*, 42(2), 91–107. 10.1177/0022466907312354

Lee, Y. J., & Recchia, S. L. (2016). Zooming in and out: Exploring teacher competencies in inclusive early childhood classrooms. *Journal of Research in Childhood Education*, 30(1), 1–14. 10.1080/02568543.2015.1105330

Lenski, S. D., Crumpler, T. P., Stallworth, C., & Crawford, K. M. (2005). Beyond awareness: Preparing culturally responsive preservice teachers. *Teacher Education Quarterly*, 32(2), 85–100.

Levine, S. C., Gibson, D. J., & Berkowitz, T. (2019). Mathematical development in the early home environment. In *Cognitive foundations for improving mathematical learning* (pp. 107–142). Academic Press. 10.1016/B978-0-12-815952-1.00005-0

Lieberman, A. F., & Van Horn, P. (2005). Don't hit my mommy!: A manual for child-parent psychotherapy with young witnesses of family violence. *Zero to Three*.

Light, J. C., Parsons, A. R., & Drager, K. (2002). "There's more to life than cookies," Developing interactions for social closeness with beginning communicators who use AAC. In J. Reichle, D. Beukelman, & J. Light *Eds)., *Exemplary practices for beginning communicators: Implications for AAC* (pp. 187--218). Paul H. Brookes.

Light, J., & Drager, K. (2007). AAC technologies for young children with complex communication needs: State of the science and future research directions. *Augmentative and Alternative Communication*, 23(3), 204–216. 10.1080/07434610701553635175701740

Light, J., Drager, K., McCarthy, J., Mellott, S., Millar, D., Parrish, C., Parsons, A., Rhoads, S., Ward, M., & Welliver, M. (2004). Performance of typically developing four- and five-year-old children with AAC systems using different language organization techniques. *Augmentative and Alternative Communication*, 20(2), 63–88. 10.1080/07434610410001655553

Light, J., & McNaughton, D. (2013). Putting people first: Re-thinking the role of technology in augmentative and alternative communication intervention. *Augmentative and Alternative Communication*, 29(4), 299–309. 10.3109/07434618.2013.84893524229334

Light, J., Wilkinson, K. M., Thiessen, A., Beukelman, D. R., & Fager, S. K. (2019). Designing effective AAC displays for individuals with developmental or acquired disabilities: State of the science and future research directions. *Augmentative and Alternative Communication*, 35(1), 42–55. 10.1080/07434618.2018.155828330648896

Lin, S. C., & Gold, R. S. (2017). Assistive technology needs, functional difficulties, and services utilization and coordination of children with developmental disabilities in the United States. *Assistive Technology*, 30(2), 100–106. 10.1080/10400435.2016.126502328140832

Lin, V. W., Lin, J., & Zhang, X. (2016). U.S. social workforce report card: Forecasting nationwide shortages. *Social Work*, 61(1), 7–15. 10.1093/sw/swv04726897994

Little, C. (2020). Collaboration. In Spandagou, I., Little, C., Evans, D., & Bonati, M. L. (Eds.), *Inclusive education in schools and early childhood settings* (pp. 85–92). Springer. 10.1007/978-981-15-2541-4_8

Lizana, P. A., & Lera, L. (2022). Depression, anxiety, and stress among teachers during the second COVID-19 wave. *International Journal of Environmental Research and Public Health*, 19(10), 5968. 10.3390/ijerph1910596835627505

Lloyd, C., King, R., & Chenoweth, L. (2009). Social work, stress, and burnout: A review. *Journal of Mental Health (Abingdon, England)*, 11(3), 255–265. 10.1080/09638230020023642

Lomotey, K. (2023, April 27). *A Conversation on Black education.* Invited talk, Towson University.

Lomotey, K. (1990). *Going to school: The African-American experience.* State University of New York Press.

Lomotey, K. (2022). *Justice for Black students: Black principals matter.* Myers Education Press.

Lorang, E., Maltman, N., Venker, C., Eith, A., & Sterling, A. (2022). Speech-language pathologists' practices in augmentative and alternative communication during early intervention. *Augmentative and Alternative Communication*, 38(1), 41–52. 10.1080/07434618.2022.204685335422176

Love, H. R., & Beneke, M. R. (2021). Pursuing justice-driven inclusive education research: Disability critical race theory (DisCrit) in early childhood. *Topics in Early Childhood Special Education*, 41(1), 31–44. 10.1177/0271121421990833

Luo, R., Alper, R. M., Hirsh-Pasek, K., Mogul, M., Chen, Y., Masek, L. R., Paterson, S., Pace, A., Adamson, L. B., Bakeman, R., Golinkoff, R. M., & Owen, M. T. (2019). Community-Based, Caregiver-Implemented Early Language Intervention in High-Risk Families: Lessons Learned. *Progress in Community Health Partnerships*, 13(3), 283–291. 10.1353/cpr.2019.005631564669

Magee, R. V. (2019). *The inner work of racial justice: Healing ourselves and transforming our communities through mindfulness.* TarcherPerigee.

Mandak, K., O'Neill, T., Light, J., & Fosco, G. M. (2017). Bridging the gap from values to actions: A family systems framework for family-centered AAC services. *Augmentative and Alternative Communication*, 33(1), 32–41. 10.1080/07434618.2016.127145328081651

Marshall, J., & Goldbart, J. (2008). 'Communication is everything I think.' parenting A child who needs augmentative and alternative communication (AAC). *International Journal of Language & Communication Disorders*, 43(1), 77–98. 10.1080/1368282070126744417852533

Marshall, N. L., Dennehy, J., Starr, E., & Robeson, W. W. (2005). *Preparing the early education and care workforce: The capacity of Massachusetts institutions of higher education.* Wellesley Center for Women.

Marshall, T. R. (2023). *Understanding Your Instructional Power: Curriculum and Language Decisions to Support Each Student.* ASCD.

Martin, D. B. (2007). Beyond Missionaries or Cannibals: Who Should Teach Mathematics to African American Children? *High School Journal*, 91(1), 6–28. 10.1353/hsj.2007.0023

Mas, J. M., Dunst, C. J., Hamby, D. W., Balcells-Balcells, A., García-Ventura, S., Baqués, N., & Giné, C. (2020). Relationships between family-centred practices and parent involvement in early childhood intervention. *European Journal of Special Needs Education*, 37(1), 1–13. 10.1080/08856257.2020.1823165

Matusevich, H. A., Shogren, K. A., Raley, S. K., Zimmerman, K. N., Alsaeed, A., & Chapman, R. (2023). A Systematic Review of the Research: The Self-Determined Learning Model of Instruction Within MTSS. *Career Development and Transition for Exceptional Individuals*, 00(0), 1–15. 10.1177/21651434231200000

Maxwell, J. A. (2013). *Qualitative research design: An interactive approach* (3rd ed.). Sage Publications, Inc.

Mazzotti, V. L., Rowe, D. A., Kwiatek, S., Voggt, A., Chang, W. H., Fowler, C. H., Poppen, M., Sinclair, J., & Test, D. W. (2021). Secondary transition predictors of postschool success: An update to the research base. *Career Development and Transition for Exceptional Individuals*, 44(1), 47–64. 10.1177/2165143420959793

McBride, S. L., & Brotherson, M. J. (1997). Guiding practitioners toward valuing and implementing family centered practices. In Winton, P., McCollum, J., & Catlett, C. (Eds.), *Reforming personnel preparation in early intervention*. Paul H. Brookes Publishing Co.

McClain, M. P. (2021). Teacher candidates' perceptions of preparedness of teaching students who experience trauma. *Journal of Teacher Education and Educators*, 10(1), 5–23. https://files.eric.ed.gov/fulltext/EJ1310243.pdf

McCord, M. S., & Soto, G. (2004). Perceptions of AAC: An ethnographic investigation of Mexican-American families. *Augmentative and Alternative Communication*, 20(4), 209–227. 10.1080/07434610400005648

McCoy, D. C., Yoshikawa, H., Ziol-Guest, K. M., Duncan, G. J., Schindler, H. S., Magnuson, K., Yang, R., Koepp, A., & Shonkoff, J. P. (2017). Impacts of early childhood education on medium-and long-term educational outcomes. *Educational Researcher*, 46(8), 474–487. 10.3102/0013189X1773773930147124

McHendry, G. (n.d.). Interactive syllabus. *Interactive Syllabus*. https://www.interactivesyllabus.com/

McNaughton, D., Rackensperger, T., Benedek-Wood, E., Kerzman, C., Williams, M. B., & Light, J. (2008). "A child needs to be given a chance to succeed": Parents of individuals who use AAC describe the benefits and challenges of learning AAC technologies. *Augmentative and Alternative Communication*, 24(1), 43–55. 10.1080/07434610701421007018256963

McWayne, C., Sunah, H., Diez, V., & Jayanthi, M. (2022). "We feel connected... and like we belong:" A parent-led, staff-supported model of family engagement in early childhood. *Early Childhood Education Journal*, 50(3), 445–457. 10.1007/s10643-021-01160-x

McWilliam, R. A. (2010). *Routines-based early intervention: Supporting young children and their families*. Brookes.

Meadan, H., Douglas, S. N., Kammes, R., & Schraml-Block, K. (2018). "I'm a different coach with every family": Early interventionists' beliefs and practices. *Infants and Young Children*, 31(3), 200–214. 10.1097/IYC.0000000000000118

Meek, S. E., & Gilliam, W. S. (2016). *Expulsion and suspension in early education as matters of social justice and health equity.* (Discussion Paper). Washington, DC. National Academy of Medicine. 10.31478/201610e

Meek, S., Iruka, I. U., Allen, R., Yazzie, D., Fernandez, V., Catherine, E., McIntosh, K., Gordon, L., Gilliam, W., Hemmeter, M. L., Blevins, D., & Powell, T. (2020). Fourteen priorities to dismantle systemic racism in early care and education. The Children's Equity Project. https://fpg .unc.edu/sites/fpg.unc.edu/files/resource-files/14-priorities-equity-121420.pdf

Meek, S., Iruka, I. U., Catherine, E., Yazzie, D., Gilliam, W., McIntosh, K., Fernandez, V., Blevins, D., Jimenez Castellanos, O., & Garcia, G. (2021). Advancing equity in early care and education systems with the american rescue plan act. The Children's Equity Project. https://c hildandfamilysuccess.asu.edu/cep/initiatives/advancing-equity-through-american-rescue-plan-

Meek, S., Smith, L., Allen, R., Catherine, E., Edyburn, K., Williams, C., Fabes, R., McIntosh, K., Garica, E., Takanishi, R., Gordon, L., Jimenez-Castellanos, O., Hemmeter, M. L., Gilliam, W., & Pontier, R. (2020). *Start with equity: From the early years to the early grades.* Children's Equity Project; Bipartisan Policy Center. https://bipartisanpolicy.org/download/?file=/wp-content/ uploads/2020/07/cep-report-071320-final.pdf

Merriam-Webster. (n.d.). Inclusion. In *Merriam-Webster.com com dictionary.* Merriam-Webster. https://www.merriam-webster.com/dictionary/inclusion

Mesibov, G. B., Shea, V., & Schopler, E. (2004). *The TEACCH approach to autism spectrum disorders.* Springer. 10.1007/978-0-306-48647-0

Miles, M. B., & Huberman, A. M. (1994). *Qualitative Data Analysis: An Expanded Sourcebook.* SAGE Publications.

Miller, D. (2018). *The space between: Current practices and perceptions regarding trauma-informed supports and special education services* [Doctoral dissertation, University of Illinois at Urbana-Champaign]. Graduate Dissertations and Theses at Illinois. http://hdl.handle.net/2142/ 102769

Mitchell, C. L., & Hedge, V. A. (2007). Beliefs and practices of in-service preschool teachers in inclusive settings: Implications for personnel preparation. *Journal of Early Childhood Teacher Education*, 28(4), 353–366. 10.1080/10901020701686617

Mitsch, M. K., Collins, B., Friesen, A., & Hermoso, J. C. R. (2023). Social emotional development and mental health: Special education and social work interdisciplinary collaboration. In Slanda, D., & Pike, L. (Eds.), *Handbook of research on interdisciplinary preparation for equitable special education* (pp. 468–494). IGI Global. 10.4018/978-1-6684-6438-0.ch023

Mitsch, M. K., Weglarz-Ward, J., & Branch, J. (2022). "I'm new here": Leveraging responsibilities, relationships, and resources for new faculty leaders. *Young Exceptional Children*, 26(4), 193–206. 10.1177/10962506221111362

Moje, E. B., & Wade, S. E. (1997). What case discussions reveal about teacher thinking. *Teaching and Teacher Education*, 13(7), 691–712. 10.1016/S0742-051X(97)00015-2

Moll, L. C., Amanti, C., Neff, D., & Gonzalez, N. (1992). Funds of knowledge for teaching: Using a qualitative approach to connect homes and classrooms. *Theory into Practice*, 31(2), 132–141. 10.1080/00405849209543534

Moorcroft, A., Scarinci, N., & Meyer, C. (2020). 'We were just kind of handed it and then it was smoke bombed by everyone': How do external stakeholders contribute to parent rejection and the abandonment of AAC systems? *International Journal of Language &amp. International Journal of Language & Communication Disorders*, 55(1), 59–69. 10.1111/1460-6984.1250231553126

Moorcroft, A., Scarinci, N., & Meyer, C. (2021). "I've had a love-hate, I mean mostly hate relationship with these PODD books": Parent perceptions of how they and their child contributed to AAC rejection and abandonment. *Disability and Rehabilitation. Assistive Technology*, 16(1), 72–82. 10.1080/17483107.2019.163294431250678

Moore, R. C. (2017). *Childhood's domain: Play and place in child development* (Vol. 6). Routledge. 10.4324/9781315121895

Moran, K. K., & Sheppard, M. E. (2023). Finding the on ramp: Accessing early intervention and early childhood special education in an urban setting. *Journal of Early Intervention*, 45(4), 391–407. 10.1177/10538151221137801

Mosle, A., & Sims, M. (2021). *State of the field: Two-generation approaches to family well-being*. Aspen Institute.

Muhammad, G. E. (2022). Cultivating genius and joy in education through historically responsive literacy. *Language Arts*, 99(3), 195–204. 10.58680/la202231623

Mumbardó-Adam, C., Guàrdia-Olmos, J., Giné, C., Raley, S. K., & Shogren, K. A. (2018). The Spanish version of the Self-Determination Inventory Student Report: Application of item response theory to self-determination measurement. *Journal of Intellectual Disability Research*, 62(4), 303–311. 10.1111/jir.1246629282783

Murphy, P. K., & Alexander, P. A. (2007). Contextualizing learner-centered principles for teachers and teaching. In Hawley, W. D. (Ed.), *The keys to effective schools: Educational reform as continuous improvement* (pp. 13–32). Corwin Press. 10.4135/9781483329512.n2

Muttiah, N., Seneviratne, A., Drager, K. D., & Panterliyon, N. A. (2022). Parent perspectives on augmentative and alternative com-munication in Sri Lanka. *Augmentative and Alternative Commu-nication,38*(3), 173–183. https://doi.org/. 212194010.1080/07434618.2022

NAEYC. (2019). *Position Statement on Advancing Equity in Early Childhood Education*. National Association for the Education of Young Children. https://www.naeyc.org/sites/default/files/globally-shared/downloads/PDFs/resources/position-statements/advancingequitypositionstatement.pdf

NAEYC. (2020). *Developmentally Appropriate Practice: A position statement of the National Association for the Education of Young Children*. NAEYC. https://www.naeyc.org/resources/position-statements/dap/contents

NAEYC. (2021). *Learning Stories: Observation, Reflection, and Narrative in Early Childhood Education. Association for the Education of Young Children*. NAEYC. https://www.naeyc.org/resources/pubs/yc/summer2021/learning-stories

National Academies of Sciences, Engineering, and Medicine. (2022). *Addressing the Impact of COVID-19 on the Early Care and Education Sector*. Washington, DC: The National Academies Press. https://doi.org/10.17226/26463

National Association for the Education of Young Children & National Council of Teachers of Mathematics. (2010). *Early childhood mathematics: Promoting good beginnings*. Washington DC: NAEYC National Association for the Education of Young Children. (2020). Developmentally Appropriate Practice [PDF file]. https://www.naeyc.org/sites/default/files/globallyshared/downloads/PDFs/resources/position-statements/dap-statement_0.pdf

National Association for the Education of Young Children. (2019). *Advancing equity in early childhood education* [Position statement]. NAEYC. https://www.naeyc.org/sites/default/files/globally-shared/downloads/pdfs/resources/position-statements/advancingequitypositionstatement.pdf

National Association for the Education of Young Children. (2019). *Advancing equity in early childhood education A position statement of the National Association of the Education of Young Children*. NAEYC. https://www.naeyc.org/sites/default/files/globally-shared/downloads/PDFs/resources/position-statements/advancingequitypositionstatement.pdf

National Association for the Education of Young Children. (2019). *Early learning program accreditation standards and assessment items*. NAEYC. https://www.naeyc.org/sites/default/files/globally-shared/downloads/PDFs/accreditation/early-learning/standards_assessment_2019.pdf

National Association for the Education of Young Children. (2020a). *Developmentally appropriate practice: A position statement of the National Association of the Education of Young Children*. NAEYC. https://www.naeyc.org/sites/default/files/globally-shared/downloads/pdfs/resources/position-statements/dap-statement_0.pdf

National Association for the Education of Young Children. (2020b). *Professional standards and competencies for early childhood educators*. NAEYC. https://www.naeyc.org/sites/default/files/globally-shared/downloads/pdfs/resources/position-statements/standards_and_competencies_ps.pdf

National Association for the Education of Young Children. (n.d.). *Position statements*. NAEYC. https://www.naeyc.org/resources/position-statements

National Association of Social Work. (2015). *Standards and indicators for cultural competence*. NASW. https://www.socialworkers.org/linkclick.aspx?fileticket=7dvckzayumk%3d&portali=0

National Child Traumatic Stress Network. (n.d.). *About child trauma*. NCTSN. https://www.nctsn .org/what-is-child-trauma/about-child-trauma

National Research Council. (2001). *Educating children with autism*. Committee on Educational Interventions for Children with Autism. Division of Behavioral and Social Sciences and Education. Washington, DC: National Academy Press.

Neitzel, J. (2018). Research to practice: Understanding the role of implicit bias in early childhood disciplinary practices. *Journal of Early Childhood Teacher Education*, 39(3), 232–242. 10.1080/10901027.2018.1463322

Nelson, C. A., Scott, R. D., Bhutta, Z. A., Harris, N. B., Danese, A., & Samara, M. (2020). Adversity in childhood is linked to mental and physical health throughout life. *BMJ (Clinical Research Ed.)*, 371, m3048. 10.1136/bmj.m304833115717

Neufeld, B., & Roper, D. (2003). *Coaching: A strategy for developing instructional capacity*. The Aspen Institute.

Newton, P. M. (2015). The learning styles myth is thriving in higher education. *Frontiers in Psychology*, 6, 1908. 10.3389/fpsyg.2015.0190826696947

Nicholson, J., Kuhl, K., Maniates, H., Lin, B., & Bonetti, S. (2020). A review of the literature on leadership in early childhood: Examining epistemological foundation and considerations of social justice. *Early Child Development and Care*, 190(2), 91–122. 10.1080/03004430.2018.1455036

Nicolopoulou, A., Cortina, K. S., Ilgaz, H., Cates, C. B., & de Sá, A. B. (2015). Using a narrative-and play-based activity to promote low-income preschoolers' oral language, emergent literacy, and social competence. *Early Childhood Research Quarterly*, 31, 147–162. 10.1016/j. ecresq.2015.01.00625866441

Nieto, S. (2000). Placing equity front and center: Some thoughts on transforming teacher education for a new century. *Journal of Teacher Education*, 51(3), 180–187. 10.1177/0022487100051003004

Nieto, S., & Bode, P. (2018). *Affirming diversity: The sociopolitical context of multicultural education* (7th ed.). Pearson.

O'Neill, T., & Wilkinson, K. M. (2020). Preliminary investigation of the perspectives of parents of children with cerebral palsy on the supports, challenges, and realities of integrating augmentative and alternative communication into Everyday Life. *American Journal of Speech-Language Pathology*, 29(1), 238–254. 10.1044/2019_AJSLP-19-0010331961702

Obiakor, F. E., & Rotatori, A. F. (2014). *Multicultural education for learners with special needs in the twenty-first century*. Information Age Publishing.

Odom, S. L., Vitztum, J., Wolery, R., Lieber, J., Sandall, S., Hanson, M. J., Beckman, P., Schwartz, I., & Horn, E. (2004). Preschool inclusion in the United States: A review of research from an ecological systems perspective. *Journal of Research in Special Educational Needs*, 4(1), 17–49. 10.1111/J.1471-3802.2004.00016.x

Odom, S., Buysse, V., & Soukakou, E. (2011). Inclusion for young children with disabilities: A quarter century of research perspectives. *Journal of Early Intervention*, 33(4), 344–356. 10.1177/1053815111430094

Olson, J. R., & Singer, M. (1994). Examining teacher beliefs, reflective change, and the teaching of reading. *Literacy Research and Instruction*, 34(2), 97–110.

Oluo, I. (2018). *So you want to talk about race*. Seal.

Ondrasek, N., Carver-Thomas, D., Scott, C., & Darling-Hammond, L. (2020). *California's special education teacher shortage* (report). Palo Alto, CA: Policy Analysis for California Education.

Orange County Department of Education. (n.d.). *California MTSS framework*. OCDE. https://ocde.us/MTSS/Pages/CA-MTSS.aspx

Orr, R., Williams, M. R., & Pennington, K. (2009). Institutional efforts to support faculty in online teaching. *Innovative Higher Education*, 34(4), 257–268. 10.1007/s10755-009-9111-6

Ortega, L. (2014). Ways forward for a bi/multilingual turn for SLA. In May, S. (Ed.), *The multilingual turn: Implications for SLA, TESOL, and bilingual education* (pp. 32–52). Routledge.

Osborne, K. R., Caughy, M. O., Oshri, A., Smith, E. P., & Owen, M. T. (2021). Racism and preparation for bias within African American families. *Cultural Diversity & Ethnic Minority Psychology*, 27(2), 269–279. 10.1037/cdp000033932297761

Otheguy, R., García, O., & Reid, W. (2015). Clarifying translanguaging and deconstructing named languages: A perspective from linguistics. *Applied Linguistics Review*, 6(3), 281–307. 10.1515/applirev-2015-0014

Ou, S. R. (2005). Pathways of long-term effects of an early intervention program on educational attainment: Findings from the Chicago longitudinal study. *Journal of Applied Developmental Psychology*, 26(5), 578–611. 10.1016/j.appdev.2005.06.008

Palmer, S. A., Wehmeyer, M. L., & Shogren, K. A. (2017). The development of self-determination during childhood. In Wehmeyer, M. L., Shogren, K. A., Little, T. D., & Lopez, S. J. (Eds.), *Development of self-determination through the life-course* (pp. 71–88). Springer. 10.1007/978-94-024-1042-6_6

Palmer, S. B., Summers, J. A., Brotherson, M. J., Erwin, E. J., Maude, S. P., Stroup-Rentier, V., Hsiang-Yi, W., Peck, N. F., Zheng, Y., Weigel, C. J., Chu, S.-Y., McGrath, G. S., & Haines, S. J. (2013). Foundations for self-determination in early childhood: An inclusive model for children with disabilities. *Topics in Early Childhood Special Education*, 33(1), 38–47. 10.1177/0271121412445288

Pang, Y., & Wert, B. Y. (2010). Preservice teachers' attitudes towards family- centered practices in early intervention: An implication for teacher education. *Educational Research*, 1(8), 253–262.

Papay, C., Unger, D. D., Williams-Diehm, K., & Mitchell, V. (2015). Begin with the end in mind: Infusing transition planning and instruction into elementary classrooms. *Teaching Exceptional Children*, 47(6), 310–318. 10.1177/0040059915587901

Parette, H. P.Jr, Brotherson, M. J., & Huer, M. B. (2000). Giving families a voice in augmentative and alternative communication decision-making. *Education and Training in Mental Retardation and Developmental Disabilities*, 177–190.

Park, E.-Y., & Shin, M. (2020). A meta-analysis of special education teachers' burnout. *SAGE Open*, 10(2). Advance online publication. 10.1177/2158244020918297

Parker, J. S., Garnes, J. N., Oliver, E. D., Amabile, A., & Sarathy, A. (2020). It takes a village: Understanding African American high school students' self-determination in school. *School Psychology Review*, 49(2), 111–129. 10.1080/2372966X.2020.1717371

Park, H. (2021). "I kept questioning it in the first 6th months": The process of AAC acceptance in parents of children with complex communication needs. *Communication Sciences & Disorders (Seoul, Korea)*, 26(1), 120–136. 10.12963/csd.21801

Park, S., Lee, S., Alonzo, M., & Adair, J. K. (2021). Reconceptualizing assistance for young children of color with disabilities in an inclusion classroom. *Topics in Early Childhood Special Education*, 41(1), 57–68. 10.1177/0271121421992429

Parlakian, R. (2021). Promoting inclusion in infant toddler settings. *Young Children*, 90–94.

Paschall, K., Madill, R., & Halle, T. (2020). *Demographic characteristics of the early care and education workforce: Comparisons with child and community characteristics*. OPRE Report #2020-108. Washington, DC: Office of Planning, Research, and Evaluation, Administration for Children and Families., U.S. Department of Health and Human Services.

Passmore, A. H., & Tejero Hughes, M. (2022). Using eCoaching to Support Mothers' Pretend Play Interactions at Home. *Early Childhood Education Journal*. 10.1007/s10643-022-01420-436439906

Paterson, C. R., & Arco, L. (2007). Using video modeling for generalizing toy play in children with autism. *Behavior Modification*, 31(5), 660–681. 10.1177/0145445507301651117699123

Peisner-Feinberg, E. S., Burchinal, M. R., Clifford, R. M., Culkin, M. L., Howes, C., Kagan, S. L., & Yazejian, N. (2001). The relation of preschool childcare quality to children's cognitive and social developmental trajectories through second grade. *Child Development*, 72(5), 1534–1553. 10.1111/1467-8624.0036411699686

Pérez, M. S., & Saavedra, C. (2017). A call for onto-epistemological diversity in early childhood education and care: Centering global South conceptualizations of childhood/s. *Review of Research in Education*, *41*, 1–29. https://doi./10.3102/0091732X16688621org

Perry, B. D., & Szalavitz, M. (2006). *The boy who was raised as a dog: And other stories from a child psychiatrist's notebook—What traumatized children can teach us about loss, love, and healing*. Basic.

Perry, T., & Steele, C. (2004). *Young, gifted and black: Promoting high achievement among African-American students*. Beacon Press.

Peshkin, A. (1988). In search of subjectivity: One's own. *Educational Researcher*, 17(7), 17–21.

Pianta, R., Howes, C., Burchinal, M., Bryant, D., Clifford, R., Early, D., & Barbarin, O. (2005). Features of pre-kindergarten programs, classrooms, and teachers: Do they predict observed classroom quality and child-teacher interactions? *Applied Developmental Science*, 9(3), 144–159. 10.1207/s1532480xads0903_2

Pickl, G. (2011). Communication intervention in children with severe disabilities and multilingual backgrounds: Perceptions of pedagogues and parents. *Augmentative and Alternative Communication*, 27(4), 229–244. 10.3109/07434618.2011.63002122136362

Podolsky, A., & Kini, T. (2016). *How effective are loan forgiveness and service scholarships for recruiting teachers?* [Policy brief]. Learning Policy Institute. https://learningpolicyinstitute.org/media/185/download?inline&file=how_effective_are-loan_forgiveness_and_service-scholarships_recruiting_teachers.pdf

Pope, L., Light, J., & Franklin, A. (2022). Black Children with Developmental Disabilities Receive Less AAC Intervention than their White Peers: Preliminary Evidence of Racial Disparities from a Secondary Data Analysis. *American Journal of Speech-Language Pathology*, 31(5), 2159. 10.1044/2022_AJSLP-22-0007936044883

Power to the Profession Task Force. (2020). *Unifying framework for the early childhood profession*. Power to the Profession Task Force. https://powertotheprofession.org/wp-content/uploads/2020/03/power-to-profession-framework-03312020-web.pdf

Prendeville, J., Prelock, P., & Unwin, G. (2006). Peer play interventions to support the social competence of children with autism spectrum disorders. *Seminars in Speech and Language*, 27(1), 32–46. 10.1055/s-2006-93243716440243

Pretti-Frontczak, K., & Grisham, J. (2022). *Assessing young children in inclusive settings* (2nd ed.). Brookes Publishing.

Purtle, J. (2018). Systematic review of evaluations of trauma-informed organizational interventions that include staff trainings. *Trauma, Violence & Abuse*, 21(4), 725–740. 10.1177/152483801879130430079827

Pyle, A., & DeLuca, C. (2017). Assessment in play-based kindergarten classrooms: An empirical study of teacher perspectives and practices. *The Journal of Educational Research*, 110(5), 457–466. 10.1080/00220671.2015.1118005

Pyles, L. (2020). Healing justice, transformative justice, and holistic self-care for social workers. *Social Work*, 65(2), 178–187. 10.1093/sw/swaa01332236450

Raab, M., & Dunst, C. J. (2006). Influence of child interests on variations in child behavior and functioning. *Bridges*, 4(4), 1–22.

Raley, S. K., Shogren, K. A., Rifenbark, G. G., Lane, K. L., & Pace, J. R. (2021). The impact of the self-determined learning model of instruction on student self-determination in inclusive secondary classrooms. *Remedial and Special Education*, 42(6), 363–373. 10.1177/0741932520984842

Raulston, T. J., & Machalicek, W. (2018). Early intervention for repetitive behavior in autism spectrum disorder: A conceptual model. *Journal of Developmental and Physical Disabilities*, 30(1), 89–109. 10.1007/s10882-017-9566-9

Rausch, A., Joseph, J., Strain, P. S., & Steed, E. A. (2021). Fostering engagement within inclusive settings. *Young Children*, 76(4), 16–21.

Raver, C. C., Garner, P. W., & Smith-Donald, R. (2007). The roles of emotion regulation and emotion knowledge for children's academic readiness: Are the links causal?

Raver, S. A., & Childress, D. C. (2015). *Family-centered early intervention*. Brookes Publishing.

Reagan, E. M., & Hambacher, E. (2021). Teacher preparation for social justice: A synthesis of the literature, 1999–2019. *Teaching and Teacher Education*, 108, 103520. 10.1016/j.tate.2021.103520

Reska, S. S., Odom, S. L., & Hume, K. A. (2012). Ecological features of preschools and the social engagement of children with autism. *Journal of Early Intervention*, 34(1), 40–56. 10.1177/1053815112452596

Reyes, C.C., Haines, S.J., & Clark/Keefe, K. (2021). *Humanizing methodologies in educational research: Centering non-dominant communities*. Teachers College Press.

Rios-Aguilar, C., & Kiyama, J. M. (2012). Funds of knowledge: An approach to studying Latina(o) students' transition to college. *Journal of Latinos and Education*, 11(1), 2–16. 10.1080/15348431.2012.631430

Rios, K., & Tu, W.-M. (2023). Navigating IEP meetings: Effective approaches for supporting Asian families of children with IDD in special education. *The Journal of Special Education Apprenticeship*, 12(3), 27–38. 10.58729/2167-3454.1179

Riser-Kositsky, M. (2019, January 3). *Education statistics: Facts about American schools*. EdWeek. https://www.edweek.org/leadership/education-statistics-facts-about-american-schools/2019/01

Rivera, C. J., Haughney, K. L., Clark, K. A., & Werunga, R. (2022). Culturally responsive planning, instruction, and reflection for young children with significant disabilities. *Young Exceptional Children*, 25(2), 74–87. 10.1177/1096250620951767

Rivers, S. E., Brackett, M. A., Reyes, M. R., Mayer, J. D., Caruso, D. R., & Salovey, P. (2012). Measuring emotional intelligence in early adolescence with the MSCEIT-YV: Psychometric properties and relationship with academic performance and psychosocial functioning. *Journal of Psychoeducational Assessment*, 30(4), 344–366. 10.1177/0734282912449443

Roberts, M. Y., & Kaiser, A. P. (2011). The Effectiveness of Parent-Implemented Language Interventions: A Meta-Analysis. *American Journal of Speech-Language Pathology*, 20(3), 180–199. 10.1044/1058-0360(2011/10-0055)21478280

Robinson, N. B., & Solomon-Rice, P. L. (2009). Supporting collaborative teams and families. In G. Soto & C. Zangari (Eds.)., *Practically speaking: Language, literacy, and academic development for students with AAC needs.* (pp. 289–312). Paul H. Brooks Publishing.

Rogoff, B. (2003). *The cultural nature of human development.* Oxford University Press.

Romano, N., & Chun, R. Y. (2018). Augmentative and alternative communication use: Family and professionals' perceptions of facilitators and barriers. *CoDAS*, 30(4), 1–9. 10.1590/2317-178 2/2016201713830043827

Romski, M., & Sevcik, R. A. (2005). Augmentative communication and early intervention: Myths and realities. *Infants and Young Children*, 18(3), 174–185. 10.1097/00001163-200507000-00002

Romski, M., Sevcik, R. A., Adamson, L. B., Cheslock, M., Smith, A., Barker, R. M., & Bakeman, R. (2010). Randomized comparison of augmented and nonaugmented language interventions for toddlers with developmental delays and their parents. *Journal of Speech, Language, and Hearing Research: JSLHR*, 53(2), 350–364. 10.1044/1092-4388(2009/08-0156)20360461

Roper, N., & Dunst, C. J. (2003). Communication intervention in natural environments. *Infants and Young Children*, 16(3), 215–225. 10.1097/00001163-200307000-00004

Rossetti, Z., Redash, A., Sauer, J. S., Bui, O., Wen, Y., & Regensburger, D. (2020). Access, accountability, and advocacy: Culturally and linguistically diverse families' participation in IEP meetings. *Exceptionality*, 28(4), 243–258. 10.1080/09362835.2018.1480948

Roth, F. P., & Worthington, C. K. (2023). *Treatment resource manual for speech-language pathology.* Plural Publishing.

Roybal-Lewis, A. (2022). Moving towards proficiency: A grounded theory study of early childhood teacher candidates and professional development schools. *Early Childhood Education Journal*, 50(6), 913–924. 10.1007/s10643-021-01229-7

Safir, S. (2017). *The listening leader: Creating the conditions for equitable school transformation.* John Wiley & Sons.

Safir, S., & Dugan, J. (2021). *Street data: A next-generation model for equity, pedagogy, and school transformation.* Corwin.

Sandall, S. R., Schwartz, I. S., Joseph, G. E., & Gauvreau, A. N. (2019). *Building blocks for teaching preschoolers with special needs* (3rd ed.). Brookes.

Sansanwal, S. (2014). Pretend play enhances creativity and imagination. *Journal of Arts and Humanities*, 3(1), 70–83.

Sarason, S. B. (1996). *Revisting "The Culture of the School and the Problem of Change.".* Teachers College Press.

Schladant, M., & Dowling, M. (2020). Parent perspectives on augmentative and alternative communication integration for children with fragile X syndrome: It starts in the home. *Intellectual and Developmental Disabilities*, 58(5), 409–421. 10.1352/1934-9556-58.5.40933032315

Schochet, O. N., Johnson, A. D., & Phillips, D. A. (2020). The effects of early care and education settings on the kindergarten outcomes of doubly vulnerable children. *Exceptional Children*, 87(1), 27–53. 10.1177/0014402920926461

Schön, D. A. (1987). *Educating the reflective practitioner*. Jossey-Bass.

Schore, A. N. (2003). *Affect regulation and the repair of the self*. W.W. Norton & Company.

Sethi, S., Johnson-Staub, C., & Robbins, K. G. (2020). *An anti-racist approach to supporting child care through COVID-19 and beyond*. The Center for Law and Social Policy (CLASP). https://www.clasp.org/publications/report/brief/anti-racist-approach-supporting-child-care -through-covid-19-and-beyond/

Sevcik, R. A., Romski, M. A., & Adamson, L. B. (2004). Research directions in augmentative and alternative communication for preschool children. *Disability and Rehabilitation*, 26(21-22), 1323–1329. 10.1080/09638280412331280352155513732

Shillingsburg, M. A., Bowen, C. N., & Shapiro, S. K. (2014). Increasing social approach and decreasing social avoidance in children with autism spectrum disorder during discrete trial training. *Research in Autism Spectrum Disorders*, 8(11), 1443–1453. 10.1016/j.rasd.2014.07.013

Shogren, K. A., Gerasimova, D., Lachapelle, Y., Lussier-Desrochers, D., Hagiwara, M., Petit-pierre, G., Fontana-Lana, B., Piazza, F., Courbois, Y., Desbiens, A., Haelewyck, M., Geurts, H., Pace, J. R. & Hicks, T. (2019a). *Preliminary reliability and validity of the self-determination inventory*. Student report (trans.).

Shogren, K. A., Zimmerman, K. N., & Toste, J. R. (2021). The potential for developing and supporting self-determination in early childhood and elementary classrooms. *Handbook of Effective Inclusive Elementary Schools: Research and Practice*, 390-410. Taylor & Francis. 10.4324/9781003043874-19

Shogren, K. A., Anderson, M. H., Raley, S. K., & Hagiwara, M. (2020). Exploring the Relationship between Student and Teacher/Proxy-Respondent Scores on the Self-Determination Inventory. *Exceptionality*, 29(1), 47–60. 10.1080/09362835.2020.1729764

Shogren, K. A., Palmer, S. B., Wehmeyer, M. L., Williams-Diehm, K., & Little, T. D. (2012). Effect of intervention with the self-determined learning model of instruction on access and goal attainment. *Remedial and Special Education*, 33(5), 320–330. 10.1177/0741932511141007224771963

Shogren, K. A., & Raley, S. K. (2022). Assessment of Self-Determination. In *Self-Determination and Causal Agency Theory: Integrating Research into Practice* (pp. 63–75). Springer International Publishing., 10.1007/978-3-031-04260-7_6

Shogren, K. A., Raley, S. K., Burke, K. M., & Wehmeyer, M. L. (2019b). *The self-determined learning model of instruction: Teacher's guide*. Kansas University Center on Developmental Disabilities.

Shogren, K. A., Shaw, L. A., Raley, S. K., & Wehmeyer, M. L. (2018). Exploring the effect of disability, race-ethnicity, and socioeconomic status on scores on the self-determination inventory: Student-report. *Exceptional Children*, 85(1), 10–27. 10.1177/0014402918782150

Shogren, K. A., Wehmeyer, M. L., Palmer, S. B., Forber-Pratt, A., Little, T. J., & Lopez, S. (2015). Causal agency theory: Reconceptualizing a functional model of self-determination. *Education and Training in Autism and Developmental Disabilities*, 50(3), 251–263. https://www.jstor.org/stable/24827508

Shogren, K. A., Wehmeyer, M. L., & Singh, N. N. (Eds.). (2017). *Handbook of Positive Psychology in Intellectual and Developmental Disabilities: Translating Research Into Practice*. Springer. 10.1007/978-3-319-59066-0

Shonkoff, J. P., Garner, A. S., Siegel, B. S., Dobbins, M. I., Earls, M. F., Garner, A. S., McGuinn, L., Pascoe, J., & Wood, D. L. (2012). The lifelong effects of early childhood adversity and toxic stress. *Pediatrics*, 129(1), e232–e246. 10.1542/peds.2011-266322201156

Shonkoff, J. P., & Hauser-Cram, P. (1987). Early intervention for disabled infants and their families: A quantitative analysis. *Pediatrics*, 80(5), 650–658. 10.1542/peds.80.5.6503313255

Simmons-Mackie, N., King, J. M., & Beukelman, D. (2013). *Supporting communication for adults with acute and chronic aphasia*. Paul H. Brookes Publishing Co.

Sisk-Hilton, S. (2024). *Teaching Climate Science in the Elementary Classroom: A Place-Based, Hope-Filled Approach to Understanding Earth's Systems*. Routledge.

Sleeter, C. E. (2001). Preparing teachers for culturally diverse schools: Research and the overwhelming presence of whiteness. *Journal of Teacher Education*, 52(2), 94–106. 10.1177/0022487101052002002

Sleeter, C. E. (2016). Critical family history: Situating family within contexts of power relationships. *Journal of Multidisciplinary Research*, 8(1), 11–23.

Sleeter, C. E. (2017). Critical race theory and the whiteness of teacher education. *Urban Education*, 52(2), 155–169. 10.1177/0042085916668957

Smilansky, S., & Shefatya, L. (1990). *Facilitating play: a medium for promoting cognitive, socio-emotional, and academic development in young children*. Psychological & Educational Publications.

Solomon-Rice, P. L., & Soto, G. (2014). Facilitating vocabulary in toddlers using AAC: A preliminary study comparing focused stimulation and augmented input. *Communication Disorders Quarterly*, 35(4), 204–215. 10.1177/1525740114522856

Soto, G., & Yu, B. (2014). Considerations for the provision of services to bilingual children who use augmentative and alternative communication. *Augmentative and Alternative Communication*, 30(1), 83–92. 10.3109/07434618.2013.87875124471987

Souto-Manning, M. (2010). *Freire, teaching, and learning: Culture circles across contexts* (Vol. 350). Peter Lang.

Souto-Manning, M. (2013). *Multicultural teaching in the early childhood classroom: Approaches, strategies, and tools, preschool-2nd grade*. Teachers College Press.

Souto-Manning, M. (2016). Honoring and building on the rich literacy practices of young bilingual and multilingual learners. *The Reading Teacher*, 70(3), 263–271. 10.1002/trtr.1518

Souto-Manning, M., & Rabadi-Raol, A. (2018). (Re)centering quality in early childhood education: Toward intersectional justice for minoritized children. *Review of Research in Education*, 42(1), 203–225. 10.3102/0091732X187595

Souto-Manning, M., & Rabadi-Raol, A. (2018). (Re)Centering Quality in Early Childhood Education: Toward Intersectional Justice for Minoritized Children. *Review of Research in Education*, 42(1), 203–225. 10.3102/0091732X18759550

Spradley, J. P. (1979). *The Ethnographic Interview*. Harcourt Brace Jovanovich College Publishers.

Staats, C. (2016). Understanding implicit bias: What educators should know. *American Educator*, 39(4), 29–33, 43. https://files.eric.ed.gov/fulltext/EJ1086492.pdf

Stacey, S. (2018). *Emergent curriculum in early childhood settings: From theory to practice* (2nd ed.). Redleaf Press.

Steed, E. A., Rausch, A., Strain, P. S., Bold, E., & Leech, N. (2023). High-quality inclusion in preschool settings: A survey of early childhood personnel. *Topics in Early Childhood Special Education*, 43(2), 142–155. 10.1177/02711214211063921

Steele, C. M. (2010). *Whistling Vivaldi: How stereotypes affect us and what we can do*. W.W. Norton & Company.

Stockstill, C. (2023). *False starts: The segregated lives of preschoolers*. NYU Press.

Strain, P. S., & Bovey, E. H. II. (2011). Randomized, controlled trial of the LEAP model of early intervention for young children with autism spectrum disorders. *Topics in Early Childhood Special Education*, 31(3), 133–154. 10.1177/0271121411408740

Strauss, A., & Corbin, J. M. (1998). *Basics of Qualitative Research: Techniques and Procedures for Developing Grounded Theory*. SAGE Publications.

Stuart, S. A., & Parette, H. P. Jr. (2002). Native americans and augmentative and alternative communication issues. *Multiple Voices for Ethnically Diverse Exceptional Learners*, 5(1), 38–53. 10.56829/muvo.5.1.p8006861217m5414

Substance Abuse and Mental Health Services Administration. (2014). *SAMHSA's concept of trauma and guidance for a trauma-informed approach* (HHS Publication No. [SMA] 14-4884). SAMHSA. https://store.samhsa.gov/sites/default/files/sma14-4884.pdf

Sullivan, J., Wilton, L., & Apfelbaum, E. P. (2021). Adults delay conversations about race because they underestimate children's processing of race. *Journal of Experimental Psychology. General*, 150(2), 395–400. 10.1037/xge000085132757612

Summers, J. A., Brotherson, M. J., Erwin, E. J., Maude, S. P., Palmer, S. B., Haines, S. J., Stroup-Rentier, V., Wu, H.-Y., Peck, N. F., & Zheng, Y. Z. (2014). Family reflections on the foundations of self-determination in early childhood. *Inclusion (Washington, D.C.)*, 2(3), 175–194. 10.1352/2326-6988-2.03.175

Sun, F. (2015). Cultural consciousness: A Chinese immigrant teacher's understanding of culture and culturally responsive teaching in the United States. In Meier, D. R., & Kroll, L. R. (Eds.), *Educational Change in International Early Childhood Contexts* (pp. 73–88). Routledge. 10.4324/9781315848945-14

Tang, G., Savic, M., El Turkey, H., Karakok, G., Cilli-Turner, E., & Plaxco, D. (2017). Inquiry as an access point to equity in the classroom. In *Proceedings of the 20th Annual Conference on Research on Undergraduate Mathematics Education* (pp. 1098-1106). IEEE.

TASH. (2021). *TASH position statement with policy recommendations on inclusive education*. TASH. https://tash.org/tash-position-statement-with-policy-recommendations-on-inclusive-education/

Tate, W. (2012). Race, retrenchment, and the reform of school mathematics. In Gutstein, E., & Peterson, B. (Eds.), *Rethinking mathematics: teaching social justice by the numbers* (2nd ed., pp. 42–52). Rethinking Schools.

Taylor, J. L., & Sailor, W. (2023). A case for systems change in special education. *Remedial and Special Education*, 00(0), 1–11. 10.1177/07419325231181385

Taylor, S. D., Veri, M. J., Eliason, M., Hermoso, J. C. R., Bolter, N. D., & Van Olphen, J. E. V. (2019). The social justice syllabus design tool: A first step in doing social justice pedagogy. *Journal Committed to Social Change on Race and Ethnicity*, 5(2), 133–166.

Teasley, M. L. (2016). Related services personnel and evidence-based practice: Past and present challenges. *Children & Schools*, 38(1), 5–8. 10.1093/cs/cdv039

The Council for Exceptional Children and The Division for Early Childhood. (2020). *Initial practice-based professional preparation standards for early interventionists/early childhood special educators (EI/ECSE) (initial birth through age 8)*. The Council for Exceptional Children and The Division for Early Childhood. https://exceptionalchildren.org/standards/initial-practice-based-standards-early-interventionists-early-childhood-special-educators

Tilstone, C., Florian, L., & Rose, R. (1998). *Promoting Inclusive Practice*. Routledge; London.

Tip sheets - inclusive child care. (2020). Center for Inclusive Child Care. https://www .inclusivechildcare.org/sites/default/files/courses/swf/Social%20Scripts.pdf

TODOS. (2020). *The Mo(ve)ment to Prioritize Antiracist Mathematics: Planning for this and every school year.* Tempe, AZ. https://www.todos-math.org/statements

Tominey, S. L., O'Bryon, E. C., Rivers, S. E., & Shapses, S. (2017). Teaching emotional intelligence in early childhood. *Young Children*, 72(1), 6–12.

Tomlinson, M. (2015). Infant mental health in the next decade: A call for action. *Infant Mental Health Journal*, 36(6), 538–541. 10.1002/imhj.2153726514552

Tomporowski, P. D., McCullick, B., Pendleton, D. M., & Pesce, C. (2015). Exercise and children's cognition: The role of exercise characteristics and a place for metacognition. *Journal of Sport and Health Science*, 4(1), 47–55. 10.1016/j.jshs.2014.09.003

Trauma Transformed. (n.d.). *Trauma informed systems.* https://traumatransformed.org/communities -of-practice/communities-of-practice-tis.asp

Trawick-Smith, J. (2014). *The physical play and motor development of young children: A review of literature and implications for practice.* Center for Early Childhood Education, Eastern Connecticut State University.

Trent, M., Dooley, D. G., Dougé, J., Cavanaugh, R. M.Jr, Lacroix, A. E., Fanburg, J., Rahmandar, M. H., Hornberger, L. L., Schneider, M. B., Yen, S., Chilton, L. A., Green, A. E., Dilley, K. J., Gutierrez, J. R., Duffee, J. H., Keane, V. A., Krugman, S. D., McKelvey, C. D., Linton, J. M., & Wallace, S. B. (2019). The impact of racism on child and adolescent health. *Pediatrics*, 144(2), e20191765. 10.1542/peds.2019-176531358665

Tuck, E., & Yang, K. W. (2012). Decolonization is not a metaphor. *Decolonization*, 1(1), 1–40.

Turnbull, A. P., Summers, J. A., & Brotherson, M. J. (1984). Working with families with disabled members: A family systems approach. Research & Training Center on Independent Living, University of Kansas.

Turnbull, A. P., Summers, J. A., & Brotherson, M. J. (1984). *Working with families with disabled members: A family systems approach.* University of Kansas.

Turnbull, A. P., Turnbull, R., Erwin, E. J., Soodak, L. C., & Shogren, K. A. (2015). *Families, professionals, and exceptionality: Positive outcomes through partnerships and trust* (7th ed.). Pearson.

U.S. Bureau of Labor Statistics. (2021a). *Social workers.* BLS. https://www.bls.gov/ooh/community -and-social-service/social-workers.htm

U.S. Bureau of Labor Statistics. (2021b). *Special education teachers.* BLS. https://www.bls.gov/ ooh/education-training-and-library/special-education-teachers.htm

U.S. Department of Education & U.S. Department of Health and Human Services. (2023). *Policy Statement on Inclusion of Children with Disabilities in Early Childhood Programs.* USDoE.

U.S. Department of Education, Office of Special Education and Rehabilitative Services, Office of Special Education Programs. (2021). *42nd annual report to Congress on the implementation of the Individuals With Disabilities Education Act, 2020.*

U.S. Department of Education. (2016). *Racial and ethnic disparities in special education: A multi-year disproportionality analysis by state, analysis category, and race/ethnicity.* USDoE. https://www2.ed.gov/programs/osepidea/618-data/LEA-racial-ethnic-disparities-tables/disproportionality-analysis-by-state-analysis-category.pdf

U.S. Department of Education. (2017). *Teacher shortage areas nationwide: Listing 1990–1991 through 2017–2018.* USDoE. https://www2.ed.gov/about/offices/list/ope/pol/ateachershortageareasreport2017-18.pdf

U.S. Department of Education. (2021). *Individuals with Disabilities Education Act (IDEA) database: Digest of Education Statistics 2020.* Office of Special Education Programs. https://data.ed.gov/dataset/idea-section-618-data-products-state-level-data-files

U.S. Department of Health and Human Services, & U.S. Department of Education. (2015a). *Policy statement on inclusion of children with disabilities in early childhood programs.* USDoE. https://www2.ed.gov/policy/speced/guid/earlylearning/joint-statement-full-text.pdf

U.S. Department of Health and Human Services, & U.S. Department of Education. (2015b). *Policy statement on expulsion and suspension policies in early childhood settings.* OESE. https://oese.ed.gov/files/2020/07/policy-statement-ece-expulsions-suspensions.pdf

U.S. Department of Health and Human Services. (2022). *Protective factors and adverse childhood experiences.* USDoE. https://www.childwelfare.gov/topics/preventing/preventionmonth/about/protective-factors-aces/

United Nations. (2006). *Convention on the rights of persons with disabilities.* UN.

Urbani, J. M., Collado, C., Manalo, A., & Gonzalez, N. (2022). Building the on-ramp to inclusion: Developing critical consciousness in future early childhood educators. *Issues in Teacher Education,* 31(2), 91–121. https://www.itejournal.org/wp-content/pdfs-issues/summer-2022/09urbanietal.pdf

Vacca, J. L., Vacca, R. T., Gove, M. K., Burkey, L., Lenhart, L. A., & McKeon, C. (2003). *Reading and learning to read* (5th ed.). Pearson Education, Inc.

Vacca, R. T., Vacca, J. L., & Bruneau, B. (2004). Teachers Reflecting on Practice. In *Handbook of Research on Teaching Literacy Through the Communicative and Visual Arts* (pp. 445–450). Routledge.

van der Kolk, B. (2014). *The body keeps the score: Brain, mind, and body in the healing of trauma.* Penguin Books.

Van Mensel, L. (2018). 'Quiere koffie? 'The multilingual familylect of transcultural families. *International Journal of Multilingualism,* 15(3), 233–248. 10.1080/14790718.2018.1477096

Van Oers, B., & Duijkers, D. (2013). Teaching in a play-based curriculum: Theory, practice and evidence of developmental education for young children. *Journal of Curriculum Studies*, 45(4), 511–534. 10.1080/00220272.2011.637182

Vandell, D., & Wolfe, B. (2000). *Child care quality: Does it matter and does it need to be improved?* Institute for Research on Poverty.

Vélez-Agosto, N. M., Soto-Crespo, J. G., Vizcarrondo-Oppenheimer, M., Vega-Molina, S., & García Coll, C. (2017). Bronfenbrenner's bioecological theory revision: Moving culture from the macro into the micro. *Perspectives on Psychological Science*, 12(5), 900–910. 10.1177/174 5691617704397289728838

Venet, A. S. (2019). *Role-clarity and boundaries for trauma-informed teachers* (EJ1206249). ERIC. https://files.eric.ed.gov/fulltext/EJ1206249.pdf

Venet, A. S. (2021). *Equity-centered trauma-informed education (equity and social justice in education)*. W. W. Norton & Company.

Verschaffel, L., Greer, B., & De Corte, E. (2000). *Making sense of word problems*. Swets & Zeitlinger.

Vygotsky, L. S. (1978). *Mind in society: The development of higher psychological processes*. Harvard University Press.

Vygotsky, L. S., & Cole, M. (1978). *Mind in society: Development of higher psychological processes*. Harvard University Press.

Walker, H. M., Calkins, C., Wehmeyer, M. L., Walker, L., Bacon, A., Palmer, S. B., & Johnson, D. R. (2011). A social-ecological approach to promote self-determination. *Exceptionality*, 19(1), 6–18. 10.1080/09362835.2011.537220

Walker, M. L. (1993). Participatory action research. *Rehabilitation Counseling Bulletin*, 37, 2–2.

Watson-Vandiver, M. J., & Wiggan, G. (2021). *The healing power of education: Afrocentric pedagogy as a tool for restoration and liberation*. Teachers College Press.

Weglarz-Ward, J., Mitsch, M. K., Branch, J., Yarczower, M. B., & Anang, C. (2024). Family practices in educator licensure: A content analysis of U.S. state requirements. *Journal of Early Childhood Teacher Education*, 1–19. 10.1080/10901027.2024.2314290

Wehmeyer, M. L. (1992). Self-determination and the education of students with mental retardation. *Education and Training in Mental Retardation*, 27(4), 302–314. https://www.jstor.org/stable/23878861

Wertsch, J. V. (1998). *Mind as action*. Oxford University Press.

Wesley, P. W., & Buysse, V. (1996). Supporting early childhood inclusion: Lessons learned through a statewide technical assistance project. *Topics in Early Childhood Special Education*, 16(4), 476–499. 10.1177/027112149601600407

Westby, C., Burda, A., & Mehta, Z. (2003). Asking the right questions in the right ways: Strategies for ethnographic interviewing. *ASHA Leader*, 8(8), 4–17. 10.1044/leader.FTR3.08082003.4

WestEd. (2012). *Early childhood mental health: Raising awareness, taking action. R & D Alert*, *13*(3), 1–3. https://www.wested.org/wp-content/uploads/2016/11/1372730177article_earlyc hildhoodmentalhealth_2012-3.pdf

Wetherby, A. M., & Woods, J. J. (2006). Early social interaction project for children with autism spectrum disorders beginning in the second year of life: A preliminary study. *Topics in Early Childhood Special Education*, 26(2), 67–82. 10.1177/02711214060260020201

Whitebrook, M., Phillips, D., Bellm, D., Crowell, N., Almaraz, M., & Jo, J. Y. (2004). *Two years in early care and education: A community portrait of quality and workforce stability: Alameda County, California*. University of California.

Whitford, B. L., & Wood, D. R. (2010). *Teachers Learning in Community: Realities and Possibilities*. SUNY Press. 10.1353/book518

Woodhead, M. (2006). Changing perspectives on early childhood: Theory, research and policy. *International Journal of Equity and Innovation in Early Childhood*, 4(2), 1–43.

Wood, J. L., Hilton, A. A., & Nevarez, C. (2015). Faculty of color and white faculty: An analysis of service in colleges of education in Arizona public university system. *Journal of the Professoriate*, 8(1), 85–109. https://caarpweb.org/wp-content/uploads/2015/06/8-1_Wood_p85.pdf

World Health Organization. (2011). *World report on disability*. WHO. https://www.who.int/disabilities/world_report/2011/en/

World Health Organization. (2020, June 30). *Self-care interventions for health*. World Health Organization. https://www.who.int/news-room/fact-sheets/detail/self-care-health-interventions #:~:text=Self%2Dcare%20interventions%20promote%20individuals,convenience%2C%20 confidentiality%2C%20and%20cost

Wright, B. L., & Ford, D. Y. (2016). "This little light of mine": Creating early childhood education classroom experiences for African American boys prek-3. *Journal of African American Males in Education*, 7(1), 5–19.

Wright, B., & Counsell, S. (2018). *The brilliance of Black boys: Cultivating school success in the early grades*. Teachers College Press.

Wright, C. A., Kaiser, A. P., Reikowsky, D. I., & Roberts, M. Y. (2013). Effects of a naturalistic sign intervention on expressive language of toddlers with down syndrome. *Journal of Speech, Language, and Hearing Research: JSLHR*, 56(3), 994–1008. 10.1044/1092-4388(2012/1 2-0060)23275419

Wu, M. Y. H., Alexander, M. A., Frydenberg, E., & Deans, J. (2020). Early childhood social-emotional learning based on the Cope-Resilience program: Impact of teacher experience. *Issues in Educational Research*, 30(2), 782–807.

Yeh, C., Ellis, M., & Mahmood, D. (2020). From the margin to the center: A framework for rehumanizing mathematics education for students with dis/abilities. *The Journal of Mathematical Behavior*, 58, 100758. 10.1016/j.jmathb.2020.100758

Yoder, P., & Stone, W. L. (2006). A randomized comparison of the effect of two prelinguistic communication interventions on the acquisition of spoken communication in preschoolers with ASD. *Journal of Speech, Language, and Hearing Research: JSLHR*, 49(4), 698–711. 10.1044/1092-4388(2006/051)16908870

Yosso, T. J. (2005). Whose culture has capital? A critical race theory discussion of community cultural wealth. *Race, Ethnicity and Education*, 8(1), 69–91. 10.1080/1361332052000341006

Yuan, T., & Jiang, H. (2019). Culturally responsive teaching for children from low-income, immigrant families. *Young Exceptional Children, 22*(3), 150—161. h 10.1177/1096250618756897

Yu, B., Epstein, L., & Tisi, V. (2021). A DisCrit-informed critique of the difference vs. disorder approach in speech-language pathology. In *Critical perspectives on social justice in speech-language pathology* (pp. 105–128). IGI Global. 10.4018/978-1-7998-7134-7.ch006

Yull, D., Blitz, L., Thompson, T., & Murray, C. (2014). Can we talk? Using community-based participatory action research to build family and school partnerships with families of color. *School Community Journal*, 24(9).

Zack, N. (2023). Social Construction and Racial Identities. In *Philosophy of Race*. Palgrave Philosophy Today. Palgrave Macmillan., 10.1007/978-3-031-27374-2_6

Zamudio, M., Russell, C., Rios, F., & Bridgeman, J. L. (2011). *Critical race theory matters: Education and ideology*. Routledge. 10.4324/9780203842713

Zermeño, B. P. (2022). I Come from Mathema*ticians and Engineers: Reclaiming Histories Towards Ethnic Studies in Early Childhood* (Publication No. 28971341) [Doctoral dissertation, Mills College]. ProQuest Dissertations & Theses Global.

Zippia: The Career Expert. (2022). *Early childhood teacher demographics and statistics in the US*. Zippia. https://www.zippia.com/early-childhood-teacher-jobs/demographics/

Ziviani, J., Feeney, R., & Kahn, A. (2011). Early intervention services for children with physical disability: Parents' perceptions of family-centeredness and service satisfaction. *Infants and Young Children*, 24(4), 364–382. 10.1097/IYC.0b013e31822a6b77

About the Contributors

Amber Friesen (she/her), PhD - Dr. Friesen is a Professor and Chair of the Department of Special Education, at San Francisco State University. Since joining SF State in 2012, her research has focused on promoting inclusive early childhood settings and strong family partnerships. With colleagues in early childhood, she co-created and is the co-coordinator of the Inclusive Early Childhood Practices Graduate Certificate. Dr. Friesen has been the principal investigator on two Office of Special Education Programs (OSEP) grants, including a more recent interdisciplinary grant with speech language therapists.

Maryssa Kucskar Mitsch, Ph.D., is an Associate Professor of Early Childhood Special Education in the Department of Special Education. Her primary teaching responsibilities includes courses in early intervention, assessment of young children at-risk and with disabilities, and family systems. Dr. Kucskar's primary research interests focus on inclusive practices, social skills interventions for young children with disabilities, implementation of evidence-based practices, and strategies for effective professional development.

Karina Du received her undergraduate degree in Psychology and Sociology at the University of California Irvine and is an alumni of the Early Childhood Special Education Credential/M.A. program at San Francisco State University. She is a lecturer for an undergraduate course on the science of early intervention. She currently works with preschoolers with autism, and also has experience in early intervention, family-centered practices and inclusion. She also had the opportunity to teach in South Africa as a part of the the CAD/ECSE summer program.

***

Serra Acar, is an Assistant Professor in the Early Care and Education in Inclusive Settings Program at the UMass Boston. She earned her doctoral degree in the Early Intervention Program from the University of Oregon. Her primary research interests are culturally and linguistically responsive assessment and personnel preparation in EI/ECSE.

Jacqueline Anton is a graduate student completing her doctorate in Special Education at San Francisco State University and University of California, Berkeley.

Tonya Gau Bartell is an associate professor of mathematics education whose research focuses on issues of culture, race, and power in mathematics teaching and learning, with particular attention to teachers' development of mathematics pedagogy for social justice and pedagogy integrating a focus on mathematics, children's mathematical thinking, and children's community and cultural knowledge.

About the Contributors

Ruby Batz specializes in the interdisciplinary study of family engagement practices, examining the intersection of race, ethnicity, language, and disability. She joined the faculty of Special Education in the College of Education and Human Development at the University of Nevada, Reno (UNR), in 2020 as an assistant professor. Dr. Batz received her undergraduate training in special education and educational psychology from Universidad del Valle and Universidad Rafael Landívar in Guatemala City, and she did her master's and doctorate studies in early intervention and early childhood special education from the University of Oregon. Dr. Batz is a former Fulbright Fellow and AAHHE (American Association of Hispanics in Higher Education) Faculty Fellow. Her work has been supported by an early career grant from the Society for Research in Child Development, a racial equity grant from the Spencer Foundation, and a National Institute of Health (NIH) sub-award to study structural inequity in Early Intervention.

Erica Bosque is an Assistant Professor for the School of Social Work at San Francisco State University and is a Clinical Supervisor. Erica is the owner of Keystone Therapy & Training Services, a non-profit & private practice providing therapeutic support and resources to women, men, families, diverse populations and professional development to people who work in the human service, mental health fields, nonprofits and business sectors. In addition, Erica is a Mother of 4 and her and her husband Ryan have grown-up and live in California. Erica also has extensive training in Trauma Informed Care/Approaches, Motivational Interviewing, a Certified Center for Mind Body Medicine Facilitator, a certified yoga instructor, birth & postpartum doula and childbirth educator. Erica earned her Educational Doctorate in Leadership and Social Justice at San Francisco State University.

Monica Brown is a Professor of Special Education at the University of Las Vegas, Nevada (UNLV). Prior to entering higher education, she spent 13 years as a classroom special education teacher. She received her Ph.D. from UNLV in 2001. Dr. Brown identifies as a Black scholar in that she focuses on research for, with, and by Black people. Specifically, her research centers on issues relative to race and disability as they relate to Black PreK – 12 students with and without disabilities and their families. Currently, she has 45+ publications, as well as 75+ conference presentations.

Melissa M. Burnham is a Professor and Department Chair of Human Development, Family Science, and Counseling at the University of Nevada, Reno. Her Ph.D. is in Human Development from the University of California, Davis, where she learned positivist approaches to studying infants and young children. Dr. Burnham's research interests involve the intersection of children and contexts (e.g., sleep development within families; children and pedagogy in early care and education settings). Dr. Burnham holds an endorsement in Infant Mental Health as a Research/Faculty Mentor and strives to hold the strengths of the child at the forefront in her work. She is committed to actively learning critical pedagogies and methods and unlearning oppressive methodologies and practices that have dominated the field and her consciousness.

Deb Carter, Ph.D., BCBA-D, is a professor in Early and Special Education at Boise State University. Dr. Carter's areas of expertise include Positive Behavioral Interventions and Supports, social-emotional development, and nature-based learning in early childhood education. Her work has been published in the Journal of Positive Behavior Interventions, Behavioral Disorders, Assessment for Effective Intervention, Intervention in School and Clinic, The Early Childhood Education Journal, Teaching Young Children, and International Journal of Early Childhood Environmental Education.

Lisa B. Fiore is Director of Post-Baccalaureate programs in the Graduate School of Arts and Sciences and affiliated faculty in the Child Study and Human Development Department at Tufts University, MA. Her current research emphasizes social-emotional learning and development, building and sustaining relationships in educational settings, and promoting strengths-based environments and awareness of the multi-generational effects of adverse childhood experiences (ACEs). Dr. Fiore is the author of several books, including: Grit, Resilience, & Motivation in Early Childhood; Assessment of Young Children: A Collaborative Approach; Your Anxious Child: How Parents and Teachers Can Relieve Anxiety in Children; and Building Trust between Faculty & Administrators: An Intercultural Perspective. Dr. Fiore obtained her Ph.D. in Developmental and Educational Psychology from Boston College, an M.A.T. from Tufts University, and a B.A. in English and American Literature from Brandeis University.

Mayumi Hagiwara is an Assistant Professor in the Extensive Support Needs (moderate/severe disabilities) Program in the Department of Special Education at San Francisco State University.

Patricia Hampshire is an Associate Professor in Special Education in the Department of Teacher Education and Leadership at Mississippi State University. She received her PhD in Special Education at Indiana University in 2011. Her research focuses on developing interventions based in Applied Behavior Analysis for young children with autism.

Sylvia Horning is a graduate student in the Department of Early and Special Education at Boise State University. She is also a Program Manager at the Boise State Children's Center.

John Kim MS CCC-SLP, ATACP (he/him) is a doctoral student in the Joint Doctoral program at San Francisco State University (SFSU) & UC Berkeley in Special Education. John's area of research is at the intersection of visual-graphic symbol acquisition, equity-centered AAC system implementation, and translanguaging practice in the exchange semiotics of AAC users of culturally and linguistically diverse individuals. John also serves as a Project Coordinator for a Federal Grant titled Project AAC for ALL at SFSU. John currently works as a clinical faculty at SFSU, speech-language pathologist and AAC specialist serving individuals, families, and communities.

Kofi LeNiles is an African American scholar, international educator, and assistant professor at Towson University. His research interests include African-centered education, culturally centered education, and educational leadership and policy. He is a former elementary school principal and early-childhood literacy specialist.

Shamaria Mosley is a Graduate Research Assistant in the Department of Teacher Education and Leadership at Mississippi State University. She is pursuing her Masters in Public Policy and Administration.

Katherine Orlando is a retired school principal, having served at all three levels: birth– elementary, middle, and high school. She is the graduate program director for the Instructional Leadership and Professional Development Department at Towson University. Her research interests include equity-centered leadership, liberatory pedagogies, teacher preparation, professional learning, coaching, intergroup dialogue, and higher education opportunities for justice-impacted persons.

Juli Lull Pool, PhD, is an Associate Professor in the Early & Special Education Department at Boise State University. Dr. Pool received her Ph.D. in Early Intervention at the University of Oregon. Her teaching focuses on early childhood assessment, inclusive and intervention methods in preschool, and foundations of practice in early childhood and early childhood special education. Dr. Pool's areas of expertise include early childhood assessment such as observational assessment, parent-completed tools, and curriculum-based assessment; and, inclusive environments and teaching methods for preschoolers. She has published in several professional journals including Young Exceptional Children, Topics in Early Childhood Special Education, Early Childhood Education Journal, Intervention in School & Clinic, and Assessment for Effective Intervention.

Angi Stone-MacDonald is a Professor and Department Chair in the Department of Special Education, Rehabilitation, and Counseling at California State University, San Bernardino. Until July 2022, she was the Associate Dean of Grants and Research for the College of Education and Human Development and Associate Professor at the University of Massachusetts Boston in the Early Education and Care in Inclusive Settings program. She received her doctorate from Indiana University in Special Education. Dr. Stone-MacDonald has worked with people with disabilities for the last two decades as a paraprofessional, teacher, consultant, and researcher. Her areas of research include early intervention, international special education for children with developmental disabilities, and teacher preparation for early intervention. Her current research agenda includes early intervention personnel preparation and inclusive early childhood education in Tanzania.

Sara Ucar is a graduate student completing her doctorate in Special Education at San Francisco State University and University of California, Berkeley.

Melissa Clucas Walter, an assistant professor of Human Development and Family Sciences at Northern Illinois University in DeKalb, IL, dedicates her research to empowering caregivers—both families and early childhood education (ECE) professionals—towards fostering nurturing and high-quality interactions in early learning environments. Her multifaceted focus seeks to fortify family dynamics and interactions, elevating the quality of home environments, while simultaneously enhancing the preparedness, skills, and methodologies of professionals guiding young learners. Dr. Walter's work encompasses strategies for improving parent-child interactions, developing innovative approaches in ECE curriculum design, and examining the impact of technology on early childhood experiences. She has also been integrally involved in pioneering methodologies for enhancing the ECE workforce, creating novel pathways for educators' professional development. Dr. Walter holds a Ph.D. and M.S. in Human Development and Family Studies, as well as a B.S. in Early Childhood Education Unified, all earned from Iowa State University.

Jennifer Ward is an associate professor of elementary mathematics education at Kennesaw State University who teaches mathematics methods coursework and coordinates the undergraduate teaching program. Her research uses a social justice lens to focus on mathematics learning with young children (Birth through Grade 3). This work includes preparing pre-service teachers to integrate justice-centered mathematics teaching in their work with young children. It aims to reconceptualize thinking around the capabilities of young learners in mathematics classrooms.

Index

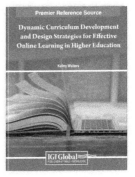
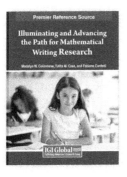

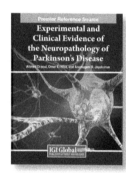

Individual Article & Chapter Downloads

US$ 37.50/each

 Easily Identify, Acquire, and Utilize Published Peer-Reviewed Findings in Support of Your Current Research

- Browse Over *170,000+ Articles & Chapters*
- *Accurate & Advanced* Search
- Affordably Acquire *International Research*
- *Instantly Access* Your Content
- Benefit from the *InfoSci® Platform Features*

THE UNIVERSITY
of NORTH CAROLINA
at CHAPEL HILL